FROMMER'S

# FROMMER'S EASYGUIDE TO
# ROME, FLORENCE & VENICE

**8th Edition**

By Elizabeth Heath,
Stephen Keeling,
and Donald Strachan

FrommerMedia LLC

Piazza Navona, Rome

# CONTENTS

The graceful stone span of the Rialto Bridge (p. 268) on Venice's Grand Canal was originally a pontoon bridge built across the canal's narrowest point.

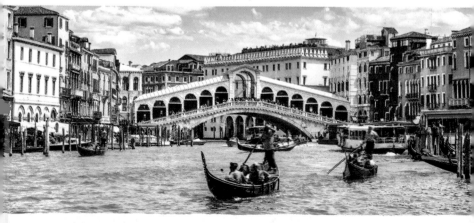

# A LOOK AT ROME, FLORENCE & VENICE

The classic itinerary that forms the heart of this guidebook—Rome, Florence, and Venice—showcases three of the world's most magical destinations. The highlights are legendary: In Rome, thrill to the ruins of the Roman Forum, best reached by first ascending the Capitoline steps designed by Michelangelo; the treasures of the Vatican; the elegant bones of the once-mighty Colosseum; and the Pantheon, designed by Hadrian in the 2nd century. In Florence, Michelangelo's "David" stands tall in the Accademia Museum, and the *Uffizi* and the Pitti Palace are packed with priceless art. In Venice, float on the canal on a gondola or watch the world go by from a cafe seat on the Piazza San Marco. Italy can support a lifetime of travel, but our EasyGuide approach gives you all the tools you need to make your trip as pleasurable and uncomplicated as possible. *Buon viaggio*!

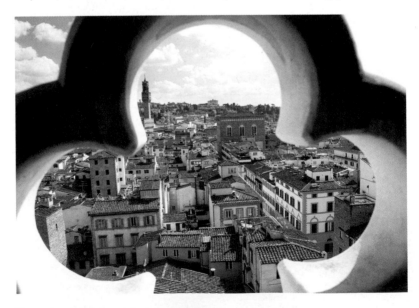

Florence's rooftops viewed through a stone trefoil.

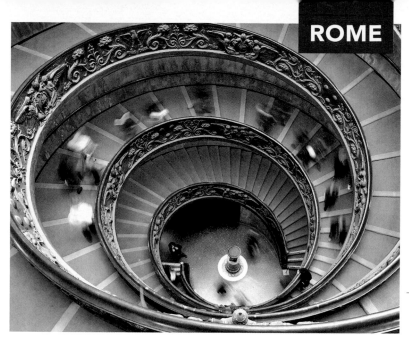

The double spiral staircase at the Vatican Museums (p. 89), inspired by a 1505 design by Bramante, allows visitors to pass in both directions without encountering one another.

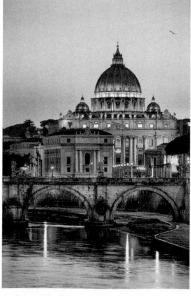

St. Peter's Basilica in Vatican City (p. 86) is one of the holiest sites in all Christendom. The church was built on the tomb of St. Peter.

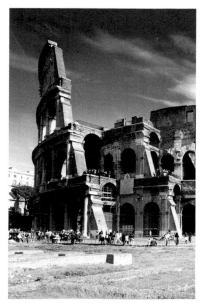

The Roman Colosseum (p. 98), inaugurated in 80 A.D., was once the site of bloody gladiator contests and wild-animal fights. It could also be flooded for mock naval battles.

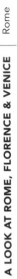

A LOOK AT ROME, FLORENCE & VENICE | Rome

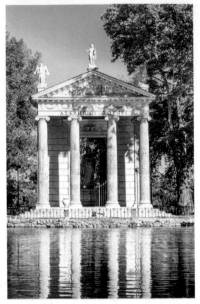

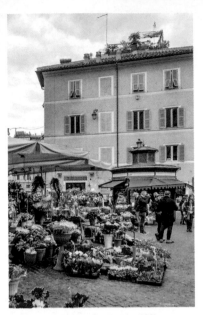

The Temple of Esculapio, Pincian Hill, at the Villa Borghese in Rome, was originally the suburban home of Scipione Borghese.

Shopping at Campo de' Fiori (p. 133), once the site of public executions. The colorful produce and souvenir market becomes a lively bar scene at night.

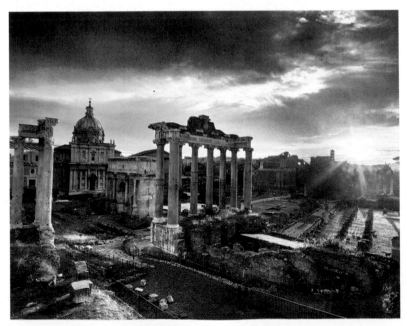

Now a jumble of ruins and fragments, the Roman Forum (p. 101) was once the center of commercial, political, and religious life in the ancient Empire.

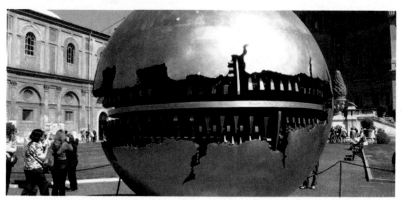

Sculptor Arnaldo Pomodoro's "Sculpture within Sculpture" ("Sfera con Sfera"), in the courtyard of the Vatican Museums (p. 89), depicts a large, cracked metal sphere holding another cracked sphere inside.

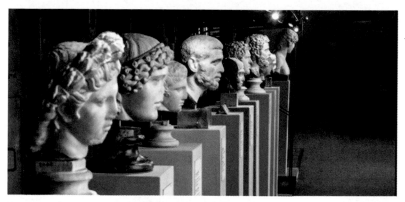

Fragments of Roman statuary are displayed in Centrale Montemartini (p. 124), Rome's original public electrical plant, transformed in 1997 into an exhibitions outpost of the Capitoline Museums that marries archaeology with industrial archaeology.

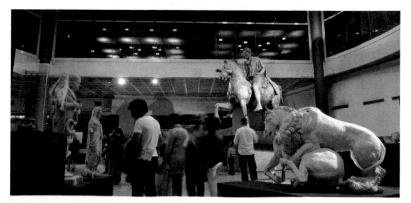

The original equestrian statue of Marco Aurelius, dating to around A.D. 180, is exhibited in a bright new wing of the Capitoline Museums (p. 96).

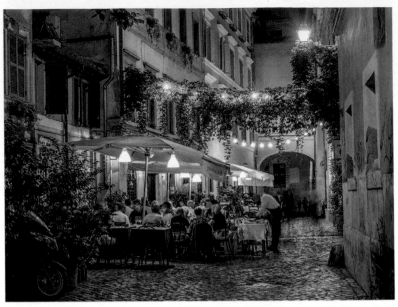

Nighttime alfresco dining on the narrow cobblestone streets of Trastevere (p. 133), once a medieval working-class district and now home to charming trattorie, clubs, and shops.

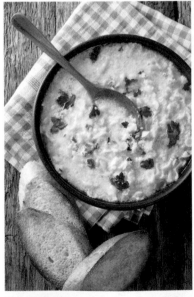

Rich and fortifying, the traditional soup known as *stracciatella alla romana*, here with farfalline and cheese, is also sometimes called Italian egg drop soup.

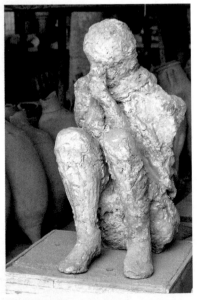

The ancient ruins of Pompeii, reachable via a day trip from Rome, reveal the preserved Roman city, including plaster casts of Vesuvius's victims in their moments of death in August, A.D. 79. See p. 137.

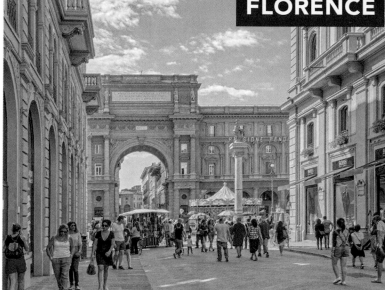

The Piazza della Repubblica was once the site of the city's Roman forum. Today this central square, lined with designer shops and cafes, is dominated by the Triumphal Arch of Vittorio Emanuele II and the Column of Plenty, which marks the site of the ancient Roman settlement. See p. 150.

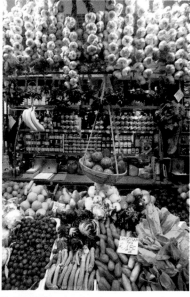

Fresh produce, exotic spices, pizza vendors, and gourmet food stalls are all on hand at Florence's Mercato Centrale (p. 204).

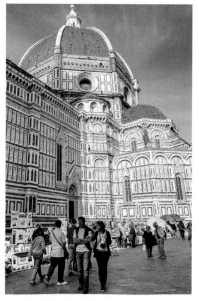

Florence's Duomo (p. 180), with its elaborate 19th-century facade, is topped by Brunelleschi's marvelous 15th-century dome and overlooks Piazza del Duomo.

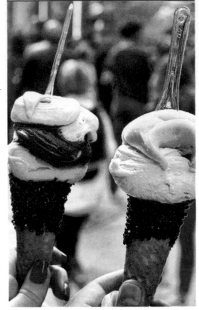

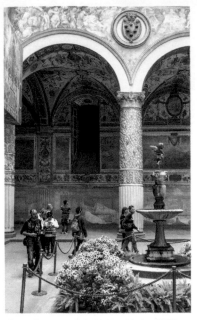

Florence is famous for its luscious artisanal gelato in a range of flavors (p. 174).

The 14th-century Palazzo Vecchio (p. 187) is a treasure-filled palace that was once the seat of pre-Renaissance Florentine Republic governments and later home to Medicis, who redecorated with fabulous frescoes by Renaissance masters such as Bronzino and Vasari.

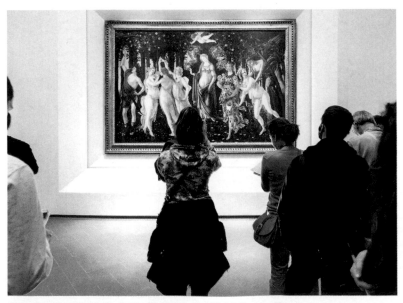

"Primavera" painting in the Botticelli room in the Uffizi Gallery (p. 181).

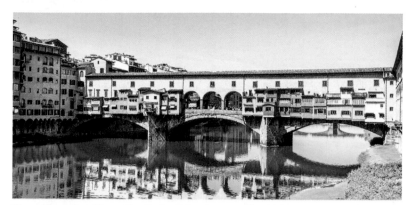

The medieval span of Ponte Vecchio (p. 188) is the city's oldest bridge across the Arno River and looks much like it did when it was built in 1345 to replace an earlier version. Since then, it's survived wars, Nazi bombers, and floods (barely).

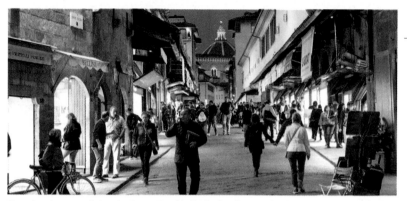

Shopping the stores lining the Ponte Vecchio bridge has been a Florentine pastime since the first span was built in the 12th century. Once home to butchers and fishmongers, in the 16th century they were replaced by gold- and silversmiths, leather workshops, and jewelers. See p. 203.

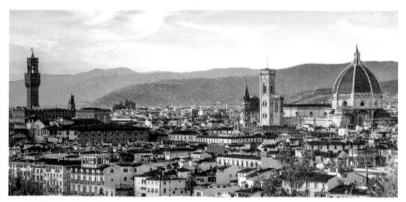

The walk, cab, or bus ride up to Piazzale Michelangelo (p. 200) affords splendid panoramic views of the Duomo and the rest of Florence.

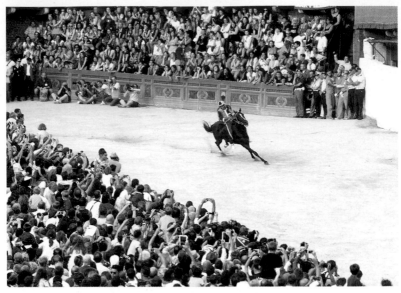

The rollicking annual horse race known as the Palio is held in the scallop-shell-shaped Piazza del Campo (p. 212), Siena's magnificent city square, little changed since the mid-1300s. Fans crowd the Campo to see bareback riders circle the square three times. See p. 40.

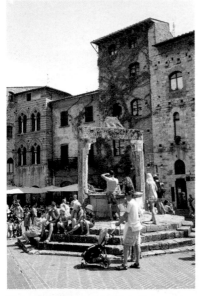

Piazza della Cisterna (p. 219), built around a well dating to 1237, is a focal point of San Gimignano, a picturesque town near Siena known for its medieval defensive towers.

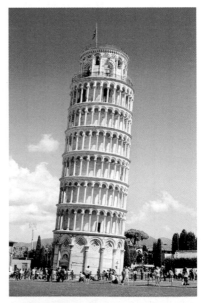

Tourists on the Campo dei Miracoli (Square of Miracles) visiting the Leaning Tower of Pisa (p. 216), the infamous Tuscan campanile with its four-degree lean, the result, engineers say, of too much heavy marble stacked on shifting subsoil.

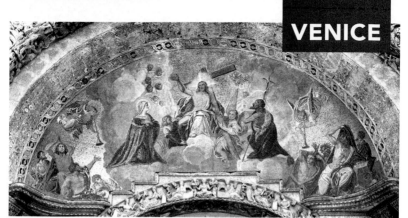

The Eastern influence on Venetian art and history is in evidence in these Byzantine mosaics on the facade of the Basilica di San Marco (p. 261).

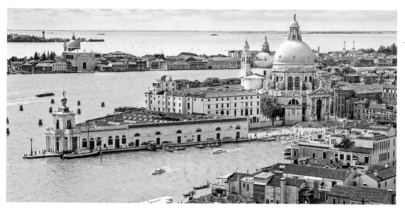

A fixture on the Venice skyline, Santa Maria della Salute (p. 276) was built in the 1630s to offer thanks for the city's deliverance from the Black Death.

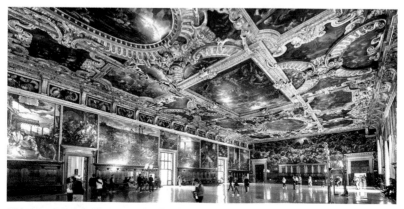

Gilded interior of the Great Council Hall in the Palazzo Ducale, former residence of the city-state heads known as doges, who ruled the maritime republic of Venice for more than a thousand years.

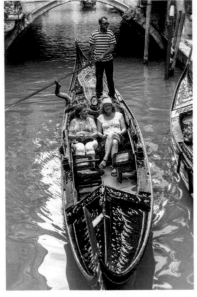

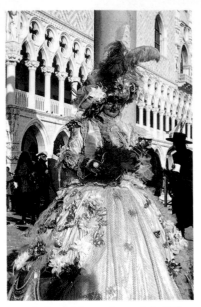

Overpriced, but not overrated, a gondola ride (p. 231) through the canals of Venice is every bit as romantic as it looks.

A reveler in an elaborate Carnevale (p. 287) costume at the Piazza San Marco; the pre-Lenten festival takes place over 10 days leading up to Fat Tuesday.

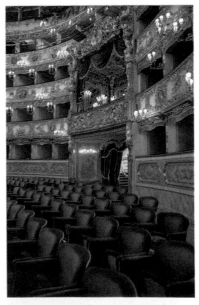

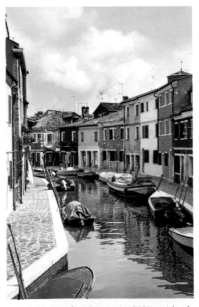

Reopened in 2003 after a devastating fire, Venice's Teatro La Fenice (p. 269) is one of Europe's great opera houses.

Colorful houses line Burano (p. 283), an island in the Venetian Lagoon known for its lacemaking tradition.

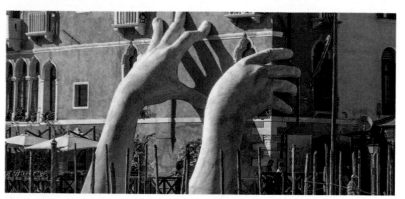

Monumental hands rise from the water in Venice, the work of sculptor Lorenzo Quinn for the 2017 Venice Biennale art show, in his effort to highlight climate change. The sculpture, called "Support," was made from an age-old process known as lost-wax casting, fashioning a mold from a wax model.

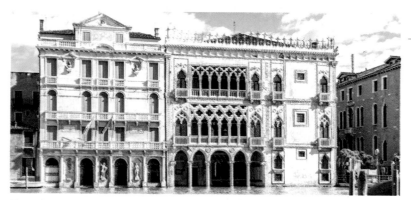

The 15th-century Venetian Gothic palace known as Ca d'Oro overlooks the Grand Canal. It's home to the Galleria Giorgio Franchetti, a museum holding the stellar art collection of a prominent Torinese baron who restored what was then a dilapidated palace to its former glory at the turn of the 20th century.

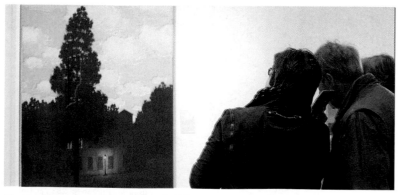

Museum-goers in front of Rene Magritte's 1954 "Empire of Light" in the Peggy Guggenheim Collection (p. 274).

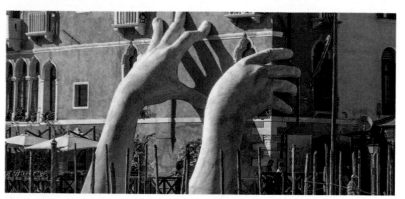

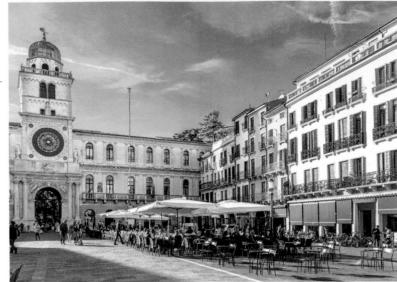

The Torre dei Lamberti clock tower overlooks Piazza delle Erbe, the market square and heart of Verona, an easy day trip from Venice. See p. 294.

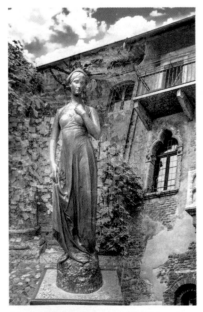

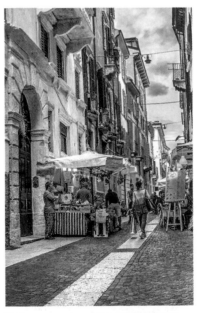

A beloved attraction in the city of Verona is Casa di Giulietta, a rustic 14th-century villa that may or may not have housed the real-life family the Capulets were based on. Juliet's balcony looks out over a bronze statue of the doomed Shakespeare heroine. See p. 295.

Shakespearean associations aside, Verona's narrow, cobbled medieval streets are well worth wandering.

# THE BEST OF ROME, FLORENCE & VENICE

By Donald Strachan

As world travel and wanderlust finally return, Italy is at the top of many must-see lists. It is easy to understand why. This southern European country needs no fanfare to introduce it. The name conjures up vivid images: the grand ruins of Ancient Rome, the paintings and panoramas of Florence, the secret canals and noble palaces of Venice. For centuries, visitors have headed to Italy looking for a slice of the good life, and these three cities supply the highpoint of any trip here.

Nowhere in the world feels the impact of the Renaissance more than in its birthplace, **Florence,** a repository of iconic art left by Michelangelo, Masaccio, Botticelli, Leonardo da Vinci, and many others. Much of the "known world" was once ruled from **Rome,** a city mythically founded by twins Romulus and Remus in 753 B.C. There is no place with more artistic monuments—not even **Venice,** an impossible floating city whose beauty and history was shaped by centuries of trade with the Byzantine world to the east.

And there's more. Long before Italy was a country, it was a loose collection of city-states. Centuries of alliance and rivalry left a legacy dotted across the hinterlands of these three great cities. Much of it lies within easy day-trip distance. It is a short hop from Venice to the "Venetian Arc": **Verona,** for Shakespearean romance and an intact Roman Arena; and **Padua** with its sublime Giotto paintings. In **Siena,** an hour from Florence, ethereal art and Gothic palaces have barely altered since the city's heyday in the 1300s. South of Rome, **Pompeii**—preserved under volcanic ash for two millennia after Vesuvius's eruption in A.D. 79—remains the best place to get up close with the ancient world.

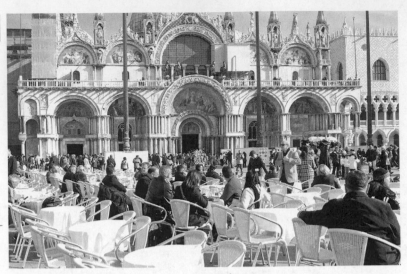

St. Mark's Square in Venice.

# ITALY'S best AUTHENTIC EXPERIENCES

- **Dining Italian Style:** No Italian pastime is more cherished than eating—even better, eating outdoors, preferably with a view of a Renaissance piazza. There's no such thing as a single "Italian" cuisine: You'll discover that each region and city has its own beloved recipes, handed down over generations. *Buon appetito!*

- **Catching an Opera at Verona's Arena:** In summer, Italians enjoy opera under the stars. The setting for Italy's largest and most famous outdoor festival is the ancient **Arena di Verona,** a Roman amphitheater grand enough to accommodate as many elephants as Verdi's "Aïda" requires. See p. 295.

- **Shopping at Rome's Working Food Markets:** Testaccio's reborn historic market is a culinary and cultural treat, where acclaimed chefs jostle with feisty *signore* for the day's best *pomodori, mozzarella di bufala,* and *trippa* (tripe). Sustain yourself with street food as you soak up a genuine neighborhood south of the Aventine. See p. 133.

- **Exploring Florence's Diverse Cocktail Scene:** You can tailor your sipping the way you like it: straight up with one of the world's great views at **Terrazza;** vintage and quirky at **Mayday;** or crafted by one of Italy's most inventive mixologists at **Bitter Bar.** See p. 206.

# THE best TASTES OF ITALY

- **Bonci Pizzarium, Rome:** Chef-entrepreneur Gabriele Bonci elevates the simple slice of pizza to extraordinary levels. There's nothing fussy about the place, or the prices, but every single ingredient is carefully sourced and expertly prepared. You can taste it from the very first bite. See p. 71.

o **Mercato Centrale, Florence:** Not simply a restaurant…more the food hall of your dreams, with a constant buzz from noon until nighttime. Pick and choose from multiple street food vendors preparing the best Tuscan and modern Italian soul food; wash it down with fine wine from a well-stocked enoteca. See p. 171.

o **Florence's Vegetarian Dining Scene:** The days when you had to be a carnivore to fully enjoy a meal in the Renaissance city are long gone. **A Crudo** (p. 173) serves vegetarian tartare alongside classic and reinvented meat versions. Vegans, as well as anyone gluten intolerant, are looked after by an inventive menu at **Brac** (p. 171).

o **Cicchetti & a Spritz in Venice:** *Cicchetti*—tapas-like small plates, usually eaten while standing at a bar—are a Venetian tradition. To make the experience complete, accompany them with a spritz made from Aperol and sparkling prosecco wine from the Veneto hills. Find some great spots on the San Polo side of Rialto Bridge. See p. 254.

o **Osteria dell'Enoteca, Florence:** When successful wine-bar owners open a restaurant, you know the *vino* will be first rate. Osteria dell'Enoteca serves food that unites Tuscany's traditional ingredients with a light, contemporary cooking style. Their stone-and-slate dining room is atmospheric enough for any special occasion. See p. 174.

o **A Tasty Tasting Trail Around Siena:** The shell-shaped Piazza del Campo is the heart of this preserved Gothic city. A **Taste Siena** walk shows you the sights via eight different encounters with Sienese gastronomy—from sweet

Grabbing a bite at Florence's Mercato Centrale.

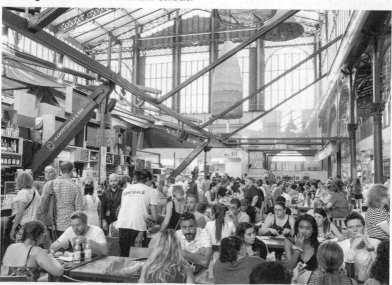

treats and artisanal cheese to hand-rolled *pici* pasta and, of course, wine. See p. 214.

o **Ai Artisti, Venice:** Venice's culinary rep is founded on the quality of fish sold at its famous market. Both *primi* and *secondi* at Ai Artisti feature the freshest catch from the lagoon and farther afield. See p. 254.

# ITALY'S most memorable HOTELS

o **Villa Spalletti Trivelli, Rome:** Recent upgrades have only enhanced the unique experience of staying in an Italian noble mansion in the middle of the capital. Opulence and impeccable service come at a price, of course. When we hit the lottery, we will be booking a stay here. See p. 64.

o **Soggiorno Battistero, Florence:** Room with a view…and then some. You can almost touch Florence's famous old Baptistery from piazza-facing rooms at this simple guesthouse with an enviable address. Off-season rates are astonishingly affordable. See p. 158.

o **Mediterraneo, Rome:** Upscale and Art Deco, Mediterraneo is the flagship of a trio of hotels near Termini Station run by the Bettoja family. Others are more budget-friendly, but all offer vintage charm, old-school comforts, and warm service from a loyal longtime staff. They don't make 'em like this anymore. See p. 65.

o **Metropole, Venice:** The Grand Old Lady of Venetian hospitality, transformed from a medieval building into a luxury hotel in the 19th century, remains a chic choice, filled with antiques and Asian art. See p. 240.

A suite at Villa Spalletti Trivelli, Rome.

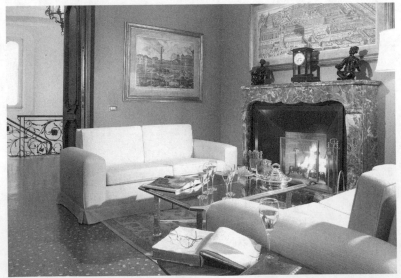

o **Palazzo Tolomei, Florence:** Raphael once stayed in this palace—and perhaps even gave its owners a painting to make rent. The place is as grand as it sounds, with a Renaissance layout and a baroque redecoration from the 1600s that remain gloriously intact. See p. 159.

# ITALY'S best FOR FAMILIES

o **Climbing Pisa's Wonky Tower:** Are we walking up or down? Pleasantly disoriented kids are bound to ask, as you spiral your way to the rooftop viewing balcony atop the world's most famous work of botched engineering. Pisa is an easy daytrip from Florence. Eight is the minimum age for heading up its *Torre Pendente,* or Leaning Tower. See p. 216

o **Boat Tripping on the Venice Lagoon:** Who doesn't like a day boating on a lake, any lake? Throw in the floating city and its bell tower of San Marco on the horizon and you have one unforgettable family moment. See p. 285.

o **Rooting for Fiorentina at Soccer:** Forget lions battling gladiators in Rome's Colosseum, or Guelphs fighting Ghibellines in medieval lanes. For a modern showdown, hit a Florence soccer game. Home side Fiorentina plays Serie A matches at the city's Stadio Comunale on alternate weekends from September to June. Wear something lilac—the team's nickname is *i viola* ("the purples"). See p. 209.

o **Visiting Rome's Centrale Montemartini:** Industrial meets ancient marble in this unique museum, where Greek and Roman statues are displayed in the restored rooms of Rome's first public electricity plant. The museum always has drawing and painting materials onsite; guided tours for children are available on request. See p. 124.

o **Road-Testing Every Artisanal Gelateria:** When it comes to Italian ice cream, choose carefully—Smurf-blue or bubblegum-pink flavors are a sure sign of color enhancers, and ice crystals and fluffy heaps betray additives and pumped-in air. Artisanal *gelaterie* make good stuff from scratch daily, with fresh seasonal produce: Look for a short, all-natural ingredient list posted proudly for all to see. Believe us, you'll taste the difference. See "Gelato," p. 75, 174, and 260.

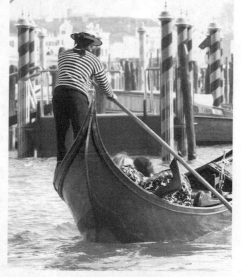

A gondolier steers his craft in Venice.

# ITALY'S best MUSEUMS

*Note:* At most major Italian museums, timed **tickets must now be booked ahead** of arrival. Please check to verify opening and closing hours, which may change to align with public health protocols.

o **Vatican Museums, Rome:** The 100 galleries of the Musei Vaticani are loaded with papal treasures accumulated over the centuries. Musts include the Sistine Chapel, such ancient Greek and Roman sculptures as "Laocoön" and "Belvedere Apollo," and room after room of Raphael's frescoes, including his masterful "School of Athens." See p. 89.

o **Galleria degli Uffizi, Florence:** This U-shaped High Renaissance building designed by Giorgio Vasari was the administrative headquarters, or *uffizi* (offices), for the Medici dukes of Tuscany. It's now the crown jewel of Europe's art museums, housing the world's greatest collection of Renaissance paintings, including icons by Botticelli, Leonardo da Vinci, and Michelangelo. See p. 181.

o **Accademia, Venice:** The "Academy" houses an unequalled array of Venetian paintings, exhibited chronologically from the 13th to the 18th century. Walls are hung with works by Bellini, Carpaccio, Giorgione, Titian, and Tintoretto. See p. 273.

o **Galleria Borghese, Rome:** The frescoes and decor of a 1613 palace in the heart of the Villa Borghese are merely a backdrop for collections that

"Sphere Within Sphere" bronze sculpture by Italian sculptor Arnaldo Pomodoro in the Courtyard of the Pigna at the Vatican Museums.

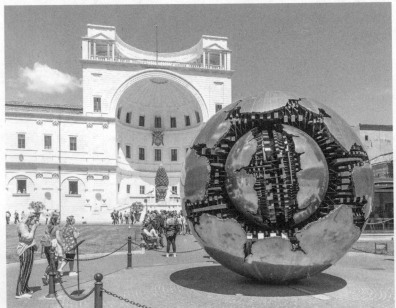

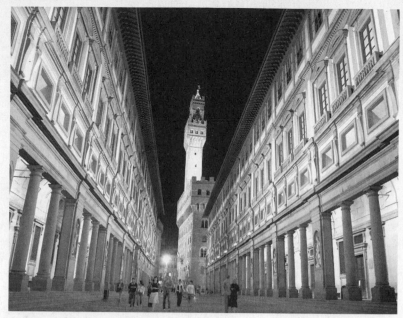

The Galleria degli Uffizi at night.

include baroque sculpture by a young Bernini and Canova, plus paintings by Caravaggio and Raphael. See p. 118.

o **Santa Maria della Scala, Siena:** The building is as much the star as its artworks—frescoed wards, ancient chapels, sacristy, and a labyrinthine basement in a medieval hospital that was treating patients until the 1990s. See p. 214.

# ITALY'S best FREE THINGS TO DO

o **Watching Sunrise at the Roman Forum:** A short stroll from the Capitoline Hill down Via del Campidoglio to Via di Monte Tarpeo rewards you with a perfect outlook: a terrace behind this Michelangelo-designed square, an ideal photo op when the sun rises behind the Temple of Saturn, illuminating this archaeological complex in pink-orange light. Complete your ideal early start with breakfast from the nearby Jewish Ghetto. See p. 100.

o **Gazing in Wonder at Caravaggio's Greatest Paintings:** Rome's French church, San Luigi dei Francesi, is home to three panels by bad boy of baroque art, Michelangelo Merisi da Caravaggio. His "Calling of St. Matthew," painted at the height of his powers, incorporates uncompromising realism and trademark *chiaroscuro* (extremes of light and dark). See p. 110.

7

o **Basking in the Lights of the Renaissance:** At dusk, make the steep climb to the ancient church of San Miniato al Monte, Florence. Sit down on the steps and watch the city begin to twinkle. See p. 200.

o **Discovering You're Hopelessly Lost:** You haven't experienced Venice until you have turned a corner, convinced you're on the way to somewhere, only to find yourself smack against a canal with no bridge, or in a little courtyard with no way out. All you can do is shrug, smile, and give the city's maze of narrow streets another try. Because getting lost in Venice is a pleasure. See p. 229.

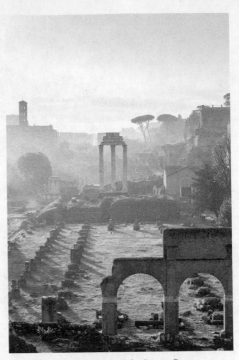

A misty morning sunrise over the Roman Forum.

# undiscovered ITALY

o **San Frediano, Florence:** Most Florentines have abandoned their *centro storico* to the visitors. But the Arno's Left Bank in San Frediano has plenty of local action after dark: Dine at **iO** (p. 172), slurp a gelato by the river at **La Carraia** (p. 175), then sip fine wines until late at **Santino** (p. 208) or catch some offbeat live music at **Libreria-Café La Cité** (p. 207).

o **Cannaregio, Venice:** This residential neighborhood has silent canals, elegantly faded mansions, hidden churches graced by Tiepolo paintings, and the old Ghetto Nuovo, a historic area of Jewish bakeries, restaurants, and synagogues. It's a great escape from the chaos around San Marco. See chapter 9.

o **The North Terrace on the Cathedral Roof, Florence:** Everyone climbs the dome, but savvy visitors can join a daily guided visit beyond normally locked doors. Crane your neck up to view the lantern, look down on the Baptistery, and gaze across Florence's rooftops to the hills of Fiesole beyond. See p. 202.

o **The View from T Fondaco dei Tedeschi:** This Venice department store—renovated by stellar architect Rem Koolhas—was once an elegant *palazzo* beside the Grand Canal. Views from its free rooftop deck are even more spectacular than the opulence inside. See p. 269.

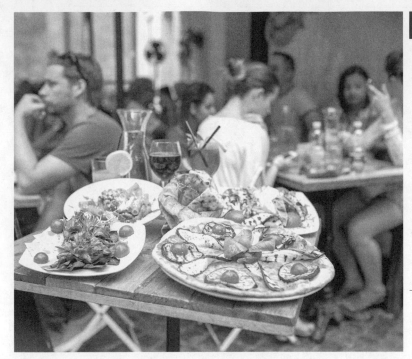

Aperitivo time in Rome.

o **A Secret Insight into Brunelleschi's Genius:** Tucked away at the top of Florence's Spedale degli Innocenti is a window with a cutaway view into a Brunelleschi-designed chapel. From this angle, you can check every ceiling strut, joint, and Renaissance nail holding it up. It's fascinating. See p. 196.

# SUGGESTED ITINERARIES

By Donald Strachan

Italy is so vast and treasure-filled, it's hard to resist the temptation to pack too much into too little time. This is a dauntingly diverse destination, and you can't even skim the surface in 1 or 2 weeks. Relax; don't try. If you're a first-time visitor with limited time, we suggest you max out on the classic trio: Rome, Florence, and Venice can be packed into one very busy week, better yet in two.

How can you accomplish that? Well, in addition to having one of Europe's better highway networks (called *autostrade*), Italy has an efficient high-speed rail network. If you're city-hopping, you need never rent a car. Rome is a key hub of this 21st-century transportation empire; from Rome's Termini station, Florence can be reached in only 90 minutes. Key routes (including the Venice–Florence–Rome line) are served by comfortable, fast trains. You only require a rental car for rural detours. Of course, some people may prefer to travel in their own vehicle than a train carriage; see p. 303 for rental tips and individual chapters for parking advice. (Spoiler: In cities, parking can be a nightmare.)

The following itineraries take you to some of our favorite places. Note that during the pandemic, many museums restricted visitor numbers with compulsory prebooking; it is likely that many of these measures will remain. Reserve ahead, and organize the rest of your days around personal must-sees.

The pace of some of our itineraries may be a bit breathless, so skip a stop occasionally and enjoy chill-out time—after all, you're on vacation. Of course, you can use any of the following itineraries as a jumping-off point to develop your own adventure.

## ROME, FLORENCE & VENICE IN 1 WEEK

Let's be realistic: It's impossible to see Italy's three iconic cities fully in a week. However, a fast, efficient, center-to-center rail network along the Rome–Florence–Venice line means it's surprisingly easy to see much of their best. This weeklong itinerary

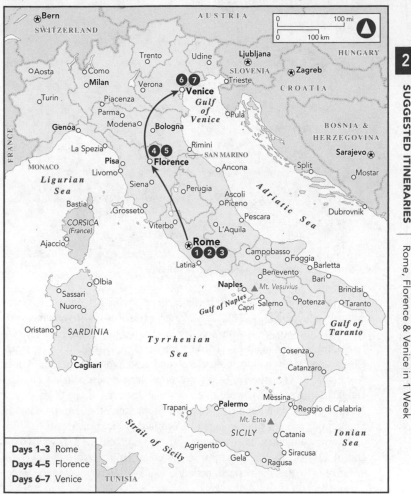

Days 1–3 Rome
Days 4–5 Florence
Days 6–7 Venice

treads familiar highlights, but there's a reason why these are Italy's most-visited sites: They're sure to provide memories that will last a lifetime.

## Days 1, 2 & 3: Rome: The Eternal City ★★★

You could spend a month touring Italy's capital, but 3 days is enough to get the flavor. There are two essential areas to focus on. The first is the legacy of Imperial Rome, including the **Forum, Campidoglio,** and **Colosseum** (p. 95). Bookend your day with the Forum and Colosseum (one first, the other last) to avoid the busiest crowds. One ticket is good for

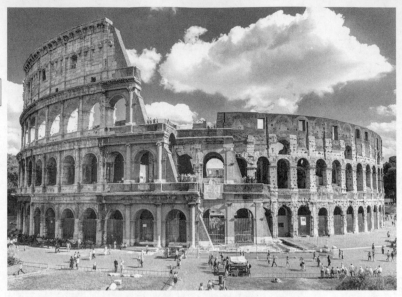

Rome's Flavian Amphitheater, better known as the Colosseum.

both; or buy the new Full Experience ticket, which includes House of Augustus, too. On **Day 2,** tackle **St. Peter's Basilica** (p. 86) and the **Vatican Museums** (p. 89), with a collection unlike any other in the world (including Michelangelo's **Sistine Chapel**). On **Day 3,** it's a toss-up: Choose between visiting the underground catacombs of the **Via Appia Antica** (p. 127) or the well-trod streets of the **Centro Storico** (p. 108) and **Tridente** (p. 113), where you can wander (and shop) from Piazza Navona to the Pantheon, the Spanish Steps, and the Trevi Fountain. Spend your evenings in the bars of **Campo de' Fiori** or **Monti** (p. 135) and the restaurants of **Trastevere** (p. 80) or **Testaccio** (p. 81). Toward the end of Day 3, catch a late train to Florence. Be sure to buy tickets in advance: On the high-speed network, walk-up fares are much more expensive than prebooked tickets.

## Days 4 & 5: Florence: Cradle of the Renaissance ★★★

You have 2 whole days to explore the city of Giotto, Leonardo, Botticelli, and Michelangelo. Start with their masterpieces at the **Uffizi** (p. 181; definitely prebook tickets, weeks or even months ahead if possible), then explore the **Duomo** complex (p. 180): Scale Brunelleschi's ochre dome and follow up with a visit to the adjoining **Battistero di San Giovanni,** the **Museo dell'Opera del Duomo,** and the **Campanile di Giotto** (p. 177). Start the next day with "David" at the **Accademia** (p. 194; another essential advance reservation). Spend the rest of your day getting to know the intimate wall paintings of **San Marco** (p. 194), paintings hanging at the **Palazzo Pitti** (p. 199), and Masaccio's revolutionary frescoes in the **Cappella Brancacci** (p. 201). In the evenings, head south of the Arno, to **San Frediano** or **San Niccolò,** for lively wine bars and better restaurants than you generally find in the historic center (p. 172).

## Days 6 & 7: Venice: City That Defies the Sea ★★★

Head to Venice via early train in the morning. You'll ride into the heart of Venice on a *vaporetto* (water bus), taking in the **Grand Canal,** the world's greatest main street. Begin your sightseeing at **Piazza San Marco** (p. 268): The **Basilica di San Marco** is right there, and after exploring it, visit the nearby **Palazzo Ducale** (**Doge's Palace;** p. 263) before walking over the **Bridge of Sighs.** Begin your evening with the classic Venetian *aperitivo,* an Aperol spritz (Aperol with sparkling prosecco wine and soda), followed by *cicchetti* (Venetian tapas) before a late dinner. Make your second day all about the city's art—the **Gallerie dell'Accademia** (p. 273), the modern **Peggy Guggenheim Collection** (p. 274), and **San Rocco** (p. 278)—or take in offbeat history at the quirky, multimedia **Casanova Museum and Experience** (p. 263). Catch the latest train you can back to Rome. Or add another night—you can never stay too long in Venice.

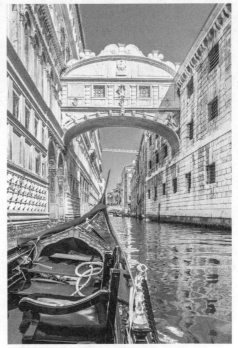

The Bridge of Sighs, Doge's Palace, Venice.

# A 2-WEEK ITINERARY

It's obviously difficult to see the top sights of Italy—and see them properly—in just 2 weeks. But in this itinerary, we show you many of the best. We add significant detours from the Rome–Florence–Venice trail, heading south to Pompeii, Europe's most complete Roman ruins, and north to Pisa (for the Leaning Tower and more); and making day trips to Padua (with its Giotto art) and Verona (city of lovers since *Romeo and Juliet*).

# Italy in 2 Weeks

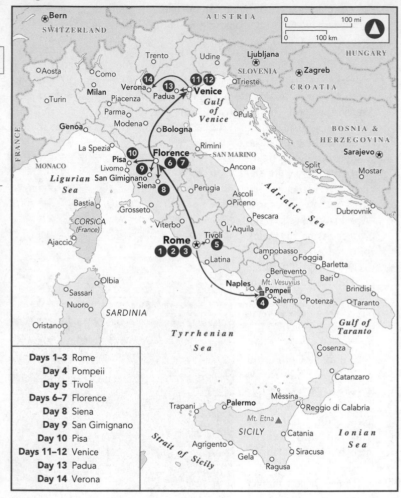

Days 1–3   Rome
Day 4   Pompeii
Day 5   Tivoli
Days 6–7   Florence
Day 8   Siena
Day 9   San Gimignano
Day 10   Pisa
Days 11–12   Venice
Day 13   Padua
Day 14   Verona

## Days 1, 2 & 3: Rome ★★★

Follow the Rome itinerary suggested in "Italy in 1 Week," above. Rome will actually be your base for 5 nights (days 4 and 5 will be day trips from Rome); for this longer stay, consider apartment rental rather than a hotel room in the capital (see "Self-Catering Apartments," p. 55).

## Day 4: Pompeii: A Day Trip to Europe's Best-Preserved Roman Ruins ★★

Early on **Day 4,** take the high-speed Frecciarossa or Italo train from Rome to Naples (1½ hr.), then a Circumvesuviana train 24km (15 miles) southeast of Naples to wander the archaeological remains at **Pompeii** (p. 137). Pack water and a lunch if you can—on-site services aren't great. Buried for almost 2,000 years, after nearby Vesuvius erupted in A.D. 79, Pompeii exhibits some of the great archaeological treasures of Italy, including the patrician **Casa dei Vettii** and the frescoed **Villa dei Misteri.** You'll return to Rome at night. *Tip:* This is a very long day; it may be easier to do as an escorted visit by bus from Rome, especially with kids or mobility-impaired travel companions. Several operators offer Pompeii tours; ask at your hotel or at one of Rome's tourist information points (see "Visitor Information," p. 44). Doing it by rental car is another option, but only for those confident behind the wheel. Driving in and around both Rome and Naples can be hair-raising.

## Day 5: Tivoli: A Day Trip to Rome's Imperial Villa ★★

Take your foot off the gas with a more relaxed day trip, 32km (20 miles) northeast of Rome to **Tivoli** (p. 142). Emperor Hadrian's serene rural retreat here, the **Villa Adriana** (p. 143), is the grandest retirement residence you'll ever see, complete with theaters, baths, fountains, and gardens. This emperor had a fine eye for design.

## Days 6 & 7: Florence ★★★

Take an early train to Florence, where you will spend the next 5 nights. Follow the 2-day itinerary in "Rome, Florence & Venice in 1 Week," p. 10, then use Florence as a base for exploring Siena, San Gimignano, and Pisa. We suggest using public transportation for day trips out of Florence. But all three towns are easily reached by rental car, too, if you prefer having your own wheels. See p. 149 for parking tips in Florence; discuss options with your accommodation provider. The roads of central Tuscany are pretty at any time of year, and there's well-signposted parking just outside the historic core in all three recommended day-trip destinations.

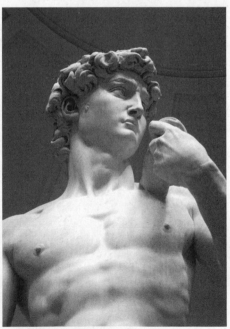

Michelangelo's "David" in the Accademia, Florence.

## Day 8: A Day Trip to Gothic Siena ★★★

It's just over an hour to **Siena** (p. 212) on the *rapida* bus from Florence. On arrival, set out immediately for **Piazza del Campo,** the shell-shaped main square, including its art-filled **Museo Civico** (inside the **Palazzo Pubblico**). You still have time to squeeze in a look at the **Duomo** and **Museo dell'Opera Metropolitana,** where you'll find Sienese master Duccio's giant "Maestà" painting. Stop on the Campo for a late-afternoon drink, then grab an early dinner at a restaurant in Siena's atmospheric back streets. The last bus back to Florence departs at 8:45pm, arriving back in Florence at 10pm. (*Note:* On weekends, the last bus is usually 7:10pm, so you may want to schedule dinner in Florence.)

## Day 9: San Gimignano: A Town Stuck in the 1300s ★★

It's another day on buses, but well worth it to see one of the best-preserved Gothic towns in Europe. You change buses in Poggibonsi for the last, outrageously pretty leg through vine-clad hills to **San Gimignano** (p. 218). In its medieval heyday, the "city of beautiful towers" had over 70 turrets spiking the sky above its tiny, crowded plot. Now just a handful remain, including the **Torre Grossa** (which you can climb). The frescoed **Collegiata** is the essential art stop. You can dine early at **Chiribiri** (it's open all day), then leave on the late bus.

## Day 10: Pisa & Its Leaning Tower ★★

A fast train from Florence takes only 1 hour to Pisa, with its set-piece piazza, one of the most photographed slices of real estate on the planet. Pisa's **Campo dei Miracoli** ("Field of Miracles") is home to the **Leaning Tower** (p. 216) of course; book a slot ahead of time if you want to climb it. A combination ticket admits you to the rest of the piazza's sights, including the **Duomo,** with its Arab-influenced Pisan-Romanesque facade, and the **Battistero,** with a carved pulpit and crazy acoustics. Head away from the piazza for dining *alla pisana*—the "real Pisa" lies in the warren of streets around the market square, **Piazza delle Vettovaglie.** Finish your visit with a stroll on the handsome promenade along the **River Arno.** Take a late train back to Florence (the last fast service departs at 9:30pm).

## Days 11 & 12: Venice ★★★

Set out early the next morning for Venice, where you'll spend the next 4 nights. For the first 2 days, follow the itinerary suggested in "Rome, Florence & Venice in 1 Week," p. 10.

## Day 13: Padua & Its Giotto Frescoes ★

Lying only 40km (25 miles) west of Venice, **Padua** (p. 292) is a fairly relaxed day trip by train. Visit the **Basilica di Sant'Antonio** (p. 293) to see Donatello bronzes and the **Cappella degli Scrovegni** (p. 292) for its Giotto frescoes—perhaps the most important paintings in the history of pre-Renaissance Italian art. Return to Venice for the night.

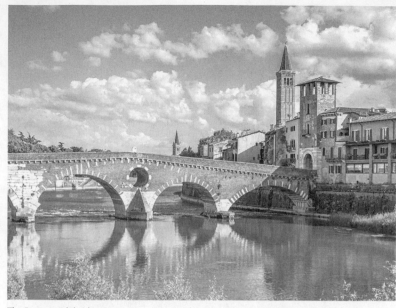

The Roman arch bridge Ponte Pietra crosses the Adige River in Verona.

### Day 14: Verona: City of Lovers & Gladiators ★★★

Although he likely never set foot in the place, Shakespeare set his epic love story, "Romeo and Juliet," in Verona. Wander **Piazza dei Signori** and **Piazza delle Erbe** before descending on the **Arena di Verona** (p. 295), the world's best-preserved gladiatorial arena: It's still packed out for monumental opera performances on summer evenings. Aim to catch a Regionale Veloce train: It costs the same (under 10€) as a Regionale service, but takes just 1½ hours compared with over 2 hours for the slower train.

# ITALY FOR FAMILIES

Italy is probably the friendliest family vacation destination in Europe. Logistically, it presents few challenges. If you're traveling by rental car with young children, request safety car seats ahead of time, so the rental company can arrange for a seat that complies with EU regulations. Reduced-price family fares are available on much of the high-speed rail network; ask when you buy your tickets or contact a booking agent. You won't need to hunt for "child-friendly" restaurants or special kids' menus. There is always plenty available for little ones, even dishes not on the grownup menu. If you have a fussy eater, never be afraid to ask; pretty much any request is met with a smile.

A few **tips** from parents who've been here: Space out your museum visits so you get a chance to see the masterpieces, but your youngsters don't suffer a meltdown from too many paintings of saints and holy *bambini*. You **must**

# Italy for Families

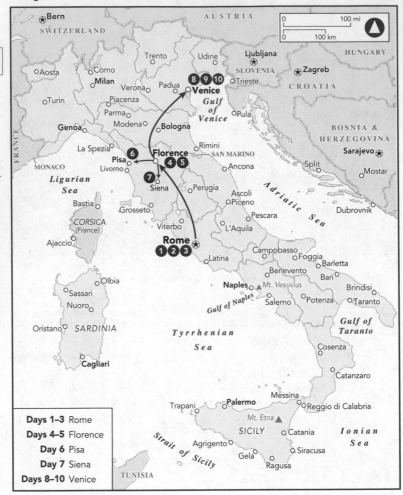

Days 1–3 Rome
Days 4–5 Florence
Day 6 Pisa
Day 7 Siena
Days 8–10 Venice

**now book** many major museum targets ahead of arrival; leave plenty of time between them if you are traveling with young children. And punctuate every day with a **gelato** stop—Italy makes the world's best ice cream (you'll easily find soy-milk options for the lactose intolerant). It's a good idea to limit long, tiring day trips out of town, especially by public transportation. End your trip in Venice, which for many kids is every bit as magical as a Disney theme park: It's a city. That floats. (Kinda.)

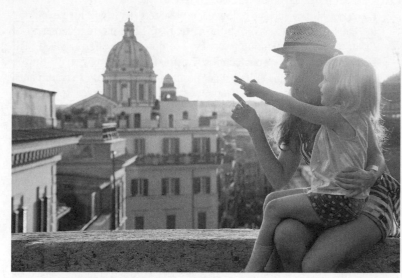

Overlooking the rooftops of Rome.

## Day 1: Rome's Ancient Ruins ★★★

History is on your side here: The wonders of **Ancient Rome** (p. 95) should appeal as much to kids as to adults. There are gory tales to tell at the **Colosseum** (p. 98), where the bookshop also has city guides aimed at kids. (And a new ticketing system has reduced wait times.) After that, little ones can let off steam wandering the **Roman Forum** and **Palatine Hill.** (The roadside ruins of the **Imperial Forums** can be viewed at any time.) Cap the afternoon by exploring the **Villa Borghese** (p. 118), a monumental park in the heart of the city; rent bikes or visit the small zoo in the park's northeast section. For dinner, tuck into crispy crusts at an authentic Roman **pizzeria,** such as **Li Rioni** (p. 72).

## Day 2: Rome After the Romans ★★★

Head early to **St. Peter's Basilica** (p. 86) before long lines form. Kids will find it spooky wandering the Vatican grottoes and relish the opportunity to climb up to Michelangelo's dome. After lunch, begin your assault on the **Vatican Museums** (p. 89) and the **Sistine Chapel** (be sure to book advance tickets). Even if your kids don't like art museums, they will gawp at the grandeur. Later in the day, head for the iconic **Spanish Steps** (p. 116), then wander over to the **Trevi Fountain** (p. 118). Give the kids coins to toss into the fountain, which is said to ensure their return to Rome—perhaps when they are older and can better appreciate the city's many more artistic attractions.

## Day 3: Rome Underground ★★★

Layers of history survive below the city streets. Kids will love exploring the catacombs of the **Via Appia Antica** (p. 127), the first cemetery of Rome's Christian community, where the devout secretly practiced their faith during periods of persecution. **Context Travel** (www.contexttravel. com; see p. 130) runs an excellent family tour of the city's subterranean layers ($362 per party). Eat more **pizza** before you leave; Rome's pizzerias are bested only by those in Naples, to the south…and our next recommended stops all lie north. *Note:* Rome's underground sites were closed through the pandemic. Restrictions may return at short notice.

## Days 4 & 5: Florence: City of the Renaissance ★★★

Take the early train to Florence. Although it's usually thought of as more of an adult city, there's enough here to fill 2 family days, plus a couple of day trips. (With day trips, you'll be staying 4 nights in Florence: Consider taking an apartment rather than a hotel room, so you have space to spread out; see p. 55.) Begin with the city's monumental main square, **Piazza della Signoria,** an open-air museum of statues with the **Palazzo Vecchio** (p. 187) towering over one side; you can tour the palace on special child-friendly itineraries. Turn your afternoon visit to the **Uffizi** (p. 181; must be prebooked) into a treasure hunt by first buying postcards of key artworks. On the second morning, kids will delight in climbing to the top of Brunelleschi's dome on the **Duomo** (p. 180) for a classic panorama. Book your slot for as early as possible; waiting times often lengthen during the day. If the kids still have energy to burn, climb the 414 steps up to the **Campanile di Giotto** (p. 177), run around in the **Giardino di Boboli** (p. 198), eat some of Italy's best gelato (p. 174), and take the bus to **Piazzale Michelangiolo** (p. 200) at dusk.

## Day 6: Pisa & Its Leaning Tower ★★

With children seven or under, you may want to skip **Pisa** (p. 215): Eight is the minimum age for a disorienting ascent up the bell tower of Pisa's cathedral, more commonly known as the **Leaning Tower.** Older kids will appreciate the hyperreal monuments of the **Campo dei Miracoli** and learning about the city's Galileo links: He was born here, and supposedly discovered his law of pendulum motion while watching a swinging lamp inside the **Duomo.** Before returning to Florence, sample a local specialty, *cecina*—a pizzalike flatbread made of garbanzo-bean flour—at **Il Montino.** Rail connections between Florence and Pisa are frequent, fast (50–90 min.), and affordable (around 9€ each way).

## Day 7: Gothic Siena ★★★

Count yourself lucky if you can visit **Siena** (p. 212) around July 2 or August 16 for the famous 4-day **Palio** celebrations, when horses race around **Piazza del Campo.** Year-round, however, a couple of epic climbs will thrill the kids. The **Torre del Mangia**—the bell tower of the **Palazzo**

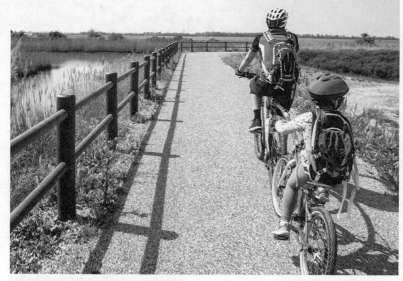

Bike riding in the countryside near Venice.

**Pubblico**—yields a dramatic view of the city and countryside. Through the **Museo dell'Opera Metropolitana,** they can scale the "Facciatone" for a dizzying view down into the Campo. At **Santa Maria della Scala,** they will find **Bambimus,** the art museum for kids, with paintings hung at child-friendly heights. The zebra-striped **Duomo** is jazzy enough to pique their curiosity, and Siena's bakeries are famed for sweet treats. Ride the bus back to Florence after an early dinner. (*Note:* Bus service is reduced on Sundays.)

## Days 8, 9 & 10: Venice, City on the Lagoon ★★★

Leave Florence early for Venice, the most kid-pleasing city in Italy. The fun begins the moment you arrive and take a *vaporetto* ride along the **Grand Canal.** Head straight for **Piazza San Marco** (p. 268), where kids delight in an elevator ride up the **Campanile.** Catch the sparkly mosaics inside the **Basilica di San Marco;** at the **Palazzo Ducale,** walk over the infamous **Bridge of Sighs** after checking out the pint-size knights' armor. Make time for art: Visit the **Gallerie dell'Accademia** (p. 273) and **San Rocco** (p. 278), where kids can "read" the Tintoretto paintings like a comic book. For a modern break, the **Peggy Guggenheim Collection** (p. 274) has pop art, an open courtyard, and a rooftop cafe. In summer, save time for the beach at the **Lido** (p. 284). And yes, splurge on a story-book view of Venice's canals from the seat of a **gondola** (p. 277) or ride the waters DIY-style with a **kayak rental** (p. 285).

# ITALY IN CONTEXT

By Donald Strachan

Many stereotypes you have heard about this charming country are accurate. Children are fussed over wherever they go; food and soccer are practically a religion; the north–south divide is alive and well; and (alas) bureaucracy is a frustrating feature of daily life for many families and businesses. Some stereotypes, however, are wide of the mark: Not every Italian you meet will be open and effusive. Just occasionally, they do taciturn pretty well, too.

One important fact to remember is that, for a land so steeped in history—3 millennia and counting—Italy has only a short history *as a country.* In 2021 Italy celebrated its 160th birthday. Prior to 1861, the map of this boot-shaped peninsula was in constant flux. War, alliance, invasion, and disputed successions caused the political map to change color as often as a chameleon crossing a field of Tuscan wildflowers. Republics, mini-monarchies, client states, Papal states, and city-states, as well as Islamic emirates, colonies, dukedoms, and Christian theocracies, roll onto and out of the pages of Italian history with regularity. In some regions, you'll hear languages and dialects other than Italian. It all combines to form an identity often more regional than it is national.

This confusing history explains why your Italian experience will differ wildly if you visit, say, Rome rather than Venice. (And why you should visit both, if you can.) The architecture is different; the food is different; the legends and historical figures are different, as are many local issues of the day, even in times of shared experience. And the people are different: While the north–south schism is most often written about, cities as close as Florence and Siena can feel dissimilar. This chapter tries to help you understand why.

## ITALY TODAY

Recent Italian experience has been dominated by the novel coronavirus (SARS-CoV-2) and the disease it causes, Covid-19. Daily life in hill-town olive groves, wine cellars, and medieval city streets has been profoundly impacted. Italians are a friendly, tactile people; the virus hit at the heart of their social and sociable culture.

Italy was the first European country—indeed, the first outside Asia—to feel the force of the virus. The country's first official death from Covid-19 was recorded in late February 2020. By March, pictures showing the virus's terrible impact on emergency rooms, hospital wards, and ordinary Italians were beamed around the world.

Localized lockdowns in first-hit towns, in the Lombardy and Veneto regions, failed to contain the virus—hardly surprising, when so little was known about how it spread and the risks it posed. Daily deaths attributed to Covid-19 topped out at more than 900 in March and April 2020, with Lombardy the epicenter of the outbreak. Hit especially hard was one of the world's oldest populations. Doctors, nurses, and healthcare workers also fell victim to the virus, as hospitals in municipalities like Bergamo struggled to cope.

Having been caught initially off-guard, Italy's federal government quickly passed emergency powers and implemented strenuous measures to control the contagion. A national lockdown was strictly policed, turning Rome, Florence, and all urban Italy into ghost cities. In many places—and later, nationally—masks and social distancing were enforced, both indoors and, at times, outside. By late May 2020, the first wave of infections had receded. Official figures put the death toll at over 33,000. Excess mortality data suggests this is a significant underestimate.

On/off national and local lockdowns, mask mandates bolstered by stiff fines, strict enforcement of social distancing in shops and businesses, quarantine, and a national test-and-trace regime were deployed through 2020 and 2021. Further major virus peaks in November 2020 and April 2021 grew progressively smaller. Vaccine rollout kept pace with Italy's European neighbors, driven by altruism and a growing realization that such treasured rituals as eating indoors, attending soccer stadia, even entering museums would be barred to the unvaccinated or those without proof of exemption. Still, 18-plus months of Covid-19 had claimed more than 130,000 Italian lives, one of the developed world's gravest tolls.

And yet, 2021 was not entirely gloomy. A more optimistic summer saw the virus pushed off the front pages by a national obsession from happier times: soccer. Italian national team coach Roberto Mancini had promised to make a wounded country proud again. He delivered in style, with "the *Azzurri*" winning football's European Championship. Soccer success was closely followed by Italy's best Olympics in recent memory, including a Texas-born sprinter capturing the gold in the men's 100m. The first dribbles of data showed a much better summer for tourism than expected, driven perhaps by the success of Italy's vaccination plan and the European Union's multi-country Digital COVID Certificate scheme.

These are only the first small steps on what may well be a long road to recovery. Bouncing back is critical for an economy that draws visitors from every corner of the globe. For detailed guidance on the latest pandemic protocols, see "Visiting Italy in the Covid-19 Era," in chapter 10.

# THE MAKING OF ITALY

## Etruscans & Villanovans: Prehistory to the Rise of Rome

Among all early inhabitants of Italy, the most significant legacy was left by the **Etruscans.** No one knows exactly where they came from (although some evidence points to origins in what is now Turkey) and the inscriptions they left behind (often on tombs in necropoli) are too bland to be of much help. Whatever their origins, within 2 centuries of appearing on the peninsula around 800 B.C., they had subjugated lands in modern **Tuscany** (to which they leave their name), northern Lazio, and Campania, along with the so-called **"Villanovan"** tribes that lived there. They also made Rome the governmental seat of Latium. "Roma" is an Etruscan name, and the mythical ancient kings of Rome had Etruscan names: Numa, Ancus, even Romulus.

The Etruscans ruled until the **Roman Revolt** around 509 B.C., which expelled Rome's Etruscan kings. By 250 B.C. Romans and their allies had vanquished or assimilated the Etruscans, wiping out their language and religion. Many of their manners and beliefs remained, however, and are integral to what we now think of as "Roman culture."

Rome's **Museo Nazionale Etrusco** (p. 120) and the Etruscan collection in Rome's **Vatican Museums** (p. 89) are a logical starting point to see remnants of Etruscan civilization. Florence's **MAF Museo Archeologico** (p. 194) houses one of the greatest Etruscan bronzes unearthed, the "Arezzo Chimera."

The Arezzo Chimera, star attraction of Florence's archaeological museum.

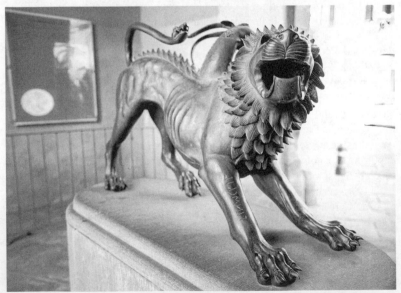

# THE ESSENTIALS OF italian FOOD

Italians know how to cook—just ask one. But be sure to leave plenty of time: Once Italians start talking food, they don't pause for breath. Italy does not really have a unified national cuisine; it's a loose grouping of delicious regional cuisines which share a few staples, notably pasta, bread, tomatoes, and pig meat cured in endlessly creative ways.

**Rome** can be the best place to introduce yourself to Italian food, because it has restaurants from every region. There are some authentic Roman specialties, however, such as *saltimbocca alla romana* (literally "jump-in-your-mouth"—thin slices of veal with sage, cured ham, and cheese), *carciofi alla romana* (tender artichokes cooked with herbs), and the ubiquitous *spaghetti alla carbonara*—pasta coated in a silky sauce of cured pork cheek, egg, and *pecorino Romano* (sheep's milk cheese). Historical migration has also infused Roman food with a strong current of Jewish cuisine.

To the north, in **Florence and Tuscany,** you'll find seasonal ingredients served simply. One main ingredient for almost any savory dish is the local olive oil, feted for its low acidity. The typical Tuscan pasta is wide, flat *pappardelle*, generally tossed with a game sauce such as *lepre* (hare) or *cinghiale* (boar). Tuscans are fond of their own local pecorino, a strong ewe's-milk cheese made in Pienza. The classic main course is a *bistecca alla fiorentina*, a T-bone–like slab of meat from the white Chianina

breed of cattle. Sweet treats are also good here, particularly Siena's *panforte* (a dense, sticky cake) and *biscotti di Prato* (hard, almond-flour biscuits for dipping in dessert wine).

While **Venice** is rarely celebrated for its cuisine, the fresh seafood is usually excellent. Grilled fish is often served with red radicchio, a bitter lettuce that thrives around nearby Treviso. Two classic Venetian non-fish dishes are *fegato alla veneziana* (liver and onions) and *risi e bisi* (rice and fresh peas). The traditional carbohydrate here isn't pasta but *risotto* (rice), delectably flavored with seasonal vegetables or seafood.

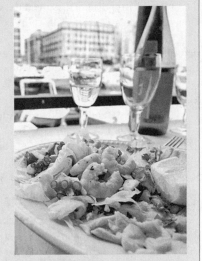

Fresh seafood and alfresco dining in Italy.

## The Roman Republic: ca. 509–27 B.C.

After the Roman Republic was established around 509 B.C.—it's impossible to date precisely—the Romans continued to increase their power by conquering neighboring communities in the highlands and forming alliances with other Latins in the lowlands. They gave to their allies, and then to conquered peoples, partial or complete Roman citizenship, with a corresponding obligation of military service. This further increased Rome's power and reach.

Citizen colonies were established as settlements of Roman farmers or veterans, among them both **Florence** and **Siena.** The all-powerful Senate presided as Rome defeated rival powers one after another and came to rule the Mediterranean Sea.

No figure was more towering during the late Republic, nor more instrumental in its transformation into Empire (see below), than **Julius Caesar,** the charismatic conqueror of Gaul—"the wife of every husband and the husband of every wife," according to scurrilous rumors reported by 1st-century historian Suetonius. After defeating the last resistance of the Pompeiians in 45 B.C., he came to Rome and was made dictator and consul for 10 years. Conspirators, led by Brutus, stabbed him to death at the Theater of Pompey on March 15, 44 B.C., the "Ides of March." The site (now **Largo di Torre Argentina**) is an Instagrammers' hotspot these days. Not for the history: It is home to a photogenic feral cat colony.

The conspirators' motivation was to restore power to the Republic and topple dictatorship. But they failed: **Mark Antony,** a Roman general, assumed control. He made peace with Caesar's willed successor, **Octavian,** and after the Treaty of Brundisium dissolved the Republic, he found himself married to Octavian's sister, Octavia. This didn't prevent him from also marrying Egyptian queen Cleopatra in 36 B.C. A furious Octavian gathered legions and defeated Antony at the **Battle of Actium** on September 2, 31 B.C. Cleopatra fled to Egypt, followed by Antony, who committed suicide in disgrace a year later. Cleopatra, unable to retain her rule of Egypt, followed suit with the help of an asp.

Many of the standing buildings of Ancient Rome are from later periods, but parts of the **Roman Forum** (p. 101) date to the Republic, including the **Temple of Saturn.** The adjacent **Capitoline Hill** and **Palatine Hill** have been sacred religious and civic places since the earliest days of Rome. Rome's best Republican-era artifacts are inside the **Musei Capitolini** (p. 96).

## The Roman Empire in Its Pomp: 27 B.C.–A.D. 395

Born Gaius Octavius in 63 B.C., then known as Octavian, **Augustus** became the first Roman emperor in 27 B.C. and reigned until A.D. 14. His autocratic rule ushered in the so-called *"Pax Romana,"* 2 centuries of peace. In Rome you can still see the remains of the **Forum of Augustus** (p. 100) and admire his statue in the **Vatican Museums** (p. 89).

By now, Rome ruled the entire Mediterranean world, either directly or indirectly. All political, commercial, and cultural pathways led to Rome, a sprawling city set on seven hills: the Capitoline, Palatine, Aventine, Caelian, Esquiline, Quirinal, and Viminal. It was during this period **Virgil** wrote his epic poem "The Aeneid," supplying a grandiose founding myth for the city and empire; **Ovid** composed erotic poetry; and **Horace** wrote his "Odes."

The emperors brought Rome to new heights. Yet without the counterbalance once provided by the Senate and legislatures, success bred corruption. The centuries witnessed a steady decay in the ideals and traditions on which

# 10 EARLY ROMAN emperors

**Augustus** (ruled 27 B.C.–A.D.14): First, "divine" emperor to whom all later emperors aspired

**Tiberius** (r. A.D. 14–37): Former general whose increasingly unpopular reign was infused with paranoia

**Caligula** (r. A.D. 37–41): This young emperor's reign of spite and terror ended in assassination by his own Praetorian Guard

**Claudius** (r. A.D. 41–54): A sickly man who turned into a wise and capable emperor, as well as the conqueror of Britain

**Nero** (r. A.D. 54–68): Last emperor of the Julio-Claudian dynasty, a cruel megalo-maniac who killed his own mother and may have started the Great Fire of Rome (A.D. 64)

**Vespasian** (r. A.D. 69–79): First emperor of the Flavian dynasty, who built the Colosseum and lived as husband-and-wife with a freed slave, Caenis

**Domitian** (r. A.D. 81–96): Increasingly paranoid populist and authoritarian who became fixated on the idea he would be assassinated—and was proven right

**Trajan** (r. A.D. 98–117): Virtuous soldier-ruler who presided over the empire at its widest geographical spread and also rebuilt much of the city

**Hadrian** (r. A.D. 117–138): Humanist, general, and builder who redesigned the Pantheon and added the Temple of Venus and Roma to the Forum

**Marcus Aurelius** (r. A.D. 161–180): Phi-losopher-king, and last of the so-called Five Good Emperors, whose statue is in the Musei Capitolini

the Empire was founded. The army became a fifth column of unruly merce-naries, tax collectors became the scourge of the countryside, and for every good emperor (Augustus, Claudius, Trajan, Vespasian, and Hadrian, to name a few) there were also cruel, debased, or simply incompetent tyrants (Calig-ula, Nero, Caracalla, and many others).

After Augustus died (by poison, perhaps), his widow, **Livia**—a shrewd operator who had divorced her first husband to marry Augustus—used intrigues and poisonings to set up her son, **Tiberius,** as ruler. A series of mur-ders ensued and Tiberius, who ruled during Pontius Pilate's trial and crucifix-ion of Christ, was eventually murdered in his late 70s. Murder was so common that a short time later, **Domitian** (ruled A.D. 81–96) became so gripped by the fear of assassination, he ordered his palace walls covered in mica, so he could see behind himself at all times. (He was killed anyway.)

Excesses ruled the day—at least, if you believe surviving tracts written by biased contemporary chroniclers: **Caligula** supposedly committed incest with his sister Drusilla; appointed his horse to the Senate; and proclaimed himself a god. Caligula's successor, his uncle **Claudius,** was poisoned by his final wife—Agrippina the Younger, who was also his niece—to secure the succession of **Nero,** her son by a previous marriage. Nero's thanks were later to murder not only his mother but also his wife (Claudius's daughter) and his rival, Claudius's 13-year-old son Britannicus. An enthusiastic persecutor of Christians, Nero sup-posedly committed suicide with the cry, "What an artist I destroy!"

By the 3rd century A.D., corruption and rivalry became so poisonous there were 23 emperors in 73 years. Few were as twisted as **Caracalla,** who to secure control, had his brother Geta slashed to pieces while Geta was in the arms of their mother, former empress Julia Domna.

**Constantine the Great,** who became emperor in A.D. 306, made Constantinople (or Byzantium) the new capital of the Empire in 330, moving administrative functions away from Rome altogether, partly because of the growing menace of barbarian attacks. Constantine was the first Christian emperor, allegedly converting after he saw the True Cross in a dream, accompanied by the words, IN THIS SIGN SHALL YOU CONQUER. He defeated rival emperor Maxentius and his followers at the **Battle of the Milvian Bridge** (A.D. 312), a victory memorialized by Rome's triumphal **Arco di Costantino** (p. 95). Constantine formally ended the persecution of Christians with the **Edict of Milan** (A.D. 313).

During the Imperial period Rome flourished in architecture. **Classical orders** were simplified into forms of column capitals: **Doric** (a plain capital), **Ionic** (a capital with a scroll), and **Corinthian** (a capital with acanthus leaves). Much of this development was enabled by the invention of concrete and fine-tuning the arch, which was used with a logic, rhythm, and ease never before seen. Many of these monumental buildings still stand in Rome, notably **Trajan's Column** (p. 101), the **Colosseum** (p. 98), and Hadrian's **Pantheon** (p. 110). Elsewhere in Italy, Verona's massive **Arena** (p. 295) bears witness to huge crowds the brutal sport of gladiatorial combat could draw. Three **Roman cities** have been preserved, with street plans and in some cases even buildings intact: doomed **Pompeii** (p. 137) and its neighbor **Herculaneum,** both buried by Vesuvius's cataclysmic A.D. 79 eruption; and Rome's ancient seaport, **Ostia Antica** (p. 140). At Herculaneum, one of Rome's greatest writers, **Pliny the Elder** (A.D. 23–79), perished. It's thanks to him; his nephew, **Pliny the Younger,** and satirist **Juvenal;** and historians **Tacitus, Suetonius, Cassius Dio,** and **Livy** that knowledge of ancient Roman life and history was not lost.

Surviving Roman **art** had a major influence on the painters and sculptors of the Renaissance (p. 32). In Rome itself, look for the marble *bas-reliefs* (sculptures projecting slightly from a flat surface) on the **Arco di Costantino** (p. 95); the sculpture and mosaic collections at the **Palazzo Massimo alle Terme** (p. 122); and the gilded equestrian statue of Marcus Aurelius at the **Musei Capitolini** (p. 96). The Florentine Medici were avid collectors of Roman statuary, much of it now at the **Uffizi** (p. 181).

## The Fall of the Empire Through the "Dark Ages"

The Eastern and Western sections of the Roman Empire split in A.D. 395, leaving the Italian peninsula without support it once received from east of the Adriatic. When the **Goths** moved toward Rome in the early 5th century, citizens in the provinces, who had grown to hate the bureaucracy set up by **Diocletian,** welcomed the invaders. And then the pillage began.

# ALL ABOUT VINO (& birra, too)

Italy is the largest **wine**-producing country in the world; as far back as 800 B.C., the Etruscans were vintners. However, it wasn't until 1965 that laws were enacted to guarantee consistency in winemaking. Quality wines are labeled **"DOC"** (Denominazione di Origine Controllata). If you see **"DOCG"** on a label (the "G" stands for *Garantita*), this denotes an even higher-quality wine region (in theory, at least). **"IGT"** (Indicazione Geografica Tipica) indicates a more general wine zone—for example, Umbria—but still with mandatory quality control.

Below we cite a few of the best Italian wines around Venice, Rome, and Florence. Rest assured there are hundreds more—have fun sampling to find your own favorites. Even a pitcher of a local *vino della casa* (house wine) can be a delight.

**Tuscany:** Tuscan red wines rank with the world's finest. **Sangiovese** is the king of grapes here; **Chianti** from the hills south of Florence is the most widely known Sangiovese wine. The premium zone is **Chianti Classico,** where a lively ruby-red DOCG wine has a bouquet of violets. More concentrated and powerful are the handful of **Chianti Classico Gran Selezione** wines chosen every year. The Tuscan south houses two even finer DOCGs: mighty, robust **Brunello di Montalcino,** a garnet red ideal for roasts and game; and almost purple **Vino Nobile di Montepulciano,** with its rich, velvet body. End a meal with the Tuscan dessert wine **Vin Santo,** often accompanied by hard *biscotti* to dunk in your glass.

**The Veneto:** Reds around Venice vary from light, lunchtime-friendly **Bardolino** to **Valpolicella,** which can be particularly intense if grapes are partially dried before fermentation to make an **Amarone.** White, Garganega-based **Soave** has a pale amber color and a peachlike flavor. **Lugana** at its best has a sparkle of gold and a rich but dry structure. **Prosecco** is the classic Italian sparkling white, the base for both a Bellini and a Spritz (joints that use Champagne are doing it wrong).

**Latium:** Many of Rome's rustic wines come from the Castelli Romani, hill towns around the capital. These wines are best drunk young and are most often white, mellow, and dry. The golden wines of **Frascati** are the most famous.

Italy's drink isn't all about wine, however. Especially among the young, there's a boom in popularity for artisanal **beer.** Although supermarket shelves are still stacked with mainstream brands Peroni and Moretti, smaller stores and bars increasingly offer craft microbrews. Italy had fewer than 50 breweries in 2000; the count was over 1,000 by 2018. Craft-beer consumption has more than tripled since 2012, according to brewers' association, Unionbirrai. Look for Unionbirrai's official seal on the label of genuine craft brewery products. For more on breweries and styles to look out for, browse the annual winners' list at **www.birradellanno.it**.

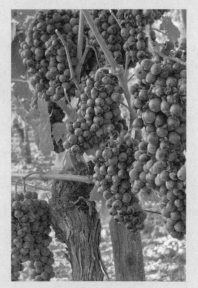

Italy's climate is perfect for vineyards.

Rome was first sacked by **Alaric I,** king of the Visigoths, in 410. The populace made no attempt to defend their city (other than trying vainly to buy him off, a tactic that worked 3 years earlier); most people fled into the hills. The feeble Western emperor **Honorius** hid out in **Ravenna,** which in 402 he declared capital of the Western Roman Empire.

More than 40 troubled years passed. Then **Attila the Hun** invaded Italy to besiege Rome. Attila was dissuaded from attacking, thanks largely to a peace mission headed by Pope Leo I in 452. Yet relief was short-lived: In 455, **Gaiseric,** king of the **Vandals,** sailed from Carthage in North Africa to carry out a 2-week sack of unparalleled thoroughness. The empire of the West limped on for another 20 years; finally, in 476, the sacks and chaos ended the once-mighty city. Rome itself was left to the popes, though ruled nominally from Ravenna.

Although little detailed history of Italy in the immediate post-Roman period is known—and few buildings survive—it is certain the spread of **Christianity** was creating a new society. The religion was probably founded in Rome about a decade after the death of Jesus and gradually gained strength despite Roman persecution. To relive the early Christian era, visit Rome's Appian Way and its Catacombs, along the **Via Appia Antica** (p. 127), just outside Rome's ancient walls. A church on the Appian Way marks the spot where the disciple Peter, fleeing persecution, is said to have had a pivotal vision of Christ; the nearby **Catacombs** (p. 128), the first cemeteries of Rome's Christian community, house remains of early popes and martyrs.

We have Christianity, along with the influence of Byzantium, to thank for the appearance of Italy's next great artistic style: the **Byzantine.** Painting and mosaic work in this era was stylized and static, but also ornate and ethereal. Churches in the Byzantine style include Venice's **Basilica di San Marco** (p. 261) and Rome's **Basilica di San Clemente** (p. 104).

## The Middle Ages: 9th–14th Centuries

A ravaged Rome entered the Middle Ages, its population scattered. A modest number of residents continued to live around the swamps of the **Campus Martius.** The Seven Hills—now without water because aqueducts were cut—stood abandoned and crumbling.

The pope turned toward Europe, where he found a powerful ally in **Charlemagne,** king of the Franks. In 800, Pope Leo III crowned him emperor. Although Charlemagne pledged allegiance to the church and made the pope the final arbiter in most religious and cultural matters, he also set Western Europe on a course of bitter opposition to papal meddling in affairs of state.

The successor to Charlemagne's empire was a political entity known as the **Holy Roman Empire** (962–1806). The new Empire defined the end of the Dark Ages but ushered in a long period of bloody warfare. Magyars from Hungary invaded Lombardy and, in turn, were defeated by an increasingly powerful **Venice,** which, having defeated its naval rival Genoa in the 1380 Battle of Chioggia, reigned over most of the eastern Mediterranean. Venetian merchants ruled a republic that lasted for a millennium and built a city of imposing architecture like the **Doge's Palace** (p. 263).

While Venice flourished, **Rome** during the Middle Ages was a quaint backwater. Narrow lanes with overhanging buildings filled areas that had once been showcases of imperial power. The forums, markets, temples, and theaters of the Imperial era slowly disintegrated. It remained the seat of the Roman Catholic Church, a state almost completely controlled by priests who aggressively expanded Church influence and acquisitions. The result was an endless series of power struggles.

In the mid–14th century, the **Black Death** ravaged Europe, killing perhaps a third of Italy's population; the preservation of Tuscan towns like **San Gimignano** (p. 218) and **Siena** (p. 212) owes much to the fact they never fully recovered from the devastations of this 1348–49 plague. Despite such setbacks, Italian city-states grew wealthy from Crusades booty, trade, and banking. The **Florin,** a gold coin minted in Florence, became the first truly international currency for centuries, dominating trade all over the continent.

The medieval period marks the beginning of building in stone on a mass scale. Flourishing from 800 to 1300, **Romanesque architecture** took its inspiration and rounded arches from Ancient Rome. Architects built large churches with wide aisles to accommodate the masses. Pisa's **Campo dei Miracoli** (p. 216) is typical of Pisan-Romanesque style, with stacked arcades of mismatched columns in the cathedral facade (and wrapped around the **Leaning Tower of Pisa**) and blind arcading set with diamond-shaped lozenges. The influence of Arab architecture is obvious—Pisa was a city of seafaring merchants.

**Romanesque sculpture** is often wonderfully childlike in its narrative simplicity, frequently mixing biblical scenes with the myths and motifs of pagan traditions. Among Italy's greatest surviving examples of Romanesque sculpture are 48 relief panels on the bronze doors of the **Basilica di San Zeno Maggiore** in Verona (p. 295).

As the appeal of Romanesque and Byzantine faded, the **Gothic** style flourished between the 13th and 15th centuries. Gothic architecture was characterized by flying buttresses, pointed arches, and delicate stained-glass windows. These engineering developments freed architecture from the heavy, thick walls of the Romanesque and allowed ceilings to soar, walls to thin, and windows to proliferate. Many secular Gothic buildings arose, including palaces designed to show off the prestige of various ruling regimes, like Siena's **Palazzo Pubblico** (p. 213) and a number of great buildings of **Venice** (see chapter 8). **San Gimignano** (p. 218) has a remarkably preserved Gothic center.

Painters such as **Cimabue** (1251–1302) and **Giotto** (1266–1337) in Florence, **Pietro Cavallini** (1259–ca. 1330) in Rome, and **Duccio di Buoninsegna** (ca. 1255–1319) in Siena lifted art from Byzantine rigidity and set it on the road to realism. Giotto's finest work is his fresco cycle at Padua's **Cappella degli Scrovegni** (p. 293); he was the harbinger of the oncoming Renaissance, which would forever change art and architecture. Duccio's "Maestà,"

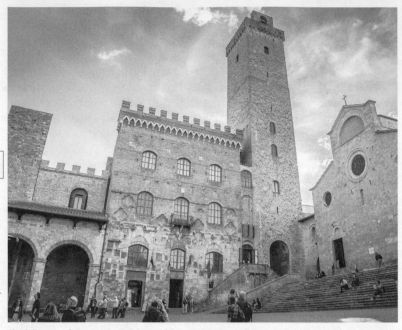

The hill town of San Gimignano is a 14th-century time capsule.

now in Siena's **Museo dell'Opera del Duomo** (p. 213), influenced Sienese painters for centuries. Ambrogio Lorenzetti painted the greatest civic frescoes of the Middle Ages—his "Allegories of Good and Bad Government" in Siena's **Palazzo Pubblico** (p. 213)—before he succumbed to the Black Death, along with almost every significant Sienese artist of his generation.

The medieval period saw the birth of literature in the Italian language, a written version of the **Tuscan dialect**—primarily because the great writers of the age were Tuscans. Florentine **Dante Alighieri** wrote his "Divine Comedy" in the 1310s, and Boccaccio's "Decameron"—a kind of Florentine "Canterbury Tales"—appeared in the 1350s.

## Renaissance & Baroque Italy: 1400s–1700s

The story of Italy from the dawn of the Renaissance in the early 15th century to the Age of Enlightenment in the 17th and 18th centuries is as fascinating and complicated as that of the rise and fall of the Roman Empire.

During this period, **Rome** underwent major physical changes. The old centers of culture reverted to pastures; new churches and palaces were built with the recycled stones of Ancient Rome. This construction boom did more damage to the temples of the Caesars than any barbarian sack ever had. Rare marbles were stripped from Imperial-era baths and used as altarpieces or sent to limekilns. So enthusiastic was the popes' destruction of Imperial Rome, it's a miracle anything is left.

# RENAISSANCE reading

Whole libraries have been written on the Renaissance—and it's worth acquainting yourself with some of the themes and styles before you visit. The most accessible introductions include Peter and Linda Murray's **The Art of the Renaissance** (1963), Michael Levey's **Early Renaissance** (1967), Evelyn Welch's **Art in Renaissance Italy 1350–1500** (2000), and Peter Murray's **The Architecture of** **the Italian Renaissance** (1969). Giorgio Vasari's **Lives of the Artists,** first published in 1550, remains the definitive work on Renaissance artists, written by one who knew some of them personally; it's still a good read. In **The Stones of Florence** (1956), Mary McCarthy mixes architectural insight with no-holds-barred opinion.

Around 1400 the most significant power in Italy was the city where the Renaissance began: **Florence** (see chapter 6). The **Medici** family rose to become the most powerful of the city's ruling oligarchy, gradually usurping the trades guilds and republicans. They reformed law and commerce, expanded the city's power by taking control of neighbors such as **Pisa** (see chapter 7), and financed a "renaissance," or rebirth, in painting, sculpture, and architecture. Christopher Hibbert's *The Rise and Fall of the House of Medici* is the most readable historical account of the era. Netflix's *Medici: Masters of Florence* and *The Magnificent* serve up a fictionalized, sensationalized, but fun "history" of power plays in the Renaissance city.

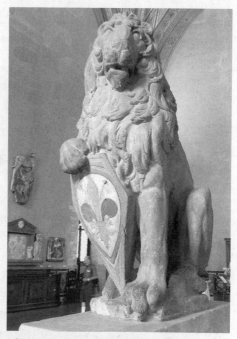

Under the patronage of the Medici and other rich Florentine families, innovative painters and sculptors pursued expressiveness and naturalism. In Florence, **Donatello** (1386–1466) cast the first free-standing nude since antiquity (now in the **Museo Nazionale del Bargello;** see p. 184). **Lorenzo Ghiberti** (1378–1455) labored for 50 years on two sets of doors for the **Baptistery** (p. 175), the most famous of which were dubbed the "Gates of Paradise"; and **Masaccio** (1401–28) produced the first painting

A lion holds Florence's coat of arms, Museo Nazionale del Bargello.

to realistically portray linear perspective, on the nave wall of **Santa Maria Novella** (p. 192).

Next followed a brief period known as the **High Renaissance.** The epitome of Renaissance Man, Florentine **Leonardo da Vinci** (1452–1519) painted his "Last Supper" in Milan and an "Annunciation" now hanging in Florence's **Uffizi** (p. 181), beside countless Renaissance masterpieces from such great painters as Paolo Uccello, Sandro Botticelli, and Piero della Francesca. **Raphael** (1483–1520) produced a sublime body of work in his 37 years. Skilled in sculpture, painting, and architecture, **Michelangelo** (1475–1564) marks the apogee of the Renaissance. His giant "David" at the **Galleria dell'Accademia** (p. 194) in Florence is the world's most famous statue; his **Sistine Chapel** frescoes have lured millions to the **Vatican Museums** (p. 89) in Rome.

The father of Venice's High Renaissance was **Titian** (1485–1576), known for his mastery of color and tone. Venice (see chapter 8) offers up a trove of Titian's art, along with works by earlier Venetian masters **Gentile Bellini** (1429–1507), **Giorgione** (1477–1510), and **Vittore Carpaccio** (1465–1525).

As in painting, Renaissance **architecture** stressed proportion, order, and classical inspiration. In the early 1400s, **Filippo Brunelleschi** (1377–1446) grasped the mathematics of "perspective" and provided artists with ground rules for creating an illusion of three dimensions on a flat surface. (Read Ross King's *Brunelleschi's Dome* for the story of his greatest achievement, the crowning of Florence's cathedral with its iconic ochre dome.) Even **Michelangelo** took up architecture late in life, designing the Laurentian Library and New Sacristy at the **Medici Chapels** in Florence (p. 190) then moving to complete the soaring dome of Rome's **St. Peter's Basilica** (p. 86). The third

"Annunciation" by Leonardo da Vinci in the Galleria degli Uffizi, Florence.

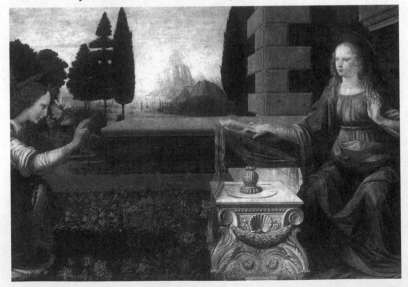

great Renaissance architect—and most influential of them all—**Andrea Palladio** (1508–80) worked in a classical mode of columns, porticoes, pediments, and other ancient-temple-inspired features. His masterpiece is the elegant **Il Redentore** church (p. 281) in Venice.

In time, the High Renaissance evolved into the **baroque.** Stuccoes, sculptures, and paintings were carefully designed to complement each other—and the space itself—to create a unified whole. The baroque movement's spiritual home was Rome, and its towering figure was **Gian Lorenzo Bernini** (1598–1680), the greatest baroque sculptor, a fantastic architect, and a more-than-decent painter. Among many fine sculptures, you'll find his best in Rome's **Galleria Borghese** (p. 118) and **Santa Maria della Vittoria** (p. 122) church.

In **music,** the most famous baroque composer was Venetian **Antonio Vivaldi** (1678–1741), whose "Four Seasons" is among the most performed classical compositions of all time. In **painting,** baroque often mixed a kind of super-realism—using peasants as models, exaggerating light and shadow with a technique called *chiaroscuro*—with complex composition and dynamic explosions of movement and color. The period produced many fine painters, notably **Caravaggio** (1571–1610). Among his masterpieces are a "St. Matthew" cycle in Rome's **San Luigi dei Francesi** (p. 110). The baroque also had an outstanding female painter: **Artemisia Gentileschi** (1593–1652), whose brutal "Judith Slaying Holofernes" hangs in Florence's **Uffizi** (p. 181).

Frothy and ornate, **rococo** art was the baroque taken to flamboyant extremes and had few serious proponents in Italy. **Giambattista Tiepolo** (1696–1770), arguably the best of the rococo painters, specialized in ceiling frescoes and canvases with cloud-filled heavens of light, as in Venice's **Scuola Grande dei Carmini** (p. 276). For rococo building—more a decorative than an architectural movement—look no further than Rome's **Spanish Steps** (p. 116) or **Trevi Fountain** (p. 118).

## At Last, a United Italy: the 1800s

By the 1800s Renaissance glories were a fading memory. Chunks of Italy had changed hands many, many times—between the Austrians, the Spanish, and the French, among autocratic thugs and enlightened princes, between the noble and the merchant classes. The 19th century witnessed the final collapse of many Renaissance city-states. The last of the Medici, Gian Gastone, died in 1737, leaving Tuscany in the hands of foreign Lorraine and Habsburg princes. In 1797 French emperor **Napoleon** brought an end to a millennium of republican government in **Venice,** installing puppet rulers across the Italian peninsula. Napoleon's military even oversaw a brief return of the **Roman Republic** (1796–98). After a British/Prussian/Dutch alliance defeated Napoleon, the **Congress of Vienna** (1814–15) parceled out various parts of Italy once again.

Political unrest became a fact of Italian life, spurred by insurrectionaries like **Giuseppe Mazzini.** Europe's year of revolutions, **1848,** rocked Italy with violent uprisings. After decades of political intrigue, thanks to the efforts of statesman **Camillo Cavour** and rebel general **Giuseppe Garibaldi,** the

Rome's rococo Trevi Fountain.

Kingdom of Italy was proclaimed in 1861 with **Vittorio Emanuele II** of Savoy as its first monarch. The kingdom's first capital was **Turin** (1861–65), followed by **Florence** (1865–71).

The establishment of a kingdom, however, didn't signal a complete unification of Italy—Latium (including Rome) was still under papal control and Venetia was held by Austria. In 1866, Venetia joined the rest of Italy after the **Seven Weeks' War** between Austria and Prussia. Then on September 20, 1870, Rome was taken—present-day **Via XX Settembre** is the very street up which patriots advanced after breaching the gates. It became the capital in 1871. The **Risorgimento**—the "resurgence," Italian unification—was complete.

Political heights in Italy seemed to correspond to creative depths in art and architecture. Among few notable practitioners of this era was Venetian **Antonio Canova** (1757–1822), Italy's major neoclassical sculptor, who became notorious for painting both Napoleon and his sister Pauline as nudes. His best work is in Rome's **Galleria Borghese** (p. 118).

Music, however, was experiencing its Italian golden age: **Opera** is the major legacy of the 19th century. *Bel canto* composer **Gioachino Rossini** (1792–1868) found success with his 1816 "The Barber of Seville," and the fame of **Gaetano Donizetti** (1797–1848) was assured when his "Anna Bolena" premiered in 1830. Both were later overshadowed by **Giuseppe Verdi** (1813–1901), whose works such as "Rigoletto" and "La Traviata" assumed profound nationalist symbolism. At the turn of the century, the Romantic movement that had dominated music gave way to the *verismo* ("realism") of others including **Giacomo Puccini** (1858–1924), whose operas "La Bohème," "Tosca," "Madama Butterfly," and the unfinished "Turandot" still pack houses worldwide.

# The 20th Century: Two World Wars & One Duce

In 1915, Italy entered **World War I** on the side of the Allies, joining Britain, Russia, and France to help defeat Germany and Italy's traditional enemy to the north—now the Austro-Hungarian Empire—and so to "reclaim" Trentino and Trieste. (Mark Thompson's *The White War* [2008] tells the story of Italy's catastrophic, though victorious, campaign.) In the aftermath of war's carnage, Italians suffered further with rising unemployment and horrendous inflation. As in Germany, political crisis led to the emergence of a dictator.

On October 28, 1922, **Benito Mussolini,** who started his Fascist Party in 1919, gathered 30,000 Black Shirts for his **March on Rome.** Inflation was soaring and workers had called a general strike, but rather than recognize a state under siege, **King Vittorio Emanuele III** (1900–46) proclaimed Mussolini the new government leader. In 1929 "Il Duce" ("the chief")—a moniker Mussolini began using from 1925—defined the divisions between the Italian government and pope by signing the Lateran Treaty, which granted political, territorial, and fiscal autonomy to the microstate of **Vatican City.** During the Spanish Civil War (1936–39), Mussolini's support for General Franco's Fascists, who had staged a coup against the elected government of Spain, helped seal the Axis alliance between Italy and Nazi Germany. Italy was inexorably and disastrously sucked into **World War II.**

Deeply unpleasant though their politics were, the Fascist regime did sponsor some remarkable **rationalist architecture,** such as Rome's **EUR** suburb and Florence's **Santa Maria Novella station.** (Today a plaque at the station commemorates Jews sent from the terminus to their deaths in Nazi Germany.)

After defeat in World War II, Italy voted to establish the **First Republic**—overwhelmingly so in northern and central Italy, who outvoted a southern majority in favor of keeping the monarchy. Italy quickly succeeded in rebuilding its economy, in part because of U.S. aid under the **Marshall Plan** (1948–52). By the 1960s, as a member of the European Economic Community (founded by the **Treaty of Rome** in 1957), Italy was one of the world's leading industrialized nations, prominent in the manufacture of

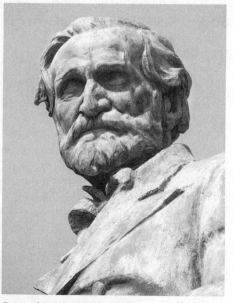

Statue of Giuseppe Verdi in his hometown of Bussetto, just outside Parma, Italy.

| The A-List of Italian Novels Available in English | |
|---|---|
| o Alessandro Manzoni, *The Betrothed* (1827) | o Italo Calvino, *If on a Winter's Night a Traveler* (1979) |
| o Alberto Moravia, *The Conformist* (1951) | o Umberto Eco, *Foucault's Pendulum* (1988) |
| o Giuseppe Tomasi di Lampedusa, *The Leopard* (1958) | o Niccolò Ammaniti, *I'm Not Scared* (2001) |
| o Elsa Morante, *History: A Novel* (1974) | o Elena Ferrante, *Neapolitan Novels* (2012–15) |

automobiles and office equipment. Fiat (from Turin), Ferrari (from Emilia-Romagna), and Olivetti (from northern Piedmont) were known around the world.

The postwar Italian **film industry** gained notice for its innovative directors. **Federico Fellini** (1920–93) burst onto the scene with a highly individual style, starting with *La Strada* (1954) and going on to such classics as *The City of Women* (1980). His *La Dolce Vita* (1961) defined an era in Rome. The gritty "neorealism" of controversial **Pier Paolo Pasolini** (1922–75) is conveyed most vividly in *Accattone* (1961), which he wrote and directed.

The country continued to be plagued, however, by economic inequality between the prosperous industrial north and depressed south. During the late 1970s and early 1980s, it was rocked by domestic terrorism: These were the so-called **Anni di Piombo (Years of Lead),** when extremists of left and right bombed and assassinated with impunity. Conspiracy theories became a staple diet; everyone from a shadow state to Masonic lodges to the CIA was accused of involvement in what became an undeclared civil war. The most notorious incident of the Anni di Piombo was the kidnap and murder of Prime Minister **Aldo Moro** in 1978. A succinct account of these murky years is in Tobias Jones's *The Dark Heart of Italy* (2003).

# WHEN TO GO

The best months for traveling in most of Italy are from **April to June** and **mid-September to October:** Temperatures are usually comfortable, rural colors are rich, and crowds aren't too intense (except around Easter). From **July through early September** the country's holiday spots teem with visitors. **Easter, May,** and **June** usually see the highest hotel prices in Rome and Florence.

**August** is the worst month in many places: Not only is it uncomfortably hot and muggy, but seemingly the entire country goes on vacation for at least 2 weeks (some Italians take off the entire month). Many family-run hotels, restaurants, and shops are closed (except at the spas, beaches, and islands, where most Italians head). Paradoxically, Florence in August can seem emptied of locals, and hotels there (and in Rome) were once heavily discounted (alas, now less so). Be aware that fashionable urban restaurants and nightspots close for the whole month.

From **late October to Easter,** many attractions operate on shorter (sometimes *much* shorter) winter hours, and some hotels close for renovation or redecoration, although this is less likely to be a problem in a city. Many family-run restaurants take a week or three off sometime between **November** and **February;** beach destinations become padlocked ghost towns. Deals are often available then, if you avoid Christmas and New Year.

## Weather

It's warm all over Italy in summer; landlocked cities in Tuscany can be stifling during a July or August hot spell. Higher temperatures (measured in Italy in degrees Celsius) usually begin in May, often lasting until early October. Winters in the north of Italy are cold, with rain and snow, and a biting wind whistles over the mountains into Venice and, less often, Florence. In Rome and farther south, the weather is mostly warm (or at least, warm-ish) all year, averaging 10°C (50°F) in winter. Even here chilly snaps are possible, as freezing temperatures and heavy snow in recent winters proved. The rainiest months are October and November.

### Italy's Average Daily High Temperature & Monthly Rainfall

| | | JAN | FEB | MAR | APR | MAY | JUNE | JULY | AUG | SEPT | OCT | NOV | DEC |
|---|---|---|---|---|---|---|---|---|---|---|---|---|---|
| **ROME** | Temp. (°F) | 55 | 56 | 59 | 63 | 71 | 77 | 83 | 83 | 79 | 71 | 62 | 57 |
| | Temp. (°C) | 12 | 13 | 15 | 17 | 21 | 25 | 28 | 28 | 26 | 21 | 16 | 13 |
| | Rainfall (in.) | 3.2 | 2.8 | 2.7 | 2.6 | 2 | 1.3 | .6 | 1 | 2.7 | 4.5 | 4.4 | 3.8 |
| **FLORENCE** | Temp. (°F) | 49 | 53 | 60 | 68 | 75 | 84 | 89 | 88 | 81 | 69 | 58 | 50 |
| | Temp. (°C) | 9 | 11 | 15 | 20 | 23 | 28 | 31 | 31 | 27 | 20 | 14 | 10 |
| | Rainfall (in.) | 1.9 | 2.1 | 2.7 | 2.9 | 3 | 2.7 | 1.5 | 1.9 | 3.3 | 4 | 3.9 | 2.8 |
| **VENICE** | Temp. (°F) | 42 | 47 | 54 | 61 | 70 | 77 | 81 | 81 | 75 | 65 | 53 | 44 |
| | Temp. (°C) | 6 | 8 | 12 | 16 | 21 | 25 | 27 | 27 | 24 | 18 | 11 | 7 |
| | Rainfall (in.) | 2.3 | 2.1 | 2.2 | 2.5 | 2.7 | 3 | 2.5 | 3.3 | 2.6 | 2.7 | 3.4 | 2.1 |

## Public Holidays

Offices, government buildings (though not usually tourist information centers), and shops in Italy generally close on: January 1 (*Capodanno,* or New Year); January 6 (*La Befana,* or Epiphany); Easter Sunday *(Pasqua)*; Easter Monday *(Pasquetta)*; April 25 (Liberation Day); May 1 (*Festa del Lavoro,* or Labor Day); June 2 (*Festa della Repubblica,* or Republic Day); August 15 (*Ferragosto,* or the Assumption of the Virgin); November 1 (All Saints' Day); December 8 (*L'Immacolata,* or the Immaculate Conception); December 25 (*Natale,* Christmas Day); and December 26 (*Santo Stefano,* or St. Stephen's Day). You'll often find businesses closed for any annual celebration dedicated to a local patron saint (for example, Jan 31 in San Gimignano, Tuscany).

*Note:* Many of the following festivals and events were cancelled or postponed in 2020 and 2021 due to the coronavirus. Be sure to use the contact info below to check on the latest updates on pandemic restrictions and any revised festival dates.

# Italy Calendar of Events

## FEBRUARY

**Carnevale,** Venice. At this riotous time, theatrical presentations and masked balls take place across Venice and on islands in its lagoon. Balls are by invitation only (except the Doge's Ball), but street events and fireworks are open to everyone. www.carnevale.venezia.it. Two weeks before Ash Wednesday.

## MARCH

**Festa di San Giuseppe,** Trionfale Quarter, Rome. A decorated statue of St. Joseph graces a fair with food stalls, concerts, and sporting events. Around March 19.

## APRIL

**Holy Week,** nationwide. Processions and ceremonies are staged—some dating to the Middle Ages. The pope leads the most notable procession, passing the Colosseum and Roman Forum; a torch-lit parade caps the observance. Beginning 4 days before Easter Sunday.

**Easter Sunday (Pasqua),** Piazza San Pietro, Rome. In an event broadcast around the world, the pope gives his blessing from the balcony of St. Peter's.

**Scoppio del Carro (Explosion of the Cart),** Florence. White oxen draw a cart laden with flowers and fireworks to the Duomo, where at the 11am Mass a mechanical dove detonates it. Easter Sunday.

## MAY

**Maggio Musicale Fiorentino (Florentine Musical May),** Florence. Italy's most prestigious music festival presents music from the 14th to the 20th centuries. www.maggiofiorentino.com. Late April to June.

**Concorso Ippico Internazionale (International Horse Show),** Piazza di Siena, Rome. Top-flight show jumping at the Villa Borghese. www.piazzadisiena.it. Late May.

## JUNE

**Festa di San Ranieri,** Pisa. The city honors its patron saint with candlelit parades, followed the next day by eight-rower teams competing in 16th-century costumes. June 16 and 17.

**Calcio Storico (Historic Football),** Florence. A revival of a raucous 15th-century form of football, pitting four teams in medieval costume against one another. Games usually culminate June 24, feast day of St. John the Baptist. www.calciostoricofiorentino.it. Late June.

**Gioco del Ponte,** Pisa. Teams in Renaissance costume take part in a long-contested push-of-war on the Ponte di Mezzo, which spans the Arno. www.giocodelpontedipisa.it. Last weekend in June.

**La Biennale di Venezia,** Venice. One of the world's most famous recurring contemporary art events takes place in alternate, odd-numbered years. www.labiennale.org. June to November.

## JULY

**Il Palio,** Piazza del Campo, Siena. Palio fever grips this Tuscan hill-town for a wild and exciting horse race from the Middle Ages. Pageantry, costumes, and celebrations for the victorious *contrada* (sort of a neighborhood social club) mark the spectacle. It's a "no rules" event: Even a horse without a rider can win. July 2 and August 16.

**Festa del Redentore (Feast of the Redeemer),** Venice. This festival marks the lifting of a 1576 plague with fireworks, pilgrimages, and boating. www.redentorevenezia.it. Third Saturday and Sunday in July.

## AUGUST

**Venice International Film Festival,** Venice. Ranking just behind Cannes, this festival brings together stars, directors, producers, and filmmakers from all over the world to the Palazzo del Cinema on Lido. www.labiennale.org. Late August to early September.

## SEPTEMBER

**Regata Storica,** Grand Canal, Venice. A maritime spectacular: Many gondolas participate in the canal procession, although gondolas don't race in the regatta itself. www.regatastoricavenezia.it. First Sunday in September.

## DECEMBER

**Christmas Blessing of the Pope,** Piazza San Pietro, Rome. Delivered at noon from the balcony of St. Peter's Basilica, the pope's words are broadcast to the faithful around the globe. December 25.

# ROME

By Elizabeth Heath

Once it ruled the Western World, and even the partial, scattered ruins of that awesome empire, of which Rome was the capital, are today among the most overpowering sights on earth. To walk the Roman Forum, to view the Colosseum, the Pantheon, and the Appian Way—these are among the most memorable, instructive, and illuminating experiences in all of travel. To see evidence of a once-great civilization that no longer exists is truly a humbling experience.

As a visitor to Rome, you will be constantly reminded of this city's extraordinary history. Take the time to get away from the crowds to explore the intimate piazzas and lesser basilicas in the back streets of Trastevere and the *centro storico*. Indulge in enogastronomic pursuits at coffee bars, trattorias, enotecas and gelaterias. Have a picnic in Villa Borghese or climb to the top of the Gianicolo for million-dollar views. Rome is so compact that without planning too much, you'll end up stumbling across its monuments and its simpler pleasures.

Walk the streets of Rome, and the city will be yours.

## Don't Leave Rome Without...

**Exploring the World's Smallest Country.** Vatican City is just .2 square miles, but what riches this tiny nation holds! From one of the finest museums on the planet, to its largest Catholic church, to the architectural masterwork that is St. Peter's Square, your trip isn't complete without at least a day spent here. See p. 84.

**Gazing over the Roman Forum and Palatine from Capitoline Hill Terraces at Night.** Yes, explore the ruins by day too, but after dark—as spotlights cast dramatic glows over solitary columns and crumbling arches—the view is truly, disarmingly spectacular. See p. 135.

**Lingering over Dinner.** Take time to unwind at a typical Roman trattoria, with a steady and wonderfully affordable flow of wine and delicious food. See p. 68.

**Downtime Spent Wandering the Streets of a Roman Neighborhood.** It's easy to over-program a visit to Rome, but time spent

## TRAVEL DISRUPTIONS IN rome

Virtually any travel guidance for Rome needs to appear with the suffix "but call ahead or check the website for the most current information." In 2020 and 2021, there were a number of pandemic-related closures and operational changes, and we cannot guarantee that everything will be back to normal by the time you read this guide. We've always encouraged readers to buy tickets in advance for the attractions they really want to see; that advice is even more pertinent now. Many attractions have switched to **advanced-ticketing only,** in order to limit crowds; though most are back to normal opening hours, check in advance, as some museums opened only on weekends in 2020 and 2021. **Proof of vaccination** (see p. 299) may be required for entry to museums and restaurants. Depending on when you arrive, **mask-wearing and social distancing** may still be advised, especially on public transportation. See p. 299 for more information, and check for the updated Covid-19 pages at **www.italia.it**.

Our hotel and restaurant listings (p. 54 and p. 68) reflect what those establishments expect to offer when you arrive, but on-again off-again pandemic restrictions may impact that. Hotels may still have reduced services, such as limited meal service or shuttered fitness rooms and saunas; if a certain amenity is important to you, check before booking. Restaurants have expanded outdoor dining areas or at least added a few sidewalk tables, but many now require reservations and may still serve only lunch or dinner rather than both; reserve ahead so you won't be disappointed.

wandering at leisure in Monti, Trastevere, or the Jewish Ghetto might be some of your most memorable.

**Mixing with Locals at the Lively Mercato di Testaccio.** No other market in the city has such a strong sense of community, coupled with the chance to sample real Roman street food. See p. 133.

# ESSENTIALS

## Arriving

**BY PLANE**    Most flights arrive to Terminal 3 of Rome's **Leonardo da Vinci International Airport (FCO)** (www.adr.it; ✆ **06-65951**), popularly known as **Fiumicino,** 30km (19 miles) from the city center. (If you're arriving from other European cities, you might land at Ciampino Airport, discussed below.) As you exit Baggage Claim, you'll see a **tourist information desk,** staffed daily from 8am to 8:45pm. A *cambio* (money exchange) operates daily from 7:30am to 11pm, but it's just as easy, and possibly less expensive, to withdraw cash from an ATM (*bancomat*) in the airport. See p. 306 for tips on using Italian ATMs.

Follow signs marked TRENI to find the airport train station, about a 10-minute walk from the arrivals area. *Pro tip:* If you have a lot of bags and opt for the train, grab a free luggage cart when you get to Baggage Claim. When you exit into the terminal, turn left instead of right, and take the elevator to the train station level. If you go right, you have to take an escalator and ditch the luggage cart.

From there, catch the delightfully named **Leonardo Express** for a 32-minute shuttle ride) to Rome's main station, **Stazione Termini.** The shuttle runs every 30 minutes from 6:23am to 11:23pm for 14€ one-way (free kids 12 and under). You can buy tickets from one of several machines (you can choose instructions in English and machines take cash or credit), or you can buy them at the Trenitalia window near the tracks. You can also buy e-tickets at www. trenitalia.com or use the Trenitalia mobile app.

A **taxi** from da Vinci airport to the city costs a flat-rate 48€ for the 45-minute to 1-hour trip, depending on traffic (hotels tend to charge 50€–60€ for pickup service). Note that the flat rate is applicable from the airport to central Rome and vice-versa, but only if your central Rome location is inside the old Aurelian Walls (most hotels are). Otherwise, standard metered rates apply, which can bump the fare to 75€ or higher. There are also surcharges for large luggage, Sunday and holiday rides, more than 4 passengers, and rides after 10pm and before 6am.

If you arrive at **Ciampino Airport** (www.adr.it/ciampino; ✆ **06-65951**), you can take a Terravision bus (www.terravision.eu; ✆ **06-4880086;** first bus at 8:35am, last bus at 11:55pm) to Stazione Termini. This takes about 45 minutes and costs 5€. (Note that the timetable for buses reflects current flight schedules and will likely expand based on demand from incoming flights.) A **taxi** from Ciampino costs a flat rate of 30€, provided you're going to a destination within the Aurelian Walls.

From either airport, ride-sharing service **Uber** is available—sort of. Because of licensing laws (and strong resistance from Rome's taxi drivers), only Uber Black or Uber Van service is offered, and it's much more expensive than a taxi.

**BY TRAIN OR BUS**    Trains and buses (including trains from the airport) arrive in the center of old Rome at **Stazione Termini,** Piazza dei Cinquecento. This is the train, bus, and transportation hub for all of Rome, and it is surrounded by many hotels, especially budget ones.

The station is filled with services. There are currency-exchange windows and ATMs on the platform level, as well as on floor -1 (subway level).

---

### Train or Taxi?

Whether to take the airport shuttle train or a taxi into Rome from FCO depends on your budget and your tolerance for schlepping. If you're traveling solo and/or traveling light, the train is the most economical option for getting into the city, and takes about the same time as a taxi. If you've got a lot of bags, however, bear in mind that the train is a long walk from the arrivals terminal—and that, once your train arrives at Termini station, you'll still have to walk, or take Metro, bus, or taxi, to your final destination. (See "By Train," above, for more on Termini station options.) Bottom line? If there are three or more in your party or you're carrying lots of luggage, go for a taxi.

**Informazioni Ferroviarie** (in the outer hall) dispenses info on rail travel to other parts of Italy. There is also a **tourist information booth,** plus baggage services, newsstands, clean public toilets (they cost 1€, and snack bars.

To get from Termini to your final destination in Rome, you have several options. If you're taking the **Metropolitana** (subway), follow the illuminated red-and-white M signs. To catch a city bus, go straight through the outer hall and enter the sprawling bus lot of **Piazza dei Cinquecento.** See p. 49 for more information about getting around Rome by public transportation.

You will also find a line of **taxis** parked out front. Use the official taxi queue right in front of the station; don't go with a driver who approaches you or get into any cab where the meter is "broken." You should be able to pay with a credit or debit card in any official taxi, but confirm this before getting in the cab. Note that taxis now charge a 2€ supplement for any fares originating at Termini, plus 1€ for each bag in the trunk.

**BY CAR**    From the north or south, the main access route is the **Autostrada A1.** This highway runs from Milan to Naples via Bologna, Florence, and Rome. At 754km (469 miles), it is the longest Italian autostrada and the "spinal cord" of Italy's road network. All the autostrade join with the **Grande Raccordo Anulare (GRA),** a ring road encircling Rome, channeling traffic into and around the congested city. *Tip:* Long before you reach the GRA, you should study your route carefully to see what part of Rome you plan to enter. Route signs along the ring road tend to be confusing.

*Warning:* If you must drive a car into Rome, return your rental car immediately on arrival, or at least get yourself to your hotel, park your car, and leave it there until you leave the city. Seriously think twice before driving in Rome—the traffic, as well as the parking options, are nightmarish. Plus, most of central Rome is a **ZTL (Zona Traffico Limitato),** off-limits to nonresidents and rigorously enforced by cameras. You will almost certainly be fined; the ticket might arrive at your home address months after your trip.

## Visitor Information

Information, maps, and the Roma Pass (p. 46) are available at the six Tourist InfoPoints maintained by **Roma Capitale** (www.turismoroma.it/en) around the city. Each kiosk keeps its own hours and none are exactly the same, but you can reliably find them open after 9:30am and before 6pm (though some stay open later). The one at Termini (daily 9:30am–7pm), is located next to platform 24 but often has a long line. See the Turismo Roma website (link above) for the locations of additional information points.

As Rome bloggers go, we like the soup-to-nuts approach of **Romewise** (www.romewise.com) and the honest assessments of expat Natalie Kennedy in her blog, **An American in Rome** (www.anamericaninrome.com).

## City Layout

The bulk of what you'll want to visit—ancient, Renaissance, and baroque Rome (as well as the train station)—lies on the east side of the **Tiber River**

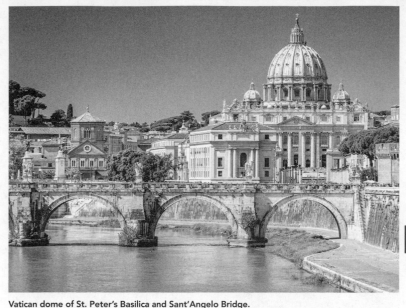

Vatican dome of St. Peter's Basilica and Sant'Angelo Bridge.

**(Fiume Tevere),** which curls through the city. However, several important landmarks are on the other side: **St. Peter's Basilica** and the **Vatican, Castel Sant'Angelo,** and the colorful **Trastevere** neighborhood. Even if those last sights are slightly farther afield, Rome has one of the most compact and walkable city centers in Europe.

That doesn't mean you won't get lost from time to time (most newcomers do). Arm yourself with a detailed street map of Rome (or a smartphone with a hefty data plan). Most hotels hand out a pretty good version of a city map.

## Rome's Neighborhoods in Brief

Much of the historic core of Rome does not fall under easy or distinct neighborhood classifications. Instead, when describing a location, the frame of reference is the name of the nearest large monument or square, like St. Peter's or Piazza di Spagna. Street numbers usually run consecutively, with odd numbers on one side of the street, evens on the other. However, in centro, the numbers sometimes run up one side and then run back down on the other side (so #50 could be potentially opposite #308).

**VATICAN CITY & PRATI** Vatican City is technically a sovereign state, although in practice it is just another part of Rome. The **Vatican Museums, St. Peter's,** and the **Vatican Gardens** take up most of the land area; the popes have lived here for 7 centuries. If you plan to spend most of your time exploring Vatican City sights, or if you just want to stay outside the city center, **Prati,** a middle-class neighborhood east of the Vatican, has a smattering of affordable hotels and shopping streets, as well as some excellent places to eat.

# roma & omnia PASSES

If you plan to do serious sightseeing in Rome (and why else would you be here?), the **Roma Pass** (www.romapass.it) is worth considering. For 52€ per card, valid for 3 days, you get free entry to the first two museums or archaeological sites you visit; "express" entry to the Colosseum; discounted entry to all other museums and sites; free use of the city's public transport network (all bus, Metro, tram, and railway lines, but transfers to Fiumicino Airport are not included), and a free map.

If your stay in Rome is shorter, you may want to opt for the **Roma Pass 48 Hours** (32€), which offers the same benefits as the 3-day pass, except that only the first museum you visit is free and the ticket is valid for just 48 hours.

The free transportation perk with the Roma Pass is not insignificant, if only because it saves you the hassle of buying paper tickets. In any case, do some quick math; one major museum or attraction entrance is 12€ to 15€, and each ride on public transportation is 1.50€. Discounts to other sites range from 20% to 50%. If you plan to visit a lot of sites and dash around the city on public transport, it's probably worth the money.

A glaring disadvantage of the Roma Pass is that it does not include access to the Vatican Museums or the paid areas of St. Peter's. That's where the **Omnia Card** comes to the rescue. The 72-hour card combines all the benefits of the Roma Pass with skip-the-line entry to the Vatican Museums and St. Peter's, an audioguide to St. Peter's, a hop-on-hop-off bus pass and admission to other Vatican properties. At 113€ it's an investment, but worth it if you want to take in all the heavy hitters of Rome and the Vatican. If you just want express entrance to the Vatican Museums and St. Peter's, there's also a 24-hour Omnia Card available for 55€ that does not include Roma Pass benefits. The cards can be purchased online at www.omniavatican rome.org and picked up at one of four Omnia Card offices in the city, including at St. Peter's Square.

You can buy Roma passes online (www.romapass.it) and pick them up at one of the city's **Tourist InfoPoints kiosks** (www.turismoroma.it/en); you can also order in advance by phone, with a credit card, at ☎ **06-060608.** Roma Passes are also sold directly at Tourist InfoPoint booths (see p. 44) or at participating museums and ATAC subway ticket offices.

Finally, Roma Pass holders intending to visit the Colosseum **must reserve timed entry** to that site. We find the easiest way to do this is as follows: On the Roma Pass website, go to the FAQ page and scroll down to question 7.1. Follow the link to CoopCulture and buy your Roma Pass directly from that site, at the same time reserving entry to the Colosseum. Otherwise, you can purchase from the Roma Pass website and then call ☎ **06-39967575,** credit card in hand, to reserve timed entry with a 2€ per person booking fee. Note that other sites included on the Roma Pass may also require advanced booking; check individual websites for the latest on opening hours and Roma Pass reservation requirements.

**CENTRO STORICO & THE PANTHEON**   One of the most desirable (and busiest) areas of Rome, the **Centro Storico** ("Historic Center") is a maze of narrow streets and cobbled alleys dating from the Middle Ages and filled with churches and palaces built during the Renaissance and baroque eras, as well as countless hotels and Airbnb rentals. The only way to explore it is by

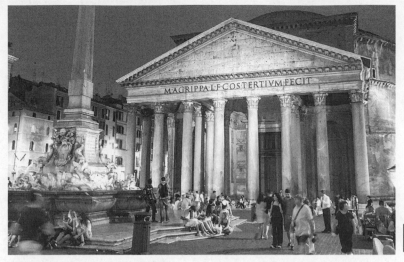

The Pantheon, on Piazza della Rotonda.

foot. Its heart is elegant **Piazza Navona,** built over Emperor Domitian's stadium and bustling with overpriced sidewalk cafes and restaurants, street artists, musicians, and milling crowds.

Nearby, the area around the ancient Roman **Pantheon** is abuzz with crowds, a cafe scene, and nightlife. South of Corso Vittorio Emanuele is the lively square of **Campo de' Fiori,** home to the famous produce market. West of Via Arenula lies the old Jewish **Ghetto,** with several good restaurants and a few interesting hotels.

**ANCIENT ROME, MONTI & CELIO**   Although no longer the heart of the city, this is where Rome began, with the **Colosseum, Palatine Hill, Roman Forum, Imperial Forums,** and **Circus Maximus.** This area offers only a few hotels and, in Monti (Rome's oldest *rione,* or quarter), a handful of very good restaurants and plenty of nightlife. Closer to the Colosseum are tour-bus traps. Just beyond the Circus Maximus, the **Aventine Hill** is now a posh residential quarter with great city views. For more of a neighborhood feel, stay in **Monti** or **Celio,** respectively located north and southeast of the Colosseum.

**TRIDENTE & THE SPANISH STEPS**   The most upscale part of Rome, full of expensive hotels, designer boutiques, and chic restaurants, lies north of Rome's center. It's often called the Tridente, because Via di Ripetta, Via del Corso, and Via del Babuino form a trident leading down from **Piazza del Popolo.** The star here is unquestionably **Piazza di Spagna,** which attracts Romans and tourists alike (though mostly the latter) to linger at its celebrated **Spanish Steps** (just don't eat lunch on the steps! See p. 76). Some of Rome's most high-end shopping streets fan out from here, including **Via Condotti.**

**VIA VENETO & PIAZZA BARBERINI**   In the 1950s and early 1960s, the tree-lined boulevard **Via Veneto** was the swinging place to be, the haunt

47

of la Dolce Vita celebrities and paparazzi. Luxury hotels, cafes, and restaurants still cluster here, although the restaurants are mostly overpriced tourist traps. Our take? If you choose to base here, you may feel just a little too far removed from the action. To the south, Via Veneto ends at **Piazza Barberini** and the magnificent **Palazzo Barberini,** begun in 1623 by Carlo Maderno and later completed by Bernini and Borromini.

**VILLA BORGHESE & PARIOLI**   **Parioli** is Rome's most elegant residential section, a setting for excellent restaurants, hotels, museums, and public parks. Bordered by the green spaces of the **Villa Borghese** to the south and the **Villa Glori** and **Villa Ada** to the north, Parioli (and just to its south, Pinciano) is one of the city's safest districts, but it's not exactly central—and not the best base if you plan to depend on public transportation.

**AROUND STAZIONE TERMINI**   For many visitors, their first glimpse of Rome is the main train station and the unappealing **Piazza del Cinquecento** out front. There are a lot of affordable hotels in this area (as well as several less-affordable ones), and the location is convenient, near the city's transportation hub and not far from ancient Rome. Hotels on the Via Marsala side often occupy floors of a *palazzo* (palace), with clean and decent, sometimes even charming, rooms. Traffic and noise are worse on the streets to the left of the station. The once-seedy neighborhoods on either side of Termini (Esquilino and Tiburtino) have slowly been cleaning up.

**TRASTEVERE**   In a Roman shift of the Latin *Trans Tiber,* Trastevere means "across the Tiber." Since the 1970s, when expats and other bohemians discovered it, this once-medieval working-class district has been gentrified and is now most definitely on the tourist map. Yet Trastevere retains its colorful appeal, with dance clubs, offbeat shops, pubs, and little *trattorie* and wine bars. Trastevere has places to stay—mostly rather quaint rentals and Airbnb's—and excellent restaurants and bars, too. The area centers on the ancient churches of **Santa Cecilia** and **Santa Maria in Trastevere.**

**TESTACCIO & SOUTHERN ROME**   Once home to slaughterhouses and Rome's port on the Tiber, the working-class neighborhood of **Testaccio** was built around one strange feature: a huge, compacted mound of broken amphorae and terracotta roof tiles, begun under Emperor Nero in A.D. 55 and added to over the centuries. Houses were built around the mound; caves were dug into its mass to store wine and foodstuffs. Now known for its authentic Roman restaurants, Testaccio is also one of Rome's liveliest areas after dark. Stay here if you want a taste of a real Roman neighborhood, but bear in mind that you're a bus, tram, or subway ride from most touristic sights.

**THE APPIAN WAY**   Farther south and east, the 2,300-year-old Via Appia Antica road once extended from Rome to Brindisi on the southeast coast. This is one of the most historically rich areas of Rome, great for a day trip, but not a convenient place to stay. Its most famous sights are the Catacombs, the graveyards of early Christians and patrician families.

# Getting Around Rome

Central Rome is perfect for exploring on foot, with sites of interest often clustered together. Much of the inner core is traffic-free, so you will need to walk whether you like it or not. *Tip:* Wear sturdy, comfortable walking shoes. In the most tourist-trod parts of the city, walking can be challenging thanks to crowds, uneven cobblestones, heavy traffic, and narrow (if any) sidewalks.

**BY SUBWAY**   The **Metropolitana (Metro)** is managed by **ATAC** (Agenzia del Trasporto Autoferrotranviario del Comune di Roma; www.atac.roma.it; ℂ **06-57003**). which also runs the city's buses, trams, and urban trains. The Metro operates daily from 5:30am to 11:30pm (until 12:30am on Sat). A big red M indicates the entrance to the subway. If your destination is close to a Metro stop, hop on, as your journey will be much faster than by taking surface transportation. There are currently three lines: **Line A** (orange) runs southeast to northwest via Termini, Barberini, Spagna, and several stations in Prati near the Vatican; **Line B** (blue) runs north to south via Termini and stops at the Colosseum; **Line C** (green) has been delayed for years, largely because crews working underground keep stumbling upon new archaeological finds that have to be researched and excavated. It will ultimately run from Monte Compatri in the southeast to Clodio/Mazzini (just beyond the Ottaviano stop on Line A) and include several stops in the Centro Storico.

Tickets are 1.50€ and are available from *tabacchi* (tobacco shops), many newsstands, and vending machines at all stations. Booklets of tickets are available at newsstands, *tabacchi,* and in some terminals. You can also buy a **pass** on either a daily or a weekly basis (see "By Bus & Tram," below). To open the subway barrier, insert your ticket. If you have a **Roma Pass** (p. 46), touch it against the yellow dot and the gates will open.

Tickets are valid for 100 minutes from the first time they're used, and can be used to transfer to buses, trams, and urban trains. See the Metro stops on the tear-out map in this guide.

**BY BUS & TRAM**   For 1.50€ you can ride to most parts of Rome on buses or trams, although it can be slow going in all that traffic, and the buses are often very crowded. A ticket is valid for 100 minutes, and you can ride many buses and trams, as well as the Metro, during that time by using the same ticket. Tickets are sold in *tabacchi,* at newsstands, and at bus stops, but there are seldom ticket-issuing machines on the vehicles themselves. Note that if you switch from a bus or tram to Metro within your 100-minute ticket time, you must revalidate your ticket before boarding the subway.

> ## Tap & Go
>
> It's now possible to ride paperless on Rome's Metro. In all stations, ATAC has installed Tap & Go payment machines for credit/debit cards and handheld devices equipped for contactless payment. For now, Tap & Go machines are only in Metro stations, but once you're tapped in, you can ride for up to 100 minutes on all public transport methods, as long as your journey begins on the Metro.

# Rome at a Glance

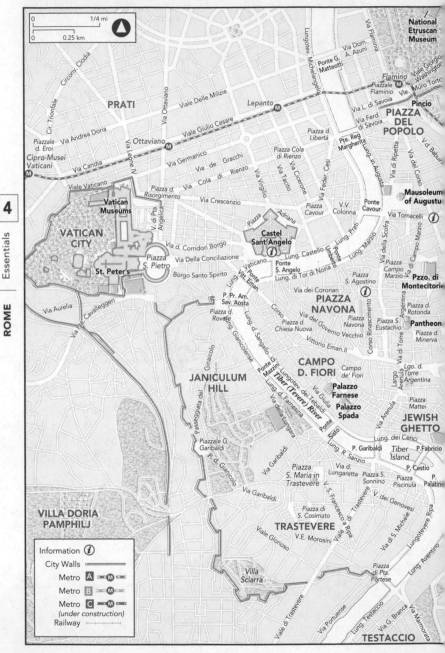

**ROME** | Essentials

**4**

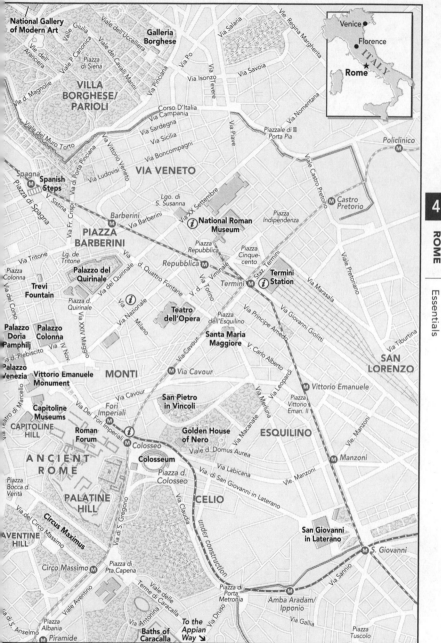

National Gallery
of Modern Art

Galleria
Borghese

Via Giulia

Viale dell'Uccelliera

Viale dell'
Aranciera

Viale P. Canonica

Viale dei Cavalli Marini

Piazza
di Siena

VILLA
BORGHESE/
PARIOLI

Vle d. Magnolie

Viale del Muro Torto

Via Pinciana

Via Po

Via Isonzo

Via Tevere

Via Salaria

Vle. Regina Margherita

Venice

Florence

ITALY

Rome

Via Savoia

Via Nomentana

Corso D'Italia

Via Campania

Via Sardegna

Via Sicilia

Via Boncompagni

Via Vittorio Veneto

Via di Porta Pinciana

Via Plave

Piazzale di
Porta Pia

Viale Castro Pretorio

Policlinico

Spagna

Spanish
Steps

Piazza di Spagna

Via Fr. Crispi

V. Sistina

Via Ludovisi

VIA VENETO

Lgo. di
S. Susanna

Via XX Settembre

Piazza
Indipendenza

Castro
Pretorio

Barberini

Via Barberini

National Roman
Museum

Via Tritone

PIAZZA
BARBERINI

Piazza d. Quattro Fontane

Viale Pretoriano

Via del Quirinale

Via del Corso

Piazza
Colonna

Lg. de
Tritone

Palazzo del
Quirinale

Repubblica

Piazza
Repubblica

Piazza
Cinque-
cento

Staz. Termini

Termini

Via Marsala

Termini
Station

Via Giovanni Giolitti

Trevi
Fountain

Piazza d.
Quirinale

Via Nazionale

Via Milano

Viminale

V. d. Torino

Via Pretoriano

SAN
LORENZO

Palazzo
Doria
Pamphilj

Palazzo
Colonna

Via IV Nov.

Via XXIV Maggio

Teatro
dell'Opera

Piazza
dell'Esquilino

Via Principe Amedeo

Santa Maria
Maggiore

V. Carlo Alberto

Via Tiburtina

Palazzo
Venezia

Via d. Plebiscito

Vittorio Emanuele
Monument

MONTI

Via Cavour

Via Cavour

Vittorio Emanuele

Piazza
Vittorio
Eman. II

Via Merulana

Via Macanate

Vle. Manzoni

Via Del Teatro di Marcello

Capitoline
Museums

Via Dei Fori Imperiali

Fori
Imperiali

San Pietro
in Vincoli

Golden House
of Nero

ESQUILINO

Via Leopardi

Manzoni

CAPITOLINE
HILL

Roman
Forum

Colosseo

Via Labicana

Via di San Giovanni in Laterano

Vle. Manzoni

ANCIENT
ROME

Colosseum

Piazza d.
Colosseo

Viale d. Domus Aurea

Piazza
Bocca d.
Verità

PALATINE
HILL

CELIO

Via Claudia

Via di S. Gregorio

Circus Maximus

Via del Circo Massimo

under construction

San Giovanni
in Laterano

S. Giovanni

AVENTINE
HILL

Circo Massimo

Piazza di
Pta. Capena

Viale Aventino

Terme di Caracalla

Viale delle

Piazza di
Porta
Metronia

Via Sannio

Via di S. Anselmo

Piazza
Albania

Piramide

Via Antonina

Baths of
Caracalla

To the
Appian
Way ↘

Amba Aradam/
Ipponio

Via Druso

Via Gallia

Piazza
Tuscolo

You can buy **special timed passes:** a 24-hour (ROMA 24H) ticket is 7€; a 48-hour ticket is 12.50€; a 72-hour ticket costs 18€; and a 7-day ticket is 24€. If you plan to ride public transportation a lot—and if you are skipping between the *centro storico,* Roman ruins, and Vatican, you likely will—these passes save time and hassle over buying a new ticket every time you ride. Purchase the appropriate pass for your length of stay in Rome. All the passes allow you to ride on the ATAC network, and are also valid on the Metro (subway). On the first bus you board, place your ticket in a small (typically yellow) machine, which prints the day and hour you boarded, and then withdraw it. The machine will also print your ticket's time of expiration ("*scad.*"—short for scadenza). One-day and weekly tickets are also available at *tabacchi,* many newsstands, and at vending machines at all Metro stations. If you plan to do a lot of sightseeing, however, the **Roma Pass** (p. 46) is a smarter choice. We also like the **MyCicero app** (www.mycicero.eu), as it allows you to search for transit options, buy e-tickets and passes, and top up your touchless tickets, all on your smartphone.

Buses and trams stop at areas marked *fermata.* Signs will display the numbers of the buses that stop there and a list of all the stops along each bus's route, making it easier to scope out your destination. Digital displays at most stops show how soon the next bus or tram will arrive. Generall---y, buses run daily from 5am to midnight. From midnight until dawn, you can ride on special night buses (look for the "N" in front of the bus number), which run only on main routes. It's best to take a taxi in the wee hours—if you can find one. Call for one (see "By Taxi," below) in a pinch. **Bus information booths** at Piazza dei Cinquecento, in front of Stazione Termini, offer advice on routes.

**BY TAXI** If you've reached your walking limit, don't feel like waiting for a bus, or need to get someplace in a hurry, taking a taxi in Rome is reasonably

## Walk or Ride?

Rome is such a walkable city, one where getting there (on foot) is half the fun. And public transportation doesn't necessarily save that much time. (For example, walking from Piazza Venezia to Piazza di Santa Maria in Trastevere takes about 25 minutes at a leisurely pace; it takes 12 minutes via bus and tram, but that doesn't include potential time spent waiting for the bus or tram to show up.) My take? On a nice day and for relatively short distances, enjoy the stroll. On the other hand, if you want to save your steps (maybe for a marathon tour of the Vatican Museums), then head to the nearest Metro, tram, or bus stop.

# ROME'S KEY bus routes

First, know that any map of the Roman bus system will likely be outdated before it's printed. Although routes may change, a few reliable bus routes have remained valid for years in Rome:

- **40 (Express):** Stazione Termini to the Vatican via Via Nazionale, Piazza Venezia and Piazza Pia, by Castel Sant'Angelo

- **64:** The "tourist route" from Termini, along Via Nazionale and through Piazza Venezia and along Via Argentina to Piazza San Pietro in the Vatican

- **75:** Stazione Termini to the Colosseum

- **H:** Stazione Termini via Piazza Venezia and the Ghetto to Trastevere via Ponte Garibaldi

affordable compared with other major world cities. Just don't count on hailing a taxi on the street. Instead, have your hotel call one, or if you're at a restaurant, ask the waiter or cashier to dial for you. If you want to phone for yourself, try the **city taxi service** at ✆ **06-0609** (Italian only), or one of the following **radio taxi numbers,** which may or may not have English-speaking operators on duty: ✆ **06-6645,** 06-3570, or 06-4994. You can also text a taxi at ✆ **366-6730000** by typing the message "Roma [address]" (assuming you know the address in Italian). Taxis on call incur a surcharge of 3.50€. Larger taxi stands are at Piazza Venezia (east side), Piazza di Spagna (Spanish Steps), the Colosseum, Corso Rinascimento (Piazza Navona), Largo Argentina, the Pantheon, Piazza del Popolo, Piazza Risorgimento (near St. Peter's), and Piazza Belli (Trastevere).

Many taxis acccpt credit cards, but it's best to check before getting in. Between 6am and 10pm, the meter begins at 3€ (4.50€ Sat–Sun), then it's 1.10€ per kilometer up to 11€. (From 10pm–6am every day, the meter starts at 6.50€.) After that, it's 1.30€ to 1.60€ per kilometer depending on the length of the ride. The first suitcase is free; every additional piece of luggage costs 1€. *Note:* Italians don't tip taxi drivers like Americans do and, at most, will simply round up to the nearest euro. If the driver is really friendly or helpful, a tip of 1€ to 2€ is sufficient.

As in the rest of the world, taxi apps have caught on in Rome. The main app for official city taxis is **it Taxi** (www.ittaxi.it), which is run by Rome's largest taxi company, **3570** (www.3570.it). It allows users to pay directly from the app using a credit card or PayPal. Popular throughout Europe, the **MyTaxi** app offers Uber-like convenience for ordering and prepaying a cab. **Uber** is currently available in Rome in a limited capacity only.

**BY CAR** All roads might lead to Rome, but you probably won't want to drive once you get here. If you do drive into the city, call or e-mail your hotel in advance to find out the best route into Rome from wherever you are starting out. You will want to get rid of your rental car as soon as possible, or park it in a garage and leave it there until you depart Rome.

If you want to rent a car to explore the countryside around Rome or drive to another city, you will save money if you reserve before leaving home (see p. 303 in chapter 10). If you decide to book a car here, most major car rental companies have desks inside Stazione Termini.

Note that rental cars in Italy may be smaller than what you are used to, including in terms of trunk space. Make sure you consider both luggage size and the number of people when booking your vehicle.

# [FastFACTS] ROME

**Banks** In general, banks are open Monday to Friday 8:30am to 1:30pm and 2:30 or 2:45 to 4pm. Note that many banks do not offer currency exchange.

**Business Hours** Most Roman shops open at 10am and close at 7pm from Monday to Saturday. Smaller shops close for 1 or 2 hours at lunch, and may remain closed Monday morning and Saturday afternoon. Many restaurants are closed for *riposo* (rest) 1 day per week, usually Sunday or Monday.

**Dentists** **American Dental Arts Rome,** Via del Governo Vecchio 73 (near Piazza Navona; www.adadentistsrome.com; ℂ 06-6832613), uses the latest technology.

**Doctors** Call the **U.S. Embassy** at ℂ 06-46741 for a list of English-speaking doctors. You'll find English-speaking doctors at the privately run **Salvator Mundi International Hospital,** Viale delle Mura Gianicolensi 67 (in the Gianicolo

neighborhood; www.salvatormundi.it; ℂ 06-588961) The **International Medical Center** is on 24-hour duty at Via Firenze 47 (near Piazza della Repubblica; www.imc84.com; ℂ 06-4882371). **Medi-Call Italia,** Via Cremera 8 (www.medi-call.it; ℂ 06-8840113), can arrange for a qualified doctor to make a house call at your hotel or anywhere in Rome.

**Emergencies** To call the police, dial ℂ 113; for an ambulance ℂ 118; for a fire ℂ 115.

**Newspapers & Magazines** The English-language expat magazine *Wanted in Rome* (www.wantedinrome.com) comes out every 2 weeks and lists current events and shows. Also look for the Rome edition of *Time Out* (www.timeout.com/rome).

**Pharmacies** Recognizable by their neon green or red cross signs, *farmacie* are generally open 8:30am to 1pm and 4 to 7:30pm,

though some stay open later. **Farmacia Piram** at Via Nazionale 228 is open 24 hours. All closed pharmacies have signs in their windows indicating any open pharmacies nearby.

**Police** Dial ℂ 113.

**Safety** Walking alone at night is usually fine anywhere in the centro storico. Violent crime is virtually nonexistent in Rome's touristed areas, though pickpocketing is common. Purse snatching happens on occasion, by young men speeding by on scooters; keep your purse on the wall side of your body with the strap across your chest. Other pickpockets dress like typical businesspeople, so always be suspicious of anyone who tries to "befriend" you in a tourist area. Thieves will also strike where you might least expect it, such as in crowded paid areas like the Colosseum or Vatican Museums. Walking alone at night is usually fine anywhere in the *centro storico.*

# WHERE TO STAY IN ROME

Hotels in Rome's *centro storico* are notoriously overpriced, and all too often the grand exteriors and lobbies of historic buildings give way to bland modern rooms. Our selections here made the cut because they offer unique experiences, highly personalized service, or extreme value—and in a few cases all of the above.

Room rates vary wildly depending on the season, and last-minute deals are common. For example, a room at a hotel we classify as "expensive" might be had for as low as 99€ if said hotel has empty beds to fill. Always **book directly with the hotel**—you'll usually get a better rate and the chance to build some rapport with reception staff.

Breakfast in all but the highest echelon of hotels is often a buffet with coffee, fruit, rolls, and cheese. It's not always included in the rate, so check the reservation options carefully. If you are budgeting and breakfast is a payable extra, skip it and go to a nearby cafe-bar, where a caffè and *cornetto* (espresso and croissant) will likely be much cheaper.

Though most Roman hotels now have **air-conditioning** (a must during the stifling summer months), some budget options still do not. If it's not listed as a room amenity, double-check.

## Self-Catering Apartments

Rental apartments have some great virtues: They're often cheaper than standard facilities, and they let you save money by preparing at least some of your own meals.

Nearly every vacation rental in Rome—and there are tens of thousands of them—is owned and maintained by a third party (that is, not the rental agency). That means that the decor and flavor of the apartments, even in the same price range and neighborhood, can vary widely. Every reputable agency, however, puts multiple photos of each property they handle on its website, so you'll have a sense of what you're getting into. The photos should be accompanied by a list of amenities. Goliath booking sites **www.airbnb.com**, **Home away.com**, and **vrbo.com**, platforms that allow individuals to rent their own apartments to guests, have thousands of listings in Rome. These will often be cheaper than apartments rented through local agencies, but they won't be vetted, and sometimes you're on your own if something goes wrong.

If you decide to rent through one of the agencies below, know that it's standard practice for them to collect 30% of the total rental amount upfront to secure a booking. When you get to Rome and check in, the balance of your rental fee is often payable in cash only. Upon booking, the agency should provide you with detailed "check-in" procedures. *Tip:* Make sure you ask for a few numbers to call in case of an emergency. Otherwise, most apartments come with information sheets that list neighborhood shops and services.

> ### A Note on a *Notte* in Rome
>
> The Rome City Council applies a sojourn tax of 3€ to 7€ (depending on hotel class) per person, per night. Many hotels will request this fee in cash upon check-in or check-out; this is perfectly normal. Children ages 10 and under are exempt.

**RECOMMENDED AGENCIES** **Cross Pollinate** (www.cross-pollinate. com; ℂ **06-99369799**) is a multi-destination agency with a roster of apartments and B&Bs in Rome. Each property is inspected before it gets listed. **Cities Reference** (www.citiesreference.com/en/rome/vacation-rentals; ℂ **06-48903612**) offers no-surprises property descriptions (with helpful and diplomatic tags like "better for young people") and even includes the "eco-footprint" for each apartment. You can expect transparency and responsiveness from the plain-dealing staff. **Rental in Rome** (www.rentalinrome.com; ℂ **06-3220068**) has an alluring website—with video clips of the apartments—and the widest selection of midrange and luxury apartments in the *centro storico* zone (there are less expensive ones, too).

## Monasteries & Convents

Staying in a convent or a monastery can be a great bargain. But remember, these are religious houses, which means the decor is most often stark and the rules inflexible. Cohabitating is almost always frowned upon—though marriage licenses are rarely required—and unruly behavior is not tolerated (so, no staggering in after too much *limoncello* at dinner). Plus, there's usually a curfew. Also, most rooms in convents and monasteries do not have private bathrooms, but ask when making your reservation in case some are available. If, however, you're planning a mellow, "contemplative" trip to Rome, and you can live with these parameters, convents and monasteries are an affordable and fascinating option. The place to start is **www.monasterystays.com**, which lays out all your monastic options for the Eternal City.

## Hotels by Price

### EXPENSIVE

Babuino 181 ★★, p. 63
Chapter Roma ★★, p. 60
Del Sole al Pantheon ★★, p. 61
Hotel De'Ricci ★★, p. 61
The Inn at the Roman Forum ★★, p. 59
The Inn at the Spanish Steps ★★★, p. 63
Palazzo Naiadi ★★★, p. 65
Residenza Paolo VI ★★, p. 57
Villa Laetitia ★★★, p. 57
Villa Spalletti Trivelli ★★★, p. 64

### MODERATE

Coronari Palace ★, p. 61
Duca d'Alba ★★, p. 59
The Glam ★★, p. 60
Hotel Adriano ★★★, p. 61
Hotel Condotti ★, p. 64

Hotel Mediterraneo ★★★, p. 65
Hotel San Francesco ★★, p. 67
La Lumière ★, p. 64
Lancelot ★★★, p. 60
La Residenza ★, p. 64
QuodLibet ★★★, p. 58
Residenza Cellini ★★, p. 66
Residenza in Farnese ★★, p. 62
Santa Maria ★★, p. 67
Teatro di Pompeo ★★, p. 62

### INEXPENSIVE

Arco del Lauro ★★, p. 68
Beehive ★★★, p. 66
Euro Quiris ★, p. 66
Giuliana ★★, p. 67
Mimosa ★★, p. 62
Panda ★, p. 64
Parlamento ★★, p. 65
Rome Armony Suites ★★★, p. 58
Seven Kings Relais ★★, p. 67

# Around Vatican City & Prati

For many, this is a rather dull area to be based in. It's well removed from the ancient sites, and though Prati has some good restaurants, the neighborhood overall is not geared to nightlife. But if the main purpose of your visit centers on the Vatican, you'll be fine here, and you will be joined by thousands of other pilgrims, nuns, and priests (see map p. 85).

## EXPENSIVE

**Residenza Paolo VI ★★**   Literally across the street from Vatican City limits, Residenza Paolo can legitimately claim it's "steps from St. Peter's." Taking breakfast on the rooftop terrace is a special treat, as this narrow strip overlooks St. Peter's Square—if your timing's right, you'll see the Pope blessing crowds on Sunday. (There's bar service on the terrace from 4pm onwards.) Old-worldy rooms feature tile or hardwood floors, heavy drapes, Oriental rugs, and quality beds, though standard guest rooms can be a bit "cozy."

Via Paolo VI 29. www.residenzapaolovi.com. ℂ **06-684870.** 35 units. 129€–429€ double. Rates include breakfast. Metro: Ottaviano (15-min. walk). Bus: 64. **Amenities:** Bar; room service; Wi-Fi (free).

**Villa Laetitia ★★★**   This elegant hotel overlooking the River Tiber is the work of Anna Fendi of the Roman fashion dynasty. Thanks to her design aesthetic, the rooms are anything but traditional, despite the 1911 villa setting surrounded by tranquil gardens. The decor features bold patterns on the beds and floors and modern art on the walls. Splurge for the black and white Giulio Cesare suite, with a round leather bed and blissful garden views. Standard rooms are on the snug side, but most have kitchenettes. Look for great last-minute rates on the hotel website. It's worth noting that the hotel is a 20-minute walk to centro and thus perhaps not the best choice for first-timers to Rome. **Enoteca la Torre** is the villa's Michelin-starred restaurant.

Lungotevere delle Armi 22–23. www.villalaetitia.com. ℂ **06-3226776.** 20 units. 149€–400€ double. Rates include breakfast. Metro: Lepanto. **Amenities:** Restaurant; bar; babysitting; bike rentals; fitness room; room service; Wi-Fi (free).

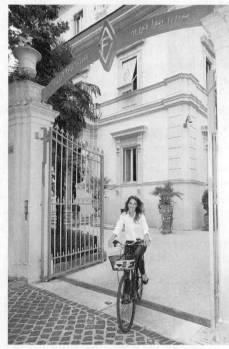

Anna Fendi's Villa Laetitia Hotel.

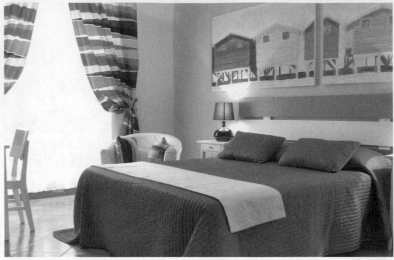

A guest room at QuodLibet.

## MODERATE

**QuodLibet** ★★★ The name is Latin for "what pleases," and we'll be frank: Everything pleases us here. This upscale B&B boasts spacious, colorful rooms, gorgeous artwork and furnishings, and generous breakfasts (served on the roof terrace, which offers evening bar service). All the rooms are set on the fourth floor of an elegant building (with elevator and air-conditioning), so it's quieter than many places. It's located just a 10-minute walk from the Vatican Museums, and a block from the Metro. Charming, conscientious hosts possess a deep knowledge of Rome and what will interest visitors. A top pick!

Via Barletta 29. https://quodlibetroma.com. © **06-1222642.** 4 units. 89€–250€ double. Rates include breakfast. Metro: Ottaviano. **Amenities:** Wi-Fi (free).

## INEXPENSIVE

**Rome Armony Suites** ★★★ A warning: Rome Armony Suites is almost always booked up months in advance, so if you're interested, book early. Why so popular? The answer starts with service; owner Luca is a charming, sensitive host, especially helpful with first-time visitors to Rome. Rooms are big, clean, and modern, with private baths, minimalist decor, tea and coffee facilities, and a fridge in each unit. Final, major perk: free loaner smartphones loaded with maps and tourist info, to help guests get the most out of their visit (calls to the U.S. and Canada included, too).

Via Orazio 3. www.romearmonysuites.com. © **348-3305419.** 6 units. 68€–150€ double (most rooms under 100€). Rates include breakfast. Metro: Lepanto. **Amenities:** Wi-Fi (free).

# Ancient Rome, Monti & Celio

There aren't many hotel rooms on earth with a view of a 2,000-year-old amphitheater, so there's a definite "only in Rome" feeling to lodging on the edge of the ancient city (see map p. 97). The negative to staying in this area—and it's a big minus—is that the streets adjacent to those ancient monuments have little life outside tourism. There's a lot more going on in **Monti**, Rome's oldest "suburb" (only 5 min. from the Forum), which is especially lively after dark. **Celio** has more of a neighborhood vibe, a local, gentrified life quite separate from tourism.

## EXPENSIVE

**The Inn at the Roman Forum ★★**   This small hotel is tucked down a medieval lane on the edge of Monti, with the forums of several Roman emperors as neighbors. Rooms are tastefully decadent, with colorful silks, rich textures, and spacious bathrooms. The posh fifth-floor Master Garden Rooms have private patios surrounded by flowers and greenery, ochre walls, and busts of emperors, and a plush apartment with a kitchen sleeps up to six people. The hotel's small **roof lounge** has views of the Campidoglio, and for archaeology buffs there's an ancient Roman *cryptoporticus* behind the lobby.

Via degli Ibernesi 30. www.theinnattheromanforum.com. ℂ **06-69190970.** 21 units. 180€–330€ double. Rates include breakfast. Metro: Cavour. **Amenities:** 2 bars; concierge; room service; Wi-Fi (free).

## MODERATE

**Duca d'Alba ★★**   Located on one of the main drags of hip Monti, with all the nightlife and authentic dining you'll need, Duca d'Alba strikes a fine balance between old-world gentility and 21st-century amenities. Rooms in the main building are snug and contemporary, with modern furniture and gadgetry and smallish bathrooms. If you want to spring for slightly higher rates,

Executive room at the Inn at the Roman Forum.

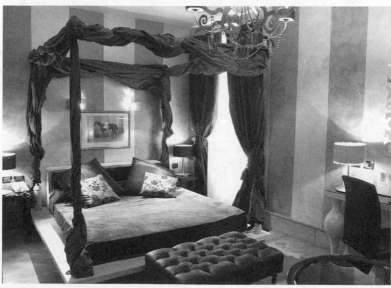

the spacious annex rooms next door have a *palazzo* character, with terracotta floors, oak and cherry furniture, and soundproofed street-facing rooms. Second-floor rooms are the brightest.

Via Leonina 14. www.hotelducadalba.com. © **06-484471**. 31 units. 79€–230€ double. Some rates include breakfast. Metro: Cavour. **Amenities:** Bar; Wi-Fi (free).

**The Glam** ★★  A decidedly modern vibe pervades at this superbly located, boutiquey hotel—right on Via Nazionale, within walking distance of Termini Station, the Colosseum and Forum, Trevi Fountain, and just about everything else you'll want to see in central Rome. Art-filled rooms are cool and functional, if a little impersonal, but a very friendly and welcoming staff more than compensates for this. A rooftop restaurant and glorious open-air bar and terrace are popular gathering spots for young Romans, and the bartender mixes a good cocktail.

Via Nazionale 82. www.theglamhotelroma.it. © **06-99345430**. 59 units. 130€–275€ double. Some rates include breakfast. Metro: Repubblica or Cavour. **Amenities:** Restaurant; bar; roof terrace; Wi-Fi (free).

**Lancelot** ★★★  Expect warmth and hospitality from the minute you walk in the door. The staff, all of whom have been here for years, are the heart and soul of Lancelot, and the reason why the hotel has so many repeat guests. The room decor is simple, and most of the units are spacious, immaculately kept, and light-filled, thanks to large windows. Bathrooms are small but serviceable. Sixth-floor rooms have private terraces overlooking Ancient Rome—well worth springing for. The 1938 building retains vestiges of its Art Deco past, most felt in the genteel, chandelier-lit common areas for meeting other travelers, *Room With a View*–style. Unusual for Rome, Lancelot also has limited private parking, for which you'll need to book ahead.

Via Capo d'Africa 47. www.lancelothotel.com. © **06-70450615**. 60 units. 130€–196€ double. Rates include breakfast. Metro: Colosseo. Bus: 53, 75, 85, 87, 118. Tram: 3. **Amenities:** Restaurant; bar; Wi-Fi (free).

## The Centro Storico & Pantheon

There's nothing like an immersion in the atmosphere of Rome's lively Renaissance heart, though you'll pay for *location, location, location*. Since many of Centro's characteristic streets are pedestrian only, expect to do a lot of walking, but that's a reason many visitors come here in the first place—to wander and discover the glory that was and is Rome. Many restaurants and cafes are an easy walk from the hotels here (see map p. 109).

### EXPENSIVE

**Chapter Roma** ★★  Stylish and irreverently hip, this design hotel is in step with the evolving character of the Rome Ghetto, where modern art galleries and concept stores are springing up next to traditional kosher restaurants. Rooms range from small to party-size, and all have wood floors, an industrial-chic vibe, original artworks, Marshall speakers, and bars stocked with booze and mixers. We appreciate the eco-friendly bath amenities and absence of tiny plastic bottles. The millennial vibe is strong in the lobby bar and adjacent **Market** cafe, which serves smoothies, wraps, and salads.

A fun rooftop restaurant, **Hey Guey,** serves margaritas and Mexican food.

Via di S. Maria De' Calderari, 47. www.chapter-roma.com. ☏ 06-89935351. 42 units. 200€–400€ double. Rates include breakfast. Bus: 40, 64 (to Largo Torre di Argentina). Tram: 8. **Amenities:** Rooftop restaurant; bar; cafe; Wi-Fi (free).

**Del Sole al Pantheon ★★** For history and atmosphere, it's hard to beat a place that's been hosting wayfarers since 1467, with past guests including Jean-Paul Sartre and Simone de Beauvoir, as well as at least one Hapsburg king. Updated rooms have lost some of their period charm but are still classic in feel, with lots of plush textures and soothing colors. Some feature million-dollar views of the Pantheon. Suites offer separate bedrooms and Jacuzzi tubs.

Piazza della Rotonda 63. www.hotelsolealpantheon.com. ☏ **06-6780441.** 32 units. 131€–300€ double. Rates include breakfast. Bus: 40, 64, 85 (to Largo Torre Argentina). **Amenities:** Bar; bike rentals; concierge; garden; Wi-Fi (free).

**Hotel De'Ricci ★★** Wine is on the menu at this oenophiles' retreat, a boutique gem tucked near Palazzo Farnese and Campo de' Fiori, from the welcome glass of bubbly in the lobby to the eight individually designed suites, each with a stocked wine fridge that can be customized to guest tastes. That's just a sampling of the more than 1,500 vintages available, thanks to the hotel's ties to nearby **Pierluigi Restaurant ★★,** a stalwart for refined seafood dining. Rooms are retro-y yet come with all the latest smart features—everything is digital—and bathrooms are done up in sleek black subway tiles. A few suites have terraces with dining areas. *Tip:* Be sure to ask for complimentary in-room snacks during happy hour.

Via della Barchetta 14. www.hoteldericci.com/en. ☏ **06-6874775.** 8 units. 270€–520€. Some rates include breakfast. Bus: 40, 64. **Amenities:** Bar; 24-hr. room service; complimentary snacks and wine (in lobby); Wi-Fi (free).

## MODERATE

**Coronari Palace ★** Once a cozy 10-room guesthouse with classic decor, Coronari Palace now sings a modern tune. Its 16 rooms feature modular furnishings and wood laminate floors; three junior suites have terraces. While some bathrooms are on the snug side, they're sleek and well-designed, most with enough counter/sink space for a toiletry bag. The communal roof terrace invites guests to BYOB and enjoy a pleasant evening looking out on the terracotta rooftops of Rome. There are no surprises here, just clean, up-to-date facilities, good prices, and amiable staff.

Via dei Coronari 231. www.coronaripalace.com. ☏ **06-68309541.** 16 units. 100€–200€ double. Rates include breakfast. Bus: 40, 64. **Amenities:** Roof terrace; Wi-Fi (free).

**Hotel Adriano ★★★** Just 5 minutes from the Pantheon, this stylish retreat occupies an elegant 17th-century *palazzo*. Rooms boast a chic and modern vibe, though standard rooms can be a tad utilitarian. A few deluxe rooms and suites have terraces with views of the Roman rooftops. In a crowded hotel market, Adriano stands out for its plush, well-designed common areas, including the **Gin Corner,** a trendy cocktail bar specializing in…you guessed it. Rooms in the nearby "Domus Adriani" share a small kitchen and common area. *Tip:* E-mail the hotel directly for the lowest rates.

Via di Pallacorda 2. www.hoteladriano.com. ⓒ **06-68802451.** 80 units. 150€–300€ double. Rates include breakfast. Bus: 70, 85. **Amenities:** Bar; babysitting; bikes; concierge; gym; Wi-Fi (free).

**Residenza in Farnese ★★** This little gem is tucked away in a 15th-century mansion across the street from the Palazzo Farnese, within stumbling distance of Campo de' Fiori but still reasonably quiet. Most rooms are spacious and artsy, with tiled floors and a vaguely Renaissance theme. Standard rooms are on the small side but come with free minibars, and prices are usually on the low end of the range shown here. The complimentary breakfast spread is downright generous. *Tip:* Last-minute rates are often much lower than those shown below.

Via del Mascherone 59. www.residenzafarneseroma.it. ⓒ **06-68210980.** 31 units. 140€–240€ double. Rates include breakfast. Bus: 40, 64. **Amenities:** Bar; concierge; room service; Wi-Fi (free).

**Teatro di Pompeo ★★** History buffs will appreciate this small hotel, built atop the ruins of the 1st-century Theatre of Pompey, where on the Ides of March Julius Caesar was stabbed to death (p. 26). The atmospheric breakfast area is actually part of the old theater's arcades, with original Roman walls. The large, simple rooms have an authentic feel, with wood-beam ceilings, cherrywood furniture, and terracotta-tiled floors. Staff members are extremely helpful.

Largo del Pallaro 8. www.hotelteatrodipompeo.it. ⓒ **06-68300170.** 13 units. 100€–220€ double. Rates include breakfast. Bus: 40, 64, 70 to Largo di Torre Argentina. **Amenities:** Bar; room service; Wi-Fi (free).

### INEXPENSIVE

**Mimosa ★★** This budget stalwart in the heart of the *centro storico* enjoys great word of mouth, so book early. Straightforward, modern rooms are bright, with private bathrooms and air-conditioning—neither a given at this price point. Larger units are suitable for families with small children. A location this close to the Pantheon at these prices is hard to beat. Mention Frommer's for a 10% discount.

Via di Santa Chiara 61. www.hotelmimosa.net. ⓒ **06-68801753.** 11 units. 79€–150€ double. Rates include breakfast. Bus: 40, 64, 70 to Largo di Torre Argentina. **Amenities:** Wi-Fi (free).

## Tridente, the Spanish Steps & Via Veneto

The heart of the city is a great place to stay if you're a serious shopper or enjoy the romantic, somewhat nostalgic locales of the Spanish Steps and Trevi Fountain. But expect to part with a lot of extra euro for the privilege. This is one of the most elegant areas in Rome (see map p. 115), but we've found you a few bargains (and some worthy splurges).

## EXPENSIVE

**Babuino 181** ★★   Leave Renaissance and baroque Italy far behind at this sleek, contemporary hotel, with relatively spacious rooms and apartment-size suites outfitted with Frette bathrobes and Nespresso machines. Bathrooms are roomy and well-laid-out, and shuttered windows with hefty curtains provide a quiet and perfectly blacked-out environment for light sleepers. On-site restaurant **EMME** offers a fine dining experience. A surcharged breakfast is served on the rooftop terrace, which doubles as a cocktail bar at night.

Via del Babuino 181. www.romeluxurysuites.com/babuino. ✆ **06-32295295.** 24 units. 150€–430€ double. Metro: Flaminio or Spagna. **Amenities:** Restaurant; bar/roof terrace; babysitting; concierge; room service; Wi-Fi (free).

**The Inn at the Spanish Steps** ★★★   Set in one of Rome's most desirable locations on the famed Via dei Condotti shopping street, this hotel is the epitome of luxe. Rooms are fantasias of design and comfort, some with parquet floors and cherubim frescoes on the ceiling, others decked out with wispy fabrics draping canopied beds; upgraded units have swoon-worthy views of Piazza di Spagna. The rooftop garden provides beautiful views, to be enjoyed at breakfast—with its generous buffet spread—or for evening cocktails.

Via dei Condotti 85. www.atspanishsteps.com. ✆ **06-69925657.** 24 units. 175€–490€ double. Some rates include breakfast. Metro: Spagna. **Amenities:** Bar; roof terraces; babysitting; concierge; room service; Wi-Fi (free).

Balcony at the Inn at the Spanish Steps.

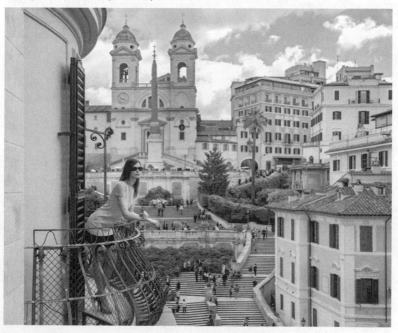

**Villa Spalletti Trivelli** ★★★  This really is an experience rather than a hotel, an early-20th-century neoclassical villa remodeled into an exclusive 14-room guesthouse, where lodgers mingle in the gardens or the great hall, as if invited by an Italian noble for the weekend. There is no key for the entrance door; ring a bell and a staff member will open it for you, often offering a glass of prosecco as a welcome. On-site is a sizeable and modern wellness oasis for those who want extra pampering, while rooms feature elegant antiques and embroidered bed linens, with sitting areas or separate lounges. And the minibar? All free, all day. A rooftop lounge boasts Jacuzzis and a bar serving light fare.

Via Piacenza 4. www.villaspalletti.it. ℂ **06-48907934.** 14 units. 300€–750€ double. Rates include breakfast. Metro: Barberini. **Amenities:** Restaurant; bar; roof terrace; concierge; exercise room; room service; Jacuzzis; sauna; Wi-Fi (free).

## MODERATE

**Hotel Condotti** ★  This cozy hotel can be a tremendously good deal depending on when you stay and how far out you book. For your money you'll get a clean, unpretentious room, though the common areas aim higher, with marble floors, antiques, tapestries, and a Venetian-glass chandelier. Standard rooms are tight; you'll get a bit more space and modernity in the nearby annex rooms. Overall, it's worth considering for its proximity to the Spanish Steps.

Via Mario de' Fiori 37. www.hotelcondotti.com. ℂ **06-6794661.** 16 units. 70€–210€. Some rates include breakfast. Metro: Spagna. **Amenities:** Bar; babysitting; Wi-Fi (free).

**La Lumière** ★  You won't be checking in for chic design or innovation— this traditional hotel just off Via dei Condotti smacks of middle-class comforts, from rooms with matchy-matchy color schemes, wood floors, and warm lighting to the glassed-in roof terrace or open-air patio where breakfast and evening aperitivo are served. For all but highest season and holidays, it's a winner on the price/location ratio.

Via Belsiana 72. www.lalumieredipiazzadispagna.com. ℂ **06-69380806.** 10 units. 120€–350€ double. Rates include breakfast. Metro: Spagna. **Amenities:** Bar; roof terrace; Wi-Fi (free).

**La Residenza** ★  Considering its location just off Via Veneto, this hotel— hosting guests since 1936—is a smart deal. Renovated, modern rooms retain a touch of Art Deco appeal, and are all relatively spacious, with a couple of easy chairs or a small couch in addition to a desk. Families with children are especially catered to, with quad rooms and junior suites on the top floor featuring a separate kids' alcove with two sofa beds, and an outdoor terrace with patio furniture. The excellent breakfast buffet includes quality charcuterie and cheeses, homemade breads, and pastries.

Via Emilia 22–24. www.hotel-la-residenza.com. ℂ **06-4880789.** 27 units. 150€–250€ double. Rates include breakfast. Metro: Barberini. **Amenities:** Bar; cafe; terrace; babysitting; room service; Wi-Fi (free).

## INEXPENSIVE

**Panda** ★  Panda has long been popular among budget travelers, so it books up quickly. Rooms are spare, but not without some old-fashioned charm, like characteristic Roman *cotto* (terracotta) floor tiles, and the odd frescoed ceiling or exposed beams—and they do have air-conditioning. Most rooms are a bit cramped, but for these prices in this neighborhood they remain a very, very good deal. Outside your doorstep are several great cafes and wine bars where you can start the day with espresso and end it with a nightcap. *Tip:* With its budget single rooms with shared baths, Panda is a good pick for solo travelers. Breakfast is 5€ extra.

Via della Croce 35. www.hotelpanda.it. ℭ**06-6780179.** 28 units (8 with shared bath). 85€–130€ double with bath. Metro: Spagna. **Amenities:** Wi-Fi (free).

**Parlamento** ★★  Set on the top floors of a 17th-century *palazzo,* this is one of the best budget deals in the area. Rooms are fresh and modern, with wood floors and monochromatic color schemes. Breakfast is served on the rooftop terrace—you can also chill up there with a glass of wine in the evening. Trevi Fountain, Spanish Steps, and the Pantheon are all within a 5- to 10-minute walk.

Via delle Convertite 5 (at Via del Corso). www.hotelparlamento.it. ℭ**06-69921000.** 19 units. 125€–230€ double. Rates include breakfast. Metro: Spagna. **Amenities:** Bar; roof terrace; concierge; room service; Wi-Fi (free).

# Around Termini

Known for its concentration of cheap hotels, the Termini area (see map p. 123) is about the only part of the center where you can score a high-season double for under 100€. Lately the area has seen the development of more upscale hotels, particularly in the zone northwest of the station. Streets close to the train station are hardly picturesque, and parts of the neighborhood are a little sketchy. Still, it's very convenient to most of Rome's top sights, and a hub for Metro lines, buses, and trams. Following are some of our favorites near Termini.

## EXPENSIVE

**Palazzo Naiadi** ★★★  We won't sugarcoat it—this is one pricey palace. But in exchange for lots of dearly departed euros, guests are treated to a regal experience from the moment they approach the porticoed neoclassical facade, which wraps in a crescent shape around a quarter of Piazza della Repubblica. Rooms and suites are studies in rich textures and subtle color, with plush carpeting and marble baths. The lofty lobby bars serves up fancy drinks and snacks, while adjacent **Tazio** restaurant and bar swims in the ambience of Fellini-era Rome. The hotel spa is top-notch.

Piazza della Repubblica, 47. www.anantara.com/en/palazzo-naiadi-rome. ℭ**06-489381.** 238 units. 243€–540€ double. Breakfast additional. Metro: Repubblica. **Amenities:** 2 restaurants (1 summer-only); 2 bars; concierge; fitness room; rooftop pool; spa; Wi-Fi (free).

## MODERATE

**Hotel Mediterraneo** ★★★  Within sight of Termini station, this surprisingly upscale hotel offers vintage Art Deco style, along with a team of long-time employees who warmly evoke the spirit of a bygone era of class and service. Freshly renovated rooms are large and well-equipped, with bathrooms of grand proportions; suites are downright palatial, and seven top-floor units have terraces with sweeping views. Read about the hotel's interesting WWII–era history as you linger over cocktails in the Wes Anderson-y bar. Sister properties **Atlantico** and **Massimo D'Azeglio,** located next door and across the street, respectively, offer lower room prices and share amenities with Mediterraneo. *Tip:* Check online for off-season or last-minute deals on those top-floor suites.

Via Cavour 15. www.romehotelmediterraneo.it. ℂ **06-4884051.** 245 units. 90€–250€ double. Rates include breakfast. Metro: Termini. **Amenities:** Restaurant; bar; roof terrace; concierge; gym; room service; Wi-Fi (free).

## Residenza Cellini ★★

It's tradition all the way at Cellini, a modest, refined hotel around the corner from Piazza della Repubblica. Antique-styled rooms are proudly 19th century, with thick walls (so no noise from your neighbors), solid furnishings, and handsome parquet floors, yet also offer modern comforts like memory-foam mattresses and air-conditioning. Bathrooms come with Jacuzzi tubs or jetted showers. Service is topnotch and wonderfully personal.

Via Modena 5. www.residenzacellini.it. ℂ **06-47825204.** 18 units. 75€–190€ double. Breakfast additional. Metro: Repubblica. **Amenities:** Concierge; room service; Wi-Fi (free).

## INEXPENSIVE

**Beehive ★★★**   Conceived as part hostel, part hotel, the Beehive is an utterly cheerful lodging experience, run by eco-minded American owners and offering rooms for a variety of budgets. Options range from fancy-for-the-price private rooms with ensuites and TVs to economical rooms with shared bathrooms, as well as both mixed and female-only dorms. All are decorated with flair, adorned with artwork or flea-market treasures, and smell heavenly (go sniff for yourself). A garden offers trees and secluded reading/relaxing space. A buzzy cafe offers breakfast a la carte, as well as occasional, budget-friendly vegan/vegetarian meals; there's also a concerted effort to maintain eco-conscious practices. Weekly pizza and pasta-making classes add to the fun.

Via Marghera 8. www.the-beehive.com. ℂ **06-44704553.** 20 units. 60€–100€ double; 20€–35€ dorm beds. Metro: Termini or Castro Pretorio. **Amenities:** Cafe; lounge; Wi-Fi (free).

**Euro Quiris ★**   There's not a frill in sight at this one-star a couple of blocks north of the station. Rooms are on the 5th floor and simply decorated with functional furniture, but they are spotless, and mattresses are a lot more comfortable than you should expect in this price bracket. Bathrooms are ensuite, too. The friendly reception staff dispenses sound local knowledge, including tips on where to have breakfast in cafes nearby. No credit cards are accepted, and you'll pay extra for air-conditioning.

Via dei Mille 64. www.euroquirishotel.com. ℂ **06-491279.** 9 units. 45€–80€ double. Metro: Termini. **Amenities:** Wi-Fi (free).

**Giuliana** ★★    The Santacroce family and their staff bend over backwards to make guests feel welcome at this moderately priced inn near the station and Santa Maria Maggiore. Basic but comfy rooms, most done up in crimson and buttercream, come with surprisingly large bathrooms. Breakfast is a simple affair, but all in all, this is a good value for this side of the (train) tracks.

Via Agostino Depretis 70. www.hotelgiuliana.com. © **06-4880795.** 11 units. 55€–125€ double, includes breakfast (with most rates). Metro: Termini or Repubblica. **Amenities:** Bar; bike rentals; concierge; Wi-Fi (free).

**Seven Kings Relais** ★★    This unfussy hotel has a slightly retro feel, kitted out with dark wooden furniture, chocolate-brown bedspreads, and modern tiled floors. Despite its location right on one of Rome's busiest thoroughfares, street noise is minimal—an external courtyard and modern soundproofing see to that. "Breakfast" is a 24-hour self-service bar with tea, coffee, and packaged cookies, but the area has plenty of inexpensive dining options. Management has several other nearby properties as well, run through **Roma Termini Suites** (www.romaterminisuites.com).

Via XX Settembre 58A. www.sevenkingsrelais.com. © **06-42917784.** 11 units. 60€–110€ double. Metro: Repubblica. **Amenities:** Wi-Fi (free).

# Trastevere

This was once an "undiscovered" neighborhood—but no longer. Being based here does give some degree of escape from the busy *centro storico,* though Trastevere's narrow streets can be packed to the gills in the evenings, as there are bars, shops, and restaurants galore in this boho section of Rome (see map p. 125). The preponderance of Airbnb-type rentals here has also changed the character of the neighborhood somewhat.

## MODERATE

**Hotel San Francesco** ★★    Lying at the edge of Trastevere, close to the Porta Portese gate in an area that hasn't (yet) been gentrified, this hotel still has a local feel that has disappeared from much of the neighborhood. All rooms are bright, with color-washed walls and modern tiling. Doubles are fairly small, but the bathrooms are quite roomy. The grand piano in the lobby adds a touch of old-time charm; a top-floor garden with a cocktail bar overlooks terracotta rooftops and pealing church bell towers. A tasty cooked breakfast costs extra here. *Tip:* Book a "charity room," and the hotel will match your 2€ donation to help Rome's shelter dogs.

Via Jacopa de' Settesoli 7. www.hotelsanfrancesco.net. © **06-48300051.** 24 units. 96€–199€ double. Bus: H, 44 or 75. Tram: 3 or 8. **Amenities:** Bar; Wi-Fi (free).

**Santa Maria** ★★    Hidden behind an ivy-covered wall, the lovely Santa Maria is built around a 16th-century cloister, now a relaxing courtyard fragrant with orange trees. Cheerful rooms, some with exposed brick walls and beamed ceilings, are mostly on the ground floor. Free breakfast and loaner bikes, a roof garden, and a cocktail bar all make this charmer a standout in hotel-deprived Trastevere. *Tip:* Several spacious, multi-bed rooms make this a fine option for families.

Vicolo del Piede 2. www.htlsantamaria.com. ⓒ **06-5894626.** 20 units. 100€–225€ double. Rates include breakfast. Tram: 8. Bus: 23, 280, H. **Amenities:** Bar; courtyard; loaner bikes; Wi-Fi (free).

### INEXPENSIVE

**Arco del Lauro** ★★ Hidden in Trastevere's snaking alleyways, this serene little B&B occupies the ground floor of a shuttered pink *palazzo*. Bright rooms have wood floors, plush beds, and simple decor, with a mix of modern and period furnishings. Rooms can't be defined as large, but they all feel spacious thanks to lofty wood ceilings. Breakfast is taken at a nearby cafe (with a 5€ surcharge); coffee and snacks are laid out around the clock. Note that minimum-stay rules may apply in high season.

Via Arco de' Tolomei 29. www.arcodellauro.it. ⓒ **06-97840350.** 6 units. 75€–145€ double. Bus: 23, 280, H. Tram: 8. **Amenities:** Wi-Fi (free).

# WHERE TO EAT IN ROME

Roman culinary specialties reflect the city's ancient past, the Italian tradition of eating locally and seasonally, and the *cucina povera*—poor people's food—legacy of making a lot from a little and wasting nothing. Here's a run-down on the basics of Roman cuisine:

o Must-try pasta dishes include delightfully simple *cacio e pepe,* made with pecorino cheese and black pepper, or hefty *carbonara,* composed of *guanciale* (pork cheek), eggs, and pecorino.

o Meat-lovers may be tempted to explore dishes made from the *quinto quarto,* which translates to the "fifth fourth" and means offal—the head, tails, and organ meats of cow, pork. and lamb. Braised oxtail (*coda alla vaccinara*) and *trippa alla Romana* (stewed tripe) are perennial favorites in Testaccio, the old slaughterhouse area that's now foodie central.

o Biting into a crispy thin-crusted Roman **pizza** is a joy you'll savor long after your vacation, especially when said pizza comes from a wood-fired oven.

o *Supplì,* deep-fried rice balls stuffed with ragù and cheese are a Roman specialty everywhere, and in the Jewish Ghetto, you'll find authentic *carciofi alla giudia*—deep-fried artichokes typically ordered as an appetizer.

o Wash it all down with **Frascati wine,** a highly drinkable white from the nearby Castelli Romani hills.

o For dessert, head to one of Rome's many **artisanal gelato**-makers. With your morning *espresso* or *cappuccino,* be sure to try a *maritozzo,* a sweet, fried pasta overflowing with whipped cream.

# Restaurants by Cuisine

4

ROME | Restaurants by Cuisine

## Near Vatican City

For restaurant locations, see map p. 85. The path leading from the Vatican Museums to St. Peter's Basilica is something of a gauntlet of bad food—overpriced tourist traps preying on the dazed crowds that have just wandered out of the museum and need sustenance before tackling the basilica. Fortunately, there are a handful of very fine options for inexpensive fast food right near the Vatican—and no, we don't mean McDonald's (though it's here, too). If you just want a quick, tasty sandwich before or after your Vatican safari, **Duecento Gradi** ★★ is a topnotch panino joint with lots of yummy choices, right across from the Vatican walls at Piazza Risorgimento 3 (www.duecentogradi.it; ✆ **06-39754239**; Sun–Thurs 10am–2am, Fri–Sat 11am–5am). Around the corner, in a friendly hole-in-the-wall at Via Dei Gracchi 7, **Pinsa 'm pò!** ★★ serves light and crispy *"pinsa"* pizzas with organic ingredients and gourmet toppings, most priced around 5€ (http://pinsampo.it; ✆ **06-88980716**; Mon–Sat 10:30am–9pm). For a caffeine jolt, head to **Pergamino Caffe** ★ (Piazza Risorgimento 7; ✆ **06-89533745**; daily 8am–8pm), which brews Fair Trade, specialty coffees from all over the world, paired with delectable pastries.

### EXPENSIVE

**Taverna Angelica** ★★ MODERN ITALIAN/SEAFOOD  In a sea of mediocre restaurants near St. Peter's, Angelica serves up surprisingly good and justly priced (though not cheap) fare. Specialties include handmade pasta with crunchy bacon and leeks, a divine lime risotto with artichokes and Parmesan, or grilled octopus, stuffed calamari, or duck breast in a port wine

Fresh mussels at Taverna Angelica.

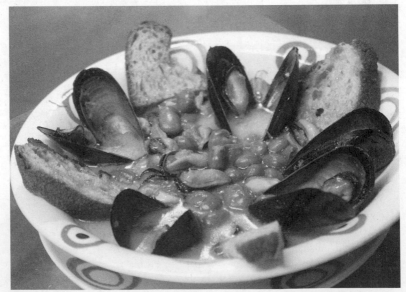

reduction. Save room for the delicious, non-run-of-the-mill dessert options. Reservations are required.

Piazza A. Capponi 6. https://tavernaangelica.com/en. © **06-6874514.** Main courses 18€–23€; tasting menus 45€. Mon–Thurs and Sun noon–3:30pm; dinner daily 6–11pm. Closed 10 days in Aug. Metro: Ottaviano.

## MODERATE

**Bonci Pizzarium** ★★★ PIZZA Celebrity chef Gabriele Bonci has always had a cult following in the Eternal City. And since he's been featured on TV shows overseas and written up by influential bloggers, you can expect long lines at his pizzeria. No matter—it's worth waiting (and walking 10 minutes west of the Vatican Museums) for some of the best pizza you'll ever taste, sold by the slice or by weight. Ingredients are fresh and organic, the crust is perfect, and the toppings often experimental (try the mortadella and crumbled pistachio). There's also a good choice of Italian craft IPAs and wheat beers, and wines by the glass. Bonci has only a handful of stand-up tables inside and benches outside for seating, and reservations aren't taken.

Via della Meloria 43. www.bonci.it. ©**06-39745416.** Pizza 12€–40€ per kilo, depending on toppings. Mon–Sat 11am–10pm. Metro: Cipro.

# Ancient Rome, Monti & Celio

For restaurant locations, see map p. 97. For a cappuccino, a quick bite, or aperitivo snacking, head to the epicenter of Monti, **La Bottega del Caffè** ★★ (© **06-4741578**) on lively Piazza Madonna dei Monti, open from 8am to the wee hours. When we hanker for something other than Italian food, we head to **Maharajah** ★★, an elegant Northern Indian eatery at Via dei Serpenti 124 (www.maharajah.it; © **06-4747144**).

## MODERATE

**Caffè Propaganda** ★ MODERN ITALIAN This stylish eatery—part lively Parisian bistro, part cocktail bar—is your best bet for scoring a good meal within eyeshot of the Colosseum. Diners lounge on caramel-colored leather banquettes and choose from a diverse menu that mixes Roman classics such as *carbonara* (pasta with cured pork, egg, and cheese) with inventive Continental fare or more familiar dishes—like an 18€ hamburger. Desserts are Instagram-worthy affairs. After dark, confident bartenders shake up Propaganda's signature cocktails. Service is relaxed by U.S. standards, so only eat here if you have time to linger.

Via Claudia 15. www.caffepropaganda.it. © **06-94534255.** Main courses 15€–24€. Tues–Sun 8:30–2am. Metro: Colosseo. Bus: 75, 81, 118. Tram: 3 or 8.

**InRoma al Campidoglio** ★ ITALIAN Once a club for Rome's film industry, InRoma sits on a cobbled lane opposite the Palatine Hill. Though the place rests heavily on its cinematic laurels, it still serves up authentic Roman and regional cuisine. Meals might start with *caprese di bufala affumicata* (salad of tomatoes and smoked buffalo mozzarella) followed by classic Roman pasta *carbonara*—they claim to do the best one in Rome—or a main

# food FOR THOUGHT: CULINARY TOURS & CLASSES

Eating out is not the only way to sample Rome's culinary bounty. Numerous food tours and cooking classes range from morning market tours and street food crawls to immersive, daylong cooking classes from which you leave with new recipes and skills to try out at home. In addition to all that eating, drinking, and cooking, the tours offer historical context and a more intimate look at Roman life as it relates to food. Here are two of our favorite ways to sample the vibrant and storied cuisine of the Eternal City:

○ **Eating Europe** (www.eating europe.com) offers in-depth, small-group food and wine tours in Rome, particularly of Testaccio and Trastevere. Guides connect Rome's culinary culture to the city's history and traditions, and guests leave with their curiosity (and hunger) sated. Tours from 79€.

○ Run by a trio of food experts, including American **Eleonora Baldwin**, a TV foodie celebrity in Italy, **Casa Mia Tours** (www.casa miatours.com) offers high-touch private tours of Rome's markets and neighborhoods, with plenty of sampling along the way. They also do private cooking classes and dinners with locals. Prices range from €160 per person for a cooking class to €390 for a 3-hour private food tour for two. Mention this guidebook for a 10% discount.

course of *tagliata* (beef strip steak) with a red wine reduction. The ambience inside is fairly generic; we recommend the terrace for a view to remember.

Via dei Fienili 56. www.inroma.eu. ✆ **06-69191024.** Main courses 10€–20€. Daily noon–3:30pm and 7–11pm. Bus: H, 81, 83, 160, 170, 628.

**La Barrique** ★★ MODERN ROMAN   This cozy, contemporary *enoteca* (wine bar with food) has a kitchen that knocks out fresh farm-to-table fare that complements the well-chosen wine list. The atmosphere is lively and informal, with rustic place settings and friendly service—as any proper *enoteca* should be. The menu offers creative takes on familiar Italian dishes, such as ricotta-stuffed ravioli with lemon, roe, and celery, or grilled octopus served over a cream of chickpeas and sesame paste.

Via del Boschetto 41B. labarriquevinoecucina.wordpress.com. ✆ **06-47825953.** Main courses 9€–16€. Mon–Fri 1–3pm and 7–11:30pm; Sat 7–11:30pm. Metro: Cavour.

## INEXPENSIVE

**Li Rioni** ★★ PIZZA   This fab neighborhood pizzeria is close enough to the Colosseum to be convenient, but just distant enough to avoid the dreaded "touristy" label that applies to so much dining in this part of town. Roman-style pizzas baked in the wood-stoked oven are among the best in town, with perfect crisp crusts. There's also a bruschetta list (from around 4€) and a range of salads. Outside tables can be cramped, but there's plenty of room inside. If you want to eat late, booking is essential, or you'll be fighting with hungry locals for a table. *Tip:* After visiting the Colosseum or the Basilica of San

Clemente, stop for an aperitivo, then head here at 7 for an early (and cheap) pizza dinner.

Via SS. Quattro 24. www.lirioni.it. ☏ **06-70450605.** Pizzas 6€–9€. Wed–Mon 7pm–midnight. Closed 2 weeks in Aug. Metro: Colosseo. Bus: 51, 85, 87. Tram: 3 or 8.

# Centro Storico

## EXPENSIVE

**Pierluigi** ★★ SEAFOOD   There's a lot of pomp and circumstance at Pierluigi, a hallowed seafood restaurant tucked near Piazza Farnese and in business since 1938. Fish that were swimming that morning and still-wiggling lobsters are brought tableside for inspection prior to being impeccably prepared to order. There's also an extensive raw bar menu, as well as items for landlubbers. The wine list is encyclopedic, and service is discreet and flawless. This is event dining, and the ambience—and prices—reflect it. *Tip:* Fresh fish is priced *per etto* (100g) and can add up fast.

Piazza de'Ricci 144. www.pierluigi.it. ☏ **06–6868717.** Main courses 30€–36€; fresh fish can go much higher. Daily 12–3pm, 7pm–midnight. Bus: 40, 64.

**Pipero Roma** ★★ MODERN ITALIAN   Whether you're accustomed to dining in Michelin-starred temples or planning a once-in-a-lifetime event, consider adding Pipero to your bucket list. This long-established foodie haven has moved to chic new digs opposite the Chiesa Nuova, in a setting that's as sophisticated as the plates paraded forth from the kitchen. Start with an antipasto of anchovies, tomato, and oregano, followed by a memorable pasta of cauliflower and vanilla ravioli with scallops. Everything is expensive here and the small, precious servings will either dazzle you or drive you nuts with their pretension—it's better to make that decision beforehand.

Corso Vittorio Emanuele II 250. www.piperoroma.it. ☏ **06-68139022.** Main courses 30€–45€. Tasting menu 130€. Mon–Sat 12:30–2:30pm and 7pm–midnight. Bus: 40, 46, 62, 64, 916.

## MODERATE

**Antica Hostaria Romanesca** ★ ROMAN   It's very easy to eat badly on Campo de' Fiori, which makes this authentic spot with ringside seats on the piazza such a pleasant surprise. Romanesca does dependable, old-school Roman fare at fair prices, including a gloriously juicy *pollo e peperoni* (stewed chicken with peppers) and *abbacchio scottadito*, lamb chops hot off the grill. Locals snatch up the tables after 9pm, so a reservation is advised.

Campo de' Fiori 40 (east side of square). ☏ **06-6864024.** Main courses 9€–15€. Daily noon–3pm and 7–11pm. Bus: 40, 64, 70. Tram: 8.

**Armando al Pantheon** ★★ ROMAN/VEGETARIAN   You know you're sure of your place in the Roman culinary pantheon (sorry, couldn't resist) when you opt to take Saturday nights and Sundays off. Despite the odd hours and a location just a few steps from the *actual* Pantheon, this family-run trattoria serves as many locals as tourists. Chef Armando Gargioli took over the place in 1961, and his sons now run the business. Roman favorites to look out for include *cacio e pepe,* marinated artichokes, and the Jewish-influenced *aliciotti all'indivia* (endive and roasted anchovies; Tues and Fri only). A Roman rarity: Vegetarians get their own, fairly extensive menu. Advance reservations are a must.

Salita dei Crescenzi 31. www.armandoalpantheon.it. ℘ **06-68803034.** Main courses 10€–25€. Mon–Fri 12:30–3pm and 7–11pm; Sat 12:30–3pm. Closed Sat night and Sun, all of Aug. Bus: 40, 64, 70. Tram: 8.

**Il Bacaro** ★ MODERN ITALIAN    Romantic and low-key, Il Bacaro's setting on a hidden backstreet near the Pantheon offers respite from the traffic and tourist crush. Insanely delicious *primi* and *secondi* (like fettucine with prawns, cherry tomatoes, and truffle, or a salmon filet with pistachios and sweet Tropea onions) are a welcome departure from the usual Roman fare. Desserts are of the creamy and fluffy variety, including the obligatory tiramisu. The wine list features well-priced varietals from all over Italy, including a couple dozen by the glass. Try to get a prized sidewalk table on a balmy summer evening.

Via degli Spagnoli 27 (near Piazza delle Coppelle). www.ilbacaroroma.com/en. ℘ **06-6872554.** Main courses 20€–24€. Daily noon–midnight. Bus: 70, 71.

**La Campana** ★★ ROMAN/TRADITIONAL ITALIAN    Family atmosphere and a classic Roman elegance prevail in Rome's oldest restaurant (feeding guests since 1518!). The atmosphere is convivial yet refined, with a lovely mixture of regulars and locals. The broad selection of *antipasti* is displayed on a long table at the entrance, and the daily menu features authentic *cucina romana* that is heavy on offal—if you're not a fan, be sure to bring your Italian/English dictionary. You'll also find classics like *cacio e pepe,* plus myriad vegetarian choices. The wine list includes interesting local labels, and the staff and service are impeccable.

Vicolo della Campana 18. www.ristorantelacampana.com. ℘ **06-6875273.** Main courses 12€–22€. Tues–Sun 12:30–3pm and 7:30–11pm. Metro: Spagna. Bus: 70.

**Nonna Betta** ★★ ROMAN/JEWISH    The history is palpable at Nonna Betta's, where photos of the Rome Ghetto of the 19th century line the walls. Traditional dishes include delicious *carciofi alla giudia:* deep-fried artichokes served with small morsels like battered cod filet, stuffed and fried zucchini flowers, carrot sticks, and whatever vegetable is in season. Don't forego the *baccalà* with onions and tomato or the tagliolini with chicory and mullet roe. Middle Eastern specialties such as falafel and couscous also show up on the menu, and all desserts are homemade, including a stellar cake with pine nuts. In keeping with kosher law, meat and dairy are on separate menus and never combined in recipes.

Via del Portico d'Ottavia 16. www.nonnabetta.it. ℘ **06-68806263.** Main courses 11€–15€. Wed–Mon 11am–5pm and 6–11pm. Bus: 40, 64, 170. Tram 8.

**Retrobottega** ★★ MODERN ROMAN    Fresh, modern, and progressive, the somewhat misnamed Retrobottega is a nice contrast to the well-worn streets of the touristy heart of town. This culinary laboratory, founded by four

# GETTING YOUR FILL OF gelato

Don't leave town without trying one (or several) of Rome's outstanding **ice-cream parlors.** Choose your gelato carefully, however: Don't buy close to the tourist-packed piazzas, and don't be dazzled by vats of brightly (and artificially) colored, air-pumped gelato. The best gelato is made only from natural ingredients, which impart a natural color—if the pistachio gelato is bright green, move on. Take your cone (cono) or small cup (coppetta) and stroll as you eat—sitting down on the premises is usually more expensive. The recommended spots below are generally open mid-morning to late, sometimes after midnight on summer weekends. Cones and small cups cost between 2.50€ and 5€—at these prices you can eat it twice a day!

Near Campo de' Fiori, one of Rome's oldest artisan gelato makers, **Gelateria Alberto Pica** ★★★ (Via della Seggiola 12; ☎ **06-6868405;** Bus H, 63, or 780; Tram 8) produces top-quality gelato churned with local ingredients, including wild strawberries grown on the family's country estate. In Monti, fabulous (and gluten-free) **Fatamorgana** ★★★ (Piazza degli Zingari 5; www.gelateria fatamorgana.com; ☎ **06-86391589;** Metro Cavour, plus other locations in Rome) is the place to try inventive flavors

like delicate lavender and chamomile, or zingy avocado, lime, and white wine.

Two exceptions to the rule about avoiding gelato in touristy areas: venerable **Old Bridge Gelateria** ★ (Viale Bastioni di Michelangelo; ☎ **328-411-9478;** gelateriaoldbridge.com), which delights customers lined up for the Vatican Museums; and, near Piazza Navona, **Frigidarium** ★★★ (Via del Governo Vecchio 112; www.frigidarium-gelateria.com; ☎ **334-995-1184**), whose intense and creamy flavors will make you weep with joy. Have a coppetta of mango and coconut for me.

In the Termini area, tiny but sleek **Come il Latte** ★★★ (Via Silvio Spaventa 24; www.comeillatte.it; ☎ **06-42903882;** Metro Repubblica or Castro Pretorio) turns out artisan gelatos in flavors ranging from salted caramel (yes, please!), to mascarpone and crumbled cookies; fruit flavors change according to season.

Trastevere's best artisan gelato, **Fior di Luna** ★★★ (Via della Lungaretta 96; www.fiordiluna.com; ☎ **06-64561314;** Bus H or 780; Tram 8), is made with natural and Fair Trade produce. Star flavors are the incredibly rich chocolates, spiked with fig or orange, and an absolutely perfect pistachio.

young, accomplished chefs, is an intimate but convivial choice. Most seats surround the open kitchen and customers interact directly with the chefs—there is no waitstaff. The day's offerings focus on local, seasonal, responsibly sourced ingredients and unexpected pairings, like risotto with bee pollen, paprika and vermouth, or duck tortellini with pimpinella herb. A new endeavor, **Pasta e Pane,** serves dine-in and takeaway pasta.

Via della Stelletta 4. www.retro-bottega.com. ☎ **06-68136310.** Entrees 25€, tasting menus 65€–110€. Tues–Sun 6pm–midnight. Adjacent pasta restaurant open daily 10:30am–6pm. Bus: 40, 70, 85.

## INEXPENSIVE

**Alfredo e Ada** ★★ ROMAN   No menus here, just the waiter—and it's usually owner Sergio explaining, in Italian, what the kitchen is preparing that day. Look for classic trattoria comfort food, like eggplant parmigiana, artichoke lasagna, excellent carbonara, or tripe. The whole place oozes character, with shared tables, scribbled walls, and the house wine poured into carafes from a tap in the wall. There are only five tables, so it's best to make a reservation or get here early. This sort of place is becoming rare in Rome—enjoy it while you can.

Via dei Banchi Nuovi 14. ℂ **06-6878842.** Main courses 8€–12€. Tues–Sat noon–3pm and 7–10:30pm. Closed Aug. Bus: 40, 64.

**Antico Forno Roscioli** ★★★ BAKERY/PIZZA The Rosciolis have been running this celebrated bakery for three generations since the 1970s, though bread has been made here since at least 1824. Today it's the home of the finest crusty sourdough in Rome, assorted cakes, and addictive pastries and biscotti, as well as exceptional Roman-style *pizza bianca* and *pizza rossa* sold by weight. This is largely a takeout joint, with limited seating—and the wider range of pizza toppings is only available from noon to 2:30pm. Around the corner is the wonderful **Roscioli restaurant and *salumeria* deli** at Via dei Giubbonari 21 and, at Piazza Benedetto Cairoli 16, **Roscioli Caffè,** the latest outpost of the family empire, which offers breakfast treats, cappuccini, and palate-pleasing panini.

Via dei Chiavari 34. www.anticofornoroscioli.it. ℂ **06-6864045.** Pizza from 5€ (sold by weight). Mon–Sat 7am–7:30pm; Sun 8am–6pm. Bus: 40, 85, 492. Tram: 8.

**Da Baffetto** ★★ PIZZA You don't come to Baffetto for cheerful service or even for comfort—tables are cramped, and you might wind up sharing one with strangers. You come for the gloriously authentic Roman pizza. Crisp-crusted, oozing with toppings, and dispatched quickly from the wood oven. This place is dirt-cheap and immensely popular with locals. If there's a line out the door, take heart: They shuffle people in and out of here pretty fast (and a lot of people are in line for takeaway). After dinner, pop next door to **Frigidarium** (p. 75) for a gelato.

Via del Governo Vecchio 114. www.pizzeriabaffetto.it. ℂ **06-6861617.** Pizzas 6€–10€. Daily 12:30–3pm and 6:30pm–12:30am. Bus: 40, 64, 70, 492.

## Tridente, the Spanish Steps & Via Veneto

For restaurant locations, see map p. 115. The historic cafes near the Spanish Steps are saturated with history but, sadly, tend to be overpriced tourist traps, where mediocre slices of cake or even a cup of coffee or tea will cost 5€. Nevertheless, you may want to pop inside the two most celebrated institutions: **Babington's Tea Rooms** ★ (www.babingtons.com; ℂ **06-6786027;** daily 10am–9:30pm), established in 1893 at the foot of the Spanish Steps by a couple of English *signore,* and **Antico Caffè Greco** ★**,** Via dei Condotti 86 (anticocaffegreco.eu/en; ℂ **06-6791700;** daily 9am–9pm), Rome's oldest bar, which opened in 1760 and has hosted Keats, Ibsen, Goethe, and many other historical *cognoscenti.* In the heart of the Villa Borghese park, on Piazzale delle Canestre, **Pic Nic** ★★ (ℂ **06-855-7493;** daily 9am–7pm) is a great spot for lunch or a snack.

## EXPENSIVE

**Al Ceppo** ★★ MARCHIGIANA/ROMAN   The setting of this Parioli dining institution is an elegant 19th-century parlor, with dark wood furnishings, chandeliers, fresh flowers, family portraits on the walls, and an open kitchen with a wood-stoked hearth. The menu features regional dishes from the owners' home, the Le Marche region northeast of Rome: fish stews, fresh seafood, and grilled meats, all artfully prepared and presented, along with pastas both hearty and delicate. It's reason enough to head north to explore Parioli's many charms.

Via Panama 2 (near Piazza Ungheria). www.ristorantealceppo.com. ⓒ **06-8419696.** Main courses 18€–30€. Tues–Sun 12:30–3pm and 7:30–11pm; Mon 7:30–11pm. Closed last 2 weeks in Aug. Bus: 223, 360, 910. Tram: 3 or 19.

**Imàgo** ★★★ INTERNATIONAL   The views of Rome from this 6th-floor hotel restaurant are jaw-dropping, the old city laid out before you, glowing pink as the sun goes down. The food is equally special, as chef Andrea Antonini reinterprets Italian cuisine, borrowing heavily from international culinary traditions. The Michelin-star menu changes seasonally, but may include gnocchi with goat cheese, porcini mushrooms, and hazelnuts, or pigeon prepared with chocolate and tobacco. Reservations are essential; jackets required for the gentlemen.

In Hotel Hassler, Piazza della Trinità dei Monti 6. www.imagorestaurant.com. ⓒ **06-69934726.** Tasting menus 130€–160€. Tues–Sat 7–10:30pm. Closed most of Jan. Metro: Spagna.

**Views of Rome from Imàgo.**

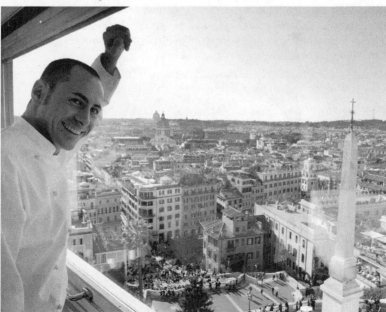

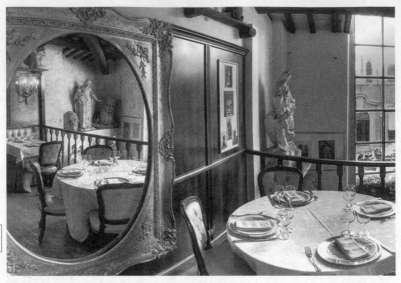

The sculpture-filled dining room at Canova Tadolini.

## MODERATE

**Canova Tadolini** ★★ ROMAN   Few restaurants are as steeped in history as this place. Antonio Canova's sculpture studio was kept as a workshop by the descendants of his pupil Adamo Tadolini until 1967, and even today it's littered with tools and sculptures in bronze, plaster, and marble. The whole thing really does seem like a museum, with tables squeezed between models, casts, drapes, and bas-reliefs. Menus change from summer to winter, and always feature an interesting variety of traditional Roman pastas, plus meat, fish, and vegetarian dishes.

Via del Babuino 150A–B. www.canovatadolini.com. ✆ **06-32110702.** Main courses 15€–25€. Daily noon–midnight (bar/cafe 7am–midnight). Metro: Spagna.

**Colline Emiliane** ★★★ EMILIANA-ROMAGNOLA   This family-owned restaurant tucked in an alley beside the Trevi Fountain has been serving traditional dishes from Emilia-Romagna since 1931. Service is excellent and so is the food: Classics include *tortelli di zucca* (pumpkin ravioli in butter sauce) and magnificent *tagliatelle alla Bolognese,* the mother of all Italian comfort foods. A menu of *secondi* is heavy on beef. Save room for the walnut-and-caramel cake or lemon meringue pie. Reservations are essential.

Via degli Avignonesi 22 (off Piazza Barberini). www.collineemiliane.com. ✆06-4817538. Main courses 15€–18€. Tues–Sun 12:45–2:45pm; Tues–Sat 7:30–10:45pm. Closed Aug. Metro: Barberini.

## Around Termini

For restaurant locations, see map p. 123. Mostly catering to dazed travelers toting wheeled suitcases, restaurants around Termini don't have to be good in order to bring in business. The following are some of our favorite exceptions to that norm.

## MODERATE

**Trattoria Monti** ★★ REGIONAL/MARCHIGIANA   Word is definitely out on this cozy, plain-Jane trattoria near Termini station. But that just means you need to reserve in advance to sample hearty, outstanding pastas and meat and game dishes from the Marche region. You will remember the *tortello al rosso d'uovo*—a large, delicate ravioli filled with spinach, ricotta, and egg yolk—for the rest of your life. You also may discover a few new favorites among the territory's underappreciated wines. Vegetarians take heart: There are always four or five non-meat entrees available.

Via di San Vito 13A (at Via Merulana). ⓒ**06-4466573.** Main courses 12€–22€. Tues–Sat 1–2:45pm and 8–10:45pm; Sun lunch only. Metro: Cavour or Vittorio Emanuele. Bus: 360, 714. Tram: 5 or 14.

**Trimani Il Wine Bar** ★ MODERN ITALIAN   This small bistro and well-stocked wine bar (with a 20-page wine list!) attracts white collars and wine lovers in a modern, relaxed ambience, accompanied by smooth jazz. The refined entrees might include rabbit stuffed with asparagus or Luganega sausage with a zucchini puree. The wines-by-the-glass list changes daily. If you just want a snack to accompany your vino, cheese and salami platters range from 9€ to 14€. The selection at Trimani's vast wine shop next door boggles the oenophilic mind.

Via Cernaia 37B. www.trimani.com. ⓒ**06-4469630.** Main courses 12€–24€. Mon–Sat 11:30am–3pm and 5:30pm–midnight. Closed 2 weeks in mid-Aug. Metro: Repubblica or Castro Pretorio.

## INEXPENSIVE

**Mercato Centrale Roma** ★★ GOURMET MARKET   This ambitious, three-story gourmet dining hall and street food hub is the best place to dine in Termini Station, with top-notch purveyors of everything from gourmet pizza to chocolate to truffles, plus a wine bar and a high-end restaurant. The space is inviting, if a little chaotic. Even if you don't have a train to catch, it's worth sampling lunch or a quick snack here. *Tip:* Walk through the hall and check out all the offerings, then snag a table and have members of your party take turns going to order their food.

Via Giovanni Giolitti 36 (in Termini Station). www.mercatocentrale.it/roma. ⓒ**06-46202900.** Daily 8am–midnight. Metro: Termini.

**Pinsere** ★★ PIZZA   *Pinsa* is an ancient Roman preparation: an oval focaccia made with a blend of four organic flours and olive oil that's left to rise for 2 to 3 days. The result is a crispy yet feather-light single-portion snack perfect for a light lunch. This friendly, small bakery always has an assortment of pies ready to pop in the oven. Favorites come with pureed pumpkin, smoked cheese, and pancetta; classic tomato, basil, and *bufala;* or the surprising combo of ricotta, fresh figs, raisins, pine nuts, and honey. Food to go only, or to eat standing up at one of the few small inside or outside counters. *Note:* It's closed Saturday and Sunday.

Via Flavia 98.℗ **06-42020924.** Pinsa 4€–6€. Mon–Fri 10am–4pm. Metro: Castro Pretorio. Bus: 38, 66, 90, 223.

# Trastevere

For restaurant locations, see map p. 125. The popular craft-beer bar Bir and Fud has been reimagined as **L'Elementare** (see p. 136), but still serves hungry drinkers pizzas and traditional snacks like *supplì* (fried stuffed rice croquettes). Hearts and taste buds soar at **Biscottificio Artigiano Innocenti ★★** (Via della Luce 21; ℗ **06-5803926**), where Stefania and her family have been turning out delicate handmade cookies and cakes since the 1920s.

## EXPENSIVE

**Antico Arco ★★★** CREATIVE ITALIAN   This well-known address for new Italian cuisine consistently delivers exquisite dishes made with the finest local and seasonal ingredients—like wild-game-stuffed tortelli with blueberries and sautéed cabbage, or duck breast with wild carrots, ginger, and plum chutney, accompanied by excellent wine and topnotch service. A full meal here makes for a special night out (reservations are essential), but you can also just come to the restaurant's wine bar for vino and some finger food—it pairs nicely with the rapturous *centro storico* views from the nearby terraces of the Janiculum Hill. *Tip:* It's a 15-minute walk uphill from Trastevere, but the climb is gradual and pleasant.

Piazzale Aurelio 7 (at Via San Pancrazio). www.anticoarco.it. ℗ **06-5815274.** Main courses 20€–30€. Daily noon–midnight. Bus: 75, or Tram 3 or 8 then a 15-min. walk.

**Glass ★★** CONTEMPORARY ROMAN   In an industrial-chic setting of exposed brick, stark white walls, and polished floors, Michelin-starred chef Cristina Bowerman and partner Fabio Spada serve refined food using high-quality ingredients. The menu changes seasonally, but expect carefully prepared shellfish, inventive pastas such as linguine with miso butter, eel, apple, and horseradish, or their signature dish, beef fillet with chocolate, mushrooms, and aged foie gras. A vegetarian menu is available. Reservations are essential.

Vicolo del Cinque 58. https://glasshostaria.it.℗ **06-58335903.** Main courses 38€; tasting menu 100€. Wed–Sun 7:30–11pm; also Sat–Sun for lunch. Closed 2 weeks in Jan and 2 weeks in July. Bus: H, 75. Tram: 8.

**Spirito DiVino ★★** ROMAN/SLOW FOOD   In a medieval synagogue on a 2nd-century street (which you can visit on a cellar tour), the Catalani family does exceptional modern plates using only organic ingredients. Plates like an appetizer salad of spinach, pinenuts, pomegranate, and gorgonzola, as well as ancient Roman cuisine (try the *maiale alla mazio,* a favorite pork dish of Julius Caesar's), are as warm and comforting as the ambience. Finish with the delicately perfumed lavender panna cotta, a cream-based dessert.

Via dei Genovesi 31 (at Vicolo dell'Atleta). www.ristorantespiritodivino.com. ℗ **06-5896689.** Main courses 16€–26€. Mon–Sat 7–11:30pm. Bus: H, 75. Tram: 8.

## MODERATE

**Cacio e Pepe** ★ ROMAN   This ultra-traditional trattoria, complete with paper tablecloths, a TV showing the game, the owner chatting up the ladies, and a bustling crowd of patrons waiting to be seated, is a Trastevere neighborhood stalwart. Start with cheapo plates of fried tidbits, from rice *supplì* to cod to vegetables, then move on to the namesake pasta *cacio e pepe* or other classic Roman pasta dishes—and be ready for hearty portions. For *secondo*—if you have room left—consider *polpette* (stewed meatballs), *saltimbocca alla romana* (veal cutlets with sage and ham), or grilled meats, all sold reasonably priced. They even have pizza for the kids.

Vicolo del Cinque 15. www.osteriacacioepepe.it.© **06-89572853.** Main courses 12€–17€. Daily 7:30pm–12:30am; Sat–Sun noon–3pm. Bus: H. 75. Tram: 8.

**Da Enzo** ★★ ROMAN   For traditional Roman cuisine, try this down-homey, non-touristy, family-run trattoria. *Cucina romana,* including classic *carbonara, amatriciana,* and *cacio e pepe,* win the gold, as do meat-heavy *secondi* like stewed tripe, or meatballs braised in tomato sauce. Local wines can be ordered by the jug or glass, and desserts are worth the calories (try the mascarpone with wild strawberries). A few outdoor tables look out on some of Trastevere's characteristic alleyways.

Via dei Vascellari 29. www.daenzoal29.com. © **06-5812260.** Main courses 9€–15€. Mon–Sat 12:15–3pm and 7–11:00pm. Bus: 75, 85, 170, H. Tram: 8.

**Osteria La Gensola** ★★★ SEAFOOD/ROMAN   Considered one of the best seafood destinations in Rome, this warm and welcoming family-run restaurant feels like a true Trastevere home; decor is cozy, with soft lighting and a life-size wood-carved tree in the middle of the main dining room. Fish-lovers come for heavenly spaghetti with fresh clams, *polpettine* (meatballs) made with tuna, and other traditional Roman cuisine with a marine twist. The grill churns out succulent beefsteaks, among non-fish dishes. Reservations are a must on weekends.

Piazza della Gensola 15. www.osterialagensola.it. © **06-58332758.** Main courses 15–20€. Daily 12:30–3pm and 7:45–11:30pm. Bus: 75, 85, 170, H. Tram: 8.

## INEXPENSIVE

**Dar Poeta** ★ PIZZA   Ranking among the best pizzerias in Rome, "the poet" is a fine place to enjoy a classic Roman pizza margherita (tomato sauce, mozzarella, and fresh basil) or a more creative combo like the *patataccia* (potatoes, creamed zucchini, and *speck* [a smoked prosciutto]). The lines are long to eat in, but you can also order takeout. The decadent dessert calzone is filled with fresh ricotta and Nutella.

Vicolo del Bologna 45. www.darpoeta.com.© **06-5880516.** Pizzas 5€–9€. Daily noon–midnight. Bus: 75, H.

# Testaccio

The slaughterhouses of Rome's old meatpacking district (see map p. 125) have been transformed into art venues, markets, and the museum **MACRO** (p. 126),

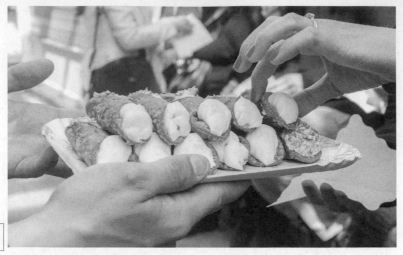
Cannelloni on the Taste of Testaccio Tour.

but restaurants here still specialize in (though are not limited to) meats from the *quinto quarto* (the "fifth quarter")—the leftover parts of an animal after slaughter, typically offal like sweetbreads, tripe, tails, and other goodies you won't find on most American menus. This is an area to eat *cucina romana*—either in the restaurants below or from the highly recommended street-food stalls in the **Nuovo Mercato di Testaccio** (p. 133). Food-themed tours of Rome invariably end up here.

## EXPENSIVE

**Checchino dal 1887** ★★ ROMAN    Often mischaracterized as an offal-only joint, this establishment, opened in 1887 across from Rome's now-defunct abattoir, is a special-night-out type of place, serving wonderful *bucatini all'amatriciana* and veal saltimbocca—as well as hearty plates of spleens, lungs, and livers. Checchino is a pricier choice than most of the other restaurants in this area, but Romans from all over the city keep coming back when they want the real thing. Despite its meat-centric leanings, Checchino also has a decent vegetarian menu. They will also make gluten-free pasta.

Via di Monte Testaccio 30 (at Via Galvani). www.checchino-dal-1887.com. ✆ **06-5746316.** Main courses 12€–28€. Wed–Sun 12:30–3pm and 7:30–1pm. Closed Aug and part of Dec–Jan. Metro: Piramide.

## MODERATE

**Flavio al Velavevodetto** ★ ROMAN    Flavio's plain dining room is burrowed out of the side of Rome's most unusual "hill": a large mound made from amphorae discarded during the Roman era (see p. 48). Food-lovers, however, come here for classic Roman pastas like *cacio e pepe* and *amatriciana,* plus *quinto quarto* (nose-to-tail) entrees at fair prices. Hearty dishes like *polpette al sugo* (meatballs in red sauce), *coda alla vaccinara* (oxtail), and fried calamari and anchovies are good for sharing. While Flavio is justly famous, it may be coasting on its reputation just a wee bit.

Via di Monte Testaccio 97–99. www.ristorantevelavevodetto.it. ✆ **06-5744194.** Main courses 9€–20€. Daily noon–3pm and 7–11pm. Metro: Piramide.

**Osteria degli Amici** ★★ MODERN ROMAN   On the corner of nightclub central and the hill of broken amphorae, this intimate and friendly *osteria* serves both traditional Roman classics and creative variations. Claudio and Alessandro base their menu on their combined experience in famous kitchens around the world, and presentations are

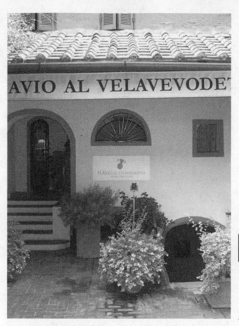

Flavio al Velavevodetto.

more sophisticated than is typical for the neighborhood. Signature musts include fish- and seafood-based pastas and mains, golden-fried mozzarella *in carrozza,* and a range of pastas from classic *carbonara* to *paccheri* tubes with squid, olives, and potatoes. Leave room for the apple tartlet with cinnamon gelato.

Via Nicola Zabaglia 25. www.osteriadegliamiciroma.it. ✆ **06-5781466.** Main courses 10€–20€. Wed–Mon 12:30–3pm and 8pm–midnight. Metro: Piramide.

**Porto Fluviale** ★ MODERN ITALIAN   This multifunctional restaurant— part trattoria, part street-food stall, part pizzeria—can accommodate pretty much whatever you fancy. The decor is vaguely industrial, with a daytime clientele made up of families and white collars—the vibe gets younger after dark. From the various menus, best bets are the 30 or so *cicchetti,* small plates that allow you to sample the kitchen's range. Both the locale and the menus are highly kid-friendly.

Via del Porto Fluviale 22. www.portofluviale.com. ✆ **06-5743199.** Cicchetti (tapas) 3€–5€, main courses 7€–21€. Daily noon–2am. Metro: Piramide.

**Trattoria Perilli** ★★ ROMAN   Dine elbow to elbow with locals and enjoy the old-school atmosphere at this beloved institution of Roman *ristorazione.* With zero pretense, Perilli's formally attired waitstaff serve unadulterated renditions of Roman classics. The menu is small and the dishes reliable, from pasta standbys like *carbonara* and *cacio e pepe* to grilled meats to that most English of Italian desserts, *zuppa inglese* (literally "English soup," or trifle). It's a fun and reasonably affordable place to go for a real four-course meal of *antipasto, primo, secondo,* and *dolce.* Reservations recommended.

Via Marmorata 39 (at Via Galvani). www.perilliatestaccio.com. ✆ **06-5742415.** Main courses 12€–22€. Thurs–Tues 12:30–3pm and 7:30–11pm. Metro: Piramide. Bus: 75. Tram: 3.

### INEXPENSIVE

**Da Remo** ★★ PIZZA   Mentioning "Testaccio" and "pizza" in the same sentence elicits one typical response from locals: Da Remo, a Roman institution. In the summer especially, come early or be prepared to wait for a table. Every crisp-crusted, perfectly foldable pizza is made for all to see behind open counters. The most basic ones (margherita and marinara) start at around 7€. If it's too crowded on a summer evening, order your pizza for takeout and eat it in the park across the street.

Piazza Santa Maria Liberatrice 44. No website. ✆ **06-5746270.** Most pizzas 6€–8€. Daily 7pm–1am. Bus: 75. Tram: 3, 8.

# EXPLORING ROME

Rome's ancient monuments are a constant reminder that this was one of the greatest centers of Western civilization. In the heyday of the Empire, all roads led to Rome, with good reason. It was one of the first cosmopolitan cities, importing food, textiles, slaves, gladiators, great art, and even citizens from the far corners of the world. Despite its brutality and corruption, Rome left a legacy of law, a heritage of art, architecture, and engineering, and a canny lesson in how to conquer enemies by absorbing their cultures.

But ancient Rome is only part of the spectacle. The Vatican has had a tremendous influence on making the city a tourism center. Although Vatican architects stripped down much of the city's ancient glory during the Renaissance, looting ruins (the Forum especially) for their precious marble, they created more treasures and occasionally incorporated the old into the new—as Michelangelo did when turning Diocletian's Baths complex into a church. And in the years that followed, Bernini adorned the city with baroque wonders, especially his glorious fountains.

## St. Peter's & the Vatican
### VATICAN CITY

The world's smallest sovereign state, **Vatican City** is a truly tiny territory, comprising little more than St. Peter's Basilica, the Vatican Museums, and the walled headquarters of the Roman Catholic Church. There are no border controls, though the city-state's 800 inhabitants (essentially clergymen and Swiss Guards) have their own radio station, daily newspaper, tax-free pharmacy and petrol pumps, postal service, and head of state—the Pope. The Pope had always exercised a high degree of political independence from the rest of Italy, formalized by the 1929 Lateran Treaty between Pope Pius XI and the Italian government to create the Vatican. The city is still protected by the

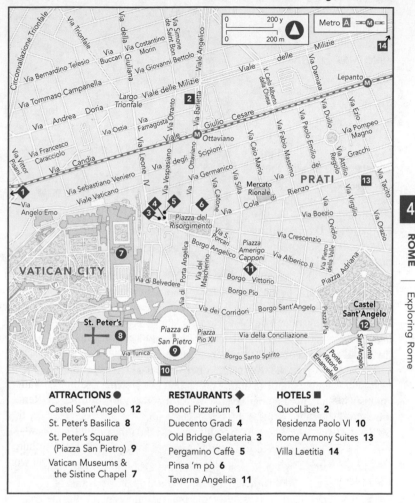

**ATTRACTIONS** ●
Castel Sant'Angelo **12**
St. Peter's Basilica **8**
St. Peter's Square
(Piazza San Pietro) **9**
Vatican Museums &
the Sistine Chapel **7**

**RESTAURANTS** ◆
Bonci Pizzarium **1**
Duecento Gradi **4**
Old Bridge Gelateria **3**
Pergamino Caffè **5**
Pinsa 'm pò **6**
Taverna Angelica **11**

**HOTELS** ■
QuodLibet **2**
Residenza Paolo VI **10**
Rome Armony Suites **13**
Villa Laetitia **14**

flamboyantly uniformed (allegedly designed by Michelangelo) Swiss Guards, a tradition dating from when the Swiss, known as brave soldiers, were often hired out as mercenaries for foreign armies. Today the Vatican remains the center of the Roman Catholic world, the home of the Pope, and the resting place of St. Peter. **St. Peter's Basilica** is obviously one of the highlights, but the only part of the Apostolic Palace itself that you can visit independently is the **Vatican Museums,** the world's biggest and richest museum complex.

On the left side of Piazza San Pietro, the **Vatican Tourist Office** (www. vatican.va; ✆ **06-69882019;** Mon–Sat 8:30am–7:30pm) sells maps and guides that will help you make sense of the treasures in the museums; it also accepts reservations for tours of the Vatican Gardens. Adjacent to the information office, the **Vatican Post Office** sells special Vatican postage stamps (open Mon–Fri 8:30am–7pm, Sat 8:30am–6pm).

The only entrance to St. Peter's for tourists is through one of the glories of the Western world: Bernini's 17th-century **St. Peter's Square (Piazza San Pietro).** As you stand in the huge piazza, you are in the arms of an ellipse partly enclosed by a majestic **Doric-pillared colonnade.** Stand in the marked marble discs embedded in the pavement near the fountains to see all the columns lined up in a

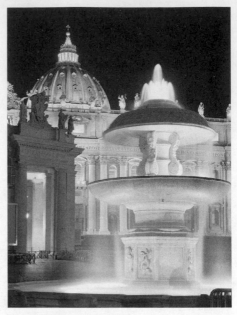

St. Peter's Square, Vatican City.

striking optical/geometrical play. Straight ahead is the facade of St. Peter's itself, and to the right, above the colonnade, are the dark brown buildings of the **papal apartments** and the Vatican Museums. In the center of the square stands a 4,000-year-old **Egyptian obelisk,** created in the ancient city of Heliopolis on the Nile delta and appropriated by the Romans under Emperor Augustus. Flanking the obelisk are two 17th-century **fountains.** The one on the right (facing the basilica), by Carlo Maderno, who designed the facade of St. Peter's, was placed here by Bernini himself; the other is by Carlo Fontana.

**St. Peter's Basilica ★★★** CHURCH  The Basilica di San Pietro, or simply **St. Peter's,** is the holiest shrine of the Catholic Church, built on the site of St. Peter's tomb by the greatest Italian artists of the 16th and 17th centuries. The line of the right side of the piazza funnels you into the basilica

### Don't Forget to Skip the Line

It used to be that going to Rome's three biggest attractions—the Colosseum, the Vatican Museums, and St. Peter's Basilica—meant waiting in line a long, long time. Now thanks to advance ticket sales for timed entry, there's absolutely no reason to wait in excessively long lines for the Colosseum or the Vatican Museums. (See individual attraction listings for more details.) Only St. Peter's offers no skip-the-line perk. The only way to jump the line there is with the **Omnia Card** (see p. 46) or by booking a private or group tour (p. 130).

## How to Visit an Entire Country in a Day

Most Vatican visitors allot a day to see its two major sights, **St. Peter's Basilica** and the **Vatican Museums** (including the Sistine Chapel). We recommend starting with the museums. **Pre-order** tickets for the earliest time slot (from 9am) available the day you wish to visit. Plan to devote several hours to see the highlights of the museum collections (see p. 89).

Next, grab a quick late lunch, either in the museum cafeteria or at a nearby sandwich shop or pizza joint. The streets leading from the museum exit to St. Peter's Basilica are lined with cheap eateries—mostly mediocre, but they'll do in a pinch. (See p. 70 for some notably good options.)

Once you enter **St. Peter's Square,** head to the back of the line (always long, but it moves fairly quickly) to enter the basilica. From the time you enter the basilica, you'll need at least 1 hour for even the most cursory tour.

By now it'll be late afternoon, and you've got 2 options: Visit the **Vatican Grottoes,** burial place of dozens of popes, or climb the 551 steps (320 if you take the elevator) to the top of the **dome of St. Peter's.** Note that the dome and grottoes are open until 6pm April to September (till 5pm Oct–Mar). If you've still got energy, head to nearby **Castel Sant'Angelo** (see p. 94)—the view of Rome from the castle's roof is a perfect way to cap off your marathon Vatican day.

Want more time at the Vatican Museums? Arrive at St. Peter's early in the morning to get in line before it opens at 7:30am; that way you can tour the basilica before the crowds get thick. Then head to a late-morning appointment at the museums and spend the rest of the day there.

(from where you can access the underground grottoes), or the dome. Whichever you opt for first, you must be **properly dressed**—a rule that is very strictly enforced.

In Roman times, the Circus of Nero, where Peter is said to have been crucified, was just to the left of where the basilica is today. He was allegedly buried here in A.D. 64, and in A.D. 324 Emperor Constantine commissioned a church to be built over Peter's tomb. That structure stood for more than 1,000 years. The present basilica, mostly completed in the 1500s and 1600s, is predominantly High Renaissance and baroque. Inside, the massive scale is almost too much to absorb, showcasing some of Italy's greatest artists: Bramante, Raphael, and Michelangelo. In a church of such grandeur—overwhelming in its detail of gilt, marble, and mosaic—you can't expect much subtlety. It is meant to be overpowering.

Going straight into the basilica, the first thing you see on the right side of the nave—the longest nave in the world, as clearly marked in the floor along with other cathedral measurements—is the chapel containing Michelangelo's graceful **"Pietà"** ★★★. Created in the 1490s when the master was still in his 20s, it clearly shows his genius for capturing the human form. (The sculpture has been kept behind reinforced glass since an act of vandalism in the 1970s.) Note the lifelike folds of Mary's robes and her youthful features; although she would've been middle-aged at the time of the Crucifixion, Michelangelo

# papal AUDIENCES

When the pope is in Rome, he gives a public audience every Wednesday beginning at 9:30am. If you want to get a good seat near the front, arrive early and prepare to wait—security begins to let people in between 7 and 7:30am but the line starts much earlier. Audiences take place in the Paul VI Hall of Audiences, although sometimes St. Peter's Basilica and St. Peter's Square are used to accommodate a large attendance in the summer. You can check on Pope Francis's appearances and the ceremonies he presides over, including celebrations of Mass, on the Vatican website (www.vatican.va). Anyone is welcome, but you must first obtain a **free ticket;** without a reservation you can try the Swiss Guards by the Bronze Doors located just after security at St. Peter's (8am–8pm in summer and 8am–7pm in winter). You can pick up tickets here up to 3 days in advance, subject to availability.

If you prefer to reserve a place in advance, visit www.vatican.va/various/prefettura/index_en.html to download a request form, which must be submitted via fax (yes, really) to the **Prefecture of the Papal Household** at ✆ **06-69885863.** Tickets can be picked up at the office located just inside the Bronze Doors from 3 to 7pm on the preceding day or on the morning of the audience from 7am.

At noon on Sundays, the Pope speaks briefly from his study window and gives his blessing to the visitors and pilgrims gathered in St. Peter's Square (no tickets are required for this). From about mid-July to mid-September, the Angelus and blessing historically takes place at the Pope's summer residence at **Castel Gandolfo,** some 26km (16 miles) out of Rome. Under Pope Francis, the residence, gardens, and villas of the castle have been opened to visitors as a museum, accessible via Metro and bus as well as a new train service that leaves from the Roma San Pietro station. Visit **biglietteriamusei. vatican.va** for information on seeing Castel Gandolfo by train.

portrayed her as a young woman to convey her purity. A few yards past the Pieta is a chapel housing the **tomb of Pope John Paul II.**

Further inside the nave, Michelangelo's dome is a mesmerizing space, rising high above the supposed site of St. Peter's tomb. With a diameter of 41.5m (136 ft.), the dome is Rome's largest, supported by four bulky piers decorated with reliefs depicting the basilica's key holy relics: St. Veronica's handkerchief (used to wipe the face of Christ); the lance of St. Longinus, which pierced Christ's side; and a piece of the True Cross.

Under the dome is the twisty-columned **baldacchino ★★,** by Bernini, sheltering the papal altar. The ornate 29m-high (96-ft.) canopy was created in part, so it is said, from bronze stripped from the Pantheon. Bernini sculpted the face of a woman on the base of each pillar; starting with the face on the left pillar (with your back to the entrance), circle the entire altar to see the progress of expressions from the agony of childbirth through to the fourth pillar, where the woman's face is replaced with that of her newborn baby.

Just before reaching the dome, on the right, the devout stop to kiss the foot of the 13th-century **bronze of St. Peter ★,** attributed to Arnolfo di Cambio.

Elsewhere the church is decorated by more of Bernini's lavish sculptures, including his monument to Pope Alexander VII in the south transept, its winged skeleton writhing under the heavy marble drapes.

An entrance off the nave leads to the Sacristy and the **Historical Museum (Museo Storico)** or **treasury ★,** which is chock-full of richly jeweled chalices, reliquaries, and copes, as well as the late-15th-century bronze tomb of Pope Sixtus IV by Pollaiuolo.

An entrance to the left of the baldacchino leads down to the **Vatican grottoes ★★,** with their tombs of the popes, both ancient and modern. Behind a wall of glass is what is considered to be the tomb of St. Peter.

After you leave the grottoes, you find yourself in a courtyard and ticket line for the grandest sight in the basilica: the climb to **Michelangelo's dome ★★★,** about 114m (375 ft.) high. You can walk all the way up or take the elevator as far as it goes (this saves you 171 steps). At this first stop, you can walk on the roof of the basilica (where there's also a restroom, a snack bar, and a gift shop) and also around the interior of the drum of the dome, which offers a bird's-eye view of the basilica below. After that, you *still* have 320 steps to go to reach the very top. Claustrophobes take note: The last part of the climb is up a very narrow spiral staircase.

After you've made it to the top, you'll have a scintillating view over the rooftops of Rome and even the Vatican Gardens and papal apartments. The elevator back down drops you into the basilica interior, near the front entrance, or you can descend via a spiral ramp, the walls of which are lined with inscriptions recalling famous visitors to the dome.

Visits to the **Necropolis Vaticana ★★** and St. Peter's tomb itself are restricted to 250 persons per day on guided tours (90 min.) You must send a fax or e-mail at least 3 weeks beforehand, or apply in advance in person at the Ufficio Scavi (⊘/fax **06-69873017;** e-mail: scavi@fsp.va; Mon–Fri 9am–6pm, Sat 9am–5pm), which is located through the arch to the left of the stairs up from the basilica. For details, check www.scavi.va/content/scavi/en/ufficio-scavi.html. Children 14 and under are not admitted to the Necropolis.

Piazza San Pietro. www.vatican.va. ⊘ **06-69881662. Basilica** (including grottoes) free. **Necropolis Vaticana** (St. Peter's tomb) 13€. **Stairs** to the dome 8€; **elevator** (part-way) to the dome 10€; **sacristy** (with Historical Museum) 5€ adults, 3€ 12 and under. **Basilica** Oct–Mar daily 7am–6:30pm, Apr–Sept daily 7am–7pm. **Dome** Oct–Mar daily 7:30am–5pm, Apr–Sept daily 7:30am–6pm. **Note:** Basilica opening time may be delayed to noon or 1pm on Wed when the Pope holds an audience in the square. **Sacristy/ museum** Oct–Mar daily 9am–5:15pm, Apr–Sept daily 9am–6:15pm. **Grottoes** Oct–Mar daily 7am–5pm, Apr–Sept daily 7am–6pm. Metro: Ottaviano/San Pietro, then a 10-min. walk; or take bus 40, 46, or 62 to Piazza Pia/Traspontina, then about a 10-min. walk.

## Vatican Museums & the Sistine Chapel ★★★ MUSEUM Nothing

else in Rome quite lives up to the awe-inspiring collections of the **Vatican Museums,** a 15-minute walk from St. Peter's out of the north side of Piazza San Pietro. It's a vast treasure store of art from antiquity and the Renaissance gathered by the Roman Catholic Church through the centuries, filling a series of ornate Papal palaces, apartments, and galleries that lead to one of the world's most beautiful interiors, the justly celebrated **Sistine Chapel.**

Note that the Vatican dress code also applies to its museums (no sleeveless blouses, no miniskirts, no shorts, no hats allowed), though it tends to be less rigorously enforced than at St. Peter's.

Obviously, one trip will not be enough to see everything here. Below are previews of the main highlights, showstoppers, and masterpieces on display (in alphabetical order).

**APPARTAMENTO BORGIA (BORGIA APARTMENTS)** ★ Created for Pope Alexander VI (the infamous Borgia pope) between 1492 and 1494, these rooms were frescoed with biblical and allegorical scenes by Umbrian painter Pinturicchio and his assistants. Look for what is thought to be the earliest European depiction of Native Americans, painted little more than a year after Columbus returned from the New World and Alexander had "divided" the globe between Spain and Portugal.

**COLLEZIONE D'ARTE CONTEMPORANEA (COLLECTION OF MODERN RELIGIOUS ART)** ★ Spanning 55 rooms of almost 800 works, these galleries contain the Vatican's concession to modern art. There are some big names here and the quality is high, and themes usually have a spiritual and religious component: Van Gogh's "Pietà, after Delacroix" is here, along with Francis Bacon's eerie "Study for a Pope II." You will also see works by Paul Klee ("City with Gothic Cathedral"), Siqueiros ("Mutilated Christ No. 467"), Otto Dix ("Road to Calvary"), Gauguin ("Religious Panel"), Chagall ("Red Pietà"), and a whole room dedicated to Georges Rouault.

**MUSEI DI ANTICHITÀ CLASSICHE (CLASSICAL ANTIQUITIES MUSEUMS)** ★★★ The Vatican maintains four classical antiquities museums, the most important being the **Museo Pio Clementino** ★★★, crammed with Greek and Roman sculptures in the small Belvedere Palace of Innocent VIII. At the heart of the complex lies the Octagonal Court, where highlights include the sculpture of the Trojan priest **"Laocoön"** ★★★ and his two sons locked in a struggle with sea serpents, dating from around 40 B.C., and the exceptional **"Belvedere Apollo"** ★★★ (a 2nd-c. Roman reproduction of a Greek work from the 4th c. B.C.), the symbol of classic male beauty and a possible inspiration for Michelangelo's "David." Look out also for the

---

### When It Pays to Pay Extra

Here's a big perk of booking a private tour of the Vatican Museums and St. Peter's Basilica: Only private tour groups can use the "secret" door from the Sistine Chapel (inside the Vatican Museums) that exits right into the courtyard of St. Peter's. From here, groups go through a short security line and directly into the basilica, bypassing the long line that often stretches halfway around the piazza. For tour provider recommendations, see "Organized Tours," p. 130.

# VATICAN MUSEUMS survival GUIDE

The sheer size of the collections and vast crowds mean that seeing one of the greatest museums of art in the world isn't a leisurely, or even pleasant, experience. Visitors tend to get herded through room after room of galleries as they make their way to the Sistine Chapel, and lack of descriptive labels means they often don't know what they're looking at. Here are some tips to make sense of it all:

- Book **"skip the line"** tickets in advance through the Vatican Museums website. Once you see the entrance line stretching around the walls of Vatican City, the €4 booking will feel like money well-spent.

- Buy the **Guide to the Vatican Museums and City** book (14€) sold in museum bookstores and at the Vatican Tourist Office, on the left side of Piazza San Pietro (you can also buy it used for a lot less on Amazon.com).

- Once you're in the museum, take a few minutes to review the galleries map and decide which collections or works of art are a priority.

- If your priority is to see the Sistine Chapel, follow signs for the "PERCORSO BREVE" (short route) to the Cappella Sistina.

For a deeper experience, consider a breakfast or after-hours visit (p. 94) or springing for a private tour of the collections. These are a great way to get the most out of a visit, especially if you have limited time. They're also the only way to visit the **Vatican Gardens.** Booking online is mandatory; visit **https://biglietteriamusei.vatican.va/musei/tickets** for information. See Organized Tours (p. 130) for info on private companies offering Vatican tours.

impressive, gilded bronze statue of **"Hercules"** in the Rotunda, from the late 2nd century A.D., and the **Hall of the Chariot,** containing a magnificent sculpture of a chariot combining Roman originals and 18th-century work by Antonio Franzoni.

The **Museo Chiaramonti** ★ occupies the long loggia that links the Belvedere Palace to the main Vatican palaces, jam-packed on both sides with more than 800 Greco-Roman works, including statues, reliefs, and sarcophagi. In the **Braccio Nuovo** ★ ("New Wing"), a handsome Neoclassical extension of the Chiaramonti sumptuously lined with colored marble, lies the colossal statue of the **"Nile"** ★, the ancient river portrayed as an old man with his 16 children, most likely a reproduction of a long-lost Alexandrian Greek original.

The **Museo Gregoriano Profano** ★★, built in 1970, houses more Greek sculptures looted by the Romans (some from the Parthenon), mostly funerary steles and votive reliefs, as well as some choice Roman pieces, notably the restored mosaics from the floors of the public libraries in the **Baths of Caracalla** (p. 95).

**MUSEO ETNOLOGICO (ETHNOLOGICAL MUSEUM)** ★★　Founded in 1926, this astounding assemblage of artifacts and artwork is from cultures around the world, from ancient Chinese coins and notes, to plaster sculptures of Native Americans and ceremonial art from Papua New Guinea.

**MUSEO GREGORIANO EGIZIO** ★★ Nine rooms packed with plunder from Ancient Egypt, including sarcophagi, mummies, pharaonic statuary, votive bronzes, jewelry, cuneiform tablets from Mesopotamia, inscriptions from Assyrian palaces, and Egyptian hieroglyphics.

**MUSEO GREGORIANO ETRUSCO** ★★ The core of this collection is a cache of rare Etruscan art treasures dug up in the 19th century, dating from between the 9th and the 1st centuries B.C. The Romans learned a lot from the Etruscans, as the highly crafted ceramics, bronzes, silver, and gold on display attest. Don't miss the **Regolini-Galassi tomb** (7th c. B.C.), unearthed at Cerveteri. The museum is housed within the *palazzettos* of Innocent VIII (reigned 1484–92) and Pius IV (reigned 1559–65), the latter adorned with frescoes by Federico Barocci and Federico Zuccari.

**PINACOTECA (ART GALLERY)** ★★★ The great painting collections of the Popes are displayed in the Pinacoteca, including work from all the big names in Italian art, from Giotto and Fra' Angelico to Perugino, Raphael, Veronese, and Crespi. Early medieval work occupies Room 1, with the most intriguing piece a keyhole-shaped wood panel of the "Last Judgment" by Nicolò e Giovanni, dated to the late 12th century. **Giotto** takes center stage in Room 2, with the "Stefaneschi Triptych" (six panels) painted for the old St. Peter's basilica between 1315 and 1320. **Fra' Angelico** dominates Room 3, his "Stories of St. Nicholas of Bari" and "Virgin with Child" justly praised (check out the Virgin's microscopic eyes in the latter piece). Carlo Crivelli features in Room 6, while decent works by Perugino and Pinturicchio grace Room 7, though most visitors press on to the **Raphael salon** ★★★ (Room 8), which holds five paintings by the Renaissance master. The best are "Coronation of the Virgin," "Madonna of Foligno," and "Transfiguration" (completed shortly before his death). Room 9 has Leonardo da Vinci's **"St. Jerome with the Lion"** ★★, as well as Giovanni Bellini's "Pietà." Room 10 is dedicated to Renaissance Venice, with Titian's "Madonna of St. Nicholas of the Frari" and Veronese's "Vision of St. Helen" being paramount. Don't skip the remaining galleries: Room 11 holds Barocci's "Annunciation," while Room 12 is really all about one of the masterpieces of the baroque, Caravaggio's **"Deposition from the Cross"** ★★.

**STANZE DI RAFFAELLO (RAPHAEL ROOMS)** ★★★ In the early 16th century, Pope Julius II hired the young Raphael and his workshop to decorate his personal apartments, on the second floor of the Pontifical Palace. Completed between 1508 and 1524, the **Raphael Rooms** now represent one of the great artistic spectacles inside the Vatican.

The **Stanza dell'Incendio** served as the Pope's high court room and later, under Leo X, a dining room. Most of its lavish frescoes have been attributed to Raphael's pupils. Leo X commissioned much of the work here, which explains the themes (past Popes with the name Leo). Note the intricate ceiling, painted by Umbrian maestro Perugino, who was Raphael's first teacher.

Raphael is the main focus in the **Stanza della Segnatura,** originally used as a Papal library and private office and home to the awe-inspiring **"School of Athens"** ★★★ fresco, depicting primarily Greek classical philosophers such as Aristotle, Plato, and Socrates. Many of the figures are thought to be based on portraits of Renaissance artists, including Bramante (on the right as Euclid, drawing on a chalkboard), Leonardo da Vinci (as Plato, the bearded man in the center), and even Raphael himself (in the lower-right corner with a black hat). On the wall opposite stands the equally magnificent "Disputa del Sacramento," where Raphael used a similar technique; Dante Alighieri stands behind the pontiff on the right, and Fra' Angelico poses as a monk (which in fact, he was) on the far left.

The **Stanza d'Eliodoro** was used for the private audiences of the Pope and was painted by Raphael immediately after he did the Segnatura. His aim here was to flatter his papal patron, Julius II: The depiction of the pope driving Attila from Rome was meant to symbolize the contemporary mission of Julius II to push the French out of Italy. Finally, the **Sala di Costantino,** used for Papal receptions and official ceremonies, was completed by Raphael's students after the master's death, but based on his designs and drawings. It's a jaw-dropping space, commemorating four major episodes in the life of Emperor Constantine.

**SISTINE CHAPEL ★★★** Michelangelo labored for 4 years (1508–12) to paint the ceiling of the Sistine Chapel; it is said he spent the entire time on his feet, paint dripping into his eyes. Could he have imagined that more than 500 years later, his magnum opus would still be considered one of the greatest accomplishments in Western art? Today, the world's most famous fresco is as vibrantly colorful and filled with roiling life as it was in 1512. And the chapel is still of central importance to the Catholic Church: This is where the Papal Conclave meets to elect new popes.

The **"Creation of Adam,"** at the center of the ceiling, is one of the best-known and most reproduced images in history, the outstretched hands of God and Adam—not quite touching—an iconic symbol of not just the Renaissance but the Enlightenment that followed. Nevertheless, it is somewhat ironic that this is Michelangelo's best-known work: The artist always regarded himself as a sculptor first and foremost.

*Tip:* The ceiling **frescoes** are obviously the main showstoppers, but staring up at them tends to take a heavy toll on the neck. To relieve your neck (and your tired feet), make your way to one of the benches that line both long sides of the gallery. As soon as someone gets up, grab a seat so you can gaze upward in relative comfort.

Commissioned by Pope Julius II in 1508 and completed in 1512, the ceiling frescoes primarily depict nine scenes from the Book of Genesis (including the famed "Creation of Adam"), from the **"Separation of Light and Darkness"** at the altar end to the **"Great Flood"** and **"Drunkenness of Noah."** Surrounding the main frescoes are paintings of 12 people who prophesied the coming of Christ, from Jonah and Isaiah to the Delphic Sibyl. Once you have

Vatican Museum visitors have an extraordinary opportunity to stroll through the galleries after sunset, at least on Friday and Saturday nights until 10:30pm (last entrance at 8:30). Options are available to add on happy hours and guided tours.

Early birds should consider booking a **breakfast tour** of the museums. Starting at 7:45am (before the official opening time), breakfast visits cost 34€, and include American-style breakfast and access to all galleries.

admired the ceiling, turn your attention to the altar wall. At the age of 60, Michelangelo was summoned to finish the chapel decor 23 years after he finished the ceiling work. Apparently saddened by leaving Florence, and depressed by the morally bankrupt state of Rome at that time, he painted these dark moods in his **"Last Judgment,"** where he included his own self-portrait on a sagging human hide held by St. Bartholomew (who was martyred by being flayed alive).

Yet the Sistine Chapel isn't all Michelangelo. The southern wall is covered by a series of astonishing paintings completed in the 1480s: **"Moses Leaving to Egypt"** by Perugino, the **"Trials of Moses"** by Botticelli, **"The Crossing of the Red Sea"** by Cosimo Rosselli (or Domenico Ghirlandaio), **"Descent from Mount Sinai"** by Cosimo Rosselli (or Piero di Cosimo), Botticelli's **"Punishment of the Rebels,"** and Signorelli's **"Testament and Death of Moses."**

On the right-hand northern wall are Perugino's **"The Baptism of Christ,"** Botticelli's **"The Temptations of Christ,"** Ghirlandaio's **"Vocation of the Apostles,"** Perugino's **"Delivery of the Keys,"** Cosimo Rosselli's **"The Sermon on the Mount"** and **"Last Supper."** On the eastern wall, originals by Ghirlandaio and Signorelli were painted over by Hendrik van den Broeck's **"The Resurrection"** and Matteo da Lecce's **"Disputation over Moses"** in the 1570s.

Vatican City, Viale Vaticano (walk around Vatican walls from St. Peter's Sq.). www.museivaticani.va. ⓒ **06-69884676. Advance booking with timed entrance mandatory.** 17€ adults, 8€ ages 6–13, free for children 5 and under; 2-hr. tours of Vatican Gardens 34€ (no tours Wed or Sun). Advance tickets (reservation fee 4€) and guided tours (33€ per person) through biglietteriamusei.vatican.va. Mon–Thurs 8:30am–6:30pm (ticket office closes 4:30pm); Fri–Sat 8:30am–10:30pm (ticket office closes 8:30pm); last Sun every month 9am–2pm (free admission). Closed Jan 1 and 6, Feb 11, Mar 19, Easter, May 1, June 29, Aug 15, Nov 1, Dec 8, and Dec 25–26. Metro: Ottaviano or Cipro–Musei Vaticani. Buses 23 and 492 to Bastioni di Michelangelo (3-min. walk from entrance), or buses 590, 982, and 19 tram to Piazza del Risorgimento (10-min. walk from entrance).

**Castel Sant'Angelo** ★★ CASTLE/PALACE   Over the years, this bulky cylindrical fortress on the Vatican side of the Tiber has had many lives: as the mausoleum tomb of Emperor Hadrian in A.D. 138; as a papal residence in the

14th century; as a castle, where in 1527 Pope Clement VII hid from the looting troops of Charles V; and as a military prison from the 17th century on. Consider renting an audio guide at the entrance to fully appreciate its various manifestations.

From the entrance a stone ramp *(rampa elicoidale)* winds to the upper terraces, where you can see amazing views of the city and enjoy a coffee at the outdoor cafe. The sixth floor features the **Terrazza dell'Angelo,** crowned by a florid 18th-century statue of the Archangel Michael. It's famous to opera fans—the last act of Puccini's "Tosca" is set here.

From here you can walk back down through five floors. On levels 3 to 5 you'll see the Renaissance apartments used by some of Rome's most infamous Popes, including Alexander VI, the Borgia pope. Below the apartments are the grisly dungeons **("Le Prigioni")** used as torture chambers in the medieval period (Cesare Borgia made great use of them). The castle is connected to St. Peter's Basilica by **Il Passetto di Borgo,** a walled passage built in 1277 by Pope Nicholas III, used by popes who needed to make a quick escape to the fortress in times of danger.

Lungotevere Castello 50. www.castelsantangelo.com. ℂ **06-32810.** 15€. Daily 9am–7:30pm. Bus: 23, 40, 62, 280, 982 (to Piazza Pia).

# The Colosseum, Forum & Ancient Rome
## THE MAJOR SIGHTS OF ANCIENT ROME

Your sightseeing experience will be enhanced if you know a little about the history and rulers of Ancient Rome: See p. 24 for a brief rundown.

### Arch of Constantine (Arco di Costantino) ★★ MONUMENT   The photogenic triumphal arch next to the Colosseum was erected by the Senate in A.D. 315 to honor Constantine's defeat of the pagan Maxentius at the Battle of the Milvian Bridge (A.D. 312). Many of the reliefs have nothing whatsoever to do with Constantine or his works, but they tell of the victories of earlier Antonine rulers (lifted from other, long-forgotten memorials).

The arch marks a period of great change in the history of Rome. Converted to Christianity by a vision on the eve of battle, Constantine ended the centuries-long persecution of the Christians, during which many followers of the new religion had been put to death in a gruesome manner. Although Constantine didn't ban paganism (which survived officially for another half-century or so), he espoused Christianity himself and began the process that ended in the conquest of Rome by the Christian religion.

Btw. Colosseum and Palatine Hill. Metro: Colosseo. Bus: 51, 85, 87, 118. Tram: 3.

### Baths of Caracalla (Terme di Caracalla) ★★ RUINS   Named for Emperor Caracalla, a particularly unpleasant individual, the baths were completed in A.D. 217 after his death. The richness of decoration has faded, but the massive brick ruins and the mosaic fragments that remain give modern visitors an idea of the complex's scale and grandeur. In their heyday, the baths sprawled across 11 ha (27 acres) and included hot, cold, and tepid pools, as

well as a *palestra* (gym) and changing rooms. A museum in the tunnels below the complex—built over an even more ancient *mithraeum*, a worship site of an Eastern cult—explores the hydraulic and heating systems (and slave power) needed to serve 8,000 or so Romans per day. Summer operatic performances here are an ethereal treat (see p. 134).

Via delle Terme di Caracalla 52. www.coopculture.it/en. © **06-39967702.** 8€ (10€ online). Tues–Sun 9am–dusk (as early as 4:30pm or as late as 7:15pm). Last entry 1 hr. before closing. Bus: 118 or 628.

**Capitoline Museums (Musei Capitolini)** ★★ MUSEUM    The masterpieces here are considered Rome's most valuable (recall that the Vatican Museums are *not* technically in Rome). They certainly were collected early: This is the oldest public museum *in the world.* So try and schedule adequate time, as there's much to see.

First stop is the courtyard of the **Palazzo dei Conservatori** (the building on the right of the piazza designed by Michelangelo, if you enter via the ramp from Piazza Venezia). It's scattered with gargantuan stone body parts—the remnants of a massive 12m (39-ft.) statue of the emperor Constantine, including his colossal head, hand, and foot. It's nearly impossible to resist snapping a selfie next to the giant finger.

On the *palazzo*'s ground floor, the unmissable works are in the first series of rooms. These include "Lo Spinario" **(Room III),** a lifelike bronze of a young boy digging a splinter out of his foot that was widely copied during the Renaissance; and the "Lupa Capitolina" **(Room IV),** a bronze statue of the famous she-wolf that suckled Romulus and Remus, the mythical founders of Rome. Scholars disagree on the date of the statue: Long thought to be from around 500 B.C., recent analysis suggests it may be from the 1100s. What is certain is that the twins were not on the original statue, but were added in the 15th century. **Room V** has Bernini's famously pained portrait of "Medusa," even more compelling when you see its writhing serpent hairdo in person.

Before heading upstairs, go toward the newer wing at the rear, which houses the original **equestrian statue of Marcus Aurelius** ★★★, dating to around A.D. 180—the piazza outside, where it stood from 1538 until 2005, now has a copy. There's a giant bronze head from a statue of Constantine (ca. A.D. 337) and the foundations of the original Temple of Jupiter that stood on the Capitoline Hill since its inauguration in 509 B.C.

The second-floor **picture gallery** ★ is strong on baroque oil paintings. Masterpieces include Caravaggio's "John the Baptist" and "The Fortune Teller" (1595) and Guido Reni's "St. Sebastian" (1615).

A tunnel takes you under the piazza to the other part of the Capitoline Museums, the **Palazzo Nuovo,** via the **Tabularium** ★★. This was built in 78 B.C. to house ancient Rome's city records, and was later used as a salt mine and then as a prison. Here, the moody *galleria lapidaria* houses a well-executed exhibit of ancient portrait tombstones and sarcophagi, many of their poignant epitaphs translated into English, and provides access to one of the

# Ancient Rome, Monti & Celio

## ATTRACTIONS ●

Arch of Constantine **20**
Basilica di San
  Clemente **26**
Basilica di San Giovanni
  in Laterano **29**
Baths of Caracalla **23**
Capitoline Museums **4**
Case Romane del Celio **24**
Circus Maximus **7**
Colosseum **21**
Domus Aurea **22**
Domus Romane di
  Palazzo Valentini **10**
Imperial Forums **9**
Museum of the Imperial
  Forums & Trajan's
  Markets **11**
Museo Nazionale del
  Palazzo di Venezia **1**
Roman Forum **8**
Santa Maria in
  Aracoeli **3**
Santa Maria in
  Cosmedin **6**
St. Peter in Chains **19**
Vittoriano **2**

## RESTAURANTS ◆

Caffè Propaganda **25**
Fatamorgana **18**
InRoma al
  Campidoglio **5**
La Barrique **15**
La Bottega
  del Caffè **13**
Li Rioni **27**
Maharajah **14**
Vale la Pena Pub **30**

## HOTELS ■

Duca d'Alba **17**
The Glam **16**
Inn at the Roman
  Forum **12**
Lancelot **28**

Metro A
Metro B
Metro C

0    200 y
0    200 m

MONTI

JEWISH GHETTO

CAPITOLINE HILL

ROMAN FORUM

PALATINE HILL

CIRCO MASSIMO

AVENTINE HILL

CELIO

Colosseo

Trajan's Column

Vittoriano

Teatro di Marcello

To the Appian Way

Basilica di San Giovanni in Laterano

best balcony **views** ★★★ in Rome: along the length of the Forum toward the Palatine Hill.

Much of the Palazzo Nuovo is dedicated to statues that were excavated from the forums below and brought in from outlying areas like Hadrian's Villa in Tivoli (p. 142). If you're running short on time at this point, head straight for the 1st-century **"Capitoline Venus"** ★★, modestly covering up after a bath, in Room III, and in Rooms IV and V, a chronologically arranged row of distinct, expressive busts of Roman emperors and their families. Another favorite is the beyond handsome **"Dying Gaul"** ★★, a Roman copy of a lost ancient Greek work. Lord Byron considered the statue so lifelike and moving that he mentioned it in his poem "Childe Harold's Pilgrimage."

Piazza del Campidoglio 1. www.museicapitolini.org. ⓒ **060608.** 11:50€ (more during special exhibits). Daily 9:30am–7:30pm. Last entry 1 hr. before closing. Bus: 40, 44, 60, 63, 64, 70, 118, 160, 170, 628, 716 or any bus that stops at Piazza Venezia.

**Circus Maximus (Circo Massimo)** ★ HISTORIC SITE   The once-grand arena today is a far cry from its *Ben-Hur*-esque heyday, when some 300,000 Romans assembled in this oval-shaped field. What the Romans called a "circus" was a large arena ringed by tiers of seats and used for sports or spectacles, which the emperor observed from his box high on the Palatine Hill.

The last games were held in A.D. 549 on the orders of Totila the Goth, who had seized Rome twice. Afterwards, the Circus Maximus was never used again, and its marble and stone were pilfered by medieval and Renaissance builders. The demand for building materials reduced it, like so much of Rome, to a great dusty field, now used mostly for big-name rock concerts. An archaeological area at its eastern end (closest to the Metro station) offers insights into how the space once functioned.

A 40-minute virtual reality tour (12€, including site admission) is available at various times during the year; see www.circomaximoexperience.it for info. *Tip:* If you're crunched for time, bypass the Circus Maximus and instead take in the emperor's-eye views of the arena from atop the Palatine Hill.

Btw. Via dei Cerchi and Via del Circo Massimo. www.sovraintendenzaroma.it (search "Circo Massimo" then translate). ⓒ **060608.** Archaeological area 5€. Daily 9:30am–7pm (last entrance 5:50pm). Metro: Circo Massimo. Bus: 81, 118, 160.

**Colosseum (Colosseo)** ★★★ ICON   No matter how many pictures you've seen, your first view of the Flavian Amphitheater (the Colosseum's original name) is likely to amaze you with its sheer size and ruined grandeur. While you're still outside its massive walls, take time to walk completely around its 500m (1,640-ft.) circumference. It doesn't matter where you start, but do the circle. Look at the various stages of ruin; note the different column styles on each level. Mere photos could never convey its physical impact.

Vespasian ordered the construction of the elliptical bowl in A.D. 72; it was inaugurated by Titus in A.D. 80. Built for gladiator contests and wild-animal fights, the stadium could hold as many as 87,000 spectators by some counts;

seats were sectioned on three levels, dividing the people by social rank and gender. Some 80 entrances allowed the massive crowds to be seated and dispersed within a few minutes. When the Roman Empire fell, however, the abandoned arena was eventually overgrown. Much of the travertine that once sheathed its outside was used for palaces like the nearby Palazzo Venezia and Palazzo Cancelleria.

An ongoing conservation effort, funded in large part by the Italian design house Tod's, has scoured 2,000 years of soot from the monument's exterior and opened restored areas previously closed to the public, including the **Arena Floor** and **Underground**, which were formerly open only by guided or private tour. (The **Belvedere** [upper tier] is open periodically but was closed as of this writing.) The Arena/Underground area is ticketed separately from standard Colosseum admission and is *not* included with the RomaPass. The process for purchasing tickets online can be baffling, but essentially you reserve a ticket that includes all "normal" areas of the Colosseum plus the arena floor, to which you can opt to add, at no extra charge, a 40-minute guided tour of the Underground (there is no option for seeing the Underground without a guide). The tour includes explanations of the complex system of ramps, elevators, and trap doors that unleashed onto the arena floor the gladiators, wild animals, and array of theatrical effects that once thrilled and stunned audiences in the stands. These tours fill up very quickly. A 24€ combined tour that includes Colosseum, Forum, and Palatine Hill admission is valid for 2 days; the regular 18€ Colosseum ticket, which includes admission to the Forum and Palatine Hill, is valid for 24 hours. Though the pre-ticketing system has eliminated the long line to enter, you still must go through security screening, which can take up to an hour on busy days. **RomaPass holders** must reserve in advance a time to enter the Colosseum, either online, by calling © **06-39967575,** *or* in person at one of the Forum/Palatine ticket offices the day you wish to enter. There's a 2€ per-person reservation fee.

Piazzale del Colosseo. www.coopculture.it/en/colosseo-e-shop.cfm. © **06-39967700.** 18€ pre-purchased online, includes Roman Forum & Palatine Hill. "Full Experience" ticket including access to the Arena 24€. Open 9:30am–dusk (as early as 4:30pm in winter, as late as 7:15pm Mar–Aug). Last entry 1 hr. before closing. Metro: Colosseo. Bus: 51, 75, 85, 87, 118. Tram: 3.

## Imperial Forums (Fori Imperiali) ★ RUINS

Begun by Julius Caesar to relieve overcrowding in Rome's older forums, the Imperial Forums were, at the time of their construction, flashier, bolder, and more impressive than anything that had come before them in Rome. They conveyed the unquestioned authority of the emperors at the height of their absolute power.

Alas, Mussolini felt his regime was more important than the ancient one, and issued the controversial orders to cut through centuries of debris and buildings to carve out Via dei Fori Imperiali, linking the Colosseum to the 19th-century monuments of Piazza Venezia. Excavations under his Fascist regime uncovered countless archaeological treasures. Most ruins more recent than imperial Rome were destroyed—*argh!*

# THREE free views TO SAVOR FOR A LIFETIME

**The Forum from the Campidoglio** Standing on Piazza del Campidoglio, outside the Musei Capitolini (p. 96), walk around the right or left side of the Palazzo Senatorio to terraces overlooking the best panoramas of the Roman Forum, with the Palatine Hill and Colosseum as a backdrop. At night, the ruins look even more haunting when the Forum is dramatically floodlit.

**The Whole City from the Janiculum Hill** From many vantage points in the Eternal City, the views are panoramic. But one of the best spots for a memorable vista is the Janiculum Hill (*Gianicolo*), above Trastevere. Laid out before you are Rome's rooftops, peppered with domes ancient and modern. From up here, you will understand why Romans complain about the materials used to build the 19th-century Vittoriano (p. 107)—it's a gigantic white shock in a

sea of rose- and honey-colored stone. Walk 50 yards north of the famous balcony (favored by tour buses) for a slightly better angle, from the Belvedere 9 Febbraio 1849. Views from the 1612 Fontana dell'Acqua Paola are also splendid, especially at night.

**The Aventine Hill & the Priori dei Cavalieri di Malta** The mythical site of Remus's original settlement, the Aventine (*Aventino*) is now a leafy, upscale residential neighborhood—but also blessed with some magical views. From Via del Circo Massimo, walk through the gardens along Via di Valle Murcia, and keep walking in a straight line. Along your right side, the Giardino degli Aranci (Orange Tree Garden) offers views over the dome of St. Peter's. When you reach Piazza dei Cavalieri di Malta, look through the keyhole of the Priory gate (on the right) for a "secret" view of the Vatican.

The best view of the Forums is from the railings on the north side of Via dei Fori Imperiali; begin where Via Cavour joins the boulevard Closest to the junction are the remains of the **Forum of Nerva,** built by the emperor whose 2-year reign (A.D. 96–98) followed the assassination of the paranoid Domitian. You'll be struck by how much the ground level has risen in 19 centuries. The only really recognizable remnant is a wall of the Temple of Minerva with two fine Corinthian columns. The next along is the **Forum of Augustus ★★,** built to commemorate Emperor Augustus's victory over Julius Caesar's assassins, Cassius and Brutus, in the Battle of Philippi (42 B.C.). Continuing along the railing, you'll see the vast, multilevel semicircle of **Trajan's Markets ★★,** essentially an ancient shopping mall whose arcades were once stocked with merchandise from the far corners of the Roman world. You can visit the part that has been transformed into the **Museo dei Fori Imperiali & Mercati di Traiano** (see p. 101).

In front of the Markets, the **Forum of Trajan ★★** was built between A.D. 107 and 113, designed by Greek architect Apollodorus of Damascus (who also laid out the adjoining market building). Many statue fragments and pedestals bear still-legible inscriptions, but more interesting is the great Basilica Ulpia, whose gray marble columns rise roofless into the sky. This forum was once regarded as one of the architectural wonders of the world. Beyond the Basilica Ulpia is **Trajan's Column ★★★,** in magnificent condition, with an intricate bas-relief sculpture depicting Trajan's victorious campaign in Dacia (modern Romania).

The **Forum of Julius Caesar ★★,** the first of the Imperial Forums to be built, lies on the opposite side of Via dei Fori Imperiali, adjacent to the Roman Forum. This was the site of the stock exchange as well as the Temple of Venus.

Along Via dei Fori Imperiali. Metro: Colosseo. Bus: 51, 75, 85, 87, 118.

## Museum of the Imperial Forums (Museo dei Fori Imperiali & Mercati di Traiano) & Trajan's Markets ★★ RUINS/MUSEUM

Built on three levels, Emperor Trajan's Market housed 150 shops and commercial offices—think of it as the world's first shopping mall. Grooves still evident in the thresholds allowed merchants to slide doors shut and lock up for the night. You're likely to have the covered, tunnel-like market halls mostly to your-self—making the ancient past feel all the more present in this overlooked site. The Museum of the Imperial Forums occupies a converted section of the market, and has excellent visual displays that help you imagine what these grand public squares and temples used to look like. All in all, it's home to 172 marble fragments from the Fori Imperiali; there are also original remnants from the Forum of Augustus and Forum of Nerva.

Via IV Novembre 94. www.mercatiditraiano.it. ⓒ **060608.** 14€. Daily 9:30am–7:30pm. Last admission 1 hr. before closing. Bus: 40, 60, 64, 70, 170.

## Roman Forum (Foro Romano) & Palatine Hill (Palatino) ★★★

RUINS    Traversed by the **Via Sacra (Sacred Way) ★,** the main thorough-fare of ancient Rome, the Roman Forum flourished as the center of religious, social, and commercial life in the days of the Republic, before it gradually lost prestige (but never spiritual draw) to the Imperial Forums (see above).

You'll see ruins and fragments, some partially intact columns, and an arch or two, but you can still feel the rush of history here. That any semblance of the Forum remains today is miraculous: It was used for years as a quarry (as was the Colosseum). Eventually it reverted to a *campo vaccino* (cow pasture). Excavations in the 19th century and later in the 1930s began to bring to light one of the world's most historic spots.

You can spend at least a morning wandering the ruins of the Forum. Enter via the gate on Via dei Fori Imperiali, at Via della Salara Vecchia. (Note that an access point in front of the Colosseum is also open from time to time.) Turn right at the bottom of the entrance slope to walk west along the old Via Sacra toward the arch. Just before it on your right is the large brick **Curia ★★,** the main seat of the Roman Senate, built by Julius Caesar, rebuilt by Diocletian, and consecrated as a church in A.D. 630.

The triumphal **Arch of Septimius Severus ★★** (A.D. 203), is the next important sight, displaying time-bitten reliefs of the emperor's victories in what are now Iran and Iraq. During the Middle Ages, Rome became a provincial backwater, and frequent flooding of the Tiber helped bury (and thus

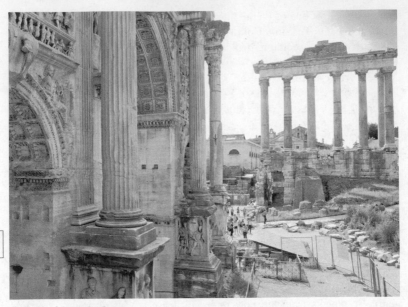

The Arch of Septimius Severus.

preserve) most of the Forum. Some bits did still stick out aboveground, including the top half of this arch, which was used to shelter a barbershop!

Just to the left of the arch, you can make out the remains of a cylindrical lump of rock with some marble steps curving off it. That round stone was the **Umbilicus Urbis,** considered the center of Rome and of the entire Roman Empire; the curving steps are those of the **Imperial Rostra ★,** where great orators and legislators stood to speak and the people gathered to listen. Nearby, a much-photographed trio of fluted columns with Corinthian capitals supports a bit of architrave from the corner of the **Temple of Vespasian and Titus ★★.** (Emperors were routinely turned into gods upon dying.)

Start heading to your left toward the eight Ionic columns marking the front of the **Temple of Saturn ★★** (rebuilt in 42 B.C.), which housed the first treasury of Republican Rome. It was also the site of one of the Roman year's biggest annual blowout festivals, the December 17 feast of Saturnalia, which, after a bit of tweaking, Christians now celebrate as Christmas. Turn left to start heading back east, past the worn steps and stumps of brick pillars outlining the enormous **Basilica Julia ★★,** built by Julius Caesar. Farther along, on the right, are the three Corinthian columns of the **Temple of the Dioscuri ★★★,** dedicated to the Gemini twins, Castor and Pollux. Forming one of the most photogenic sights of the Roman Forum, a trio of columns supports an architrave fragment. The temple's founding dates from the 5th century B.C.

Beyond the bit of curving wall that marks the site of the little round **Temple of Vesta** (rebuilt several times after fires started by the sacred flame within), you'll find the reconstructed **House of the Vestal Virgins** (A.D. 3rd–4th c.).

The temple was the home of the consecrated young women who tended the sacred flame in the Temple of Vesta. Vestals were girls chosen from patrician families to serve a 30-year-long priesthood. During their tenure, they were among Rome's most venerated citizens, with unique powers such as the ability to pardon condemned criminals. The cult was quite serious about the "virgin" part of the job description—if one of Vesta's earthly servants was found to have "misplaced" her virginity, the miscreant Vestal was buried alive, because it was forbidden to shed a Vestal's blood. (Her amorous accomplice was merely flogged to death.) The overgrown rectangle of their gardens is lined with broken, heavily worn statues of senior Vestals on pedestals.

The path dovetails back to Via Sacra. Turn right, walk past the so-called "Temple of Romulus," and then left to enter the massive brick remains of the 4th-century **Basilica of Constantine and Maxentius** ★★ (Basilica di Massenzio). These were Rome's public law courts, and their architectural style was adopted by early Christians for their houses of worship (the reason so many ancient churches are called "basilicas").

Return to the path and continue toward the Colosseum. Veer right to the Forum's second great triumphal arch, the extensively rebuilt **Arch of Titus** ★★ (A.D. 81), on which one relief depicts the carrying off of treasures from Jerusalem's temple. Look closely and you'll see a menorah among the booty. The war that this arch glorifies ended with the expulsion of Jews from the colonized Judea, signaling the beginning of the Jewish Diaspora throughout Europe. You can exit behind the Arch to continue on to the Colosseum, or head up to the Palatine Hill.

Access the **Palatine Hill** ★★ (Palatino)—where Romulus, after eliminating his twin brother Remus, founded Rome around 753 B.C. Later, emperors and other ancient bigwigs built their palaces and private entertainment facilities up here. After climbing to the top of the hill, visitors are presented with a sprawling, mostly crowd-free archaeological garden, with some shady spots for cooling off in summer.

The Palatine was where the first settlers built their huts under the direction of Romulus. In later years, the hill became a patrician residential district that attracted such citizens as Cicero. In time, however, the area was gobbled up by imperial palaces and drew an infamous roster of tenants, such as Livia (some of the frescoes in the House of Livia are in miraculous condition), Tiberius, Caligula (murdered here by members of his Praetorian Guard), Nero, and Domitian. A museum houses some of the most important finds from hill excavations.

Only the ruins of the Palatine's former grandeur remain today, but it's worth the climb for the panoramic views of both the Roman and the Imperial Forums, as well as the Capitoline Hill, the Colosseum and Circus Maximus. You can also enter from here, and do the entire tour in reverse.

> ### Famine in the Forum
>
> While there are a few water fountains on the Palatine and in the Forum, there is no place to eat—not even so much as a vending machine. If you're making a day of it, pack some snacks.

*Note:* In recent years, archaeological areas of the Palatine and Forum normally closed to visitors have been open via **S.U.P.E.R. ticket,** which allows limited, timed access to these "secret" underground sites, including the elaborately decorated **houses of Livia and Augustus ★★**. Check to see if S.U.P.E.R. (an acronym for "Seven Unique Places to Experience in Rome)" tickets have popped back up on the Coopculture site (www.coopculture.it/en).

Forum entrance on Via dei Fori Imperiali at Via della Salara Vecchia. Palatine Hill entrance at Via di San Gregorio 30 (south of the Colosseum). www.coopculture.it/en. ☎ **06-39967700.** 18€ prepurchased online (includes Colosseum), Full Experience ticket 24€. Open 9:30am–dusk (as early as 4:30pm in winter and as late as 7:15pm Mar–Aug). Last entry 1 hr. before closing. Metro: Colosseo. Bus: 51, 75, 85, 87, 118. Tram: 3, 8.

## OTHER ATTRACTIONS NEAR ANCIENT ROME

**Basilica di San Clemente ★★** CHURCH    A perfect example of how layers of history overlap in Rome, this 12-century Norman church, full of beautiful Byzantine mosaics, hides much more. Down in its eerie grottos (which you explore on your own) you'll find frescoes and mosaic floors from its previous incarnations as a 4th-century Christian church and a temple dedicated to the pagan deity Mithras—and below that, the foundations of a Roman house from the 1st century A.D., where early Christians worshiped in secret. *Note:* Access to the underground area may be limited to 10 minutes.

Via San Giovanni in Laterano (at Piazza San Clemente). www.basilicasanclemente.com. ☎ **06-7740021.** Basilica free; excavations 10€. Mon–Sat 10am–12:30pm to 3–5:30pm; Sun noon–5:30pm. Last entry 30 min. before closing. Metro: Colosseo. Bus: 51, 85, 87, 117. Tram: 3.

**Basilica di San Giovanni in Laterano ★★** CHURCH    This church, not St. Peter's, is officially the cathedral of the diocese of Rome; the Pope celebrates Mass here on certain holidays. Though it was built in A.D. 314 by Constantine, only parts of the original baptistery remain; what you see today is an 18th-century facade by Alessandro Galilei (note signs of damage from a 1993 terrorist bomb) and an interior by Borromini, built for Pope Innocent X. In a misguided redecoration long ago, frescoes by Giotto were apparently destroyed; remains attributed to Giotto, discovered in 1952, are displayed against the first inner column on the right.

---

### Strategies for Seeing Ancient Rome

Even though they're all included in the same admission fee, the ruins of the Colosseum, Roman Forum, and Palatine Hill are quite a lot to take in on a single day, particularly in the heat of Roman summer. But if a day is all you have budgeted, buy your tickets well in advance so that you can choose the earliest morning entry to the Colosseum. Then you'll have the rest of the day free for the Forum and Palatine Hill. If you've got a little more time (and interest), buy the 2-day Full Experience ticket (24€), which also gets you access to the Colosseum Arena and any S.U.P.E.R. sites currently open to visitors (see above).

# NERO'S golden HOUSE ★★★

After the Great Fire of A.D. 64, charismatic, despotic Emperor Nero staged a land grab to facilitate construction of his **Domus Aurea,** or Golden House, a massive, gilded villa complex covering all or parts of the Palatine, Esquiline, and Caelian hills and displaying a level of ostentation and excessiveness unheard of even among past emperors. After his death by noble suicide in A.D. 68, a campaign to erase all traces of Nero from the imperial city ensured that the palace was stripped of its gold, marble, jewels, mosaics, and statuary, then intentionally buried under millions of tons of rubble. It remained buried until the Renaissance, when young artists, including Raphael, descended into its "grottos" (actually the vaulted ceilings) to study the fanciful frescoes—the term grotesque (*grottoesque*) was coined here. Later excavations, both haphazard and scientific, revealed the scale and richness of the villa, but also subjected it to catastrophic moisture damage. After a years-long restoration and re-stabilization, the Domus Aurea is open for tours—but only if you time your trip well and plan ahead. Guided tours (18€; www.coopculture.it/en) of the scaffolded underground site (hardhats required) are offered on **Friday, Saturday, and Sunday only,** and with advance reservations. The tour includes a spectacular **virtual reality experience ★★★** that in itself is worth the visit. For details, go to **https://parcocolosseo.it/en/area/the-domus-aurea**.

Across the street is the **Santuario della Scala Santa (Palace of the Holy Steps),** Piazza San Giovanni in Laterano 14 (*℃* **06-7726641**), a set of 28 marble steps supposedly brought from Jerusalem by Constantine's mother, Helen. Though some historians say the stairs might date only from the 4th century, legend claims these were the stairs Christ climbed at Pontius Pilate's villa the day he was sentenced to death. Today pilgrims from the world over come here to climb the steps on their knees.

Piazza San Giovanni in Laterano 4. *℃* **06-69886433.** Free. Daily 7am–6:30pm. Metro: San Giovanni.

**Case Romane del Celio ★★** RUINS   Beneath the 5th-century Basilica of SS. Giovanni e Paolo lies a fascinating archaeological site: A complex of Roman houses of different periods—a wealthy family's townhouse from the 2nd century A.D. and a 3rd-century-A.D. apartment building for artisans. According to tradition, the latter was the home of two Roman officers, John and Paul (not the Apostles), who were beheaded during the reign of Julian the Apostate (361–63) for refusing to serve in a military campaign. They were later made saints, and their bones were said to have been buried here. The two-story construction also contains a small museum with finds from the site and fragmentary 12th-century frescoes.

Piazza Santi Giovanni e Paolo 13 (entrance on Clivo di Scauro). www.coopculture.it/en. *℃* **06-70454544.** 10€ adults. Fri–Mon and Wed 10am–4pm. Metro: Colosseo or Circo Massimo. Bus: 75, 81, 118. Tram: 3.

**Domus Romane di Palazzo Valentini** ★★ RUINS/EXHIBIT   All too often in Italy, archaeological sites are presented with little context, and it's difficult for untrained eyes to really understand what they're seeing. Not so at Palazzo Valentini, possibly Rome's best-presented ancient site. Visitors descend underneath a Renaissance palazzo and peer through a glass floor into the remains of several upscale Roman homes. With innovative use of 3D projections, the walls, ceilings, floors, and fountains of these once-grand houses spring to life, offering a captivating look at lifestyles of the ancient rich and possibly famous. Note that we dinged a star this edition because the last time we visited, several projections weren't working properly.

Via Foro Traiano 85 (near Trajan's Column). www.palazzovalentini.it. ⓒ **06-22761280.** 13.50€. Sat–Sun 10am–4pm; check website for additional opening times. Timed entrance, with guided tours in English several times daily; reservations suggested. Metro: Colosseo. Bus: 40, 63, 70, 81, 83, 87, or any bus to Piazza Venezia. Tram: 8.

**Museo Nazionale del Palazzo di Venezia** ★ MUSEUM   Best remembered today as Mussolini's Fascist headquarters in Rome, the palace was built in the 1450s as the Rome outpost of the Republic of Venice—hence the name. Today, several of its rooms house an eclectic mix of European paintings and decorative and religious objects spanning the centuries; highlights include Giorgione's enigmatic "Double Portrait" and some early Tuscan altarpieces.

Via del Plebiscito 118. www.museopalazzovenezia.beniculturali.it. ⓒ **06-6780131.** 10€. Daily 9:30am–7:30pm. Bus: 30, 40, 46, 62, 64, 70, 87, or any bus to Piazza Venezia. Tram: 8.

**Santa Maria in Aracoeli** ★★ CHURCH   This plain-on-the-outside church is worth the climb for its splendid interior. According to legend, Augustus ordered a temple erected on this spot on the Capitoline Hill, where a sibyl foretold the coming of Christ. The current church, built for the Franciscans in the 13th century, boasts a coffered Renaissance ceiling and the tomb of Giovanni Crivelli carved by the great Renaissance sculptor Donatello. The first chapel on the right, **Cappella Bufalini** ★, was frescoed by Pinturicchio with scenes of the life and death of St. Bernardino of Siena. A chapel behind the altar contains the **Santo Bambino,** a wooden figure of the Baby Jesus, which is venerated annually on Christmas Eve. The long flight of stairs leading up to the church was built in 1348 to celebrate the end of the Black Plague.

Scala dell'Arcicapitolina 12. ⓒ **06-69763838.** Free. Daily 7am–7pm (fall–winter 9:30am–5:30pm). Bus: 30, 40, 46, 62, 64, 70, 87, or any bus to Piazza Venezia.

**Santa Maria in Cosmedin** ★ CHURCH   People line up outside this ancient church (of Meklite Greek denomination) not for great art treasures (though it's worth a peek inside), but for the **"Mouth of Truth,"** a large disk on the wall of the portico. As Gregory Peck demonstrated to Audrey Hepburn in the film *Roman Holiday,* the mouth is supposed to chomp down on the hands of liars. It may have been an ancient drain cover, though one hypothesis says it was a so-called "talking statue," where anonymous notes were left to betray wrongdoers. Our take? Save this hokey photo op until after you've seen everything else you want to see in Rome.

Piazza della Bocca della Verità 18. ℰ **06-6787759.** Free. Daily 9:30am–6pm. Bus: 30, 44, 81, 83, 85, 87, 118, 160, 628, 715.

### St. Peter in Chains (San Pietro in Vincoli) ★

CHURCH Founded in the 5th century to house the chains that supposedly bound St. Peter in Jerusalem (preserved under glass below the main altar), this lovely church is mainly worth visiting to see one of the world's most famous sculptures: **Michelangelo's "Moses" ★★**, carved

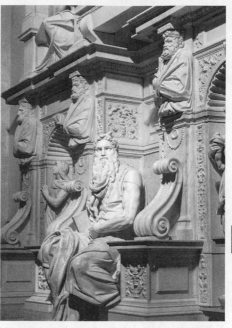

Michelangelo's "Moses," in the Basilica San Pietro in Vincoli.

for the tomb of Pope Julius II. Michelangelo never completed the 44 magnificent figures planned for the tomb, but this "minor" figure he did complete now numbers among his masterpieces.

Piazza San Pietro in Vincoli 4A. ℰ **06-97844952.** Free. Daily 8am–12:30pm and 3:30–7pm. Metro: Colosseo or Cavour. Bus: 75, 117.

### Vittoriano (Altare della Patria) ★ MONUMENT

It's impossible to miss the white marble Vittorio Emanuele monument dominating Piazza Venezia. Built in the late 1800s to honor the first king of a united Italy, this flamboyant (and widely disliked) landmark has been compared to everything from a wedding cake to a Victorian typewriter, its harsh white color glaring in a city of honey-gold hues. An eternal flame burns at the Tomb of the Unknown Soldier. For a panoramic city view, take a glass elevator to the **Terrazza delle Quadrighe (Terrace of the Chariots) ★.**

Piazza Venezia. vittoriano.beniculturali.it/en. ℰ **06-6780664.** Elevator 12€. Daily 9:30am–7:30pm (last entry 6:45pm). Bus: 30, 40, 46, 62, 64, 70, 87, or any bus to Piazza Venezia.

> ### All Roads Lead to... Piazza Venezia
>
> Love it or loathe it, the massive Vittoriano monument at Piazza Venezia is a helpful landmark for visitors to get their bearings, and almost every bus line convenient to tourists stops here. Streets fanning out from the piazza lead to Termini Station, the Colosseum, the Trevi Fountain, and across the Tiber to the Vatican and Trastevere.

# Centro Storico & the Pantheon

## CENTRO STORICO

Just across the Tiber from the Vatican and Castel Sant'Angelo lies the true heart of Rome, the **Centro Storico,** or "historic center," the triangular wedge of land that bulges into a bend of the river. Although the area lay outside the Roman city, it came into its own during the Renaissance, and today its streets and alleys are crammed with piazzas, elegant churches, and lavish fountains, all buzzing with scooters and people. It's a wonderful area in which to wander and get lost.

## PIAZZA NAVONA & NEARBY ATTRACTIONS

Rome's most famous square, **Piazza Navona** ★★★, is a gorgeous baroque gem, lined with cafes and restaurants and often crammed with tourists, street artists, and pigeons. Its long, oval shape follows the contours of the old ruined Roman Stadium of Domitian, where chariot races once took place, made over in the mid-17th century by Pope Innocent X. The twin-towered facade of 17th-century **Sant'Agnese in Agone** lies on the piazza's western side, while the **Fontana dei Quattro Fiumi (Fountain of the Four Rivers)** ★★★ opposite is one of three great fountains in the square, this one a typically exuberant creation by Bernini, topped with an Egyptian obelisk. The four stone personifications below symbolize the world's greatest rivers: the Ganges, Danube, de la Plata, and Nile. It's fun to try to figure out which is which. (*Hint:* The figure with the shroud on its head is the Nile, so represented because the river's source was unknown at the time.) At the south end is Bernini's **Fontana del Moro (Fountain of the Moor)** and the 19th-century **Fontana di Nettuno (Fountain of Neptune).**

Art lovers should make the short walk from the piazza to **Santa Maria della Pace** ★★ on Arco della Pace, a 15th-century church given the usual baroque makeover by Pietro da Cortona in the 1660s. The real gems are inside, beginning with Raphael's **"Four Sibyls"** ★★ fresco, above the arch of the Capella Chigi, and the **Chiostro del Bramante (Bramante cloister)** ★, built between 1500 and 1504 and the Renaissance master's first work in the city. The church is normally open daily from 9:30am to 6:30pm, while the cloister opens daily 10am to 8pm (to 9pm Sat and Sun). Admission to the church and cloister is free (www.chiostrodelbramante.it).

*Tip:* Waiters from Piazza Navona's many overpriced restaurants lie in wait, hoping to woo passing tourists. Buyer beware: While the setting is unmatchable, you'll have a far better meal on any of the side streets off the piazza.

**Palazzo Altemps** ★★ MUSEUM Inside this 15th-century *palazzo,* today a branch of the National Museum of Rome, is one of Rome's most charming museums. It's rarely crowded yet houses some of the city's most famous private and public art collections. Much of it was once part of the famed **Boncompagni Ludovisi Collection,** created by Cardinal Ludovico Ludovisi (1595–1632) and sold at auction in 1901.

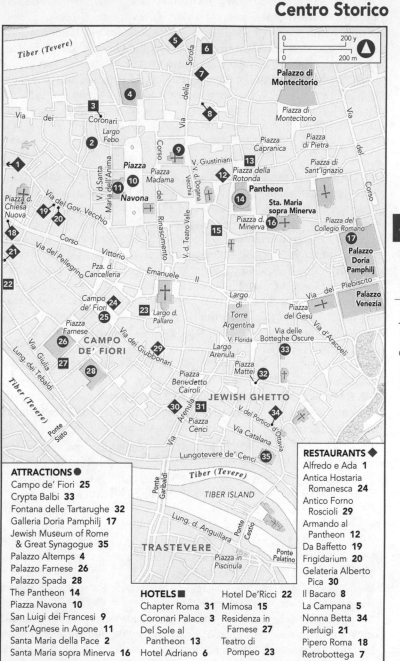

**ATTRACTIONS** ●

Campo de' Fiori **25**
Crypta Balbi **33**
Fontana delle Tartarughe **32**
Galleria Doria Pamphilj **17**
Jewish Museum of Rome
& Great Synagogue **35**
Palazzo Altemps **4**
Palazzo Farnese **26**
Palazzo Spada **28**
The Pantheon **14**
Piazza Navona **10**
San Luigi dei Francesi **9**
Sant'Agnese in Agone **11**
Santa Maria della Pace **2**
Santa Maria sopra Minerva **16**

**HOTELS** ■

Chapter Roma **31**
Coronari Palace **3**
Del Sole al
Pantheon **13**
Hotel Adriano **6**
Hotel De'Ricci **22**
Mimosa **15**
Residenza in
Farnese **27**
Teatro di
Pompeo **23**

**RESTAURANTS** ◆

Alfredo e Ada **1**
Antica Hostaria
Romanesca **24**
Antico Forno
Roscioli **29**
Armando al
Pantheon **12**
Da Baffetto **19**
Frigidarium **20**
Gelateria Alberto
Pica **30**
Il Bacaro **8**
La Campana **5**
Nonna Betta **34**
Pierluigi **21**
Pipero Roma **18**
Retrobottega **7**

Among the highlights is the **"Ludovisi Ares"** ★★, a handsome 2nd-century copy of an earlier Greek statue of Mars (Ares to the Greeks). Equally renowned is the **"Ludovisi Gaul"** ★, a marble depiction of a Gaulish warrior plunging a sword into his chest (rather than become a slave of Rome), looking backwards defiantly as he supports a dying woman with his left arm. Check out the **"Ludovisi Throne,"** a three-sided block of white marble, thought to date from the 5th century B.C., depicting Aphrodite rising from the sea.

Piazza di Sant'Apollinare 46. www.museonazionaleromano.beniculturali.it. ℰ **06-39967700.** 12€ (15€ during special exhibits), valid for 3 days; also includes Palazzo Massimo, Baths of Diocletian, Crypta Balbi. 17 and under free. Tues–Fri 2–7:45pm; Sat–Sun 10:30am–7:45pm. Last entry 1 hr. before closing. Bus: 70, 81, 87, 492, 628.

**San Luigi dei Francesi** ★★ CHURCH For a painter of such stratospheric standards as Caravaggio, it is impossible to be definitive in naming his "masterpiece." However, the **"Calling of St. Matthew"** ★★, in the far-left chapel of Rome's French church, must be a candidate. The panel dramatizes the moment Jesus and Peter "called" the customs officer to join them, in Caravaggio's distinct *chiaroscuro* (extreme light and shade) style. Around the same time (1599–1602) Caravaggio also painted the other two St. Matthew panels in the Capella Contarelli—including one depicting the saint's martyrdom. Other highlights inside include Domenichino's masterful "Histories of Saint Cecilia" fresco cycle. A free audioguide, available in English and accessible via smartphone, is at appli.lespierresparlent.com/#/list/2651.

Via di Santa Giovanna d'Arco 5. www.saintlouis-rome.net. ℰ **06-688271.** Free. Mon–Fri 9:30am–12:45pm; Sat 9:30am–12:15pm; Sun 11:30–12:45pm, plus daily 2:30–6:30pm. Bus: 30, 70, 81, 87, 492, 628.

## THE PANTHEON & NEARBY ATTRACTIONS

The Pantheon stands on **Piazza della Rotonda,** a lively square with outdoor cafes, vendors, and great people-watching.

**The Pantheon** ★★★ HISTORIC SITE Stumbling onto Piazza della Rotonda from the dark warren of streets surrounding it will likely leave you agape, marveling at one of ancient Rome's great buildings—the only one, in fact, that remains intact. The Pantheon ("Temple to All the Gods") was originally built in 27 B.C. by Marcus Agrippa but was entirely reconstructed by Hadrian in the early 2nd century A.D. This remarkable building, 43m (142 ft.) wide and 43m (142 ft.) high (a perfect sphere resting in a cylinder) is among the architectural wonders of the world, even today. Hadrian himself is credited with the basic plan. There are no visible arches or vaults holding up the dome; instead, they're sunk into the concrete of the building's walls. The ribbed dome outside is a series of cantilevered bricks.

Animals were once sacrificed and burned in the center, with the smoke escaping through the only means of light, the oculus, an opening at the top 5.5m (18 ft.) in diameter. The interior was richly decorated, with white marble statues ringing the central space in its niches. Nowadays, apart from the jaw-dropping size of the space, the main items of interest are the tombs of two

Italian kings (Vittorio Emanuele II and his successor, Umberto I) and artist **Raphael** (fans still bring him flowers), with its poignant epitaph. Since the 7th century, the Pantheon has been used as a Catholic church, the **Santa Maria ad Martyres,** informally known as "Santa Maria della Rotonda."

Piazza della Rotonda. www.pantheonroma.com/en. ℂ**06-68300230.** Free. Daily 9am–7pm. Bus: 30, 40, 62, 64, 81, 87 or 492 to Largo di Torre Argentina.

### Santa Maria sopra Minerva ★★★ CHURCH
Just one block behind the Pantheon, Santa Maria sopra Minerva is Rome's most significant Dominican church and the only major Gothic church downtown. The facade is in the Renaissance style (the church was begun in 1280 but worked on until 1725), but inside, the arched vaulting is pure Gothic. The main art treasures here are the "Statua del Redentore" (1521), a statue of Christ by **Michelangelo** (just to the left of the altar), and a wonderful fresco cycle in the **Cappella Carafa** (on the right before the altar), created by Filippino Lippi between 1488 and 1493 to honor St. Thomas Aquinas. Devout Catholics flock to the tomb of **Saint Catherine of Siena** under the high altar—the room where she died in 1380 was reconstructed by Antonio Barberini in 1637 (far left corner of the church). **Fra' Angelico,** the Dominican friar and painter, also rests here, in the **Cappella Frangipane e Maddaleni-Capiferro.** A delightful elephant statue by **Bernini** holds up a small obelisk in the piazza in front of the church.

Piazza della Minerva 42. www.santamariasopraminerva.it/en. ℂ **06-69920384.** Free. Daily 5pm–6:45pm; check website for additional opening times.

### Crypta Balbi ★ MUSEUM/RUINS
This branch of the National Museum of Rome houses the archaeological remains of the vast portico belonging to the 1st-century-B.C. **Theatre of Lucius Cornelius Balbus,** discovered here in 1981. The ground floor's exhibits chronicle the history of the site through to the medieval period and the construction of the Conservatorio di Santa Caterina della Rosa. The second floor ("Rome from Antiquity to the Middle Ages") explores the transformation of the city between the 5th and 9th centuries, using thousands of ceramic objects, coins, lead seals, bone and ivory implements, precious stones, and tools found on the site. The museum helps decode the complex layers under Rome's streets, but given its comprehensive collections, it's best recommended for history and archaeology buffs.

Via delle Botteghe Oscure 31. www.museonazionaleromano.beniculturali.it. ℂ **06-39967700.** 12€ (15€ during special exhibits), valid for 3 days; includes Palazzo Massimo, Palazzo Altemps, Baths of Diocletian. 17 and under free. Fri 2pm–7:45pm; Sat–Sun 10:30am–7:45pm. Last entry 1 hr. before closing. Bus: H, 30, 40, 46, 62, 64, 70, 81, 87, 492. Tram: 8.

### Galleria Doria Pamphilj ★★ ART MUSEUM
One of the city's finest rococo palaces, the Palazzo Doria Pamphilj is still privately owned by the aristocratic Doria Pamphilj family, but their stupendous art collection is open to the public. The *galleria* winds through the old apartments, their paintings displayed floor-to-ceiling among antique furniture and richly decorated walls. The strong Dutch and Flemish collection includes Pieter Brueghel the Elder's

"Battle in the Port of Naples," and his son Jan Brueghel the Elder's "Earthly Paradise with Original Sin." Among the best Italian works are two Caravaggio paintings, the moving "Repentant Magdalene" and his wonderful "Rest on the Flight into Egypt," hanging near Titian's "Salome with the Head of St. John." There's also Raphael's "Double Portrait," an "Annunciation" by Filippo Lippi, and a "Deposition from the Cross" by Vasari. The gallery's real treasures occupy a special room: Bernini's bust of the Pamphilj **"Pope Innocent X"** ★ and **Velázquez's enigmatic painting** ★★ of the same man. Be sure to grab a free audio guide at the entrance—it's colorfully narrated by Prince Jonathan Doria Pamphilj himself, who recalls roller-skating in the *palazzo* as a child.

Via del Corso 305 (just N of Piazza Venezia). www.doriapamphilj.it.© **06-6797323.** 15€ adults, 1€ 12 and under. Daily, except the third Wed of the month, 10am–8pm; last entry 6pm. Bus: 64 or any to Piazza Venezia.

## CAMPO DE' FIORI

The southern section of the Centro Storico, **Campo de' Fiori** is another neighborhood of narrow streets, small piazzas, and ancient churches. Its main focus remains the piazza of **Campo de' Fiori** ★★ itself, where a touristy but delightful open-air market runs daily (with fewer vendors on Sun) from early in the morning until midday, selling a dizzyingly colorful array of fruits, vegetables, and spices as well as cheap T-shirts and handbags. (Keep an eye on your valuables here.) From the center of the piazza rises a statue of the severe-looking monk **Giordano Bruno,** a reminder that heretics were occasionally burned at the stake here: Bruno was executed by the Inquisition in 1600. Curiously this is the only piazza in Rome that doesn't have a church in its perimeter.

Built from 1514 to 1589, the **Palazzo Farnese** ★, on Piazza Farnese just to the south of the Campo, was designed by Sangallo and Michelangelo, among others, and was an astronomically expensive project for the time. Its famous residents have included a 16th-century member of the Farnese family, plus Pope Paul III, Cardinal Richelieu, and the former Queen Christina of Sweden, who moved to Rome after abdicating her crown. During the 1630s, when the heirs could no longer afford to maintain the *palazzo,* it was inherited by the Bourbon kings of Naples and purchased by the French government in 1874; the French Embassy is still located here, so the building is closed to the general public, though small group tours are offered in English on Wednesday at 5pm, costing 11€ (www.inventerrome.com).

**Palazzo Spada/Galleria Spada** ★ MUSEUM   Built around 1540 for Cardinal Gerolamo Capo di Ferro, Palazzo Spada was purchased by the eponymous Cardinal Spada in 1632, who then hired Borromini to restore it—most of what you see today dates from that period. Its richly ornate facade, covered in high-relief stucco decorations in the Mannerist style, is the finest of any building from 16th-century Rome. The State Rooms are closed (the Italian Council of State still meets here), but the richly decorated courtyard and corridor, Borromini's masterful illusion of perspective *(la* *prospettiva di Borromini),* and the four rooms of the **Galleria Spada** are open to the public. Inside you will find some absorbing paintings, such as the "Portrait of Cardinale Bernardino Spada" by Guido Reni, and Titian's "Portrait of a Violinist," plus minor works from Caravaggio, Parmigianino, Pietro Testa, and Giambattista Gaulli.

Piazza Capo di Ferro 13. www.galleriaspada.beniculturali.it. © **06-6874893.** 5€. Mon–Sun 8:30am–7:30pm. Bus: 23, 280, or Tram 8 or any bus to Largo di Torre Argentina.

## THE JEWISH GHETTO

Across Via Arenula, Campo de' Fiori merges into the old **Jewish Ghetto ★★,** established near the River Tiber by a Papal Bull in 1555, which required that all the Jews in Rome live in one area. Walled in, overcrowded, prone to floods and epidemics, and on some of the worst land in the city, it was an extremely grim place to live. After the Ghetto was abolished in 1882, its walls were finally torn down and the area largely reconstructed. In the waning years of WWII, Nazis sent more than 1,000 Roman Jews to concentration camps; only a handful returned.

Today, the **Via Portico d'Ottavia** forms the heart of a flourishing Jewish Quarter, with Romans and tourists flocking here to sample the **Roman-Jewish and Middle Eastern food** for which the area is known. Head north on winding Via di S. Ambrogio to toss a coin in the **Fontana delle Tartarughe ★,** a beloved Renaissance fountain. The turtles, added in the 1600s, are thought to be by Bernini.

**Museo Ebraico di Roma (Jewish Museum of Rome) & Great Synagogue ★★** MUSEUM    On the premises of the Great Synagogue of Rome, this museum chronicles the history of not only Roman Jews but Jews from all over Italy. It displays works by 17th- and 18th-century Roman silversmiths, precious textiles from all over Europe, and a number of parchments and marble carvings that were saved when the Ghetto's original synagogues were demolished. Admission to the museum includes a guided English-language tour of the **Great Synagogue of Rome** (Tempio Maggiore), built from 1901 to 1904 in an eclectic style evoking Babylonian and Persian temples. Attacked by terrorists in 1982, the synagogue is now heavily guarded by *carabinieri,* a division of the Italian police armed with machine guns.

Via Catalana. www.museoebraico.roma.it/en. © **06-6840061.** 11€ adults, 5€ students, children 10 and under free. Apr–Sept Sun–Thurs 10am–6pm and Fri 10am–4pm; Oct and Mar Sun–Thurs 10am–5pm and Fri 9am–2pm (Nov 1–Feb 8 closes 4pm Mon–Thurs). Closed on Jewish holidays.

# Tridente & the Spanish Steps

The northern half of central Rome is known as the **Tridente,** thanks to the trident shape formed by three roads—Via di Ripetta, Via del Corso, and Via del Babuino—leading down from **Piazza del Popolo.** The area around **Piazza di Spagna** and the **Spanish Steps** was once the artistic quarter of the city, attracting English poets Keats and Shelley, German author Goethe, and film director Federico Fellini (who lived on Via Margutta). Institutions such as

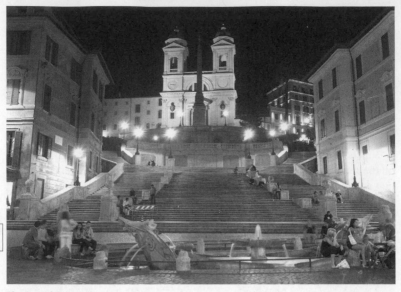

The Spanish Steps.

**Antico Caffè Greco** and **Babington's Tea Rooms** are still here (see p. 76), but between the high rents and the throngs of tourists and shoppers, you're unlikely to see many artists left.

## PIAZZA DEL POPOLO

Elegant **Piazza del Popolo ★★** is haunted with memories. Legend has it that the ashes of Nero were enshrined here, until 11th-century residents began complaining to the pope about his imperial ghost. The **Egyptian obelisk** dates from the 13th century B.C.; it was removed from Heliopolis to Rome during Augustus's reign (it once stood at the Circus Maximus).

The current piazza was designed in the early 19th century by Valadier, Napoleon's architect. Standing astride the three roads that form the "trident" are almost-twin baroque churches, **Santa Maria dei Miracoli** (1681) and **Santa Maria di Montesanto** (1679). The stand-out church, however, is at the piazza's northern curve: the 15th-century **Santa Maria del Popolo ★★,** with its splendid baroque facade modified by Bernini between 1655 and 1660. Inside, look for Raphael's mosaic series the "Creation of the World" adorning the interior dome of the **Capella Chigi** (the second chapel on the left). Pinturicchio decorated the main choir vault with frescoes such as the "Coronation of the Virgin." The **Capella Cerasi** (to the left of the high altar) contains gorgeous examples of baroque art: an altarpiece painting of "The Assumption of Mary" by Carracci, and on either side two great works by Caravaggio: "Conversion on the Road to Damascus" and "The Crucifixion of Saint Peter."

**Mausoleo di Augusto ★** RUINS  After a decades-long closure and a much-delayed restoration, the huge overgrown ruin of the **Mausoleum of**

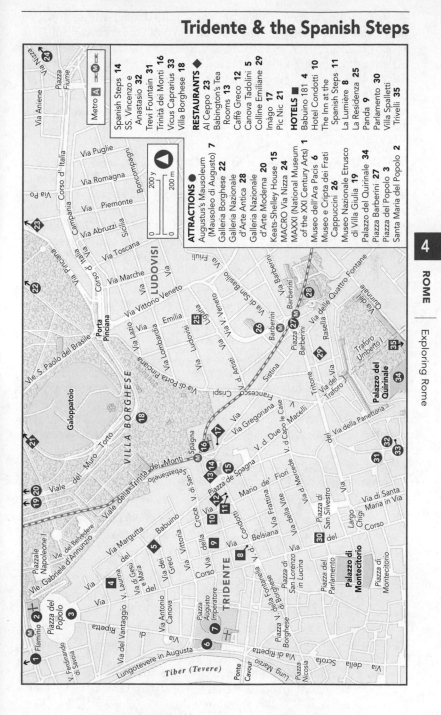

# Tridente & the Spanish Steps

Metro Ⓐ Ⓜ

Spanish Steps 14
SS. Vincenzo e
Anastasio 32
Trevi Fountain 31
Trinità dei Monti 16
Vicus Caprarius 33
Villa Borghese 18

**RESTAURANTS ◆**

Al Ceppo 23
Babington's Tea
Rooms 13
Caffè Greco 12
Canova Tadolini 5
Colline Emiliane 29
Imago 17
Pic Nic 21

**HOTELS ■**

Babuino 181 4
Hotel Condotti 10
The Inn at the
Spanish Steps 11
La Lumière 8
La Residenza 25
Panda 9
Parlamento 30
Villa Spalletti
Trivelli 35

**ATTRACTIONS ●**

Augustus's Mausoleum
(Mausoleo di Augusto) 7
Galleria Borghese 22
Galleria Nazionale
d'Arte Antica 28
Galleria Nazionale
d'Arte Moderna 20
Keats-Shelley House 15
MACRO Via Nizza 24
MAXXI (National Museum
of the XXI Century Arts) 1
Museo dell'Ara Pacis 6
Museo e Cripta dei Frati
Cappuccini 26
Museo Nazionale Etrusco
di Villa Giulia 19
Palazzo del Quirinale 34
Piazza Barberini 27
Piazza del Popolo 3
Santa Maria del Popolo 2

0 ———— 200 y
0 ———— 200 m

**4**

**ROME** | Exploring Rome

**Augustus** is finally open to the public again. Built in the 1st century B.C., the drum-shaped tomb complex once held the ashes of emperors Augustus, Caligula, Claudius, Nerva, and Tiberius. Access is by guided tour, helpful for understanding the history of the mausoleum and the area around it. Until further sections and a planned museum open, we recommend this site for ancient history afficionados rather than casual visitors.

Piazza Augusto Imperatore. www.mausoleodiaugusto.it. ✆ **06-060608.** 4€ adults. Daily 9am–7pm; last entry 5:30pm. Metro: Spagna. Bus: 30, 70, 81, 87, 119, 280, 492, 628, 913.

### MAXXI (National Museum of the XXI Century Arts) ★ MUSEUM

Ten minutes north of Piazza del Popolo by tram, leave the Renaissance far behind at MAXXI, a masterpiece of contemporary architecture with bending and overlapping oblong tubes designed by the late, great Zaha Hadid. The museum is divided into two sections, MAXXI art and MAXXI architecture, primarily serving as a venue for temporary exhibitions of contemporary work in both fields (although it does have a small permanent collection). The building is worth a visit in its own right.

Via Guido Reni 4a. www.maxxi.art/en. ✆ **06-3201954.** 12€ adults, 9€ 25 and under, children 13 and under free. Tues–Sun 11am–7pm. Metro: Flaminio, then Tram 2.

### Museo dell'Ara Pacis ★★ MUSEUM

Set in a stunning ultra-modern building designed by American architect Richard Meier (long before his #MeToo contrition), the temple-like marble "Altar of Peace" was erected in 9 B.C. to honor soon-to-be-Emperor Augustus's success in subduing tribes north of the Alps. For centuries the monument was lost to memory; signs of its existence surfaced in the 16th century, but it wasn't until the 1930s that it was fully excavated, and even so it lay virtually abandoned until a true restoration began in the 1980s. The exhibit complex provides context, with interactive displays in English.

Lungotevere in Augusta. www.arapacis.it/en. ✆ **06-060608.** 10.50€. Daily 9:30am–7:30pm (last entry 6:30pm). Metro: Spagna. Bus: 30, 70, 81, 87, 119, 280, 492, 628, 913.

### PIAZZA DI SPAGNA

The undoubted highlight of Tridente is **Piazza di Spagna,** which attracts hordes of tourists to admire its celebrated **Spanish Steps (Scalinata della Trinità dei Monti) ★★,** the widest stairway in Europe. The Steps are especially enchanting in early spring, when they are framed by thousands of blooming azaleas. At their foot lies "Fontana della Barcaccia," a fountain shaped like an old boat, the work of Pietro Bernini, father of sculptor and fountain-master Gian Lorenzo Bernini.

Built from 1723 to 1725, the monumental stairway of 135 steps and the square take their names from the Spanish Embassy (it used to be headquartered here), but were actually funded almost entirely by the French. That's because the **Trinità dei Monti** church at the top was under the patronage of the Bourbon kings of France at the time. The stately baroque facade of the

## No Swimming, Sitting, or Picnicking Allowed

In an effort to keep tourists from littering the city's monuments, or soaking their feet and even swimming (yes, it's happened) in its famous fountains, visitors are no longer permitted to picnic (or even sit) on the Spanish Steps, or perch on the edge of the Trevi and other landmark fountains. You can stop long enough for a photo or coin toss, but don't plan on getting comfortable (or taking a dip).

16th-century Trinità dei Monti is perched photogenically at the top of the Steps, behind yet another Roman obelisk, the "Obelisco Sallustiano." It's worth climbing up just for the views.

**Keats-Shelley House** ★ MUSEUM   At the foot of the Spanish Steps is the 18th-century house where the Romantic English poet John Keats died of consumption on February 23, 1821, at age 25. Since 1909, it has been a working library established in honor of Keats and fellow Romantic Percy Bysshe Shelley, who drowned off the coast of Viareggio with a copy of Keats' works in his pocket. Mementos range from kitsch to extremely moving. The apartment where Keats spent his last months, tended by his close friend Joseph Severn, shelters a death mask of Keats as well as the "deadly sweat" drawing by Severn. Both Keats and Shelley are buried in their beloved Rome, at the Protestant cemetery near the Pyramid of Cestius, in Testaccio.

Piazza di Spagna 26. www.keats-shelley-house.org. © **06-6784235.** 6€. Mon–Sat 10am–1pm and 2–6pm. Metro: Spagna.

**Palazzo del Quirinale** ★★ HISTORIC SITE   Once the palace of popes and the king of Italy, since 1946 the Quirinale has been the official residence of the President of Italy, but parts of it are open to the public.

Although it can't compare to Rome's major artistic showstoppers (there's little art or furniture in the rooms), the palace's baroque and neoclassical walls and ceilings are quite a spectacle. Few rooms anywhere are as impressive as the richly decorated 17th-century **Salone dei Corazzieri,** the **Sala d'Ercole** (once the apartments of Umberto I but completely rebuilt in 1940), and the tapestry-covered 17th-century **Sala dello Zodiaco.** Despite its Renaissance origins, this *palazzo* is rich in associations with ancient emperors and deities. The colossal statues of the "Dioscuri," Castor and Pollux, which now form part of the fountain in the piazza, were found in the nearby Baths of Constantine; in 1793 Pius VI had an ancient Egyptian obelisk moved here from the Mausoleum of Augustus. The sweeping view of the city from the piazza, which crowns the highest of the seven ancient hills of Rome, is itself worth the trip.

Piazza del Quirinale. palazzo.quirinale.it/palazzo.html. © **06-39-96-7557.** 1.50€ for basic tour; 10€ for extended tour including gardens, carriages, and special collections. Reservations must be made at least 5 days prior to visit. Tues–Wed and Fri–Sun 9:30am–4pm. Closed Aug. Metro: Barberini. Bus: 53, 60, 62-63, 70, 71, 80, 83, 85, 492.

**Trevi Fountain (Fontana di Trevi)** ★★ MONUMENT As you elbow your way through the summertime crowds around the **Trevi Fountain,** it's hard to believe that this little piazza was nearly always deserted before 1950, when it began "starring" in films. The first was *Three Coins in the Fountain;* it was later the setting for an iconic scene in the 1960 Fellini masterpiece *La Dolce Vita.* This was also where Audrey Hepburn gets her signature haircut in *Roman Holiday.* To this day, thousands of euros' worth of coins are tossed into the fountain daily. The area is always jam-packed with tourists and selfie-stick hawkers, so keep your eye (and your hands) on your belongings.

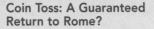

**Coin Toss: A Guaranteed Return to Rome?**

The custom of tossing a coin into the Trevi Fountain to ensure your return to Rome apparently only works if you use correct form: With your back to the fountain, toss a coin with your right hand over your left shoulder. Works for me every time!

Completed in 1762, this glorious baroque fountain centers on the triumphant figure of Neptune, standing on a shell chariot drawn by winged steeds and led by a pair of tritons. Two allegorical figures in the side niches represent good health and fertility.

On the southwestern corner of the piazza is an unimpressive church, **SS. Vincenzo e Anastasio,** with a strange claim to fame. Within it are the relics (hearts and intestines) of several popes. In an alley nearby, **Vicus Caprarius– the City of Water** ★ is a privately run archaeological area comprised of several underground levels of ancient development, including an upscale home and part of the **Acquedotto Vergine,** the aqueduct that still feeds the Trevi (www.vicuscaprarius.com; ✆ **339-7786192;** 3€ admission).

Piazza di Trevi. Metro: Barberini. Bus: 52, 62-63, 80, 83, 85, 160, 492.

## VILLA BORGHESE & PARIOLI

**Villa Borghese** ★★, just northeast of the Tridente, is actually not a villa but a large park, 6km (3¾ miles) in circumference. Cardinal Scipione Borghese created the park in the 1600s; Umberto I, king of Italy, acquired it in 1902 and presented it to the city of Rome. The greenbelt is crisscrossed by roads, but you can escape from the traffic and seek a shaded area under a tree to enjoy its landscaped vistas. On a sunny weekend, it's a pleasure to stroll here and see Romans at play, relaxing or inline skating. The park has a few casual cafes and food vendors; you can also rent bikes or Segways here. In the northeast part of the park you'll find a **zoo** and the **Galleria Borghese** (see below). The neighborhoods to the north, Parioli and Pinciano, are elegant enclaves for those wishing to stay outside the crowded city center (see p. 62).

**Galleria Borghese** ★★★ ART MUSEUM On the far northeastern edge of the Villa Borghese, the Galleria Borghese occupies the former Villa Borghese Pinciana, built between 1609 and 1613 for Cardinal Scipione Borghese, an early patron of Bernini and an astute collector of work by Caravaggio. Today the gallery displays much of his collection and a lot more besides, making this one of Rome's great art treasures. It's also one of Rome's most pleasant sites to tour, thanks to the curators' mandate that only a limited number of people be allowed in at a time.

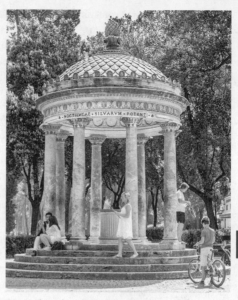

A rotunda in the Villa Borghese gardens.

The ground floor is a **sculpture gallery** par extraordinaire, housing Canova's famously risqué statue of Paolina Borghese, sister of Napoleon and wife of the reigning Prince Camillo Borghese (when asked if she was uncomfortable posing nude, she reportedly replied, "No, the studio was heated."). The genius of Bernini reigns supreme in the following rooms, with his "David" (the face of which is thought to be a self-portrait) and **"Apollo and Daphne"** ★★ both seminal works of baroque sculpture. Look also for Bernini's Mannerist sculpture next door, "The Rape of Persephone." Caravaggio is represented by the "Madonna of the Grooms," the shadowy "St. Jerome," and the frightening **"David Holding the Head of Goliath"** ★★.

Upstairs lies a rich collection of paintings, including Raphael's graceful "Deposition" and his sinuous "Lady with a Unicorn." There's also a series of self-portraits by Bernini, and his lifelike busts of Cardinal Scipione and Pope Paul V. One of Titian's best, **"Sacred and Profane Love"** ★, lies in one of the final rooms.

*Important information:* No more than 360 visitors at a time are allowed on the ground floor, and no more than 90 are allowed on the upper floor, during set 2-hour windows. **Reservations are essential,** and can be made through the museum website. Roma Pass holders need to reserve an entry time by calling ℂ **06-32810** (Mon–Fri 9am–6pm; Sat 9am–1pm). English labeling in the museum is minimal. Guided tours of the galleries in English cost an extra 6.50€, or opt for an audio guide.

Piazzale del Museo Borghese 5 (off Via Pinciana). www.galleriaborghese.it. ℂ **06-32810.** 15€; 18 and under 2€. Audio guides 5€. Tues–Sun 9am–7pm (Thurs to 9pm). Bus: 52, 53, 61, 89, 160, 490, 495, 590, 910. Tram: 3 or 19.

## Galleria Nazionale d'Arte Moderna (National Gallery of Modern Art) ★ ART MUSEUM

Housed in the monumental Bazzani Building constructed in 1911, this "modern" art collection ranges from unfashionable neoclassical and Romantic paintings and sculpture to better 20th-century works. Quality varies, but fans should seek out van Gogh's "Gardener" and "Portrait of Madame Ginoux" in Room 15, the handful of Impressionists in Room 14 (Cézanne, Degas, Monet, and Rodin), and Klimt's harrowing "Three Ages" in Room 16. Surrealist and Expressionist works by Miró, Kandinsky, and Mondrian appear in Room 22, and Pollock's "Undulating Paths" and Calder's "Mobile" hold court in Room 27. One of Warhol's "Hammer and Sickle" series is tucked away in Room 30.

Viale delle Belle Arti 131. lagallerianazionale.com/en. © **06-322981.** 10€, free ages 17 and under, 5€ for MAXXI ticket-holders. Mon–Fri 9am–7pm. Metro: Flaminio. Bus: 61, 89, 160, 490, 495. Tram: 3 or 19.

**MACRO Via Nizza** ★ MUSEUM   Rome's contemporary art museum occupies an entire block of early-1900s industrial buildings, formerly the Peroni beer factory, located near the Porta Pia gate of the Aurelian walls. The museum hosts contemporary art exhibits with edgy installations, visuals, and multimedia events. Another branch of the museum is housed in a converted slaughterhouse in Testaccio (p. 126).

Via Nizza 138. www.museomacro.org. © **06-696271.** Free (special exhibits may be ticketed). Tues–Fri and Sun 10am–8pm; Sat 10am–10pm; last entry 7pm. Bus: 38, 66, 90, 223. Tram: 3, 19.

**Museo Nazionale Etrusco di Villa Giulia (National Etruscan Museum)** ★★★ MUSEUM   The great Etruscan civilization was one of Italy's most advanced, although it remains relatively mysterious, in part because of its centuries-long rivalry with Rome. Rome definitively conquered the Etruscans by the 3rd century B.C., and though they adopted certain aspects of Etruscan culture, including religious practices, engineering innovations, and gladiatorial combat, gradual Romanization eclipsed virtually all the Etruscans' achievements.

This museum, housed in the handsome Renaissance Villa Giulia, built by Pope Julius III between 1550 and 1555, is the best place in Italy to learn about the Etruscans, thanks to a cache of precious artifacts, sculptures, vases, monuments, tools, weapons, and jewels, the vast majority of it from tombs. Fans of ancient history could spend several hours here, but for those with less time, the most striking attraction is the stunning **Sarcofago degli Sposi (Sarcophagus of the Spouses)** ★★, a late-6th-century-B.C. terracotta funerary monument featuring a life-size bride and groom, lounging at a banquet in the afterlife (Paris's Louvre has a similar monument). Equally fascinating are the **Pyrgi Tablets,** gold-leaf inscriptions in both Etruscan and Phoenician from the 5th century B.C., and the **Apollo of Veii,** a huge painted terracotta statue of Apollo dating to the 6th century B.C.

Piazzale di Villa Giulia 9. www.museoetru.it. © **06-3226571.** 10€. Tues–Sun 9am–8pm; last entry 7pm. Bus: 982. Tram: 2, 19.

## VIA VENETO & PIAZZA BARBERINI

**Piazza Barberini** lies at the foot of several streets, among them Via Barberini, Via Sistina, and Via Vittorio Veneto. It would be a far more pleasant spot were it not for the traffic swarming around its principal feature, Bernini's **Fountain of the Triton (Fontana del Tritone)** ★★. For almost 4 centuries, the figure sitting in a vast open clam has been blowing water from his triton. To one side of the piazza is the aristocratic facade of the **Palazzo Barberini,** named for one of Rome's powerful families; inside is the **Galleria Nazionale d'Arte Antica** (see below). The Barberini reached their peak when a son was elected pope as Urban VIII; he encouraged Bernini and gave him patronage.

As you walk up **Via Vittorio Veneto,** look for the small fountain on the right corner of Piazza Barberini—it's another Bernini, the **Fountain of the Bees (Fontana delle Api)** ★. At first they look more like flies, but they're the bees of the Barberini, the crest of that powerful family complete with the crossed keys of St. Peter above them. (Keys were always added to a family crest when a son was elected pope.)

## Galleria Nazionale d'Arte Antica (National Gallery of Ancient Art) ★★★ ART MUSEUM

On the southern side of Piazza Barberini, the grand **Palazzo Barberini** houses the Galleria Nazionale d'Arte Antica, which despite the "ancient" in its title is a trove of Italian art mostly from the early Renaissance to late baroque periods. Some of the art on display is wonderful, but the building itself is the main attraction, a baroque masterpiece begun by Carlo Maderno in 1627 and completed in 1633 by Bernini, with additional work by Borromini (notably a whimsical spiral staircase). The **Salone di Pietro da Cortona** in the center is the most captivating space, with a trompe l'oeil ceiling frescoed by da Cortona, a depiction of "The Triumph of Divine Providence."

The museum has intriguing works, including Raphael's "La Fornarina," a baker's daughter thought to have been the artist's lover (look for Raphael's name on her bracelet); paintings by Tintoretto and Titian (Room 15); a portrait of English King Henry VIII by Holbein (Room 16); and a couple of typically unsettling El Grecos in Room 17. Caravaggio dominates room 20 with the justly celebrated **"Judith and Holofernes"** ★★★ and **"Narcissus"** ★★.

Via delle Quattro Fontane 13. www.barberinicorsini.org. © **06-4814591.** 12€, valid for 10 days, also includes Palazzo Corsini; ages 17 and under free. Tues–Sun 10am–6pm; last entry 5pm. Metro: Barberini. Bus: 52, 53, 61–63, 80, 81, 83, 160, 492, 590.

## Museo e Cripta dei Frati Cappuccini (Museum and Crypt of the Capuchin Friars) ★★ RELIGIOUS SITE/MUSEUM

One of the most mesmerizingly macabre sights in all Christendom, this otherwise restrained museum dedicated to the Capuchin order ends with a series of six chapels in the crypt, adorned with the skulls and bones of more than 3,700 Capuchin brothers, woven into mosaic works of art. Some of the skeletons are intact, draped with Franciscan habits; others form lamps and ceiling friezes. The tradition of the friars dates to a period when Christians had a richly creative cult of the dead and great spiritual masters meditated and preached with a skull in hand. Whatever you believe, the experience is a mix of spooky and meditative. The entrance is halfway up the first staircase on the right of the church of the Convento dei Frati Cappuccini, completed in 1630 and rebuilt in the early 1930s.

*Note:* Because this site is located within a church, it maintains a strict dress code: no short pants or skirts and no bare arms—and no photos.

We don't recommend this experience for kids under 10 or so.

Via Vittorio Veneto 27. www.cappucciniviaveneto.it. ✆ **06-88803695.** 8.50€, 5€ ages 17 and under. Daily 10am–6:30pm; last entry 6pm. Metro: Barberini. Bus: 52, 53, 61, 63, 80, 83, 160, 590.

## Around Stazione Termini

**Palazzo Massimo alle Terme** ★★ MUSEUM A third of Rome's assortment of ancient art can be found at this branch of the Museo Nazionale Romano; among its treasures are a major coin collection, extensive maps of trade routes (with audio and visual exhibits on the network of traders over the centuries), and a vast sculpture collection that includes portrait busts of emperors and their families, as well as mythical figures like the Minotaur and Athena. But the real draw is on the second floor, where you can see some of the oldest of Rome's **frescoes** ★★; they depict an entire garden, complete with plants and birds, from the Villa di Livia a Prima Porta. (Livia was the wife of Emperor Augustus and was deified after her death in A.D. 29.)

Largo di Villa Peretti. www.museonazionaleromano.beniculturali.it. ✆ **06-39967700.** 12€ (15€ during special exhibits), valid for 3 days, also includes Palazzo Altemps Baths of Diocletian, Crypta Balbi. 17 and under free. Tues–Fri 2–7:45pm; Sat–Sun 10:30am–7:45pm; last entry 1 hr. before closing. Metro: Termini or Repubblica. Bus: 40, 64, or any bus that stops at Termini.

**Santa Maria della Vittoria** ★★ CHURCH A visit to this pretty little baroque church is all about one artwork: Gian Lorenzo Bernini's **"Ecstasy of St. Teresa"** ★★★. Crafted from marble between 1644 and 1647, it shows the Spanish saint at the moment of her ecstatic encounter with an angel (the so-called "Transverberation"), who gleefully pierces her with a spear. Bernini's depiction is deliciously erotic. Look for the Cornaro family, who sponsored the chapel's construction, watching the saint's ecstasy from their voyeuristic perch on the right.

Via XX Settembre 17 (at Largo S. Susanna). ✆ **06-42740571.** Free. Mon–Sat 8:30am–noon and 3:30–6pm; Sun between morning masses and from 3:30–6pm. Metro: Repubblica. Bus: 61, 62, 85, 492, 590.

**Santa Maria Maggiore (St. Mary Major)** ★★ CHURCH This imposing church, one of Rome's four papal basilicas, was founded by Pope Liberius in A.D. 358 and rebuilt on the orders of Pope Sixtus III from 432 to 440. Its 14th-century **campanile** is the city's loftiest. Don't be put off by the overdone 18th-century facade; there are treasures within, such as the 5th-century Roman mosaics in its nave, and its coffered ceiling, said to have been gilded with gold brought from the New World. The church also contains the **tomb of Bernini,** Italy's most important baroque sculptor–architect. The man who changed the face of Rome is buried in a tomb so simple that it takes a sleuth to track it down (to the right, near the altar).

Piazza di Santa Maria Maggiore. ✆ **06-69886800.** Free. Daily 7am–6:45pm. Metro: Termini or Cavour. Bus: 16, 70, 71, 75, 360, 590, 649, 714.

**4**

Exploring Rome

ROME

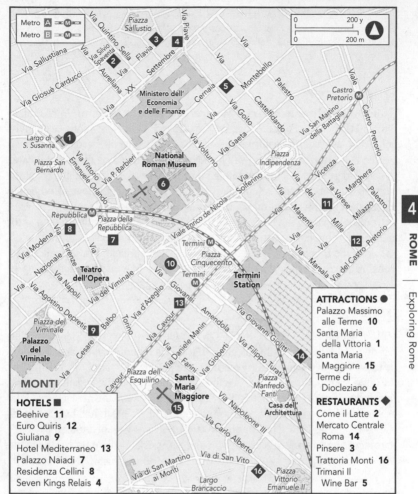

**ATTRACTIONS** ●
Palazzo Massimo
  alle Terme **10**
Santa Maria
  della Vittoria **1**
Santa Maria
  Maggiore **15**
Terme di
  Diocleziano **6**

**RESTAURANTS** ◆
Come il Latte **2**
Mercato Centrale
  Roma **14**
Pinsere **3**
Trattoria Monti **16**
Trimani Il
  Wine Bar **5**

**HOTELS** ■
Beehive **11**
Euro Quiris **12**
Giuliana **9**
Hotel Mediterraneo **13**
Palazzo Naiadi **7**
Residenza Cellini **8**
Seven Kings Relais **4**

**Terme di Diocleziano (Baths of Diocletian)** ★★ MUSEUM/RUINS
Originally this spot held the largest of Rome's baths (dating back to A.D. 298
and the reign of Emperor Diocletian). The vast baths once accommodated
3,000 at a time, and were abandoned in the 6th century after the Goth invasions. During the Renaissance a church, cloister, and convent were built
around the ruins—much of it designed by Michelangelo, no less. Today the
entire hodgepodge is part of the Museo Nazionale Romano; it's a compelling
museum stop that's usually quieter than the city's blockbusters. Exhibits

include statuary and a large collection of inscriptions and other stone carvings from the Roman and pre-Roman eras.

Viale E. di Nicola 78. www.museonazionaleromano.beniculturali.it. © **06-39967700.** 12€ (15€ during special exhibits), valid for 3 days, also includes Palazzo Massimo, Palazzo Altemps, and Crypta Balbi; 17 and under free. Tues–Fri 2–7:45pm; Sat–Sun 10:30am–7:45pm; last entry 1 hr. before closing. Metro: Termini or Repubblica. Bus: 66, 82, 85, 590, 910 or any bus to Termini.

## Trastevere

**Galleria Nazionale d'Arte Antica in Palazzo Corsini** ★ PALACE/ ART MUSEUM Palazzo Corsini first found fame—or more accurately, notoriety—as the 17th-century home of Queen Christina of Sweden, a Catholic convert who moved to Rome after abdicating the Swedish throne. (She was famously described as "Queen without a realm, Christian without a faith, and a woman without shame," referring to her open bisexuality.) Several other big names stayed in this beautiful palace, from Michelangelo to Napoleon's mother, Letizia. Today one wing houses a moderately interesting museum, with a lot of the runoff from Italy's national art collection. Worth a look is Caravaggio's "St. John the Baptist" (1606) and panels by Luca Giordano, Fra' Angelico, and Poussin; otherwise, the palace history is more interesting than the museum itself.

Via della Lungara 10. www.barberinicorsini.org. © **06-68802323.** 12€, valid for 10 days, also includes Palazzo Barberini; ages 17 and under free. Wed–Mon 8:30am–7pm. Bus: 23 or 280.

**Villa Farnesina** ★ HISTORIC HOME Originally built for Sienese banker Agostino Chigi in 1511, this elegant villa was acquired by the Farnese family in 1579. With two such wealthy Renaissance patrons, it's hardly surprising that the interior decor is top drawer. Architect Baldassare Peruzzi began the decoration, with frescoes and motifs rich in myth and symbolism. He was later assisted by Sebastiano del Piombo, Sodoma, and, most notably, Raphael. Raphael's **"Loggia of Cupid and Psyche"** ★★ was frescoed to mark Chigi's marriage to Francesca Ordeaschi—though his assistants did much of the work. The ornamental gardens are perfumed and colorful in the spring and summer.

Via della Lungara 230. www.villafarnesina.it. © **06-68077268.** 10€, includes audio guide. Mon–Sat 9am–2pm; 2nd Sun of month 9am–5pm. Bus: 23, 125, 280.

## Testaccio & Southern Rome

**Centrale Montemartini** ★★ MUSEUM The renovated boiler rooms of Rome's first thermoelectric plant now house a grand collection of Roman and Greek statues, creating a unique juxtaposition of classic and industrial archaeology. The 19th-century powerhouse was the first public plant to produce electricity for the city. Striking installation spaces include the vast boiler hall, a 1,000-sq-m (10,764-sq.-ft.) room where classical statues share space with a complex web of pipes, masonry, and metal walkways. Equally striking is the Hall of Machines, where two towering turbines stand opposite the reconstructed pediment of the **Temple of Apollo Sosiano** ★★, which illustrates a famous Greek battle.

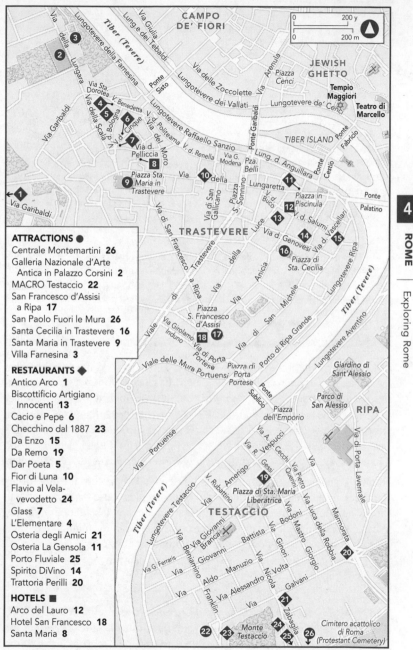

# Trastevere & Testaccio

**CAMPO DE' FIORI**

**JEWISH GHETTO**

Tempio Maggiore

Teatro di Marcello

TIBER ISLAND

Piazza Cenci

Lungotevere de' Cenci

Tiber (Tevere)

Lung. e dei Tebaldi

Via Giulia

Via della Zoccolette

Lungotevere dei Vallati

Ponte Sisto

Lungotevere Raffaello Sanzio

Ponte Garibaldi

Lung. d. Anguillara

Ponte Cestio

Ponte Fabricio

Ponte Palatino

Via della Farnesina

Lungotevere della Farnesina

Via della Lungara

Via Garibaldi

Via Sta. Dorotea

V. Benedetta

Bologna

V. d. Cinque

Via d. Pelliccia

Via d. Moro

V. d. Politeama

V. d. Renella

Via G. Modena

Pza. Belli

Via della

Lungaretta

Piazza in Piscinula

V. d. Salumi

V. d. Vascellari

Via di San Gallicano

Piazza Sonnino

S. Cosimato

Via Luce

Via d. Genovesi

Piazza di Sta. Cecilia

Lungotevere Ripa

**TRASTEVERE**

Via di San Francesco a Ripa

Via della Trastevere

Anicia

Via di San Michele

Piazza S. Francesco d'Assisi

Viale di Porta Portese

Via Girolamo Induno

Viale delle Mura Portuensi

Porto di Ripa Grande

Tiber (Tevere)

Lungotevere Aventino

Giardino di Sant'Alessio

Parco di San Alessio

**RIPA**

Piazza di Porta Portese

Ponte Sublicio

Piazza dell'Emporio

Via Portuense

Lungotevere Testaccio

Tiber (Tevere)

Via A. Cecchi

Via R. Vespucci

Via Gessi

V. Amerigo

V. Rubattino

Piazza di Sta. Maria Liberatrice

Via Pietro Querini

Via Luca della Robbia

Via di Porta Lavernale

Via Giovanni Branca

Via Benjamino Franklin

Via G. Ferraris

Via Giovanni

Aldo Manuzio

Battista

Bodoni

Nicola Volta

Ginori

Mastro Giorgio

Via Alessandro

Via Galvani

Marmorata

Via Zabaglia

**TESTACCIO**

Monte Testaccio

Cimitero acattolico di Roma (Protestant Cemetery)

---

**ATTRACTIONS** ●
Centrale Montemartini **26**
Galleria Nazionale d'Arte
  Antica in Palazzo Corsini **2**
MACRO Testaccio **22**
San Francesco d'Assisi
  a Ripa **17**
San Paolo Fuori le Mura **26**
Santa Cecilia in Trastevere **16**
Santa Maria in Trastevere **9**
Villa Farnesina **3**

**RESTAURANTS** ◆
Antico Arco **1**
Biscottificio Artigiano
  Innocenti **13**
Cacio e Pepe **6**
Checchino dal 1887 **23**
Da Enzo **15**
Da Remo **19**
Dar Poeta **5**
Fior di Luna **10**
Flavio al Vela-
  vevodetto **24**
Glass **7**
L'Elementare **4**
Osteria degli Amici **21**
Osteria La Gensola **11**
Porto Fluviale **25**
Spirito DiVino **14**
Trattoria Perilli **20**

**HOTELS** ■
Arco del Lauro **12**
Hotel San Francesco **18**
Santa Maria **8**

# A TRIO OF churches IN TRASTEVERE

Before Trastevere became bohemian and cool, it was a working-class neighborhood, separated by the Tiber from Rome's bustle. Step into the shadowy calm of any of these neighborhood churches to get a glimpse of the old Trastevere. Admission is always free, and they're open daily, though they may close at lunchtime.

On Piazza Santa Maria, the heart of Trastevere, ornate **Santa Maria in Trastevere** ★★ is one of Rome's oldest churches, founded around A.D. 350. The pride of the neighborhood, it's spectacular inside and out, with a Romanesque brick bell tower, colorful frescoes, mosaics, and loads of recycled ancient marbles. Look for Cavallini's 1293 mosaics of the "Life of the Virgin Mary" in the apse.

From there, Via di San Francisco a Ripa angles southeast to the church of **San Francesco d'Assisi a Ripa** ★ (www.sanfrancescoaripa.com), so named because it's built over a convent where

St. Francis stayed in 1219 when he came to Rome to see the pope (his simple cell is preserved inside). A Bernini treasure is tucked into the last chapel on the left: the "Tomb of Beata Ludovica Albertoni" (1675), commemorating a noblewoman who dedicated her life to the city's poor.

Next, follow Via Anicia northeast to **Santa Cecilia in Trastevere** ★★ (Piazza Santa Cecilia; www.benedettinesantacecilia.it), a still-functioning convent with a peaceful courtyard garden. Tradition holds that the saint herself once lived on this site; the church's altar has an exquisite marble sculpture of her (ca. 1600) carved by Stefano Maderno. The basilica and Roman-era ruins underneath can be visited Monday to Saturday from 10am to 12:30pm and 4 to 6pm (from 11:30am on Sun). The partial remains of a "Last Judgment," by Pietro Cavallini (ca. 1293), a masterpiece of Roman medieval painting, can be visited only in the morning.

Unless you run across a school group, this place is never crowded, and despite the cavernous setting it provides an intimate look at the ancient world.

Via Ostiense 106. www.centralemontemartini.org/en. ✆ **06-0608**. 10€, or 13€ for a 7-day ticket that includes the Capitoline Museums. Rates higher during special exhibitions. Tues–Sun 9am–7pm; last entry 30 min. before closing. Metro: Garbatella. Bus: 23 or 769.

**MACRO Testaccio/Mattatoio** ★ MUSEUM   The Testaccio outpost of Rome's contemporary art museum is housed—appropriately for this former meatpacking neighborhood—in a converted slaughterhouse (*mattatoio* in Italian). The edgy programs and exhibits are a mix of installations, visuals, events, and special viewings. Opening times are made for night owls: Make an early-evening visit before going on to dinner in Testaccio.

Piazza Orazio Guistiniani 4. www.mattatoioroma.it. ✆ **06-671070400**. 8€. Tues–Thurs and Sun 12–8pm, Fri & Sat 12–10pm, but only open when there's an exhibition. Last entry 30 min. before closing. Metro: Piramide. Bus: 23, 75, 83, 170, 280, 716. Tram: 3, 8.

**San Paolo Fuori le Mura (St. Paul Outside the Walls)** ★★ CHURCH
The giant Basilica of St. Paul, whose origins date from the time of Constantine, is Rome's fourth great patriarchal church. It was erected over the tomb of St. Paul and is the second-largest church in Rome after St. Peter's. The

basilica fell victim to fire in 1823 and was subsequently rebuilt—hence the relatively modern look. Inside, translucent alabaster windows illuminate a forest of single-file columns and mosaic medallions (portraits of the various popes). Its most important treasure is a 12th-century marble candelabrum by Vassalletto, who's also responsible for the remarkable cloisters containing twisted pairs of columns enclosing a rose garden. Miraculously, the baldacchino by Arnolfo di Cambio (1285) wasn't damaged in the fire; it now shelters the tomb of St. Paul the Apostle.

Via Ostiense 190 (at Piazzale San Paolo). www.basilicasanpaolo.org. ✆ **06-69880800.** Basilica free; cloisters 4€. Basilica daily 7am–7pm. Cloisters daily 9:30am–5:30pm. Metro: Basilica di San Paolo. Bus: 23, 769, 792.

## The Via Appia (Appian Way) & the Catacombs

Of all the roads that led to Rome, **Via Appia Antica** (begun in 312 B.C.) was the most famous. It stretched all the way to the seaport of Brindisi, through which trade with Greece and the East was funneled. (According to Christian tradition, it was along the Appian Way that an escaping Peter encountered the vision of Christ, causing him to go back into the city to face martyrdom.) The road's initial stretch in Rome is lined with the monuments and ancient tombs of patrician Roman families—burials were forbidden within the city walls as early as the 5th century B.C.—and, below ground, miles of tunnels hewn out of the soft *tufa* stone that hardens on exposure to the air.

These tunnels, or catacombs, were where early Christians buried their dead. A few are open to the public, so you can wander through tunnels whose walls are gouged out with tens of thousands of now mostly empty burial niches, including small niches made for children. Early Christians referred to each chamber as a *dormitorio*—they believed the bodies were only sleeping, awaiting resurrection (which is why they could not observe the traditional Roman practice of cremation). In some you can still discover the remains of early Christian art. The obligatory guided tours feature occasionally biased history, plus a dash of sermonizing, but the guides are very knowledgeable.

The Appia Antica park is a popular Sunday picnic site for Roman families, following the

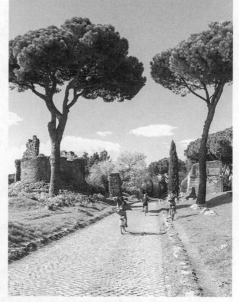

Riding bikes along the Appian Way.

Of all the monuments on the Appian Way itself, the most impressive is the **Tomb of Cecilia Metella** ★, within walking distance of the catacombs. The cylindrical tomb, clad in travertine and topped with a marble frieze, honors the wife of one of Julius Caesar's military commanders from the republican era. Why such an elaborate tomb for a figure of relatively minor historical importance? Other mausoleums may have been even more elaborate, but Cecilia Metella's earned enduring fame simply because her tomb has remained while the others have decayed. Part of the reason is its symbiotic relationship with the early-14th-century **Castle Caetani** attached to the rear. For centuries, the tomb survived being plundered for building materials because of the castle, which was built to guard the road and collect tolls; in later eras, the castle was spared because it was attached to the romantic ruin of the tomb. Admission to the tomb (10€) includes access to other sites in the archaeological park. For more info, see www.parcoarcheologico appiaantica.it (Italian only).

half-forgotten pagan tradition of dining in the presence of one's ancestors on holy days. The Via Appia Antica is closed to cars on Sundays, left for the picnickers, walkers, and bicyclists. See **www.parcoappiaantica.it** for more, including downloadable maps.

To reach the catacombs area, take bus no. 218 from the San Giovanni Metro stop or the 118 from Colosseo or Circus Maximus. *Tip:* The 118 runs more frequently than the 218 and deposits you closer to the catacombs, but runs less frequently on Sundays. If you are in a hurry to accommodate your visit to the catacombs, take a cab (p. 52).

**Catacombe di Domitilla** ★★★ RELIGIOUS SITE/TOUR   The oldest of the catacombs is the hands-down winner for most enjoyable experience. Groups are relatively small (in part because the site is not directly on the Appian Way), and guides are entertaining and personable. The catacombs—Rome's longest at 17km (11 miles)—were built below land donated by Domitilla, a noblewoman of the Flavian dynasty who was exiled from Rome for practicing Christianity. They were rediscovered in 1593, after a church abandoned in the 9th century collapsed. The visit begins in the sunken church founded in A.D. 380, the year Christianity became Rome's state religion.

There are fewer "sights" here than in the other catacombs, but this is the only catacomb where you'll still see bones; the rest have emptied their tombs to rebury the remains in inaccessible lower levels. Elsewhere in the tunnels, 4th-century frescoes contain some of the earliest representations of Saints Peter and Paul. Notice the absence of crosses: It was only later that Christians replaced the traditional fish symbol with the cross. During this period, Christ's crucifixion was a source of shame to the community. He had been killed like a common criminal.

Via delle Sette Chiese 282. www.domitilla.info. ⟨ **06-5110342.** 8€ adults, 5€ children ages 6–14. Wed–Mon 9:30am–noon and 2–5pm. Closed mid-Dec to mid-Jan. Bus: 30, 160, 714 (to Piazza dei Navigatori) or 218.

### Catacombe di San Callisto (Catacombs of St. Callixtus) ★★

RELIGIOUS SITE/TOUR "The most venerable and most renowned of Rome," said Pope John XXIII of these funerary tunnels. These catacombs are often packed with tour-bus groups, but the tunnels are phenomenal. They're the first cemetery of Christian Rome, burial place of 16 popes in the 3rd century. They bear the name of the deacon St. Callixtus, who served as pope from A.D. 217–22. The network of galleries is on four levels and reaches a depth of about 20m (65 ft.), the deepest in the area. There are many sepulchral chambers and almost half a million tombs of early Christians.

Entering the catacombs, you see the most important crypt, that of nine popes. Some of the original marble tablets of their tombs are preserved. Also commemorated is St. Cecilia, patron of sacred music (her relics were moved to her church in Trastevere during the 9th century; see p. 126). Farther on are the Cubicles of the Sacraments, with 3rd-century frescoes.

Via Appia Antica 110–26. www.catacombe.roma.it. ✆ **06-5130151.** 8€ adults, 5€ children ages 7–15. Thurs–Tues 9am–noon and 2–5pm. Closed late Jan to late Feb. Bus: 118 or 218.

### Catacombe di San Sebastiano (Catacombs of St. Sebastian) ★

RELIGIOUS SITE/TOUR Today the tomb and relics of St. Sebastian are in the ground-level basilica, but his original resting place was in the catacombs beneath it. Sebastian was a senior Milanese soldier in the Roman army who converted to Christianity and was martyred during Emperor Diocletian's persecutions, which were especially brutal in the first decade of the 4th century. From the reign of Valerian to that of Constantine, the bodies of Saints Peter and Paul were also hidden in the catacombs, which were dug from the soft volcanic rock (*tufa*). The church was built in the 4th century and remodeled in the 17th century.

In the tunnels and mausoleums are mosaics and graffiti and many pagan and Christian objects, as well as four Roman tombs with their frescoes and stucco fairly intact, found in 1922 after being buried for almost 2,000 years.

Via Appia Antica 136. www.catacombe.org. ✆ **06-7850350.** 8€ adults, 5€ children 6–15. Mon–Sat 10am–5pm. Closed Dec. Bus: 118 or 218.

## Especially for Kids

There's a real Jekyll and Hyde quality to exploring Rome with kids. On the one hand, it's a capital city, big, busy, and hot. On the other, the very best parts of the city for kids—Roman ruins, subterranean worlds, and *gelato*—are aspects you'd want to explore anyway. Seeing Rome with kids doesn't demand an itinerary redesign. And despite what you have heard about its famous seven hills, much of the center is mercifully flat, and pedestrian- (if not always stroller-) friendly.

Food is pretty easy too: Roman **pizzas** are some of the best in the world—see "Where to Eat" (p. 69) for our favorites. Ditto the ice cream, or *gelato* (p. 75). Restaurants in any price category will be happy to serve up a simple *pasta al pomodoro* (pasta with tomato sauce), and kids are welcomed virtually everywhere, including late in the evening.

# ORGANIZED tours

Forget the flag-waving guides leading a herd of dazed travelers around monuments. A better class of professionally guided tours delivers insider expertise, focused themes, and personal attention, plus perks such as skipping entry lines and visiting after hours. For **food tours and cooking classes** in Rome, see p. 72.

The affable team at **The Roman Guy** (www.theromanguy.com; 🕿 **06-342-8761859**) provides knowledgeable guides who explain thousands of years of history in an engaging, informal way. They offer small-group (most about 15 people) tours of the Colosseum (including dungeons), Vatican Museums, Catacombs, and food tours of Trastevere, among other options. Prices run from 60€ per person to much more for exclusive VIP access and/or private excursions.

**Walks of Italy** (www.walksofitaly.com; 🕿 06-95583331) also runs excellent guided tours of Rome starting from 34€; more in-depth explorations of the Colosseum, Vatican Museums, and Forum go for 60€ to 125€.

**Enjoy Rome** (www.enjoyrome.com; 🕿 06-4451843) offers a number of "greatest hits" walking tours, plus an early-evening tour of the Jewish Ghetto and Trastevere; their bus excursion to the Catacombs and Appian Way visits an ancient aqueduct that most Romans, let alone tourists, never see. Tours cost 30€ to 90€ per person; entrance fees are included with some, but not all tours.

One of the leading tour operators in Rome, **Context Travel** ★ (www.context travel.com; 🕿 **800/691-6036** in the U.S., or 06-96727371) uses local scholars—historians, art historians, archaeologists—to lead small-group walking tours around Rome's monuments, museums, and historic piazzas, as well as culinary walks and excellent family programs. Custom-designed tours are also available. Tour prices are high, beginning at about 80€ per person for 2 hours, but most participants consider the tours a highlight of their trip.

The team at **Through Eternity** (www.througheternity.com; 🕿 06-7009336) are art historians and architects; what sets them apart is their theatrical delivery, helped along by the dramatic scripts that many of the guides follow. It can be a lot of fun, but it's not for everyone. A 3½-hour tour of the Vatican is 69€; most other tours range from 42€ to 129€.

For something completely different, artist Kelly Medford runs **Sketching Rome Tours** (www.sketchingrometours. com), 3-hour small-group drawing and painting lessons in some of Rome's prettiest corners. Supplies are provided and no artistic talent is required (95€ per person).

The city is shorter on green spaces than many European cities, but the landscaped gardens of the **Villa Borghese** have plenty of room for kids to let off steam. Pack a picnic or rent some bikes (p. 118). The **Parco Appia Antica** (www.parcoappiaantica.it) is another favorite, especially on a Sunday or holiday when the old cobbled road is closed to traffic. The park's **catacombs** (p. 127) are eerie enough to satisfy young minds, but also fascinating Christian and historical sites in their own right.

Museums, of course, are trickier. My then-8-year-old was enthralled by a small museum exhibit of gory Renaissance paintings depicting biblical murders and sacrifices but could not get out of the crowded Vatican Museums fast enough—it's not much fun when you can't see over the backs of all those adults. You can probably get kids fired up more easily for the really ancient stuff. Make the bookshop at the **Colosseum** (p. 98) an early stop; it has a good selection of guides aimed at under-12s, themed on gladiators and featuring funny or cartoonish material. The **Musei Capitolini** (p. 96) invites kids to hunt down the collection's treasures highlighted on a free leaflet—it'll buy you a couple of hours to admire the exhibits and perhaps see them from a new and unexpected angle, too. The multiple levels below **San Clemente** (p. 104) and the **Case Romane del Celio** (p. 105) are also good for small visitors.

Aspiring young gladiators may want to spend a couple of hours at the **Scuola Gladiatori Roma (Rome Gladiator School)** (www.gruppostoricoromano.it/en; 89€ per person), where they can prepare for a duel in a reasonably authentic way.

Kids will also likely enjoy some of the cheesier city sights—and at the very least these will make good family photos to share on Facebook or Instagram. Build in some time to throw a coin in the **Trevi Fountain** (p. 118), or to watch the feral cats relaxing amid the ruins of **Largo di Torre Argentina.** A cat sanctuary here provides basic healthcare to Rome's many strays.

Several of the tour operators listed on p. 130 offer family-oriented tours with special activities and perks for younger travelers.

# ROME SHOPPING

Of all the sectors of the Rome economy affected by the pandemic, retail appears to have taken the hardest hit. Even businesses that had been around for decades weren't spared, and "FOR RENT" (*affittasi*) signs are posted on many once-thriving storefronts. We expect that the retail scene will eventually bounce back, but it might take longer than anyone would like.

That said, Rome is still a magnet for high-end shoppers, foodies, and lovers of antiques. In our limited space below we've summarized streets and areas known for their shops. Keep in mind that the monthly rent on the famous streets is very high, and those costs are passed on to you. Note that **sales** usually run twice a year, starting in January and July.

## The Top Shopping Streets & Areas

**AROUND PIAZZA DI SPAGNA**   Most of Rome's haute couture and seriously upscale shopping fans out from the bottom of the Spanish Steps. **Via Condotti** is probably Rome's poshest shopping street, where you'll find Prada, Gucci, Bulgari, and the like. A few more down-to-earth stores have opened, but it's still largely a playground for the super-rich. Neighboring **Via Borgognona** is another street where the merchandise is chic and ultra-expensive, but thanks to its pedestrian-only access and handsome baroque and neoclassical facades, it offers a nicer window-browsing experience. Shops are more densely concentrated on **Via Frattina,** the third member of this trio of upscale streets. Chic boutiques for adults and kids rub shoulders with ready-to-wear fashions, high-end chains, and a few tourist tat vendors. It's usually crowded with shoppers who appreciate the lack of motor traffic.

**VIA COLA DI RIENZO**   The commercial heart of the Prati neighborhood, this long, straight street runs from the Tiber to Piazza Risorgimento and is known for stores selling a variety of merchandise at reasonable prices—from jewelry to fashionable clothing, bags, and shoes. Among the most prestigious is the historic Roman perfume store (with products for men and women), **Bertozzini Profumeria dal 1913,** at no. 192 (www.bertozzinidal1913.it). The department store **Coin** is at no. 173 (with a large supermarket in the basement), the largest branch of venerable gourmet food store **Castroni** at no. 196 (www.castronicoladirienzo.com), and the smaller, more selective gourmet grocery **Franchi** at no. 200 (www.franchi.it).

**VIA DEL CORSO**   With less of a glamour quotient (and less stratospheric prices) than Via Condotti or Via Borgognona, Via del Corso boasts affordable styles aimed at younger consumers. Occasional gems are scattered amid international shops selling jeans and sportswear. The most interesting stores are toward the Piazza del Popolo end of the street (**Via del Babuino** here has a similar profile). Or turn at Largo Chigi towards Via del Tritone, and run a retail gauntlet that includes **Altariva Shoes,** for high-quality, Made-in-Italy footwear (www.altarivashoes.it); **Rinascente,** a high-end department store; **Hugo BOSS;** and **Sephora.**

Back on Corso, the farther south you walk (towards the Vittoriano monument), the narrower the sidewalks—and generally, the tackier the stores. *Tip:* If you are shopping with young children, it's useful to know that the upper part of Via del Corso (from Piazza Colonna to Piazza del Popolo) is largely car-free, save for taxis and the occasional bus.

**VIA DEI CORONARI**   An antiques-lover's souk. If you're shopping, or just window-shopping for antiques, art, or vintage-style souvenir prints, then spend an hour walking the length of this pretty, pedestrian-only street.

**CAMPO DE' FIORI**   Though the campo itself is now chockablock with restaurants, the streets leading up to it, notably **Via dei Giubbonari** and **Via Dei Baullari,** offer edgy and often one-of-a-kind fashions. Boutiques go in and out of business with dizzying frequency, but something interesting is always popping up.

**VIA DEL GOVERNO VECCHIO**   It's Vintage Valhalla on this pretty street, which winds parallel to Corso Vittorio Emanuele II. Lined with tiny resale shops that are stuffed to the gills with merchandise, Via del Governo Vecchio also has great places to eat and drink, particularly on the end closest to Piazza di San Pantaleo. Poke into vintage treasure trove **Omero e Cecilia** (at no. 110) or **Cinzia** (no. 45) before taking a restorative gelato break at **Frigidarium** (p. 75).

**VIA MARGUTTA**   This beautiful, tranquil street is home to numerous art stalls and artists' studios—Federico Fellini used to live here—though a lot of the stores tend to offer the same sort of antiques and mediocre paintings these days. You have to shop hard to find real quality.

A definite highlight is **Bottega del Marmoraro** at no. 53b, the whimsical studio of master stonecarver Sandro Fiorentini.

**MONTI**   Rome's most fashion-conscious central neighborhood has a pleasing mix of artisan retailers, vintage boutiques, and honest, everyday stores frequented by locals, with not a brand name in sight. Roam the length of **Via del Boschetto** for one-off fashions, designer ateliers, and unique homewares. In fact, you can roam in every direction from the spot where Via del Boschetto meets **Via Panisperna.** Turn on nearby **Via Urbana** or **Via Leonina,** where boutiques jostle for space with cafes that are ideal for a break or light lunch. Via Urbana also hosts the weekend **Mercatomonti** (see "Rome's Best Markets," below).

## Rome's Best Markets

**Campo de' Fiori** ★   Central Rome's food market has been running since at least the 1800s. It's no longer the place to find a produce bargain (though the fruit and veg displays are dazzling and colorful), and it tends to attract more tourists than locals, but it's still a genuine slice of Roman life in one of its most attractive squares. The market runs daily 7am to 1 or 2pm, with fewer produce vendors on Sunday. Campo de' Fiori. No phone. Bus: 40, 64, 170. Tram: 8.

**Mercatomonti** ★★   Everything from contemporary glass jewelry to vintage cameras, handmade clothes for kids and adults, and one-off designs are sold here in the heart of trendy Monti. The indoor market runs Saturday and Sunday September to June from 10am to 8pm. Via Leonina 46. www.mercato monti.com. No phone. Metro: Cavour.

**Nuovo Mercato di Testaccio (New Testaccio Market)** ★★★   Traditional food and produce stalls meet street food central in this modernist, sustainably powered market building. It's not just the best place to go produce shopping, it's also a terrific stop for a lunch of *supplì* (fried rice balls) and craft beer (at **Food Box** ★★, Box 66), meat and sauce-stuffed panini (at **Mordi e Vai** ★★, Box 15, www.mordievai.it), or an espresso and something sweet from **Chicchi e Lettere** ★ (Box 43). There are also clothes and kitchenware stalls, but the food is the star. The market runs Monday through Saturday 7am to 3:30pm. Btw. Via Luigi Galvani and Via Aldo Manuzio (at Via Benjamin Franklin). www.mercatoditestaccio.it. No phone. Metro: Piramide.

**Porta Portese** ★   Trastevere's vast weekly flea market stretches all the way from the Porta Portese gate along Via di Porta Portese to Viale di Trastevere. You have to wade through a lot of junk (and a sea of humanity—hold tight to your belongings), but there are good stalls for vintage housewares, clothing, and collectibles. It's on Sunday from dawn until midafternoon. Via di Porta Portese. No phone. Tram: 8.

# ENTERTAINMENT & NIGHTLIFE

Several English-language outlets offer current information about nightlife and cultural events in the Eternal City. *Wanted in Rome* (www.wantedinrome. com) has listings of opera, rock, English-language cinema showings, and such and gives an insider look at expat Rome. *Romeing* (www.romeing.it) is worth consulting, especially for contemporary arts and culture.

Unless you're dead set on making the Roman nightclub circuit, try what might be a far livelier and less expensive option—sitting late into the evening on **Piazza della Rotonda, Piazza del Popolo,** or one of Rome's other piazzas, all for the (admittedly inflated) cost of an espresso or a Campari and soda. If you're a clubber who likes it loud and late, jump in a cab to **Monte Testaccio** or **Via del Pigneto** and bar-hop. In Trastevere, there's always a bit of life on **Via del Politeama** where it meets **Piazza Trilussa.** In the *centro storico,* a nice *aperitivo-cena* scene unfolds along **Via del Governo Vecchio.**

## Performing Arts & Live Music

Rome's music scene doesn't have the same vibrancy as Florence's (p. 207), nor the high-quality opera of **La Fenice** in Venice (p. 288). Still, classical music fans are well catered to here. In addition to the major venues featured below, be on the lookout for concerts and one-off events in churches and salons around the city. Check **www.operainroma.com** for a calendar of opera and ballet staged by the Opera in Roma association at enchanting venues across the city. The **Pontificio Instituto di Musica Sacra** regularly runs classical music and operatic evenings.

**Alexanderplatz Jazz Club ★★**   Alexanderplatz has been the home of Rome's jazz scene since the early 1980s. Live music 7 nights a week. Via Ostia 9. www.alexanderplatzjazz.com. ✆ **06-39742171.** Cover usually 10€. Metro: Ottaviano.

**Auditorium–Parco della Musica ★★**   Designed by Renzo Piano, this exciting multipurpose center for the arts brings a refreshing breath of modernity to Rome. The schedule features lots of aging rockers and eclectic singer-songwriter acts, as well as traditional orchestras. Great cafes and a bookstore on-site, too. Viale Pietro de Coubertin 30. www.auditorium.com. ✆ **06-80241281.** Metro: Flaminio, then Tram 2. Bus: 910.

**Teatro dell'Opera di Roma ★★**   Here you'll find marquee operas such as *La Traviata, Carmen,* and *Tosca;* classical concerts from top-rank orchestras; and such ballets as *Giselle, Swan Lake,* and *The Nutcracker.* In summer the action moves outdoors for unforgettable open-air operatic performances at the ruined **Baths of Caracalla** (p. 95). Piazza Beniamino Gigli 1 (at Via del Viminale). www.operaroma.it; ✆ **06-4817003** (box office). Tickets 25€–150€. Metro: Repubblica.

## Cafes

Remember: In Rome and everywhere else in Italy, if you just want to drink a quick coffee and bolt, walk up to *il banco* (the bar), order *"un caffè, per favore"* or *"un cappuccino,"* and stay at the bar. They will make it for you to drink on the spot. It will usually cost more (at least double) to sit down to drink it (if you're in high-traffic, touristy areas—which you'll most likely be!), and outdoor table service is the most expensive way to go. Even in the heart of the city center, a short coffee *al banco* should cost no more than 1€; add around .30€ for a *cappuccino.* Expect to pay up to five times that price if you sit outdoors on a marquee piazza. Most cafes in the city serve a decent cup of coffee, but here's a small selection of places worth hunting down.

When the sun goes down, Rome's palaces, ruins, fountains, and monuments are bathed in a theatrical white light. Make time for a memorable evening stroll past old temples or Renaissance fountains glowing under the blue-black sky.

The **Fountain of the Naiads** ("Fontana delle Naiadi") on Piazza della Repubblica, the **Fountain of the Tortoises** ("Fontana della Tartarughe") on Piazza Mattei, the **Fountain of Acqua Paola** ("Fontanone") at the top of the Janiculum Hill, and the **Trevi Fountain** (p. 118) are particularly beautiful at night.

The **Capitoline Hill** (or Campidoglio) is magnificently lit after dark, with its Renaissance facades glowing like jewel boxes. The view of the Roman Forum seen from the rear of Piazza del Campidoglio is perhaps the grandest in Rome (see "Three Free Views to Remember for a Lifetime" box, p. 100). If you're across the Tiber, the Vatican's **Piazza San Pietro** (p. 86) is impressive at night without the crowds. The combination of illuminated architecture, baroque fountains, and sidewalk shows makes **Piazza Navona** (p. 108) even more delightful at night.

With its shabby-chic interior and namesake fig tree backdrop to charming outdoor seating, **Bar del Fico** ★ (Piazza del Fico 26; www.bardelfico.com; ℂ 06 6880 8413) is one of Rome's most beloved aperitivo spots. **Sant'Eustachio il Caffè** ★★ (Piazza Sant'Eustachio 82; www.santeustachioilcaffe.it; ℂ **06-68802048**) roasts its own Fair Trade Arabica beans and draws a friendly crowd a few deep at the bar. (Unless you ask, the coffee comes with sugar.) Debate still rages as to whether the city's best cup of coffee is served at Sant'Eustachio or **Tazza d'Oro** ★, near the Pantheon (Via degli Orfani 84; www.tazzadorocoffeeshop.com; ℂ **06-6789792**). Jacketed baristas work at 100mph at **Spinelli** ★ (Via dei Mille 60; ℂ **06-31055552**), a no-nonsense locals' cafe near Termini station.

# Wine Bars, Cocktail Bars & Craft Beer Bars

The mass social phenomenon of the *aperitivo* (happy hour) provides great insight into the particular ways of real Romans. It started in hard-working northern cities like Milan, where you'd go to a bar after leaving the office and, for the price of one drink, you'll be served one or more plates of high-quality food—often with cheese, cured meats, bruschetta, and pasta salad. Luckily for Rome, the custom trickled down here, and now the city is filled with casual little places to drop in for a drink (from 6 or 7pm onward) and eat to your heart's content. Aperitivo spreads vary in quantity and quality, but generally you'll pay less than 10€ per person for a drink and buffet. All the places listed here are fine for families, too—Italian kids love *aperitivo* (minus the alcohol)! Look for signs in the window and follow your nose. The **Monti** neighborhood is a good place to begin.

**Ai Tre Scalini** ★    This little *bottiglieria* (wine bar) is the soul of Monti. There's a traditional menu, as well as a wine list sourced from across Italy. Arrive early or call for a table: This place is usually jammed. Via Panisperna 251. www.aitrescalini.org. ℂ **06-48907495.** Metro: Cavour.

**Cavour 313** ★★ A wine bar that's as traditional and genuine as you will find this close to the ancient ruins serves over 30 wines by the glass (from 3.50€) as well as cold cuts, cheese, and vegetable platters, or excellent carpaccio. Closed Aug. Via Cavour 313. www.cavour313.it. ℂ **06-6785496.** Metro: Colosseo and Cavour.

**L'Elementare** ★ Formerly called Bir and Fud, this Trastevere craft-beer watering hole has taken on a new name and devoted more attention to pizza and other snacky foods. But the beers are still here—most of them Italian craft brews, some as strong as 9%. It's 5€ for a small beer. Via Benedetta 23. ℂ **06-5894016.** Bus: H. Tram: 8.

**Ex Circus** ★ This convivial hub for digital nomads, hungry tourists on a budget, and aperitivo drinkers seeking an ample spread is just a few blocks from Piazza Navona. It also does great salads, smoothies, and Sunday brunch. Via della Vetrina 15. ex-circus.business.site. ℂ **06-97619258.** Bus: 40, 64, 70.

**Freni e Frizioni** ★★ Trastevere's "Brakes and Clutches" is a former mechanics garage turned nighttime hot spot, with an ethnic-inflected *aperitivo* spread (think curried risotto). On the adjacent square, an effervescent crowd lounges against stone walls and parked *motorini*. Via del Politeama 4–6 (near Piazza Trilussa). www.freniefrizioni.com. ℂ **06-45497499.** Bus: H. Tram: 8.

**La Bottega del Caffè** ★★ Beers, wine, cocktails, *aperitivo*—there's a little of everything at one of Monti's busiest neighborhood bars. Piazza Madonna dei Monti 5. ℂ **06-64741578.** Metro: Cavour.

**Litro** ★★ This wine bar in Monteverde Vecchio (a residential area above Trastevere) serves natural wines, cocktails, and snacks sourced from Lazio-based purveyors of cured meats and cheeses, plus bruschetta and stellar alcoholic sorbets. An entire menu is devoted to mezcal, tequila's smoky cousin. Via Fratelli Bonnet 5. ℂ **06-45447639.** Bus: 75.

**Open Baladin** ★★ If anyone ever tells you "Italians don't do good beer," send them to this bar near the Ghetto. A 40-long row of taps lines the bar, with beers from its own Piedmont brewery and across Italy. Via degli Specchi 5–6. open-baladin-roma.business.site. ℂ **06-6838989.** Bus: 40, 64, 70. Tram: 8.

**Salotto42** ★★ It's all fancy cocktails and well-chosen wines at this über-hip "bookbar" set opposite the columned facade of 2nd-century Hadrian's Temple (near the Pantheon). This makes for a classy after-dinner stop. It also does shared plates, fresh juices, smoothies, and infused teas. Piazza di Pietra 42 (off Via del Corso). www.salotto42.it. ℂ **06-6785804.** Bus: 64, 85, 492.

**Stravinskij Bar** ★ An evening at this award-winning cocktail bar inside one of Rome's most famous grand hotels is always a regal affair. Mixology, ingredients, and canapés are all topnotch. Inside Hotel de Russie, Via del Babuino 9. ℂ **06-32888874.** Metro: Spagna.

**Vale la Pena Pub** ★★ This way-casual, tongue-in-cheek beer pub with a social mission offers beer from its own microbrewery, made by inmates from Rome's Rebibbia prison. It fits like a glove in the working-class Tuscolano district. Via Eurialo 22. ℂ **06-87606875.** Metro: Furio Camillo.

# SIDE TRIPS FROM ROME

By Elizabeth Heath

You could easily spend a week in Rome and still not see everything there is to see. But if you want a break from the city, there are important ruins, old towns, and ancient villas across the countryside outside Rome. A few hours south of Rome, the archaeological site of Pompeii is on many a traveler's bucket list and can be done on a long day trip. If you can't get to Pompeii, the ruins of Ostia Antica are an excellent substitute.

Note that hours, prices, and directions listed here were correct at press time. But given the possibility of pandemic-related changes, it's always best to check online or call ahead for the latest info.

**5**

## POMPEII ★★★

240km (150 miles) SE of Rome

Completely destroyed by Vesuvius on August 24, A.D. 79, the Roman city of Pompeii was one of Italy's most important commercial centers. For almost 2,000 years, the city lay frozen in time under a thick layer of solidified ash. Today, the excavated ruins provide an unparalleled insight into the everyday life of Roman Italy, especially that of its ordinary citizens and, notoriously, the erotic art that decorated its homes and villas. It is estimated that only 2,000 people actually died in the disaster, while most of the population of 20,000 escaped before the full eruption. Those who stayed perished horribly: asphyxiated by toxic gases, and buried in several feet of volcanic ash. Pliny the Elder, the celebrated Roman naturalist, was one of the registered casualties. Although parts of the city were rediscovered in 1599, full excavations only began in 1748, starting a process that has never really ended, with new finds still being made.

By making a long day of it, you can visit the famous ruins from Rome without having to spend the night near Pompeii, where the modern city has little appeal. It's a 3½ hour drive from the capital, and even less by train. Count spending at least 4 or 5 hours wandering the site to do it justice. Remember also to take plenty of water

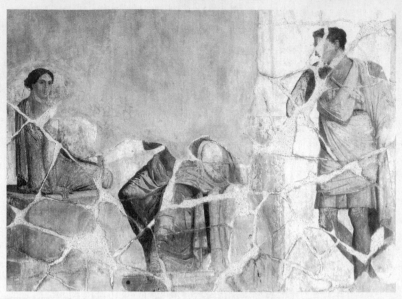

Fresco in the Villa dei Misteri, Pompeii.

with you as well as **sunscreen,** because there's not much shade anywhere among the ruins, and you'll be doing a lot of walking: Wear sturdy, comfortable shoes and a hat and/or sunglasses to shield your face/eyes/top of head from Pompeii's typically penetrating sun. Uneven stone streets make for difficult walking—consider a cane or walking stick if you're the least bit unsteady on your feet.

## Essentials

**GETTING THERE**    The best option is to take the Trenitalia "Frecciarossa" high-speed **train** from Termini to Naples (1 hr. 10 min.; from 48€ one-way), though InterCity trains are cheaper (around 27€) and take just over 2 hours—still doable if you start early. The first Frecciarossa departs at 7am. Once at Napoli Centrale (Naples Central Station), follow the signs to Napoli Piazza Garibaldi station **downstairs,** where you transfer to the **Circumvesuviana Railway** (www.eavsrl.it; website in Italian only; ℂ **800/211-388** toll-free in Italy). Note that this railway is separate from Trenitalia, so you won't be able to buy a through ticket to Pompeii from Rome; just get a return to Naples, and buy the Pompeii portion on arrival in Naples. Trains depart to Pompeii every half-hour from Piazza Garibaldi, but make sure you get on the train headed toward Sorrento and get off at Pompei Scavi/Villa Dei Misteri (*scavi* means "archaeological dig"). If you get on the "Pompei" train (toward Poggiomarino), you'll end up in the town of Pompei—which is in a totally different place—and will have to double back to get to the ruins. A ticket costs about 4€ one-way; trip time is 35 minutes.

To reach Pompeii by **car** from Rome, take the A1 *autostrada* toward Naples, then the A3 all the way to the signposted turnoff for the ruins just after the tollbooth—a straightforward and usually hassle-free drive.

**TOURS**   Consider letting someone else take care of the driving and logistics of a Pompeii trip. Plenty of tour operators run guided tours or transport to Pompeii from Rome. **Enjoy Rome** (www.enjoyrome.com; ✆ **06-4451843**) runs a Pompeii shuttle bus on Tuesday, Thursday, and Saturday (Mar–Nov) at 7:30am from its office near the Cavour Metro station, arriving at the ruins at around 11am. You can wander around independently (a guide costs extra) before leaving at 3:30pm (back around 7pm). The shuttle costs 60€ and does not include entrance fees. Most of the tour operators listed on p. 130 offer day trips to Pompeii, as does **Dark Rome** (www.darkrome.com), and some include brief stops in Naples or along the Amalfi Coast. Tours start at 129€.

**VISITOR INFORMATION**   Official tourist infopoints (pompeiisites.org/en; ✆ **081-8575347**) can be found at the Porta Marina, Piazza Esedra, and Piazza Anfiteatro entrances. The ruins are open April to October daily from 9am to 7pm and November to March 9am to 5pm. Last admission is 90 minutes before closing. Admission is 16€. The site can be crowded in the mornings, especially when tours arrive in force in July and August. Crowds thin out by early afternoon.

**PARKING**   There is no official parking lot at Pompeii, though there are several private paid lots just outside the park. Expect to pay about 2€ per hour. *Tip:* Do not leave valuables in your rental car, and if you have luggage aboard, keep it out of sight.

## Exploring Pompeii

**Pompeii** covers a large area with a lot to see, so try to be selective. Note that many of the streets run through little more than stone foundations, and although wandering the site is a magical experience, ruin fatigue can set in by the end of a frenetic day of sightseeing. Also keep in mind that even some of the best-known buildings might be temporarily closed off to the public without notice or explanation.

### In High Season, a Better Way to Pompeii

The Circumvesuviana train will get you to Pompeii, but not in style—and possibly not even in comfort. Travelers frequently complain about crowds, stifling heat, and even worse—pickpockets on board the commuter train. From spring to fall, EAV (www.eavsrl.it), which runs the Circumvesuviana, also offers the **Campania Express** train, which travels from Naples to Sorrento but only stops at tourist destinations. Trains run four times a day in each direction and tickets are about 8€ one-way for Naples to Pompeii—a small price to pay for a fast, clean, air-conditioned ride with guaranteed seating.

Entering through the **Porta Marina,** the **Forum (Foro)** ★ is a long, narrow, open space surrounded by the ruins of the **basilica** (the city's largest single structure), the **Temple of Apollo (Tempio di Apollo)** ★★, the **Temple of Jupiter (Tempio di Giove)** ★★, and, a little farther west, the **Terme Stabian (Baths)** ★★, where some plaster casts of Vesuvius's victims have been preserved.

Walk north along the Via di Mercurio to see some of Pompeii's most famous villas: The **Casa del Poeta Tragico (House of the Tragic Poet)** ★ contains some eye-catching mosaics, notably the CAVE CANEM ("Beware of the Dog") design by the main entrance. The vast **Casa del Fauno (House of the Faun)** ★★ features an amicable *"Ave"* ("welcome") mosaic and the copy of a tiny bronze faun (the original is in Naples's Archaeological Museum). Nearby, the **Casa dei Vettii** ★★★ is in excellent shape, arranged around a pretty central courtyard and containing celebrated murals, notably an image of Priapus (the fertility god) resting his ludicrously oversized phallus on a pair of scales.

Keep walking beyond the old city walls to the northwest for the **Villa dei Misteri** ★★★, Pompeii's best-preserved *insula* (Roman block of apartments), a 3rd-century-B.C. mansion containing a series of stunning depictions of the Dionysiac initiation rites. The paintings are remarkably clear, bright, and richly colored after all these years.

Walking to the eastern side of Pompeii from the Porta Marina, you'll pass the 5th-century-B.C. **Teatro Grande** ★, well-preserved and still used for performances today. Continue west on the Via dell'Abbondanza, passing the **Fullonica Stephanus** (a laundry with a large, tiered washtub); and the **Casa della Venere in Conchiglia (House of the Venus in a Shell)** ★★, named after the curious painting on its back wall. At the far western end of the town lies the **Anfiteatro** ★★, Italy's oldest amphitheater, dating from 80 B.C.

## Where to Eat

To dine really well around Pompeii, you have to go into (and stay overnight in) Naples or Sorrento. If you're doing Pompeii as a day trip, skip the so-so restaurants around Pompeii itself and pack a picnic before you set off from Rome. Of course, if you're in a bind and need a quick bite, there is a sizeable food service bar within the ruins that serves basic pastas and panini.

# OSTIA ANTICA ★★

24km (15 miles) SW of Rome

The ruins of Rome's ancient port are a must-see for anyone who can't make it to Pompeii. It's an easier daytrip than Pompeii, on a similar theme: the chance to wander around the preserved ruins of an ancient Roman settlement that has been barely touched since its abandonment.

Ostia, at the mouth of the Tiber, was the port of Rome, serving as the gateway for riches from the far corners of the Empire. Founded in the 4th century B.C., it became a major port and naval base under two later emperors, Claudius and Trajan. A prosperous city developed, full of temples, baths, theaters, and patrician homes.

Ostia flourished between the 1st and 3rd centuries, and survived until around the 9th century before it was abandoned. Gradually it became little more than a malaria bed, a buried ghost city that faded into history. A papal-sponsored commission launched a series of digs in the 19th century; however, the major work of unearthing was carried out under Mussolini's orders from 1938 to 1942. The city is only partially dug out today, but it's believed that all the chief monuments have been uncovered. There are quite a few impressive ruins, and the site is extensive.

A word to the wise: Ostia is a mostly flat site, but the Roman streets underfoot are all clad in giant basalt cobblestones—wear comfortable walking shoes.

## Essentials

**GETTING THERE** Take the Metro to Piramide, changing lines there for the Lido train to Ostia Antica. (From the platform, take the exit for "Air Terminal" and turn right at the top of the steps, where the station name changes to Porta San Paolo.) Departures to Ostia via Roma Lido trains are at minimum every half-hour; the trip takes 25 minutes and is included in the price of a Metro single-journey ticket or Roma Pass (see p. 46). It's just a 5-minute walk to the excavations from the train station: Exit the station, walk ahead and over the footbridge, and then continue straight until you reach the car park. The ticket booth is to the left.

**VISITOR INFORMATION** The site opens Tuesday to Sunday at 8:30am. Closing time is at dusk, so the time changes seasonally, ranging from 7pm in spring/summer (Apr–Aug) to 4:30pm in fall and winter (Nov–Feb 15); check at **www.ostiaantica.beniculturali.it** or call ℭ **06-56350215.** The ticket office closes 1 hour before the ruins close. Admission costs 12€ (14€ if pre-purchased online), free for ages 17 and under and 65 and over. The inexpensive map on sale at the ticket booth is a wise investment.

**PARKING** The car park, on Viale dei Romagnoli, costs a few euro per day, but it is fairly small. There's also limited street parking. Arrive early if you're driving.

## Exploring Ostia Antica

The principal monuments are all labeled. On arrival, visitors first pass the *necropoli* (burial grounds, always outside the city gates in Roman towns and cities). The main route follows the giant cobblestones of the **Decumanus ★** (the main street) into the heart of Ostia. The **Piazzale delle Corporazioni ★★** is like an early version of Wall Street: This square contained nearly 75 corporations, the nature of their businesses identified by the patterns of preserved mosaics. Nearby, Greek dramas were performed at the **Teatro,** built in the early days of the Empire. The theater as it looks today is the result of much rebuilding. Every town the size of Ostia had a **Forum ★,** and the layout is still intact: A well-preserved **Capitolium** (once the largest temple in Ostia) faces the remains of the 1st-century-A.D. **Temple of Roma and Augustus.**

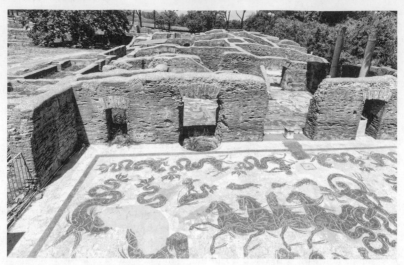
Mosaic floors at the Baths of Neptune, Ostia Antica.

Elsewhere in the grid of streets are the ruins of the **Thermopolium ★★,** which was a bar; its name means "sale of hot drinks." An *insula* (apartment block) called **Casa Diana ★** remains, its rooms arranged around an inner courtyard. The **Terme di Nettuno ★** was a vast baths complex; climb the building at its entrance for an aerial view of its well-preserved mosaics. In the enclave is a **museum** displaying Roman statuary along with fragmentary frescoes.

## Where to Eat

There is no real need to eat by the ruins—a half-day here should suffice, and Ostia is within easy reach of the abundant restaurants of Rome's city center. The obvious alternative is a picnic; the well-stocked foodie magnet **Eataly** is only a couple of minutes from the Lido platform at Piramide Metro station, making it easy to grab provisions when you make the Metro interchange. There are perfect picnic spots beside fallen columns or old temple walls. If you crave a sit-down meal, trattoria **Allo Sbarco di Enea,** Viale dei Romagnoli 675 (www.allosbarcodienea.it; ✆ **06-5650034**), is right outside the archaeological park. There's also a snack and coffee bar at the site.

# TIVOLI & THE VILLAS ★★

32km (20 miles) E of Rome

Perched high on a hill east of Rome, Tivoli is an ancient town that has always been something of a retreat from the city. In Roman times it was known as Tibur, a retirement town for the wealthy; later during the Renaissance, it again became the playground of the rich, who built their country villas out here. You need a full day to do justice to the gardens and villas that remain—especially if Villa Adriana is on your list, as indeed it should be—so set out early.

# Essentials

**GETTING THERE**   Tivoli is 32km (20 miles) east of Rome on Via Tiburtina, about an hour's drive with traffic (the Rome–L'Aquila *autostrada*, A24, is usually faster). If you don't have a car, take Metro Line B to Ponte Mammolo. After exiting the station, transfer to a Cotral bus for Tivoli (www.cotralspa.it). Cotral buses depart every 15 to 30 minutes during the day, and the trip will take less than an hour. Villa d'Este is in Tivoli itself, close to the bus stop; to get to Villa Adriana you need to catch a regional bus from town. Or take the Cotral bus that runs on Via Prenestina; this stops a short walk from the Villa Adriana entrance.

## Exploring Tivoli & the Villas

**Villa Adriana (Hadrian's Villa) ★★★** HISTORIC SITE/RUINS   The globe-trotting Emperor Hadrian spent the last 3 years of his life in the grandest style. Less than 6km (3¾ miles) from Tivoli, between A.D. 118 and 134, he built one of the greatest estates ever conceived, filling acre after acre with some of the architectural wonders he'd seen on his many travels. Hadrian erected theaters, baths, temples, fountains, gardens, and canals bordered with statuary, adorning the palaces and temples with sculpture, some of which now rest in the museums of Rome. In later centuries, barbarians, popes, and cardinals, as well as anyone who needed a slab of marble, carted off much that made the villa so spectacular. But enough of the fragmented ruins remain to inspire a real sense of awe. For a glimpse of what the villa used to be, see the plastic reconstruction at the entrance.

The most outstanding remnant is the **Canopo ★★★**, a re-creation of the Egyptian town of Canopus with its famous Temple of the Serapis. The ruins of a rectangular area, **Piazza d'Oro**, arc still surrounded by a double portico. Likewise, the **Edificio con Pilastri Dorici (Doric Pillared Hall)** remains, with its pilasters with bases and capitals holding up a Doric architrave. The apse and the ruins of some magnificent vaulting are found at the **Grandi Terme (Great Baths)**, while only the north wall remains of the **Pecile ★**, otherwise known as the *Stoà Poikile di Atene* or "Painted Porch," which Hadrian discovered in Athens and had reproduced here. The best is saved for last—the **Teatro Marittimo ★★★**, a circular maritime theater in ruins, with its central building enveloped by a canal spanned by small swing bridges.

For a closer look at some of the items excavated, visit the museum on the premises and a visitor center near the villa parking area.

Largo Marguerite Yourcenar 1, Tivoli. www.levillae.com/en. *©* **0774-312070.** 10€. Daily 8:30am–sunset (about 7:30pm in May–Aug); Oct–May, closing at 2pm. Bus: 4 from Tivoli or see directions above.

**Villa d'Este ★★** PARK/GARDEN   Like Hadrian centuries before, Cardinal Ippolito d'Este of Ferrara ordered this villa built in the mid-16th century on a Tivoli hillside. The dank Renaissance structure, with its second-rate paintings, is not that interesting; the big draw for visitors are the **spectacular gardens ★★★,** designed by Pirro Ligorio.

As you descend the cypress-studded garden slope, you're rewarded with everything from lilies to gargoyles spouting water, torrential streams, and waterfalls. The loveliest fountain is the **Fontana dell Ovato** ★★, by Ligorio. But nearby is the most spectacular engineering achievement: the **Fontana dell'Organo Idraulico (Fountain of the Hydraulic Organ)** ★★, dazzling with its music and water jets in front of a baroque chapel, with four maidens who look tipsy (the fountain "plays" every 2 hours from 10:30am).

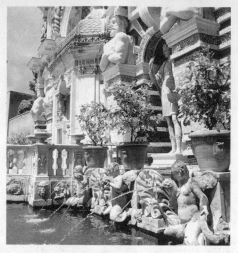

A fountain at the Villa d'Este.

The moss-covered **Fontana dei Draghi (Fountain of the Dragons),** also by Ligorio, and the so-called **Fontana di Vetro (Fountain of Glass),** by Bernini, are worth seeking out, as is the main promenade, lined with 100 spraying fountains. The garden warrants hours of exploration, but it involves a lot of walking, with some steep climbs.

Piazza Trento 5, Tivoli. www.levillae.com/en. ☎ **0774-312070.** 10€ (13€ during special exhibitions). Tues–Sun 8:30am to 1 hr. before sunset; Mon from 2pm. Bus: Cotral service from Ponte Mammolo (Roma–Tivoli); the bus stops near the entrance.

**Villa Gregoriana** ★ PARK/GARDEN   Villa d'Este dazzles with artificial glamour, but the Villa Gregoriana relies more on nature. Originally laid out by Pope Gregory XVI in the 1830s, its main highlight is the panoramic waterfall of Aniene, with the trek to the bottom studded with grottoes and balconies that open onto the chasm. The only problem is that if you do make the full descent, you might need a helicopter to pull you up again (the climb back up is fierce). From one of the belvederes, there's a view of the **Temple of Vesta** on the hill.

Largo Sant'Angelo, Tivoli. www.fondoambiente.it/parco-villa-gregoriana-eng.☎ **0774-332650.** 8€. Daily late Apr to mid-Dec 10am–dusk (from 9am July–Aug). Closed mid-Dec to late Apr. Bus: Cotral service from Ponte Mammolo (Roma–Tivoli); the bus stops near the entrance.

## Where to Eat

Tivoli's gardens make for a pleasant picnic venue, but if you crave an upscale meal with a view, **Ristorante Sibilla,** Via della Sibilla 42 (www.ristorante sibilla.com; ☎ **0774-335281;** closed Mon), sits in the shadow of the Temple of Vesta and is a 10-minute walk from the station. In the center of town, **La Fornarina,** Piazza Palatina 8 (www.pizzerialafornarina.it; ☎ **0774-312786**), is a casual choice for pizza, pasta, and Roman specialties.

# FLORENCE

Florence may be small, but over the centuries it has packed a major punch in European history. Its center—which you can easily cross on foot—still evokes this illustrious past, packed as it is with monuments from the city's golden age. In the 15th and 16th centuries, Florence's achievements in art and architecture, science, literature, and even banking were unmatched—and the rest of Europe knew it.

This was the center of the Renaissance movement and the hometown of its leading figures, Michelangelo, Brunelleschi, Leonardo da Vinci, Galileo, and others. Florence built up a store of riches that still dazzles today: the **Uffizi Gallery** heaving with masterpieces, the ingenious domed Cathedral, Michelangelo's **"David,"** and any number of decorated palaces and chapels. These treasures are still representative of the best humankind can achieve. And because of this, Florence remains a must-visit destination for every first-time traveler to Italy, and a must-return destination for anyone who cares about art and architecture.

Florence is also well located for exploring the Tuscany region. For the best day trips from Florence, see chapter 7.

## Strategies for Seeing Florence

You want to make the most of your time in Florence, but also get the most for your money, know the best ways to get around, and avoid hassles like long lines. The following essential strategies and hardworking tips will help you enrich your time and travels in Florence.

o **Avoid the lines.** If I was to give one single piece of advice to a friend visiting Florence, it would be this: **Book Uffizi and Accademia tickets in advance.** Reserving a timed entrance slot is relatively easy (see box p. 149) and at some venues and/or on certain days, compulsory. Failing to book at the Uffizi, especially, could cost you a half-day in a queue. No joke. And your best (or only) chance of standing alone in front of a popular artwork is to enter at 8:15am.

o **Save on unnecessary booking fees.** Conversely, apart from the Uffizi, Accademia, and Brunelleschi's dome (where it's always required; see p. 149), you won't usually need a timed admission slot anywhere else. Save the booking fee.

o **Discount tickets.** Do you need one? The answer, unfortunately, is "it depends." To decide whether the 85€ **Firenzecard** is for you, turn to p. 148.

o **Walk.** Florence's tortuous one-way road system makes taxis expensive, and the city has no metro. Pack comfortable shoes and hit the streets on foot. *Note:* The hill up to Piazzale Michelangelo is fairly steep: If this sounds daunting, buses 12 and 13 go there.

o **Mondays.** Italian state museums are traditionally closed on Mondays, which means no Uffizi, no Pitti Palace, and no "David." Monday, then, is a good time to visit Florence's other sights, like the Palazzo Vecchio, Santa Maria Novella, and churches including the Duomo complex—all of which are open as usual. One caveat: With the big-hitters closed, other sights are inevitably busier, so Mondays also make a perfect day-trip day; see chapter 7 for our recommended short trips from the city.

o **Eat lunch and *aperitivo;* skip dinner.** Unless you have a huge appetite, you likely won't need three big meals a day. To save money, eat a full, late lunch, which is usually cheaper, and swap dinner for an *aperitivo.* These are often generous and appear around 6:30pm at bars all over the city. Buy one drink and you can nosh as much as you like. Florentines even have a name for this: *apericena* (*cena* means "dinner").

o **First Sundays.** Like elsewhere in Italy, the first Sunday of every month is #domenicalmuseo, meaning admission to state-owned museums is free (*note:* this is not the same as *city*-owned). So, you can enter the Uffizi, Bargello, Medici Chapels, Pitti Palace, Boboli Garden, and more without paying a cent. The downside? Queues and crowds, of course—mostly Italians taking advantage of the promotion. Forget the Uffizi, which will be packed, and try your luck at others. The **tourist office** (see p. 149) has a full list. And obviously, if you're here for one day only and it's a First Sunday, do not buy a Firenzecard.

The Ponte Vecchio, seen from the banks of the River Arno.

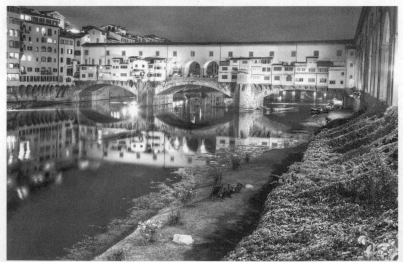

## TRAVEL DISRUPTIONS IN florence

As a popular city and busy rail hub, Florence was hit relatively hard by the coronavirus pandemic—although on nothing like the scale of Lombardy and other northern hotspots. See p. 299 for websites explaining Italy's latest regulations. Your hotel desk staff can also advise on local guidelines.

The major change for visitors is a widespread requirement to **book museums in advance,** so venues can control numbers and avoid long lines. See "Essential: Reservations for the Uffizi, Accademia & More," p. 149. As we went to press, you must also show a **Green Pass** to **enter a museum or public building; use long-distance trains;** **attend the theater** or **enter a sports stadium; eat indoors at a restaurant;** or **access many other services or venues.** While the Green Pass itself is only available to EU citizens and those from participating non-EU countries, carrying national proof of vaccination status will suffice. Mask mandates, including on public transportation, may return at any time, if public health policy requires it. **Note:** You may need to share a few personal details for contact-tracing purposes, including the contact info for those you've traveled with and your lodging.

For further details on Italy protocols, see chapter 10.

# ESSENTIALS

## Arriving

**BY PLANE**   Most international travelers will reach Florence via the airports in Rome (see p. 42) or Milan, proceeding on to Florence via train (see below). There are also direct international flights into Pisa's **Galileo Galilei Airport** (see p. 298), 97km (60 miles) west of Florence; several budget airlines fly here from European cities. Around six to eight daily **Sky Bus Lines** (www.sky buslines.it; ✆ 366/126-0651) buses connect Florence with Pisa Airport in just over 1 hour (14€ adults; 7€ children 2–10). Florence drop-off/pick-up is at the Guidoni tram stop near Florence Airport (T2 line; see below), except during the night, when the bus runs to/from Florence's main rail station.

A few European airlines, including British Airways, KLM, and Vueling, also serve **Florence Airport (FLR)** (sometimes called **Peretola;** www.aero porto.firenze.it/en; ✆ 055/306-15), just 5km (3 miles) northwest of town. A modern **tram line (T2)** is the most cost-efficient way to reach the center from there (1.50€ each way). Trams depart every 4 to 9 minutes from 5am to midnight. Journey time to Florence's rail station is 20 minutes. **Taxis** line up outside the arrivals terminal: Exit and turn immediately to the right to find the rank. Taxis charge a regulated flat rate of 22€ for the 15-minute journey to the city center (24€ on holidays, 25.30€ after 10pm; additional 1€ per bag).

Florence is also connected with Bologna Airport, by the **Appennino Shuttle** (www.appenninoshuttle.it; ✆ 055/5001-302), which runs 10 times each day and takes between 80 and 90 minutes; tickets cost 20€, 8€ ages 5 to 10, free ages 4 and under (25€/10€ if you pay on board, cash only). Buses

## DISCOUNT tickets FOR FLORENCE

It may seem a little odd to label the **Firenzecard** ★★ (www.firenzecard.it) a "discount" ticket, since it costs a substantial 85€. Is it a good buy? If you are planning a busy, museum-packed break here, the Firenzecard is a good value. If you only expect to see a few highlights, skip it.

The details: This card (valid for 72 hr.) allows one-time entrance to 60-plus sites, including some that are free anyway, but also the Uffizi, Accademia, Cappella Brancacci, Palazzo Pitti, Brunelleschi's dome, San Marco, and many more. In fact, *everything* we recommend in this chapter is included with the card, even sites in **Fiesole** (p. 210). A Firenzecard gets you into shorter "fast track" lines everywhere. It includes ticket prebooking fees—another saving of 3€ to 4€ for museums like the Uffizi and Accademia. However, many museums (including those two, but also other

popular sites) now **require Firenzecard holders to prebook** a timed admission slot. The "Museums" section at www.firenzecard.it/en has an easy-to-follow traffic light system for tracking exactly which places require prebooking.

**Don't** buy a Firenzecard for anyone ages 17 and under: With a full-priced card you can take immediate family members ages 17 and under for free. Any companions under 18 can join the express queue with you and pay only the "reservation fee" at state-owned museums (it's 4€ at the Uffizi, for example). Those under 17 gain free admission to civic museums (such as the Palazzo Vecchio) anyway. Private museums and sites have their own payment rules, but it will not add up to 85€ per child.

*Warning:* Do not buy **"skip the line" or other tickets for Brunelleschi's dome on the street.** These are not valid, and you will be turned away.

arrive at and depart from Piazzale Montelungo, between Florence's Santa Maria Novella rail station and the Fortezza da Basso.

**BY TRAIN**   Most travelers arrive in Florence by train. This is the Tuscany region's rail hub, with regular connections to all Italy's major cities. To get here from Rome or Milan, take a high-speed **Frecciarossa** or **Frecciargento** train (1½ hr.; www.trenitalia.com) or rival high-speed trains operated by **Italo** (www.italotreno.it). High-speed trains run from Venice (2 hr.) via Padua and Bologna; and also direct from Rome's Fiumicino Airport. On high-speed trains, you must sit in the seat prescribed on your reservation.

Most Florence-bound trains roll into **Stazione Santa Maria Novella,** Piazza della Stazione, which you'll see abbreviated as **S.M.N.** The station is an architectural masterpiece, albeit one dating to Italy's Fascist period, rather than the Renaissance. It lies on the northwestern edge of the city's compact historic center, a 10-minute walk from the Duomo and a brisk 15-minute walk from Piazza della Signoria and the Uffizi.

**BY CAR**   The **A1 autostrada** runs north from Rome past Arezzo to Florence and continues to Bologna. Unnumbered superhighways run to and from Siena (the *SI-FI raccordo*) and Pisa (the so-called *FI-PI-LI*). To reach Florence from Venice, take the A13 southbound, then switch to the A1 at Bologna.

Driving *to* Florence is easy; the problems begin once you arrive. Almost all cars are banned from the historic center for much of the time; only residents or merchants with special permits are allowed into this clearly marked, camera-patrolled *zona a trafico limitato* (ZTL). You can enter the ZTL to drop off baggage at your hotel or go direct to a prebooked parking garage (either can organize a temporary ZTL permit when provided with your license plate). Usual ZTL hours are Monday to Friday 7:30am to 8pm, Saturday 7:30am to 4pm. The ZTL also operates Thursday through Saturday evenings until 3am the following morning. It's a real hassle, so **only rent a car if you're leaving town to visit somewhere off the rail network.**

If you do drive here, your best bet for overnight or longer-term parking is one of the city-run garages. The best deal—better than most hotels' garage rates—is at the **Parterre parking lot** under Piazza Libertà at Via del Ponte Rosso 4 (✆ **055/5030-2209**). Open around the clock, it costs 2€ per hour, 15€ per day. Find more info on parking at **www.fipark.com**.

Don't park your car overnight on the streets in Florence without local knowledge. If you're ticketed and towed, the fine is hefty and the headaches to retrieve your car are beyond description—and a near-impossible task on weekends. If this happens to you, start by calling the vehicle removal department (**Recupero Veicoli Rimossi**) at ✆ **055/422-4142.** One more reason **you should not drive around Florence.**

## Visitor Information

**TOURIST OFFICES**   The most convenient tourist office is opposite Florence's main rail terminus at Piazza della Stazione 4. With your back to the tracks, take the left exit and then bear right; it's across the tram tracks and road junction ahead. This office is usually open Monday through Saturday 9am to 7pm and Sunday 9am to 2pm, and provides useful free street maps. Another

---

### Essential: Reservations for the Uffizi, Accademia & More

As soon as you set a date for your visit Florence, consider making advance reservations for the **Uffizi** and the **Accademia** museums—it's the best way to avoid spending hours in line, and walk-ups are either no longer allowed or strongly discouraged at many major museums. (Buying a cumulative ticket—see "Discount Tickets for Florence," above—is your other smart strategy.) Book via **Firenze Musei** at **www.uffizi. it**. This is the **only official ticketing agent for state museums:** Do not buy from elsewhere. There's a 4€ fee; you can pay by credit card. Reservations are also possible for the Galleria Palatina in the Pitti Palace, the Bargello, and several others. If you arrive in Florence without reservations, you can also reserve in person at a kiosk in the facade of Orsanmichele, on Via dei Calzaiuoli (Mon–Sat); or from the bookshop **Libreria My Accademia,** Via Ricasoli 105R (✆ **055/288-310**), almost opposite the Accademia (Tues–Sun). For prebooking timed-admission slots at city museums such as the Palazzo Vecchio or Cappella Brancacci, visit the city's separate ticketing hub at **ticketsmuse ums.comune.fi.it**.

The address system in Florence has a split personality. Private homes, some offices, and hotels are numbered in black (or blue), but businesses, shops, and restaurants are numbered independently in red. (That's the theory anyway. In reality, the division between black and red numbers isn't so clear-cut.) The result is that 1, 2, 3 (black) addresses march up the block numerically oblivious to their 1R, 2R, 3R (red) neighbors. You might find doorways on one side of a street numbered 1R, 2R, 3R, 1, 4R, 2, 3, 5R. The color codes occur only in the *centro storico* and other old sections of town. Outlying districts didn't bother with this confusing system.

office, close to Santa Croce church at Borgo Santa Croce 29R, is open the same hours. A third central office at Via Cavour 1R, two blocks north of the Duomo, is open only Monday through Friday 9am to 1pm. There's a central **phone number for all tourist assistance:** ✆ **055/000** (daily 9am–7pm).

**WEBSITES**  Florence's official tourism website, **www.feelflorence.it**, contains up-to-date information, including on local events. In the "Organize Your Trip" section of the site, you can download a PDF with opening hours for city sights; the document is updated and uploaded daily. The **Feel Florence app** is available for Android and Apple mobile devices. For one-off exhibitions and culture, **Art Trav** (www.arttrav.com) is an essential blog, written in English. For more Florence info, go to **www.frommers.com/destinations/florence**.

## City Layout

Florence is a smallish city, sitting on the Arno River and petering out rather quickly to olive-planted hills to the north and south, but extending farther west and east along the Arno valley with suburbs and light industry. Its compact center is best negotiated on foot. No two major sights are more than a 25-minute walk apart, and most of the hotels and restaurants in this chapter are in the relatively small *centro storico* (historic center), a compact tangle of medieval streets and *piazze* (squares) where visitors spend most of their time. The bulk of Florence, including most of the tourist sights, lies north of the river, with the **Oltrarno,** an old working artisans' neighborhood, hemmed in between the Arno and the hills on the south side.

## Florence Neighborhoods in Brief

**The Duomo**  The area surrounding Florence's gargantuan cathedral is as central as you can get. The Duomo itself is halfway between the churches of Santa Maria Novella and Santa Croce, as well as at the midpoint between the Uffizi Gallery to the south and the Accademia (home of Michelangelo's "David") to the north. A medieval tangle of streets south of the Duomo head toward Piazza della Signoria (see below). Southwest of the Duomo, Piazza della Repubblica lies in an even older part of town, still laid out in its Roman-era grid, though the square itself was "modernized" in the 19th century. It's also a bit of a tourist trap. The Duomo neighborhood is one of the most hotel-heavy parts of town, offering a range from luxury inns to student dives, but beware: Many hotels and restaurants here rely on location, rather than quality, for success.

**Piazza della Signoria**   The city's civic heart is prime territory for museum hounds: The Uffizi Gallery, Palazzo Vecchio, Bargello sculpture collection, and Ponte Vecchio are all nearby. A few blocks just north of the Ponte Vecchio have good shopping but unappealing modern buildings, thanks to post–World War II reconstruction. The neighborhood is crowded in peak season, but in rare moments when it's empty of tour groups, these narrow lanes remain the romantic heart of pre-Renaissance Florence. As in the Duomo neighborhood, be very choosy when picking a restaurant (or even an ice cream shop!) around here.

**San Lorenzo & the Mercato Centrale**   Centered on the Medici family church of San Lorenzo, this wedge of streets between the train station and the Duomo is market territory, with the vast indoor Mercato Centrale food hall and the San Lorenzo street market. It's a colorful but rarely quiet area, with many budget hotels and some very good, affordable dining.

**Piazza Santa Trínita**   This piazza is just north of the river at the south end of Florence's high-end shopping mecca, Via de' Tornabuoni. It's a quaint, well-to-do, and still medieval neighborhood—and if you're a shopping fiend, there's no better place to be.

**Santa Maria Novella**   Bounding the western edge of the *centro storico*, this neighborhood has two characters: a bland, busy zone around the train station and a nicer area south of it. The noisy rail-station area lacks atmosphere, but it does have more budget hotel options than any other quarter,

especially around Via Faenza. Try to avoid staying on traffic-heavy Via Nazionale. The situation improves dramatically as you head south, where Piazza Santa Maria Novella and its tributary streets have several stylish hotels.

**San Marco & Santissima Annunziata**   On the northern edge of the *centro storico*, you'll find Piazza San Marco, a busy transport hub; and Piazza Santissima Annunziata, the city's most architecturally unified square. The neighborhood is home to Florence's university, the Accademia, the San Marco paintings of Fra Angelico, and quiet streets with some hotel gems. It's just far enough from the action to escape tourist crowds.

**Santa Croce**   Few tourists roam east beyond Piazza Santa Croce, so if you want to feel like a Florentine, head here. Streets around the Mercato di Sant'Ambrogio get lively after dark, especially Via Pietrapiana and the northern end of Via de' Macci. Some of the city's best restaurants and bars are here; aperitivo time is vibrant along Via de' Benci.

**The Oltrarno, San Niccolò & San Frediano**   "Across the Arno" is the artisans' neighborhood, and still dotted with workshops. It began as a working-class neighborhood to catch overflow from the medieval city, and later became a chic area for aristocrats to build palaces with country views. The largest of these, the Pitti Palace, today houses a set of paintings second only to the Uffizi. The Oltrarno's tree-shaded center, Piazza Santo Spirito, is surrounded with great restaurants and nightlife. West of here, the neighborhood of San Frediano is ever more fashionable, and San Niccolò at the foot of Florence's southern hills has popular bars. Oltrarno's hotel range isn't great, but you can eat and drink better here than in the *centro storico*.

## Getting Around Florence

Florence is a **walking** city. You can stroll between the two top sights, Piazza del Duomo and the Uffizi, in 5 minutes or so. The hike from the most northerly major sights, San Marco and the Accademia, to the most southerly, the

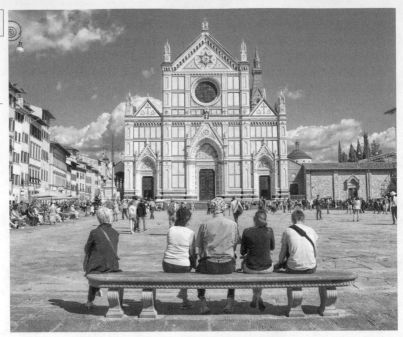

The area around Piazza Santa Croce has a genuine neighborhood feel.

Pitti Palace across the Arno, will take no more than 25 minutes for most. From Santa Maria Novella eastward to Santa Croce is a flat 20- to 30-minute walk. But beware: **Flagstones,** some of them uneven, are everywhere. Wear sensible shoes with good padding and foot support.

**BY BUS & TRAM**　You'll rarely need Florence's efficient **AT Bus** network (www.at-bus.it; ✆ **800/142424** in Italy) since the city is so compact. Bus tickets cost 1.50€ (2.50€ on board) and are good for 90 minutes, irrespective of how many changes you make (even if you switch to a tram). Tickets are sold at *tabacchi* (tobacconists), automatic machines, some bars, and most newsstands. *Note:* Once on board, validate a paper ticket in the box to avoid a steep fine. Since traffic is restricted in most of the center, buses make runs on principal streets only, except for four tiny electric bus lines (*bussini* services C1–4) that trundle about the *centro storico*. The most useful routes to outlying areas are no. 7 (for Fiesole) and nos. 12 and 13 (for Piazzale Michelangelo). Buses run from 7am until 9 or 9:30pm daily, with a limited night service on a few key routes.

　**Tram** lines (www.gestramvia.com) run until after midnight. Route T1 connects Santa Maria Novella station with the Opera di Firenze, Cascine Park, and Florence's southwestern suburbs. Line T2 and the T1 extension head northward from the station: T2 to Peretola airport and T1 to Careggi via the Fortezza.

**BY TAXI**   Taxis aren't cheap, and with the city so small and the one-way system forcing drivers on convoluted routes, they aren't an economical way to get about. They are most useful to get you and your bags between the train station and a hotel. It's 3.30€ to start the meter (which rises to 5.30€ on Sun, or to 6.60€ 10pm–6am), plus 1€ per bag or for a fourth passenger in the cab. Taxi stands are outside the train station, on Borgo San Jacopo, and in Piazza Santa Croce; otherwise, call **Radio Taxi SOCOTA** at ⓒ **055/4242** (hail a cab by WhatsApp on ⓒ **334/662-2550**), or **Radio Taxi COTAFI** at ⓒ **055/4390.** For the latest tariff information, see **www.4242.it**.

**BY BICYCLE & SCOOTER**   Florence had already begun expanding its network of marked cycle lanes before the pandemic, and the project has accelerated since. The app-powered, dockless **bike-sharing** scheme **Movi by Mobike** (www.ridemovi.com) operates in Florence. When you've downloaded the app and registered, you're free to rent: Simply scan the QR code and ride. All payments are handled inside the app, which also displays prices for longer rentals (from 1€ per 20 min.). The Movi fleet includes standard city bikes and e-bikes.

Fully electric, Italian-made e-scooters can also be rented by the minute, hour, or full day using a similar dockless sharing scheme. You can register for **MiMoto** (www.mimoto.it) at the website or by using the app.

In addition, a handful of private bike-rental specialists are located around San Lorenzo and San Marco, including **Florence by Bike,** Via San Zanobi 54R (www.florencebybike.it; ⓒ **055/488-992**), which rents city bikes (12€ per day), as well as touring bikes (29€) and e-bikes (39€). Multiday rentals work out cheaper. Advanced reservations are essential. They also provide detailed route maps for rides into the hills north and south of the center. Make sure to use the lock provided with your rental: Bike theft is depressingly common.

**BY CAR**   Trying to drive in the *centro storico* is a frustrating, useless exercise, and moreover, for most of the time unauthorized cars will be fined if they enter the restricted traffic zone (ZTL). You need a permit to do anything beyond dropping off and picking up bags at your hotel. Park your vehicle in one of the underground lots on the center's periphery and pound the sidewalk. (See "By Car" under "Arriving," p. 148.)

# [FastFACTS] FLORENCE

**Business Hours**   Hours mainly follow the Italian norm (see p. 306), although many larger and/or central shops stay open through the midday *riposo* (note the sign ORARIO NONSTOP).

**Doctors & Dentists**
Tourist-oriented **Medical Service Firenze,** at Via

Roma 4 (www.medicalservice.firenze.it; ⓒ **055/475-411**), is usually open without an appointment Monday to Friday 11am to noon, 1 to 3pm, and 5 to 6pm; Saturday 11am to noon and 1 to 3pm. During pandemic restrictions, **all visits should be arranged in advance by**

**phone.** A similar rule operates at **Dr. Stephen Kerr,** Piazza Mercato Nuovo 1 (www.dr-kerr.com; ⓒ **335/836-1682** or 055/288-055), open Monday to Friday 3 to 5pm without an appointment (appointments are available 9am–3pm). His consultation fee is 77€, or 49€ if you show student ID.

**Hospitals** The most central hospital is **Santa Maria Nuova,** a block northeast of the Duomo on Piazza Santa Maria Nuova (www.uslcentro.toscana.it; © **055/69-381**), with an emergency room (*pronto soccorso*) open 24 hours. **Do not walk into any hospital if you are showing Covid-19 symptoms;** instead, call the national coronavirus advice line on © **1500.**

**Left Luggage** At Santa Maria Novella Station, you can leave luggage at **KiPoint** (www.kipoint.it), open daily 6am to 11pm; the cost is 6€ per item for the first 5 hours, 1€ per hour

thereafter. Even cheaper (1€/hr.; 6€/day) is **Left Luggage Florence,** Via de' Boni 5R (www.leftluggage florence.com).

**Mail** Florence's **main post office** (© **055/273-6481**) is at Via Pellicceria 3, off the southwest corner of Piazza della Repubblica. It's open Monday to Friday 8:20am to 1:35pm and Saturday 8:20am to 12:35pm.

**Pharmacies** There is a 24-hour pharmacy (also open Sun and state holidays) in **Stazione Santa Maria Novella** (© **055/216-761;** ring the bell across from the taxi rank 11pm–7am). On holidays and at night, look for the sign in any pharmacy window

telling you which ones are open locally.

**Police** To report a crime or a lost passport, call the *questura* (police headquarters) at © **055/49-771.** General lost property might find its way to the *Ufficio oggetti ritrovati:* © **055/334-802.**

**Safety** As in any city, pickpockets are a risk in Florence, often light-fingered youngsters (especially around the train station). Otherwise it's a fairly safe city, but steer clear of the Cascine Park after dark, and in the wee hours when nightlife is finished, avoid the area around Piazza Santo Spirito and the backstreets behind Santa Croce.

# WHERE TO STAY IN FLORENCE

Even before the pandemic, a fast-growing stock of hotel beds had kept lodging prices in Florence stable in recent years. But the pandemic hit small hotels and B&Bs hard, and it remains difficult to find a high-season double you'd want to sleep in for much less than 100€. Once-irresistible August deals have mostly dried up: Florence no longer seems to get much quieter in its hottest month. Rooms everywhere are smaller than many North American travelers are used to.

In 2020, Florence's government increased the additional city tourist levy on room bookings. It now costs an extra 3€ to 5€ **per person per night,** depending on the hotel's official star rating, for the first 7 nights of any stay. It is payable on departure and is not usually included in quoted rates. Children below age 12 are exempt from the tax. Airbnb and other holiday rentals are **not** exempt.

Peak hotel season is Easter through early July, September through late October, and Christmas through January 6. May, June, and September are very popular; January and February are the months to grab a bargain—never be shy to haggle if you're coming then. A room at 140€ in June could be as low as 50€ in February, especially if you stay multiple nights. **Booking direct** via phone, e-mail, or the hotel's own website is often key to unlocking the lowest rates or complimentary extras.

To help you decide in which area you'd like to base yourself, consult "Florence Neighborhoods in Brief," p. 150. Note that we have included parking information below only for those places that offer it. Note, too, that many hotels offer babysitting services, but almost always "on request." At least a couple of days' notice is advisable—and like almost any hotel service, this may be curtailed if the pandemic resurges. Minibars have mostly disappeared, at least for now. Many hotels offer table or room service at breakfast instead of a buffet. Safe operation and cleaning protocols have been put in place at all reputable accommodations; check individual booking websites for details.

## Apartment Rentals & Alternative Accommodations

It's the way of the modern world: Global players in apartment rentals have overtaken most of the local specialists in Florence. **HomeAway.com**, TripAdvisor–owned **HolidayLettings.co.uk**, **Airbnb**, and others are well stocked with central and suburban apartments. Online agency **Cross Pollinate ★** (www.cross-pollinate.com; ✆ **800/270-1190** in U.S., 06/9936-9799 in Italy) has built a Florence apartment portfolio over 2 decades. Apartments are all handpicked and service is personal from the Rome-based team. The budget range is especially good.

*Tip:* For basic grocery shopping in the center, try PAM Local, Via Cavour 66R, or any central branch of Carrefour Express or Conad City. Both the Mercato Centrale and Mercato di Sant'Ambrogio sell farm-fresh produce (see "Florence's Best Markets," p. 204).

An alternative budget option (offering a unique perspective) is to stay in a **religious house ★**. A few monasteries and convents in the center receive guests for a modest fee. Our favorites are the **Suore di Santa Elisabetta,** Viale Michelangiolo 46 (near Piazza Ferrucci; ✆ **055/681-1884**), in a colonial villa just south of the Ponte San Niccolò; and close to Santa Croce, the **Istituto Oblate dell'Assunzione,** Borgo Pinti 15 (✆ **055/2480-582**), which has simple, peaceful rooms in a Medici-era building ranged around a courtyard garden. The easiest way to build a monastery and convent itinerary in Florence and beyond is via agent **MonasteryStays.com ★**. Note that most religious houses have a curfew, generally 11pm or midnight.

## Hotels by Price
### EXPENSIVE

Continentale ★★★, p. 160
Grand Hotel Minerva ★★, p.160
Palazzo Tolomei ★★★, p. 159
Residence Hilda ★★, p. 162

### MODERATE

Alessandra ★★, p. 160
Antica Dimora Johlea ★, p. 163
Davanzati ★★, p. 160
Garibaldi Blu ★★, p. 161
Il Guelfo Bianco ★★, p. 159
La Casa di Morfeo ★, p. 163

La Dimora degli Angeli ★★★, p. 158
Loggiato dei Serviti ★★, p. 162
L'Orologio ★, p. 161
Morandi alla Crocetta ★★, p. 163
Palazzo Galletti ★★, p. 158
Residenza della Signoria ★, p. 158
Riva Lofts ★★, p. 164

### INEXPENSIVE

Alloro ★★, p. 159
Soggiorno Battistero ★, p. 158
Tourist House Ghiberti ★, p. 163

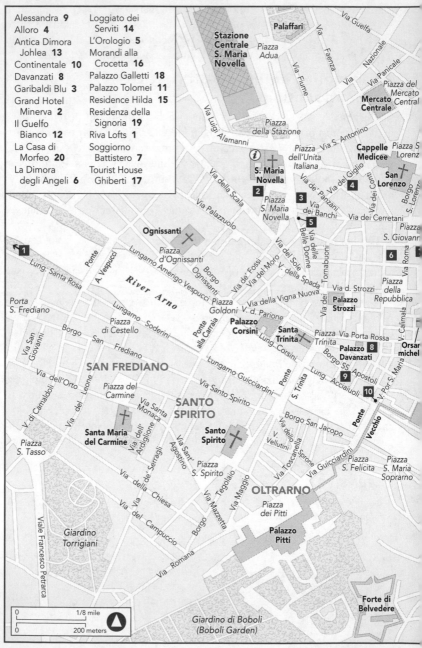

| | |
|---|---|
| Alessandra **9** | Loggiato dei |
| Alloro **4** | Serviti **14** |
| Antica Dimora | L'Orologio **5** |
| Johlea **13** | Morandi alla |
| Continentale **10** | Crocetta **16** |
| Davanzati **8** | Palazzo Galletti **18** |
| Garibaldi Blu **3** | Palazzo Tolomei **11** |
| Grand Hotel | Residence Hilda **15** |
| Minerva **2** | Residenza della |
| Il Guelfo | Signoria **19** |
| Bianco **12** | Riva Lofts **1** |
| La Casa di | Soggiorno |
| Morfeo **20** | Battistero **7** |
| La Dimora | Tourist House |
| degli Angeli **6** | Ghiberti **17** |

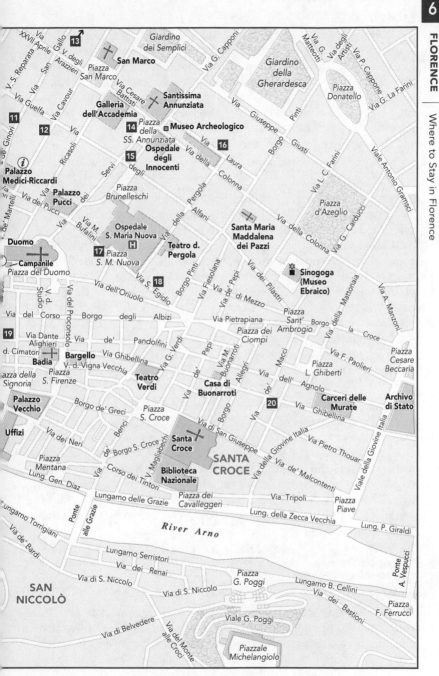

# Near the Duomo
## MODERATE

**La Dimora degli Angeli** ★★★  This B&B occupies two levels of a grand apartment building in one of the city's busiest shopping districts. Rooms on the original floor are for romantics; bright wallpaper contrasts pleasingly with iron-framed beds and classic furniture. (Beatrice is the largest, with a view of Brunelleschi's dome—just.) The floor below is totally different, with sharp lines and leather or wooden headboards throughout. Breakfast is available at a local cafe—or if you prefer, you can grab a coffee in the B&B and use your token for a light lunch instead.

Via Brunelleschi 4. www.dimoredeicherubini.it. ⓒ **055/288-478.** 12 units. 58€–198€ double. Breakfast (at cafe) 7€–12€. Parking 26€. Bus: C2. **Amenities:** Wi-Fi (free).

**Palazzo Galletti** ★★  Not many hotels within a sensible budget give you the chance to live like a Florentine noble. Rooms here have towering ceilings and an uncluttered arrangement of carefully chosen antiques. Most have frescoed or painted-wood showpiece ceilings. Bathrooms, in contrast, have a contemporary design, decked out in travertine and marble. Aside from two street-facing suites, every room has a small balcony, ideal for a pre-dinner glass of wine. If you're here for a once-in-a-lifetime trip, spring for the large suites "Giove" or (especially) "Cerere"; the latter has walls covered in frescoes from the 1800s. Snag a free bottle of their own organic estate wine when you book direct and show this Frommer's guide.

Via Sant'Egidio 12. www.palazzogalletti.it. ⓒ **055/390-5750.** 11 units. 100€–170€ double; 170€–240€ suite. Rates include breakfast. Parking 30€–35€. Bus: C1, C2, 14, 23. **Amenities:** Babysitting; Wi-Fi (free).

**Residenza della Signoria** ★  Location and value take center-stage at this small inn on an upper floor of an old palace. It's right on Florence's main drag, but thanks to modern soundproofing you'd never know. Rooms are spacious with antique-styled furnishings and ceilings, parquet flooring, luscious drapes, and king-size beds with firm mattresses. Only the junior suites have a proper panorama of Brunelleschi's cathedral dome, but for a smaller outlay, room 6 has a view from its bathroom window. A simple but tasty Continental breakfast is served next door at one of our favorite cafe-bars, **Cantinetta dei Verrazzano** (p. 207).

Via dei Tavolini 8. www.residenzadellasignoria.com. ⓒ **055/264-5990.** 7 units. 89€–159€ double. Some rates include breakfast in cafe (otherwise 3.50€). Parking 25€. Bus: C2. **Amenities:** Wi-Fi (free).

## INEXPENSIVE

**Soggiorno Battistero** ★  The Baptistery is almost close enough to touch when you take a room with a view at this super-central B&B—a modest investment you'll remember forever. Location and value are hard to beat: You lodge mere paces from the Duomo steps. Rooms are simple and spacious (though some bathrooms are a squeeze), with traditional decor of terracotta tiling and antique armoires. The square below can be noisy at night, but soundproofing keeps the racket out. Note the early checkout time: 10:30am.

Piazza San Giovanni 1. www.soggiornobattistero.it. ℭ **349/552-5390.** 6 units. 70€– 230€ double. Rates include breakfast. Bus: C2. **Amenities:** Free Wi-Fi.

## Near San Lorenzo & the Mercato Centrale

### EXPENSIVE

**Palazzo Tolomei** ★★★ In its heyday, this palace was at the heart of Medici power. In 1505 it even welcomed the painter Raphael as a guest (probably in two rooms at the front, now Barocco 1 and 2). Guest rooms are all large, with Renaissance wooden ceilings and terracotta floors. Modern fittings—leather sofas, soft mattresses, and florid crystal chandeliers—chime perfectly with a 17th-century baroque redecoration, complete with ceiling frescoes by Alessandro Gherardini. The lower floor is given over to opulent public rooms, just like when it was the *piano nobile* of the family palazzo. These days you'll find a music room, art books, a welcoming host, and probably an open bottle of Tuscan red wine. Book direct for deals—perhaps free nightly *aperitivo,* free late checkout, or a discounted room rate.

Via de' Ginori 19. www.palazzotolomei.it.ℭ **055/292-887.** 8 units. 120€–378€ double. Rates include breakfast (in nearby cafe). Bus: C1. **Amenities:** Concierge; Wi-Fi (free).

### MODERATE

**Il Guelfo Bianco** ★★ Decor in this former noble home retains its authentic palazzo feel, though carpets have been added for comfort and warmth and there's full hotel service. No two rooms are the same—stone walls this thick cannot be knocked through—and several have antiques integrated into their individual schemes. Grand rooms at the front (especially 101, 118, and 228) have Renaissance coffered ceilings and masses of space. Sleep at the back and you'll wake to an unusual sound in Florence: birdsong.

Via Cavour 29 (near corner of Via Guelfa). www.ilguelfobianco.it.ℭ **055/288-330.** 40 units. 90€–280€ double. Rates include breakfast. Parking 27€–33€. Bus: C1, 14, 23. **Amenities:** Restaurant; bar; babysitting; room service; Wi-Fi (free).

### INEXPENSIVE

**Alloro** ★★ Officially a "bed-and-breakfast," this feels more like a small hotel, whose modern rooms inside a Renaissance palace overlook a silent inner courtyard—neatly soundproofing them in a noisy neighborhood. Rooms offer an excellent value for the price and location, with high ceilings, color-washed walls, and air-conditioning. Breakfast is a traditional spread of fresh fruit and pastries. A friendly ghost from the Renaissance era reputedly roams part of the palace; you're unlikely to get a discount if you spot him, but there's no harm in asking.

Via del Giglio 8. www.allorobb.it. ℭ **055/211-685.** 5 units. 62€–183€ double. Rates include breakfast. Bus: C1. **Amenities:** Concierge; Wi-Fi (free).

# Near the Ponte Vecchio
## EXPENSIVE

**Continentale ★★★** Everything about the Continentale is cool, and the effect is achieved without even a hint of frostiness. Rooms are uncompromisingly modern, decorated in bright white and bathed in natural light. Deluxe units, which are built into a medieval riverside tower, have mighty walls and medieval-size windows (that is, small). Standard rooms are large (for Florence), and there's a retro-1950s feel to the overall styling. Communal areas are a major hit, too: A relaxation room has a glass wall with a front-row view of the Ponte Vecchio. Seasonal **Terrazza** (p. 208) is our favorite rooftop cocktail bar in the city.

Vicolo dell'Oro 6R. www.lungarnocollection.com. ⓒ **055/27-262.** 43 units. 230€–750€ double. Parking 35€. Bus: C3 or C4. **Amenities:** Bar; concierge; spa; Wi-Fi (free).

## MODERATE

**Alessandra ★★** This typical Florentine *pensione* transports you back to the age of the gentleman and lady traveler. Decor has grown organically since it opened as a hotel in 1950; Alessandra is a place for evolution, not revolution. A pleasing mix of styles is the result: some rooms have carved headboards, gilt frames, and gold damask; others eclectic postwar furniture, like a midcentury period movie set. A couple have views of the Arno, while frontside rooms overlook Borgo SS. Apostoli, one of the center's most atmospheric streets. Five additional rooms with all-out contemporary decor—including, across the street, two mezzanine mini-apartments with kitchenettes—have a separate website, **www.residenzaalessandra.com**.

Borgo SS. Apostoli 17. www.hotelalessandra.com. ⓒ **055/283-438.** 27 units. 160€–180€ double. Rates include breakfast. Parking 25€. Bus: C3, C4, 6, 11, 36, 37. Closed a few days around Christmas. **Amenities:** Wi-Fi (free).

**Davanzati ★★** Although installed inside a historic building, the Davanzati never rests on its medieval laurels: There is a laptop and an iPad with cellular data in every room for free guest use around the city, and movies to stream to your TV. Rooms are simply decorated in the Tuscan style, with color-washed walls and half-canopies over the beds. Room 100 is probably the best family hotel room in Florence, full of nooks, crannies, and split-levels that give adults and the kids some private space. A free *aperitivo* for guests is part of the Davanzati's family welcome.

Via Porta Rossa 5 (on Piazza Davanzati). www.hoteldavanzati.it. ⓒ **055/286-666.** 27 units. 99€–216€ double. Rates include breakfast. Parking 26€. Bus: C2. **Amenities:** Bar; babysitting; concierge; use of nearby gym; Wi-Fi (free).

# Near Santa Maria Novella
## EXPENSIVE

**Grand Hotel Minerva ★★** American poet Henry Wadsworth Longfellow stayed in lodgings on the site of this hotel, on what is now one of Florence's most prestigious squares. I doubt the service he experienced was

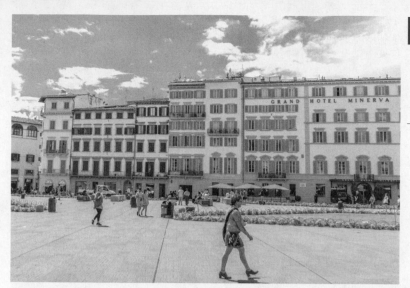

The Grand Hotel Minerva presides over Piazza Santa Maria Novella.

anywhere near the international corporate standards now set here. Quietly stylish rooms were mostly revamped in 2016, with cream tones, natural wood, tan leather, and travertine bathrooms. Each one is well soundproofed against neighbors and outdoor noise. A major bonus from May to September: a rooftop pool with panoramic sundeck, bar, and evening *aperitivo* service.

Piazza Santa Maria Novella 16. www.grandhotelminerva.com. ℂ**055/27-230.** 97 units. 240€–465€ double. Parking 30€–40€. Bus: C2, 6, 11, or 22. **Amenities:** Restaurant; 2 bars; concierge; outdoor pool; use of nearby gym; Wi-Fi (free).

## MODERATE

**Garibaldi Blu ★★**   The hotels of Piazza Santa Maria Novella are frequented by fashion models, rock stars, and blue-chip business folk. You can get a taste of that, for a fraction of the price, at this boutique hotel with attitude. Each of the mostly midsized rooms has a "warm denim" palette, with retro 1970s furniture, parquet floors, and marble bathrooms. It's well worth paying 30€ extra for a deluxe room at the front: These have much more space and a view over Florence's prettiest church facade, Santa Maria Novella. Dotted around the hotel, life-size models of superheroes like Captain America add a fun surreal touch.

Piazza Santa Maria Novella 21. www.hotelgaribaldiblu.com. ℂ**055/277-300.** 21 units. 130€–350€ double. Rates include breakfast. Parking 35€–48€. Bus: C2, 6, 11, 22. **Amenities:** Bar; babysitting (prebooking essential); concierge; Wi-Fi (free).

**L'Orologio ★**   As the name suggests, this hotel is an homage to the clock, with historic timepiece designs scattered artfully about. The color palette is rich, with mahogany wood and natural leather everywhere. The cheapest rooms ("superior") are not large, but their marble bathrooms are, and library-like wood-paneled common areas are spacious and comfortable. Staff is superb. L'Orologio is atmospheric and close to the train station; the view from its top-floor breakfast room is a showstopper.

Piazza Santa Maria Novella 24. www.hotelorologioflorence.com. ℂ **055/277-380.** 55 units. 95€–350€ double. Rates include breakfast. Parking 35€–48€. Bus: C2, 6, 11, 22. **Amenities:** Bar; babysitting; concierge; gym; sauna; Wi-Fi (free).

## Near Santissima Annunziata
### EXPENSIVE

**Residence Hilda ★★**    With no hint of the Renaissance, these luxe mini-apartments are all bright-white decor and designer furnishings, with natural wood flooring, hypoallergenic mattresses, Starck chairs, and modern gadgetry. Each is spacious, cool in summer, and soundproofed against Florence's perma-noise. Every unit has a mini-kitchen equipped for preparing a simple meal—ideal if you have kids in tow. The top-floor Executive unit has a Nespresso machine, yoga mat, and an exercise bike. *Bonus:* Unusual for apartments, all are bookable by the single night.

Via dei Servi 40. www.residencehilda.com.ℂ **055/288-021.** 12 units. 90€–400€ for 2- to 4-person apartment. Parking 31€. Bus: C1. **Amenities:** Airport transfer; babysitting; concierge; room service; Wi-Fi (free).

### MODERATE

**Loggiato dei Serviti ★★**    Stay here to experience Florence as the gentleman and lady visitors of the Grand Tour did. For starters, the building is a genuine Renaissance landmark, built by Sangallo the Elder in the 1520s. There is a sense of faded grandeur and unconventional luxury throughout—no gadgetry or chromatherapy showers, but you will find rooms with writing desks and bags of vintage ambience. No unit is small, but standard rooms are missing a view, of either Brunelleschi's dome or the perfect piazza outside. Air-conditioning is pretty much the only concession to the 21st century—and you will love it that way. Book direct for the best deal.

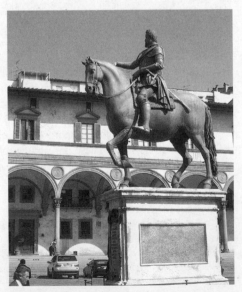

Piazza Santissima Annunziata 3. www.loggiatodeiservitihotel.it. ℂ **055/289-592.** 37 units. 120€–330€ double. Rates include breakfast. Valet parking 22€. Bus: C1, 6, 14, 19, 23, 31, 32. **Amenities:** Babysitting; concierge; Wi-Fi (free).

Loggiato dei Serviti overlooks Piazza Santissima Annunziata.

**Morandi alla Crocetta** ★★ Like many Florence inns, Morandi alla Crocetta was built in the shell of a former convent, and it has retained the original convent layout, meaning some rooms are snug. But what you lose in size, you more than gain in character: Every single one oozes *tipico fiorentino*—even the "new" breakfast room feels like you're on the Grand Tour. Rooms have parquet floors, throw rugs, and antique wood furniture. Original 1744 Zocchi prints of Florence are scattered around the place. Superior rooms have more space and either a private courtyard terrace or, in one, original frescoes decorating an entrance to the former convent chapel (the chapel itself is sealed off). The hotel is set on a quiet street.

Via Laura 50. www.hotelmorandi.it.© **055/234-4747.** 12 units. 90€–177€ double. Rates include breakfast. Parking 25€. Bus: 6, 19, 31, 32. **Amenities:** Bar; babysitting; concierge; Wi-Fi (free).

### INEXPENSIVE

**Tourist House Ghiberti** ★ A pleasing mix of traditional and modern prevails at this backstreet guesthouse named after a famous former resident: The creator of the Baptistery's "Gates of Paradise" had workshops on the top floor of this *palazzo*. Rooms have plenty of space, with herringbone terracotta floors, whitewashed walls, and high, painted wood ceilings in a vaguely Renaissance style. E-mail direct for the best room rate.

Via M. Bufalini 1. www.touristhouseghiberti.com. © **055/284-858.** 6 units. 64€–179€ double. Rates include breakfast. Parking 20€–30€. Bus: C1. **Amenities:** Wi-Fi (free).

## Near Santa Croce
### MODERATE

**La Casa di Morfeo** ★ For a cheery, affordable room in the lively eastern part of the center, look no further than this small hotel on the second floor of a grand, shuttered palace. There is no huge difference in quality among the guest rooms: All are midsized, with modern gadgetry, and painted in bright, contemporary colors, each individual scheme corresponding to a flower after which the room is named. Our favorite is Mimosa, painted in light mustard, with a ceiling fresco and a view over Via Ghibellina. Colored lighting adds a sense of fun.

Via Ghibellina 51. www.lacasadimorfeo.it. © **055/241-193.** 9 units. 79€–189€ double. Rates include breakfast. Parking 25€. Bus: C2 or C3. **Amenities:** Wi-Fi (free).

## North of the Center
### MODERATE

**Antica Dimora Johlea** ★ There's a real neighborhood feel to the streets around this *dimora* (traditional Florentine home) guesthouse, which means evenings are lively and Sundays are quiet (although it's less than a 10-min. walk to San Lorenzo). Standard-size rooms are snug; upgrade to a deluxe if you need more space, but there is no difference in the standard of decor, a mix of Florentine and earthy boho. Head up to a roof terrace for knockout views over the terracotta rooftops to the center and hills beyond.

Dusk is pure magic as the scent of lavender drifts by on the evening breeze. No credit cards.

Via San Gallo 80. www.antichedimorefiorentine.it. ✆ **055/463-3292.** 6 units. 90€–220€ double. Rates include breakfast. Parking 25€. Bus: C1, 1, 6, 11, 14, 17, 23. **Amenities:** Bar; Wi-Fi (free).

## West of the Center
### MODERATE

**Riva Lofts ★★**  The traditional Florentine alarm call—a morning mix of traffic and tourism—is replaced by birdsong when you awake in one of these stylish rooms on the banks of the River Arno. A former artisan workshop, Riva had a refit to earn its "loft" label. Mellow colors predominate, with laminate flooring, floating staircases, marble bathrooms with rainfall showers, and clever integration of natural materials such as original wooden workshop ceilings. Noon checkouts are standard—a traveler-friendly touch. The center is a 30-minute walk, or hop on one of Riva's vintage-style bikes and cycle along the river to the Uffizi. Another standout feature in this price bracket: a shaded garden with outdoor plunge pool.

Via Baccio Bandinelli 98. www.rivalofts.com. ✆ **055/713-0272.** 10 units. 145€–335€ double. Rates include breakfast. Parking 20€. Bus: 6. Tram: T1 (3 stops from central station). **Amenities:** Bar; bike rental (free); outdoor pool; Wi-Fi (free).

# WHERE TO EAT IN FLORENCE

Florence is well supplied with restaurants, though in the most touristy areas (around the Duomo, Piazza della Signoria, Piazza della Repubblica, and the Ponte Vecchio), you must choose carefully—many eateries are of below-average quality or charge high prices, sometimes both. The highest concentrations of excellent *ristoranti* and *trattorie* are east of Santa Croce around **Piazza Ghiberti,** and across the river in the **Oltrarno** and **San Frediano.** There's much improved dining around **San Lorenzo** since the reopening of the Mercato Centrale top floor (see p. 171) with a wealth of street-food counters. The city has also become much more **gluten-savvy.** If you have a food intolerance, just ask. **Vegan** food is widely available.

   **Reservations** are strongly recommended if you have your heart set on somewhere in particular, especially at dinner on weekends. Bear in mind that restaurant menus can change weekly or even daily. Opening hours may be trimmed during a Covid-19 spike; below, we list the "usual" schedules, but check individual websites or call ahead to verify. For the foreseeable future, eating at an indoor table will require you to prove you have been vaccinated. *Tip:* You can book at many Florence restaurants, including several of our favorites below, via **The Fork** (www.thefork.it) or **Quandoo** (www.quandoo.it).

**FLORENTINE CUISINE**  Florentine cuisine is increasingly cosmopolitan, but flavors are often Tuscan at heart. Even in fine restaurants, meals may kick off with country concoctions like *ribollita* (seasonal vegetable stew) before moving on to the chargrilled delights of a *bistecca alla fiorentina* (Florentine beefsteak on the bone), washed down with a robust **Chianti Classico.** A plate of cold cuts and Pecorino cheese makes a classic light lunch, or for the adventurous, *lampredotto alla fiorentina,* a sandwich of cow's stomach stewed in tomatoes and garlic.

## Restaurants by Cuisine

### CAFES
Cantinetta dei Verrazzano ★★, p. 207
Ditta Artigianale ★★, p. 208
La Menagère ★, p. 208
Procacci ★, p. 208
Rivoire ★, p. 208
Terrazza-Rooftop @Rinascente ★,
  p. 208

### FLORENTINE
Bondi ★, p. 170
Da Rocco ★, p. 172
Da Tito ★★, p. 171
Il Magazzino ★, p. 173
La Gratella ★★, p. 170
Mario ★, p. 170

### GELATO
Gelateria della Passera ★★, p. 174
Gelateria de' Neri ★, p. 175
La Carraia ★★, p. 175

### GRILL
La Gratella ★★, p. 170
Il Nutino ★★, p. 170

### JAPANESE
Koto Ramen ★, p. 172

### LIGHT FARE/SANDWICHES
Bondi ★, p. 170
I Due Fratellini ★, p. 168

Pugi ★, p. 171
SandwiChic ★★, p. 171

### MODERN ITALIAN
A Crudo ★, p. 173
Fishing Lab Alle Murate ★★, p. 168
Il Santo Bevitore ★, p. 174
Mercato Centrale ★★, p. 171

### MODERN TUSCAN
iO: Osteria Personale ★★★, p. 172
Osteria dell'Enoteca ★★★, p. 174
Osteria di Giovanni ★★, p. 169

### PIZZA
Gustarium ★★, p. 165
Mercato Centrale ★★, p. 171

### RAW FOOD
A Crudo ★, p. 173
Fishing Lab Alle Murate ★★, p. 168

### SEAFOOD
Fishing Lab Alle Murate ★★, p. 168

### TRADITIONAL TUSCAN
Coquinarius ★★, p. 165
Da Tito ★★, p. 171
Il Nutino ★★, p. 170
Osteria del Porcellino ★, p. 169

### VEGETARIAN/VEGAN
Brac ★★, p. 171

## Near the Duomo

For a lunchtime slice of fresh pizza on the move, call in at **Gustarium ★★,** Via de' Cimatori 24R (✆ **055/283-469**), where toppings are modern and creative, and all ingredients are organic. Official closing time is 5pm, but Gustarium shutters when the pizza runs out—often by midafternoon.

### MODERATE
**Coquinarius ★★** TUSCAN   There is a regular menu here, offering pasta, main courses (such as beef cheeks with red wine and caramelized onions), and traditional desserts. But it's equally pleasurable just tucking into a couple of sharing plates and quaffing from the excellent wine list. Go for something from an extensive carpaccio selection (beef, boar, octopus, swordfish), and

A Crudo **10**
Bondi **2**
Brac **15**
Coquinarius **19**
Da Rocco **22**
Da Tito **25**
Fishing Lab
  Alle Murate **20**
Gelateria della
  Passera **13**
Gelateria de'
  Neri **16**
Gustarium **18**
I Due Fratellini **17**
Il Magazzino **12**
Il Nutino **5**
Il Santo
  Bevitore **9**

iO: Osteria
  Personale **7**
Koto Ramen **21**
La Carraia **8**
La Gratella **1**
Mario **4**
Mercato
  Centrale **3**
Osteria dell'
  Enoteca **11**
Osteria del
  Porcellino **14**
Osteria di
  Giovanni **6**
Pugi **24**
SandwiChic **23**

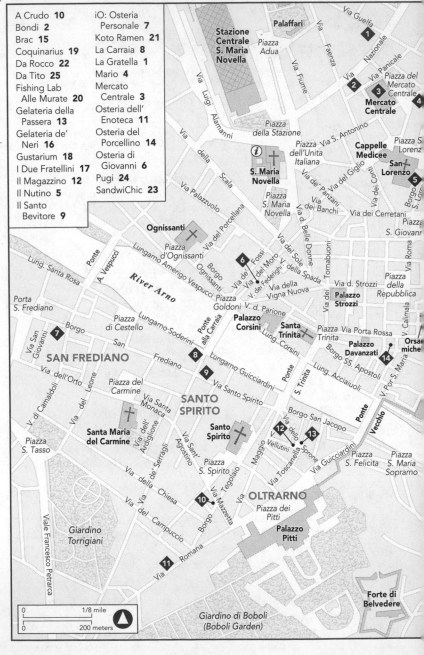

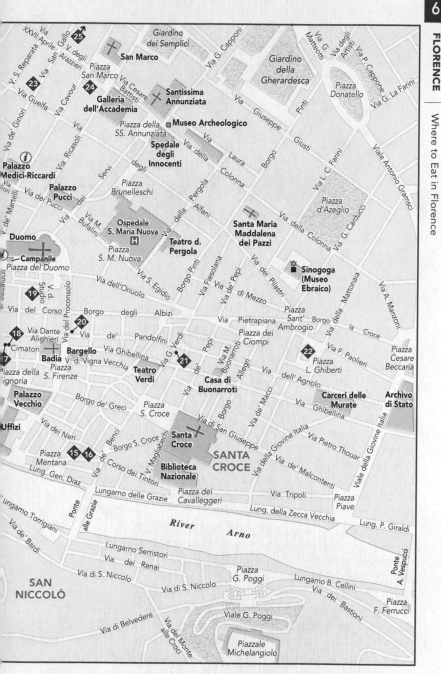

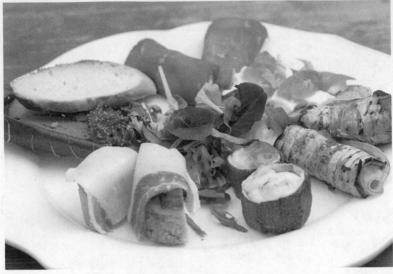

A plate of mixed appetizers at Coquinarius.

maybe pair a *misto di salumi e formaggi* (mixed Tuscan salami and cheeses) with a full-bodied red wine, to cut through the strong flavors of the deliciously fatty, salty pork and Tuscan sheep's milk cheese, pecorino.

Via delle Oche 11R. www.coquinarius.it. ⓒ **055/230-2153.** Entrees 15€–20€. Daily 12:30–3pm and 6:30–10:30pm. Bus: C1 or C2.

**Fishing Lab Alle Murate ★★** SEAFOOD/MODERN ITALIAN   This contemporary-styled temple to seafood serves fish any way you like (almost). Shrimp, tuna, bream, bass, and salmon dominate; fish are carefully sourced and preparation is modern. Tartare and carpaccio are both super-fresh and dressed delicately with citrus fruit. Hot main courses include grilled fillets, fishy pastas, and *fritto misto* (a mixed fry of baby squid, shrimp, and sardines served in a skillet). Both clientele and staff are young and lively, matching the decor of urban furniture amid frescoes. Service is brisk. Reservations highly recommended.

Via del Proconsolo 16R. www.fishinglab.it. ⓒ **055/240-618.** Entrees 12€–16€. Daily 11am–11pm. Bus: C1 or C2.

### INEXPENSIVE

**I Due Fratellini ★** PANINI/LIGHT FARE   This hole-in-the-wall has been serving sandwiches to go since 1875 (and fed Conan O'Brien on his 2018 Italian gastronomic tour). The drill is simple: Choose a filling, pick a drink, then eat your fast-filled roll on the curb opposite or find a nearby piazza to perch. There are around 30 combos to choose from, including the usual Tuscan meats and cheeses—salami, pecorino, cured ham—and more flamboyant options such as goat cheese and Calabrian spicy salami or *bresaola* (air-dried beef) and wild arugula. A glass of wine to wash it down costs from 2€. No credit cards. Lunchtime lines can be long.

Via dei Cimatori 38R (at corner of Via Calzaiuoli). ✆ **055/239-6096.** Sandwiches 4€. Daily 10am–7pm. Bus: C2.

## Near the Ponte Vecchio

**MODERATE**

**Osteria del Porcellino** ★ TUSCAN   So many characterful restaurants of "old Florence" have dropped standards in the age of mass tourism, but not this place. Traditional Tuscan is what they do best, and pasta dishes such as *pappardelle* with wild boar sauce are always tasty. Follow that with a *tagliata* (sliced steak) with arugula and Parmigiano to savor the city's carnivorous traditions. Lighter options include sublime "flan"—a potato cake with cured ham, Vin Santo wine, and *stracchino* cheese sauce—and house salads. All-day dining means you (or the kids) can eat when you choose.

Via Val di Lamona 7R. www.osteriadelporcellino.com. ✆ **055/264-148.** Entrees 16€–24€. Daily noon–11pm. Closed 1 week Feb. Bus: C2.

## Near Santa Trinita

**MODERATE**

**Osteria di Giovanni** ★★ MODERN TUSCAN   If only every Tuscan restaurant in town was this good. Family-run Osteria di Giovanni is a standout in its category and therefore always buzzing: You should reserve even in low season. Meat is a specialty, both traditional (the *bistecca alla fiorentina* is legendary) and modern interpretations like *faraona all'arancia* (guinea hen stewed in slightly sweet orange). Portions are large, so only the very brave should attempt a *primo/secondo/dolce* route. A steep cover charge (4€) is actually a good deal, because it includes a couple of tasty snacks and all the mineral water you can drink.

Via del Moro 22. www.osteriadigiovanni.com. ✆ **055/284-897.** Entrees 18€–28€. Daily 7–10:30pm; Sat–Sun also 12:30–2:30pm. Bus: 6, 11.

---

### Talking Tripe

New York has the hot dog. London has pie and mash. Florence has...cow's intestine in a sandwich. The city's traditional street food, *lampredotto* (the cow's fourth stomach), stewed with tomatoes, has made a big comeback of late, including in some fine-dining establishments. The best places to sample it affordably are the city's *trippai*, tripe vendors who sell from food trucks around the center. The most convenient vendors are in **Piazza de' Cimatori** and on **Via de' Macci** at Piazza Sant'Ambrogio. A hearty, nutritious lunch should come in around 5€. Most are open Monday through Saturday but close in August, when Florentines flee the city.

# Near San Lorenzo & the Mercato Centrale
## MODERATE

**Il Nutino** ★★ TUSCAN/GRILL   This tiny, traditional joint has been in business since the 1950s. It's become our go-to for *bistecca alla fiorentina,* in both classic and marbled styles. Whichever you choose, your meat spends a short time on the grill and is best served simply with roasted potatoes and *fagioli al fiasco* (beans stewed in olive oil). There's also a full Tuscan menu of fresh pasta, *crostini,* soups, and the like. Service is attentive and knowledgeable, especially when it comes to selecting a wine to wash down the red meat (Chianti Rufina Nipozzano is our choice). The location is one of Florence's most heavily touristed areas, but with over 6 decades behind it, Il Nutino is doing things the right way.

Borgo San Lorenzo 39R. ⓒ **349/453-6035.** Entrees 12.50€–22€. Daily 10am–11pm. Bus: C1.

**La Gratella** ★★ FLORENTINE/GRILL   It doesn't look like much—a workers' canteen on a nondescript side street—but looks don't matter much when you can source and cook meat like they do here. Star of the show is the *fiorentina* steak, a large T-bone-like cut grilled on the bone and brought to the table over coals. It is sold by weight and made for sharing; expect to pay about 50€. Pair this or any market-fresh meat on the menu with simple Tuscan sides like beans stewed in olive oil. They cater to gluten-free diets, too.

Via Guelfa 81R. www.lagratella.it. ⓒ **055/211-292.** Entrees 12€–20€. Daily noon–3pm and 7–11pm. Bus: 1, 6, 11, 14, 17, 23.

## INEXPENSIVE

**Bondi** ★ FLORENTINE/LIGHT FARE   To label this place opposite the Mercato Centrale a mere sandwich shop is like describing the Super Bowl as a football game. Bondi is an institution, specializing in *piadine* (flatbread sandwiches) in the Florentine style. Choose from a long list of traditional and unusual sandwiches, toasted or not, then order at the counter and take a seat on rustic wooden benches to await its arrival. Filling combos include anchovies with mozzarella, capers, and tomatoes or eggplant Parmigiana. Wash it down with a glass of Chianti at 2€ a pop. No credit cards.

Via dell'Ariento 85.ⓒ **055/287-390.** Sandwiches 3€–4.50€. Daily 11am–11pm. Bus: C1.

**Mario** ★ FLORENTINE   There is no doubt this market workers' trattoria is firmly on the tourist trail. But Mario's is as authentic Florentine as you'll find: They even changed their brand of pasta when it started sponsoring soccer rivals, Juventus. Food here clings to the traditions and ethos Mario adopted when the burners first fired up 60 years ago. Food is simple, hearty, and served at communal tables—"check in" on arrival and you will be offered seats together wherever they come free. Think *passato di fagioli* (bean puree soup) followed by traditional Tuscan beef stew, *peposo,* or *coniglio arrosto* (roast rabbit). No reservations or credit cards.

Via Rosina 2R (north corner of Piazza Mercato Centrale). www.trattoriamario.com. ⓒ **055/218-550.** Entrees 8.50€–14€. Mon–Sat noon–3:30pm. Closed Aug. Bus: C1.

**Mercato Centrale** ★★ MODERN ITALIAN   The upper floor of Florence's produce market is a bustling shrine to modern street food. Counters offer dishes from all over Italy: authentic Neapolitan pizza, vegetarian and vegan fare, pasta, meats, and cheeses, fresh fish, Chianina burgers, Florentine boiled beef dripping in its own juices, and much more. It's a perfect choice for families who can't agree on dinner. Or just stop by for a drink and soak up the buzz: There's a beer bar and a superb enoteca where you can buy by the glass or bottle.

Piazza Mercato Centrale. www.mercatocentrale.it. ℰ **055/239-9798.** Dishes 5€–20€. Daily 10am–midnight. Bus: C1.

**SandwiChic** ★★ LIGHT FARE   Perhaps Florence's best sandwich bar, SandwiChic succeeds because it keeps things simple, with freshly baked bread and expertly sourced ingredients including Tuscan cured meats and savory preserves. Try combinations like *finocchiona* (salami spiked with fennel), pecorino cheese, and *crema di porri* (a creamy leek relish). The inside of this former haberdashery is a tight squeeze: Go for takeout.

Via San Gallo 3R. https://en-gb.facebook.com/sandwichic. ℰ **055/281-157.** Sandwiches 4€–5.50€. Daily 11:30am–6pm. Bus: C1.

# Near San Marco

San Marco is the place to head for *schiacciata,* olive-oil flatbread loaded with savory toppings. You will find some of the best at **Pugi ★,** Piazza San Marco 9B (www.fornopugi.it; ℰ **055/280-981**), open Monday to Saturday 7:30am to 8pm, but closed most of August.

## MODERATE

**Da Tito** ★★ FLORENTINE/TUSCAN   Every night feels like party night at one of central Florence's rare genuine neighborhood trattorias. (For that reason, it's usually packed—book ahead.) The dishes are classic Florentine, with a few modern Italian curveballs: Start, perhaps, with the *risotto con piselli e guanciale* (rice with fresh peas and cured pork cheek) before going on to a traditional grill such as *lombatina di vitella* (veal chop steak). The neighborhood location, a 10-minute walk north of San Lorenzo, and a mixed clientele keep quality very consistent.

Via San Gallo 112R. https://trattoriadatito.business.site. ℰ **055/472-475.** Entrees 10€–18€. Mon–Sat 12:30–3pm and 7–11pm. Bus: C1, 1, 7, 20, 25.

# Near Santa Croce
## MODERATE

**Brac** ★★ VEGETARIAN/VEGAN   An artsy cafe-bookshop for most of the day, at lunch and dinner this place turns into one of Florence's best spots for vegetarian and vegan food. A *piatto unico* works out best for hungry diners: one combo plate loaded with three different dishes from the menu, perhaps pear carpaccio with Grana Padano cheese and a balsamic reduction; *tagliatelle* with broccoli, pecorino, and lemon; plus a *pane carasau* (Sardinian flatbread) with eggplant and buffalo mozzarella. The courtyard atmosphere is intimate and romantic, yet singletons won't feel out of place eating at the counter out front. Reservations are a must at dinner or for Brac's popular Sunday brunch.

Via dei Vagellai 18R. www.libreria brac.net. ✆ **055/094-4877.** Entrees 11€–15€. Daily noon–midnight. Bus: C1, C3, 23.

**Koto Ramen** ★ JAPA-NESE Ramen's march to world domination continues, in a city whose culinary traditions could hardly be further from Japan. The cooking here is authentic, however, with each item on the short menu floating in a deep, rich broth that's made in-house (as are the noodles). The *tantan* ramen, with chopped pork, sesame pesto, and Japanese hot pepper, is a spicy treat. Sides are also traditional, including edamame, filled

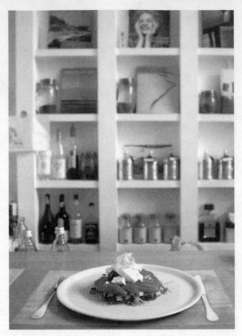

The Caprese salad at Brac.

*gyoza* dumplings, and *kara-age* (fried marinated chicken thighs); there's a strong sake list, too.

Via Verdi 42R. www.kotoramen.it. ✆ **055/247-9477.** Entrees 11€–17€. Daily 12:30–2:30pm and 7–10pm. Closed Aug. Bus: C3. Also at Borgo San Frediano 41R.

### INEXPENSIVE

**Da Rocco** ★ FLORENTINE  This tiny trattoria inside Sant'Ambrogio Market is our favorite place for a bargain lunch. Behind a takeout counter is an enclosed seating area with snug booths. Hearty dishes of lasagne, roast meats like *coniglio* (rabbit), and salt cod stewed with tomatoes cost 5€ to 7€. The house wine is farmhouse Chianti; a bottle is left on your table and you pay for whatever you drink. Get here by 1pm if you want a table; lingering is gently discouraged.

Mercato di Sant'Ambrogio. No phone. Entrees 6€–7.50€. Mon–Sat noon–2:30pm. Bus: C2, C3, or 14.

## In the Oltrarno, San Niccolò & San Frediano
### EXPENSIVE

**iO: Osteria Personale** ★★★ MODERN TUSCAN  There's a definite hipster atmosphere here, with the whitewashed brick and young staff, but a fine dining ethos is ingrained, too. Ingredients are familiar to Tuscan cooking but combined in a way you may not have seen before. The menu always has a range of seafood, meat, and vegetarian dishes: perhaps tempura artichoke flowers stuffed with taleggio cheese and marjoram, followed by smoked chestnut ravioli with wild fennel, then roasted octopus with celeriac, green apple, and cardamom. Reservations are advised: This place's reputation has only grown in the decade since we first recommended it.

Borgo San Frediano 167R. www.io-osteriapersonale.it. ⓒ **055/933-1341.** Entrees 21€–22€; tasting menus 42€–58€. Mon–Sat 7:30–10pm. Closed 10 days Jan and all of Aug. Bus: D or 6.

## MODERATE

**A Crudo** ★ MODERN ITALIAN/RAW FOOD  The name means "raw," which provides a clue to the strengths of this inventive spot. The real star is the meat tartare, done in traditional style as well as in such creative combos as Kathmandù (with lime and avocado). There's also vegetarian raw food tartare, plus a wide choice of beef or fish carpaccio. A Crudo is a perfect example of modern Florence doing what it does best: tapping into local food traditions and letting them breathe some 21st-century air.

Via Mazzetta 5R. ⓒ **055/265-7483.** Entrees 12€–22€. Daily noon–midnight. Bus: C3, 11, 36, 37.

**Il Magazzino** ★ FLORENTINE  A traditional *osteria* that specializes in the flavors of old Florence, it looks the part, too, with a terracotta tiled floor and barrel vault, chunky wooden furniture, and hanging lamps. If you dare, this is a place to try tripe or *lampredotto* (intestines), the traditional food of working Florentines, prepared expertly in ravioli or meatballs, boiled, or *alla fiorentina* (stewed with tomatoes and garlic). The rest of the menu is carnivore-friendly too: Follow *tagliatelle al ragù bianco* (pasta ribbons with a "white" meat sauce

The stylish dining room of iO: Osteria Personale.

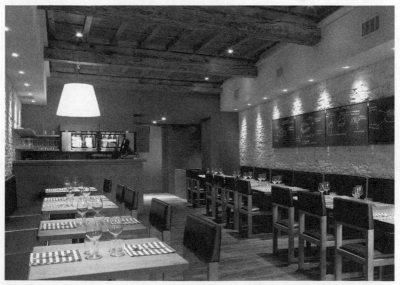

made with a little milk instead of tomatoes) with *guancia di vitello in agrodolce* (veal cheek stewed with baby onions in a sticky-sweet sauce).

Piazza della Passera 3. ✆ **055/215-969**. Entrees 10€–20€. Daily noon–3pm and 7:30–11pm. Bus: C3 or C4.

**Il Santo Bevitore** ★ MODERN ITALIAN   Sure, this place has lost its original in-the-know, local buzz. But the commitment to top produce served simply, and a trademark take on Tuscan ingredients, is unwavering—and reservations are still a must. Carefully sourced cold cuts make an ideal sharing antipasto: *prosciutto crudo* from the Casentino forests, *pecorino* cheese from Pienza in southern Tuscany. Main courses are eclectic, seasonal, and come in all appetite sizes, from a whole *burrata* (fresh cheese) served with crispy spinach to veal cutlet with artichokes, borlotti beans, and pear. There is a long, expert wine list, with about 10 offered by the glass, plus craft beers.

Via Santo Spirito 66R (at Piazza N. Sauro). www.ilsantobevitore.com. ✆ **055/211-264**. Entrees 12€–27€. Daily 12:30–2:30pm and 7:30–11pm. Closed 10 days mid-Aug. Bus: C3, C4, 6, 11, 36, or 37.

**Osteria dell'Enoteca** ★★★ MODERN TUSCAN   Opened in 2017 by experienced wine bar owners, this place majors in reasonably priced, refined dining. Traditional flavors dominate, although combinations are just as often modern, in such dishes as a poached egg yolk "*affogato*," floating in a pecorino cheese cream with wild mushrooms. Portions are not large, so cut loose and order three courses. There's also no wine list; an English-speaking waiter leads you to a chiller stocked with boutique labels—strong on Tuscan as well as Langhe/Piedmont reds. The dining room itself is elegant and refined, with slate floors, stripped brick, and soft jazz: This is the place for a special occasion or romantic meal that won't bust your budget.

Via Romana 70R. www.osteriadellenoteca.com. ✆ **055/228-6018**. Entrees 14€–18€. Thurs–Mon 7–10:30pm; also Sat–Sun 12:30–2:30pm. Bus: 11, 36, 37.

# Gelato

Having a fair claim to being the birthplace of gelato, Florence has some of the world's best *gelaterie*—but many, many poor imitations, too. Steer clear of spots around the major attractions, where air-fluffed mountains of ice cream are so full of artificial colors and flavors they practically glow in the dark. If you can see the Ponte Vecchio or Piazza della Signoria from the front door of the gelateria, you may want to move on. You might only have to walk a block, or duck down a side street, to find a genuine artisan in the gelato kitchen. Trust us, you'll taste the difference. Opening hours tend to be discretionary: On warm evenings, many places stay open beyond 11pm.

**Gelateria della Passera** ★★   Milk-free water ices here are among the most intensely flavored in the city, and with a sweetness that doesn't overpower the flavor. Try the likes of pink grapefruit or jasmine tea gelato. Via Toscanella 15R (at Piazza della Passera). www.gelateriadellapassera.it. ✆ **055/291-882**. Cone from 2€. Bus: C3 or C4.

**Gelateria de' Neri ★** There's a large range of fruit, white, and chocolate flavors here, but nothing overly elaborate. If the seasonal ricotta and fig flavor is offered, you are in luck. There's also a restroom. Via dei Neri 9R. www.gelateria deineri.it. *℡***055/210-034.** Cone from 2€. Bus: C1, C3, 23.

**La Carraia ★★** It's packed with locals late into the evening on summer weekends—for good reason. The range is vast, the quality high. Piazza N. Sauro 25R. www.lacarraiagroup.eu. *℡***055/280-695.** Cone from 2€. Bus: C3, C4, 6, 11, 36, 37. Closed Jan. Also at: Via de' Benci 24R (*℡***329/363-0069**).

# EXPLORING FLORENCE

In the wake of the pandemic, most major museums now require advance reservations. Check individual museum websites and see "Advance Reservations for the Uffizi, Accademia & More," p. 149, for details. **Proof of vaccination** will likely remain a condition of entry almost everywhere for the foreseeable future.

**Precise opening times can change** without notice, especially at city churches (e.g., the Baptistery sometimes remains open until 11pm in summer). Tourist offices distribute a list of opening hours, updated daily and also free to download from **www.feelflorence.it**. We **strongly advise** downloading this PDF or collecting it from any tourist office (p. 149) on arrival. In the listings below we list opening times that *usually* apply. You should, alas, treat these as somewhat provisional. Last admission everywhere is usually between 30 and 45 minutes before the official closing time.

## Piazza del Duomo

The cathedral square is always lively—filled with tourists and caricature artists during the day, strolling pedestrians in the early evening, and students strumming guitars on the Duomo's steps at night. The piazza's vivacity amid the glittering facades of the cathedral and the Baptistery doors makes this an eternal Florentine sight.

**Battistero (Baptistery) ★★★** CHURCH In choosing a date to mark the beginning of the Renaissance, art historians often seize on 1401, the year Florence's powerful wool merchants' guild held a contest for the commission to design the **North Doors ★★** of the Baptistery to match its Gothic **South Doors,** cast 65 years earlier by Andrea Pisano. The era's foremost Tuscan sculptors each cast a bas-relief bronze panel depicting their vision of the "Sacrifice of Isaac." Twenty-two-year-old Lorenzo Ghiberti, competing against Donatello, Jacopo della Quercia, and Filippo Brunelleschi, won. He spent the next 21 years casting 28 bronze panels and building his doors. The restored originals are inside the **Museo dell'Opera del Duomo** (see p. 180).

The result so impressed the merchants' guild—not to mention the public and Ghiberti's fellow artists—that they asked him in 1425 to do the **East Doors ★★★,** facing the Duomo, this time giving him artistic freedom to realize his Renaissance ambitions. Twenty-seven years later, just before his death,

# A MAN & HIS dome

**Filippo Brunelleschi,** a diminutive man whose ego was as big as his talent, managed in his arrogant, quixotic, and brilliant way to invent Renaissance architecture. Having been beaten by Lorenzo Ghiberti in the contest to cast the **Baptistery** doors (see p. 175), Brunelleschi decided he would rather be Florence's top architect than its second-best sculptor and took off for Rome to study the buildings of the ancients. On returning to his home city, he combined subdued gray *pietra serena* stone quarried close to Fiesole with smooth white plaster to create airy arches, vaults, and arcades of perfect classical proportions, in his own variant on the ancient Roman orders of architecture. He designed **Santo Spirito** (p. 202), the elegant **Spedale degli Innocenti** (p. 196), a chapel at **Santa Croce** (p. 197), and a new sacristy for **San Lorenzo** (p. 191), but his greatest achievement was erecting the dome over Florence's cathedral.

The Duomo—at that time the world's largest church—had already been built, but nobody had figured out how to cover the daunting octagonal space over its center without spending a fortune. No one was even sure they could create a dome that would hold up under its own weight. Brunelleschi insisted he knew how, and once granted the commission, delivered on his ingenious plan, probably inspired by close study of Rome's **Pantheon** (p. 110). He never revealed his method in full, but certainly built the dome in two shells, the inner one thicker than the outer, both shells thinning as they near the top, thus leaving the center hollow and removing much weight. He also planned to construct the dome from giant vaults with ribs crossing them, and dovetailed the bricks making up the dome's fabric in a herringbone pattern. In this way his dome supported itself as it grew, with little need for scaffolding. In the process of building, Brunelleschi found himself as much an inventor as an architect, constantly designing winches and hoists to carry the materials (plus food and drink) faster and more efficiently up to the workmen. Reputedly, only one person died during construction—a drunken worker who fell.

His finished work speaks for itself: This is still the world's largest brick-and-mortar dome, 45m (148 ft.) wide at the base, 90m (295 ft.) high, and built with an estimated 4 million bricks. The marble lantern—which Brunelleschi did not live to see dropped into place in 1446—serves as the structure's keystone. For his achievement, Brunelleschi was accorded the honor of a burial inside Florence's cathedral. Unfortunately, many construction secrets lie there with him. Academics still debate his techniques.

Ghiberti finished 10 dramatic Old Testament scenes in gilded bronze, each a masterpiece of Renaissance sculpture and some of the finest examples of low-relief perspective in Italian art. Each illustrates episodes in the stories of Noah (second down on left), Moses (second up on left), Solomon (bottom right), and others. The panels mounted here are also copies, created using historically accurate techniques, with the originals displayed in the Museo dell'Opera del Duomo. Years later, Michelangelo was standing before these doors, and someone asked his opinion. His response sums up Ghiberti's accomplishment as no art historian could: "They are so beautiful that they would grace the entrance to Paradise." They've been nicknamed the Gates of Paradise ever since.

The octagonal building itself is ancient, first mentioned in city records in the 9th century but probably 300 years old by then. Its exterior is clad in gleaming white Carrara and green Prato marble; even the roof is marble, making this the world's only building completely covered in marble.

The interior is ringed with columns pilfered from ancient Roman buildings, with a riot of mosaic-work above and below. The floor was inlaid in 1209, and between 1225 and the early 1300s the ceiling was covered with glittering **mosaics** ★★, most crafted by Venetian or Byzantine-style workshops working off designs by the era's best artists. Coppo di Marcovaldo drew sketches for a 7.8m-high (26-ft.) "Christ in Judgment" and a "Last Judgment" that fills over a third of the ceiling. Four separate, concentric registers tell stories from the Old and New Testaments. Bring binoculars for a closer look. Until the 1700s, this was the only place in Florence you could be legally baptized.

Piazza San Giovanni. www.duomo.firenze.it. ℂ **055/230-2885.** 10€ (includes Museo dell'Opera). Daily 11:15am–5:30pm. Bus: C2.

### Campanile di Giotto (Giotto's Bell Tower) ★★ ARCHITECTURE

In 1334, Giotto started the cathedral bell tower but completed only the first two levels before his death in 1337. A painter by trade, he was out of his league with the engineering aspects of architecture, and the tower was saved from falling by Andrea Pisano, who doubled the thickness of the walls. Pisano also changed the design to add statue niches—he even carved a few of the statues himself—before quitting the project in 1348. Francesco Talenti finished the job between 1350 and 1359. The **reliefs** and **statues** in the lower levels—by Andrea Pisano, Donatello, Luca della Robbia, and others—are all copies; the weatherworn originals are housed in the Museo dell'Opera (p. 180). We recommend climbing the 414 steps to the top; the **view** ★★ is memorable as you ascend, and offers one of the city's best close-ups of Brunelleschi's dome.

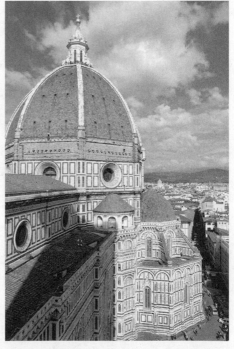

Piazza del Duomo. www.duomo. firenze.it. ℂ **055/230-2885.** 15€. Daily 8:15am–7pm. Bus: C2, 14, 23.

Brunelleschi's dome, seen from the top of Giotto's bell tower.

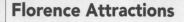

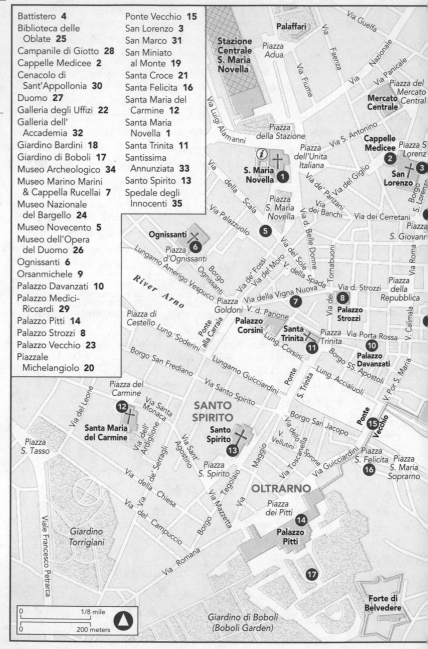

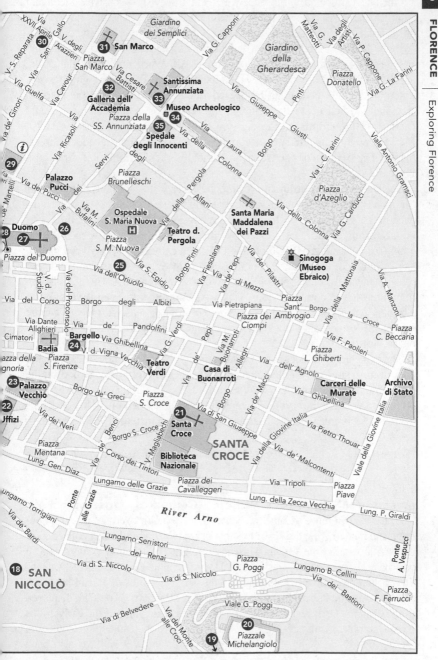

## Duomo (Cattedrale di Santa Maria del Fiore) ★★★ CATHEDRAL

By the late 13th century, Florence was feeling peevish: Archrivals Siena and Pisa had flamboyant new cathedrals while it was saddled with a tiny 5th- or 6th-century cathedral dedicated to Santa Reparata. So, in 1296, the city hired Arnolfo di Cambio to design a new Duomo, and he raised the facade and the first few bays before his death (around 1310). Work continued under the auspices of the Wool Guild and architects Giotto di Bondone (who concentrated on the bell tower) and Francesco Talenti (who expanded the planned size and finished up to the drum of the dome). Over the centuries, many designs for the unfinished facade were offered and rejected. For one lavish Medici wedding the family even commissioned a temporary facade in papier-mâché. The permanent one is a neo-Gothic design by Emilio de Fabris, built from 1871 to 1887.

The Duomo's most distinctive feature, however, is its enormous **dome ★★★** (or *cupola*), which dominates the skyline and has become the symbol of Florence itself. The raising of this dome, the largest in the world in its time, was no mean architectural feat, tackled by Filippo Brunelleschi between 1420 and 1436 (see "A Man & His Dome," p. 176). You can climb up between its two shells for one of the classic panoramas across the city—something that is not recommended for claustrophobes or anyone with no head for heights. Booking a time slot to climb the dome is **always compulsory, even if you hold a Firenzecard.** Book as far ahead as you can in peak seasons. Queues can be long, but your best shot at a short wait or late availability comes with the first or last slots of the day.

The cathedral is rather spartan inside, though check out the optical-illusion equestrian "statue" of English mercenary soldier Sir John Hawkwood on the north wall, painted in 1436 by Paolo Uccello. The remains of old **Santa Reparata ★** are in the crypt, with mosaic floors revamped in 2018. For details of highly recommended small-group visits to the **Cathedral Roof Terraces,** see p. 202.

Piazza del Duomo. duomo.firenze.it. ✆ **055/230-2885.** Church free; dome 20€. Church Mon–Sat 10:45am–5pm. Cupola Mon–Fri 8:15am–7pm; Sat 8:15am–4:30pm; Sun 12:45–5pm. Bus: C1 or C2.

## Museo dell'Opera del Duomo (Cathedral Museum) ★★★

MUSEUM    Florence's Cathedral Museum has a major overhaul in 2015, doubling and modernizing the space to show off Italy's second-largest collection of devotional art after the Vatican Museums (p. 89). The location is significant: It was once the workshop where Michelangelo sculpted his statue of "David." Today the museum's prize exhibits are the original **Gates of Paradise ★★★** cast by Lorenzo Ghiberti in the early 1400s (see "Baptistery," p. 175), displayed as the centerpiece of an extraordinary, life-sized re-creation of the early 1400s piazza, complete with a re-imagined version of what the cathedral's Gothic-era facade looked like. Ghiberti's Baptistery **North Doors ★★** have also been moved inside, scrubbed to reveal rose gold below years of soot and dirt. In 2020, Pisano's restored **South Doors ★★** joined them to complete an

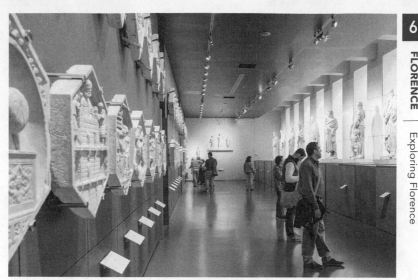

Sacred sculpture and statuary at the Museo dell'Opera del Duomo.

unparalleled set of bronze relief sculpture. Also on the ground floor, freshly restored in 2021, is Michelangelo's **"Bandini Pietà"** ★★ that nearly wasn't. Early in the process he had told students that he wanted this "Pietà" to stand at his tomb, but when he found an imperfection in the marble, he began attacking it with a hammer (look at Christ's left arm). The master never returned to the work, but his students later repaired the damage. The figure of Nicodemus was untouched—legend has it because it was a self-portrait of the artist—a Michelangelo myth that, for once, is probably true. Elsewhere are a restored early Giotto **"Madonna"** ★ with damage from the 1993 Uffizi car bomb and works by Donatello—including his restored **"Magdalen"** ★—Andrea del Verrocchio, and Luca della Robbia, plus multimedia displays which focus on the genius of Brunelleschi and his dome. They explain and show in incredible detail the engineering process behind it and the machines that built it.

Piazza del Duomo 9 (behind cathedral). www.duomo.firenze.it. ☏ **055/230-2885.** 10€ (with Battistero). Daily 9am–7pm. Closed 1st Tues of month. Bus: C1.

## Around Piazza della Signoria & Santa Trínita

**Galleria degli Uffizi (Uffizi Gallery)** ★★★ MUSEUM   There is no collection of Renaissance art on the planet to match the Uffizi. Period. For this reason, **you must reserve a timed admission slot** as soon as you can. Despite all its crowds and other inconveniences, the Uffizi remains a must-see. And what will you see? Some 60-plus rooms and marble corridors—built in the 16th century as the Medici's private offices, or *uffici*—all packed with famous paintings, among them Botticelli's "Birth of Venus," Leonardo da Vinci's "Annunciation," Michelangelo's "Holy Family," and many, many more.

Start with **Room 2** for a look at the pre-Renaissance, Gothic style of painting born in the Middle Ages. Compare Cimabue's "Santa Trínita Maestà," painted around 1280, with his student Giotto's **"Ognissanti Madonna"** ★★★, done in 1310. Both paintings have a similar subject and setting but Giotto transformed Cimabue's icon-like Byzantine style into something more human. Giotto's Madonna looks like she's sitting on a throne, her clothes emphasizing the curves of her body, whereas Cimabue's Madonna and angels float in space, like portraits on coins, with stiff positioning. A third great Madonna, Duccio's **"Rucellai Madonna"** ★ (1285), was a founding, ethereal work for the Sienese School of painters.

**Room 3** showcases the Sienese School at its peak, with Simone Martini's dazzling **"Annunciation"** ★★ (1333) slathered in gold ground and Ambrogio Lorenzetti's "Presentation at the Temple" (1342). Tragically, the Black Death of 1348 wiped out this entire generation of Sienese painters (and most of Siena's population along with them). **Rooms 5–6** show Florentine painting at its most decorative, in a style now termed International Gothic. The iconic work, Gentile da Fabriano's **"Procession of the Magi"** ★★★ (1423), depicts the line to see newborn Jesus as full of decorative and comic elements. It is even longer than the line waiting outside the Uffizi.

The unflattering profiles of the Duke Federico da Montefeltro of Urbino and his duchess, painted by **Piero della Francesca** around 1465, are the centerpiece of **Room 8.** Using newfangled oils rather than the standard tempera (a mix of egg yolk and pigment) enabled Piero to portray his subjects in a starkly realistic way—the duke exposes his warts and his crooked nose, which was broken in a tournament. A focus on earthly, rather than Christian, elements recalls the secular teachings of Greek and Roman times and is made more vivid by a depiction (on the back) of the couple riding chariots driven by the humanistic virtues of faith, charity, hope, and modesty (for her) and prudence, temperance, fortitude, and justice (for him). The same room displays works by **Filippo Lippi** from the mid–15th century. The best backstory belongs to his **"Madonna and Child with Two Angels"** ★★, from around 1465. The work was a celebrity scandal: The woman who modeled for Mary was said to be Filippo's lover—would-be nun Lucrezia Buti, whom he spirited away from a convent before she took vows—and the child looking toward the viewer the product of their union. (That son, Filippino Lippi, would also become a painter of note.) Note the background, with distant mountains on one side and water on the other framing the portrait of a woman's face; Leonardo da Vinci shamelessly stole the idea 40 years later for his "Mona Lisa."

**Rooms 10 to 14** (two linked spaces, despite the numbering) are devoted to the works of Filippo's student (and later Filippino's teacher) Sandro Filipepi, better known by his nickname "Little Barrels," or Botticelli, one of the most famous artists of the 15th century. Botticelli's 1485 **"Birth of Venus"** ★★ hangs like a billboard you have seen a thousand times. Venus's pose is taken from classical statues, while the winds Zephyr and Aura blowing her to shore, and the muse welcoming her, are from Ovid's "Metamorphosis." Botticelli's

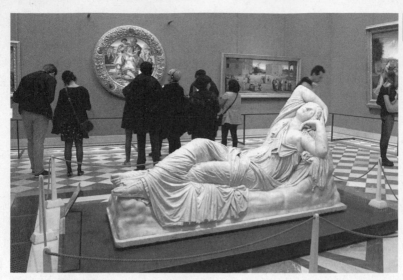

Galleria degli Uffizi, interior.

1478 **"Primavera"** ★★★, its dark, bold colors a stark contrast to filmy, pastel "Venus," defies definitive interpretation. But again it features Venus (center), alongside Mercury, with the winged boots, the Three Graces, and the goddess Flora—as well as staggering botanical detail.

The **Tribuna** ★★ is an architectural oddity, an ornate octagonal room local architect Buontalenti built on the orders of Grand Duke Francesco I. Its centerpiece is the **"Medici Venus"** ★★, a Greek marble crafted in the 1st century B.C. Botticelli copied her pose for his famous Venus (as have many others over the centuries).

To cross to the Uffizi's west wing, you pass picture windows with views of the Arno River to one side and the perfect Renaissance perspective of the Uffizi piazza to the other—plus an often-overlooked Roman sculpture gallery most museums would kill for.

The Uffizi's west wing houses two true Renaissance heavyweights. **Room 35** displays Leonardo da Vinci's magnificent, unfinished **"Adoration of the Magi"** ★★★—much of the master's line drawing is still visible— beside his **"Annunciation"** ★★. In the latter, completed in the early 1470s while Leonardo was still a student in Verrocchio's workshop, da Vinci's ability to orchestrate the viewer's focus is masterful: The line down the middle of the brick corner of the house draws your glance to Mary's delicate fingers, which themselves point along the top of a stone wall to the angel's two raised fingers. Those, in turn, draw attention to the mountain between the two parallel trees dividing Mary from the angel, representing the gulf between the worldly and the spiritual. Its apparently warped perspective was in fact painted to be viewed from the lower right.

In **Room 41** is Michelangelo's 1505–08 **"Holy Family"** ★. The twisting shapes of Mary, Joseph, and Jesus recall those in the Sistine Chapel for their sculpted form and bright colors. The Uffizi has several Raphaels; this room displays his often-copied **"Madonna of the Goldfinch"** ★★, with a background landscape lifted from Leonardo and Botticelli.

The torsion and tensions of Michelangelo's painting and sculpture inspired the next generation of Florentine painters, known as the **Mannerists.** Andrea Del Sarto, Rosso Fiorentino, and Pontormo are the focus of a suite of rooms downstairs, inaugurated in 2021 and dedicated to the **Cinquecento** (1500s). Farther on, you'll find Titian's reclining nude **"Venus of Urbino"** ★★. It's no coincidence that the edge of the curtain, the angle of her hand and leg, and the line splitting floor and bed all intersect at the forbidden part of her body. It's the highlight of a large collection of Venetian art, which also includes Lotto and Giorgione.

The final big-bats are in the **Sale Seicento (1600s Rooms):** paintings by Caravaggio, notably his crazed **"Medusa"** ★ self-portrait and an enigmatic **"Bacchus"** ★. These rooms also explore the 17th-century artists who aped his *chiaroscuro* (bright light and dark shadows) style. Greatest among them was Artemisia Gentileschi, a rare female painter from this period. Her **"Judith Slaying Holofernes"** ★ (ca. 1612), is one of the bloodiest paintings in the gallery.

If you find yourself flagging at any point (it happens to us all), there is a **coffee shop** at the far end of the upper floor's west wing. Prices are in line with the piazza below, plus you get a great close-up of the Palazzo Vecchio's facade from the terrace. Fully refreshed, you can return to discover works by the many great artists we haven't space to cover here: Cranach and Dürer; Velazquez, El Greco, and Goya; Bellini, and Mantegna; and Uccello, Masaccio, Bronzino, and Veronese. The coffered neoclassical ceiling in the **Niobe Room (42)** is another often-missed gem. There are original Greek and Roman friezes, too, notably in a room dedicated to the Medici garden at San Marco. Or save these all for your next visit. In short, there is nowhere like the Uffizi—in Italy or anywhere else in the world.

Piazzale degli Uffizi 6 (off Piazza della Signoria). www.uffizi.it. (Reserve tickets at www. firenzemusei.it or ✆ **055/294-883.**) Mar–Oct 20€; Nov–Feb 12€. Tues–Sun 8:15am–6:50pm; prebooking compulsory on weekends. Bus: C1 or C2.

### Museo Nazionale del Bargello (Bargello Museum) ★★ MUSEUM

This is the most important museum anywhere for Renaissance **sculpture**—yet it's often inexplicably quieter than other museums in the city. Originally the city's prison, torture chamber, and execution site, the Bargello now stands as a three-story art museum containing some of the best of Michelangelo, Donatello, and Ghiberti, as well as of their most successful Mannerist successor, Giambologna.

In the ground-level Michelangelo room, you'll scope out the variety of his craft, from a whimsical 1497 **"Bacchus"** ★★ to a severe, unfinished "Brutus" of 1539. "Bacchus," created when Michelangelo was just 22, genuinely looks drunk, leaning back a little too far, his head off kilter, with a cupid about to bump him over. Nearby is Giambologna's twisting **"Mercury"** ★ taking flight, propelled by the breath of Zephyr. Cellini's bronze "Cosimo I" casts the Florentine Grand Duke in the role of Roman imperial general. It was created around the same time as his "Perseus" (see below).

Upstairs a vaulted hall is filled with some of Donatello's most accomplished sculptures, including his original "Marzocco" (once outside the Palazzo Vecchio; p. 187), and **"St. George"** ★, from an exterior niche on Orsanmichele (below). Notable among them is his bronze **"David"** ★★ (which some think might actually be the god Mercury), done around 1440, the first freestanding nude sculpture after Roman times. The classical detail of these sculptures, as well as their naturalistic poses and reflective mood, is the essence of the Renaissance style.

Side by side on the back wall are the contest entries submitted by Ghiberti and Brunelleschi for the commission to do the Baptistery doors in 1401. With the "Sacrifice of Isaac" as their Biblical theme, both displayed innovative use of perspective. Ghiberti won the contest, perhaps because his scene is more thematically unified. Brunelleschi could have ended up a footnote in art history, but instead he gave up the chisel and turned his attention to architecture instead (see "A Man & His Dome," p. 176).

Via del Proconsolo 4. www.bargellomusei.beniculturali.it. ✆ **055/064-9440.** 8€ (10€ during temporary exhibitions). Sun–Fri 8:45am–1:30pm; Sat 8:45am–6:30pm. Closed 1st and 3rd Tues of each month. Bus: C1 or C2.

**Orsanmichele** ★★ CHURCH    This bulky structure halfway down Via dei Calzaiuoli looks less like a church than a Gothic warehouse—which is exactly what it was, built as a granary and grain market in 1337. After a miraculous image of the Madonna appeared on a column inside, the lower level was turned into a shrine and chapel. The city's merchant guilds each undertook the task of decorating a Gothic tabernacle around the lower level with a statue of their guild's patron saint. Masters such as Ghiberti, Donatello, Verrocchio, and Giambologna all cast or carved masterpieces to set here (those remaining are mostly copies, including Donatello's "St. George"). In the dark interior, an elaborate Gothic stone **Tabernacle** ★ (1349–59) by Andrea Orcagna protects a luminous 1348 "Madonna and Child" painted by Giotto's student Bernardo Daddi, to which miracles were ascribed during the Black Death of 1348–50.

*Tip:* On Tuesdays (9:30am–1:50pm) and Saturdays (2:15–4:35pm) only, you can also access the upper floors via an accompanied group visit (25 people max.). These airy rooms house many of the original sculptures that once adorned Orsanmichele's exterior niches. Among the treasures of this so-called **Museo di Orsanmichele** ★ are a trio of bronzes: Ghiberti's "St. John the Baptist" (1412–16), the first life-size bronze of the Renaissance; Verrocchio's "Incredulity of St. Thomas" (1483); and Giambologna's "St. Luke" (1602). Climb up one more floor, to the top, for an unforgettable **360° panorama** ★★ of the city.

Via Arte della Lana 1. www.bargellomusei.beniculturali.it. ✆ **055/238-8610.** 2€. Hours vary. Bus: C2.

# PIAZZA DELLA signoria

When the medieval Guelph party came out on top after a long political struggle with the Ghibellines, they razed part of Florence's old city center to build a new palace for civic government. It's reputed that Guelphs ordered architect Arnolfo di Cambio to build what we now call the **Palazzo Vecchio ★★** (p. 187) in the corner of this space to make sure not an inch would sit on Ghibelline land. (This odd legend was probably fabricated to explain Arnolfo's off-center architecture.) At any rate, the L-shaped space around the *palazzo* became the new civic center of town, **Piazza della Signoria ★★,** named after the medieval city's oligarchic ruling body (the "Signoria"). Today, it's an outdoor sculpture gallery, teeming with tourists, postcard stands, horse-and-buggies, and outdoor cafes. If you want to catch the square at its serene best, arrive by 8am and have it to yourself.

The statuary on the piazza is particularly beautiful, starting on the far left (as you face the Palazzo Vecchio) with Giambologna's 1594 equestrian statue of Grand Duke Cosimo I. To its right is one of Florence's favorite sculptures to hate, the **Fontana del Nettuno** (Neptune Fountain; 1560–75), created by Bartolomeo Ammannati as a tribute to Cosimo I's naval ambitions. "Il Biancone" ("Big Whitey") is whiter than ever and spurting water enthusiastically, after a restoration funded by the Ferragamo fashion house. A **porphyry plaque** in the ground in front of the fountain marks the site where puritanical monk Savonarola held the Bonfire of the Vanities: With fiery apocalyptic preaching, he whipped Florentines into a frenzy, and hundreds filed into this piazza, arms loaded with their "decadent" possessions to throw it all on the flames.

To the right of Neptune, a raised platform fronting the Palazzo Vecchio was known as the *arringheria,* from which soapbox speakers would lecture to crowds (from where we get our word "harangue"). On its far-left corner is a copy (original in the Bargello, p. 184) of Donatello's "Marzocco," symbol of the city, with a Florentine lion resting his raised paw on a shield emblazoned with the city's emblem, the *giglio* (lily). To its right is another Donatello replica, "Judith Beheading Holofernes." Farther down is a man who needs little introduction, Michelangelo's **"David,"** a 19th-century copy of the original now in the Accademia (p. 194). Near enough to David to look truly ugly in comparison is Baccio Bandinelli's lumpy "Hercules and Cacus" (1534).

**Palazzo Davanzati ★★** PALACE/MUSEUM One of the best-preserved 14th-century palaces in the city offers a glimpse of domestic life during the medieval and Renaissance period. It was originally built for the Davizzi family in the mid-1300s, then bought by the Davanzati clan; the latter's family tree, dating back to the 1100s, is emblazoned on the ground-floor courtyard walls. The palace's painted wooden ceilings and murals have aged well (even surviving World War II damage), but the emphasis here is not on decor, but on insights into the medieval life of a noble Florentine family: feasts and festivities in the **Sala Madornale;** a private internal well to secure water supply when things in Florence got sticky; and magnificent 14th-century bedchamber frescoes that recount, comic-strip style, "The Chatelaine of Vergy," a medieval morality tale. Interesting footnote: In 1916, a New York auction of furnishings

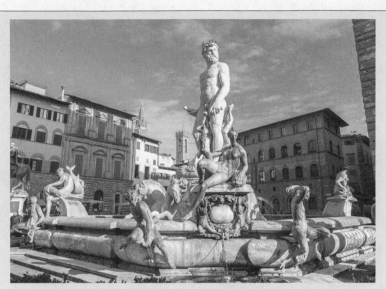

The controversial Fountain of Neptune in Piazza della Signoria.

At the piazza's south end, the **Loggia dei Lanzi** ★★ (1376–82) is named after the Swiss guard of lancers (*lanzi*) whom Cosimo de' Medici stationed here. (It's also called the Loggia della Signoria or the Loggia di Orcagna, after its designer Andrea Orcagna.) At front left stands Benvenuto Cellini's masterpiece in bronze, **"Perseus"** ★★★ (1545), holding up the severed head of Medusa. On the far right is Giambologna's **"Rape of the Sabines"** ★★, one of the most successful Mannerist sculptures in existence. You must walk all the way around to appreciate it, catching the action and artistry of its spiral design from different angles. Talk continues about moving it indoors, safe from the elements, and a copy has been commissioned...but for now, it's still here.

from this palace launched a "Florentine style" trend in U.S. interior design circles, and 2 years later, the set for the Metropolitan Opera premiere of Puccini's "Gianni Schicchi" was based on Palazzo Davanzati interiors.

Via Porta Rossa 13. www.bargellomusei.beniculturali.it. ℂ **055/064-9460.** 6€. Fri–Mon 1:45–6:30pm; Wed & Thurs 8:45am–1:30pm. Closed 1st, 3rd, and 5th Sun of each month. Bus: C2.

**Palazzo Vecchio** ★★ PALACE/MUSEUM   The core of Florence's fortress-like town hall was built from 1299 to 1302 to the designs of Arnolfo di Cambio, Gothic master builder. Home to various Florentine governments, the palace still houses the city government. When Duke Cosimo I and his Medici family moved to the *palazzo* in 1540, they redecorated: Michelozzo's 1453 **courtyard** ★ was left architecturally intact but frescoed by Vasari with scenes of Austrian cities, to celebrate the 1565 marriage of Francesco I de' Medici and Joanna of Austria. A grand staircase leads up to the **Sala dei Cinquecento ★,** named for a 500-man assembly that met here in the pre-Medici days of the Florentine Republic. It's also the site of the greatest fresco cycle that ever wasn't: Leonardo da Vinci was commissioned in 1503–05 to paint one long wall with a scene celebrating Florence's victory at the 1440 Battle of Anghiari. Always trying new methods and materials, he decided to mix wax into his pigments. Leonardo had finished painting part of the wall, but it wasn't drying fast enough, so he brought in braziers stoked with hot coals to hurry the process. As onlookers watched in horror, the wax in the fresco melted under the heat and colors ran to a puddle on the floor. The search for what remains of his work continues; some hope was provided in 2012 with the discovery of pigments similar to those used by Leonardo in a cavity behind the current wall. Michelangelo was also supposed to paint a fresco on the opposite wall, but he never got past preparatory drawings before Pope Julius II called him to Rome to paint the Sistine Chapel. Vasari and his assistants covered the bare walls from 1563 to 1565, with subservient frescoes exalting Cosimo I and the military victories of his regime, against Pisa (on the near wall) and Siena (far wall). Opposite the door you enter is Michelangelo's statue of **"Victory" ★,** carved from 1533 to 1534 for Pope Julius II's tomb but later donated to the Medici.

The first series of rooms on the upper floor is the **Quartiere degli Elementi,** frescoed with allegories and mythological characters, again by Vasari. Crossing the balcony overlooking the Sala dei Cinquecento, you enter the **Apartments of Eleonora di Toledo ★,** decorated for Cosimo's Spanish wife. Her **private chapel ★★★** is a masterpiece of mid–16th-century fresco painting by Bronzino. Under the coffered ceiling of the **Sala dei Gigli** is Ghirlandaio's fresco of "St. Zenobius Enthroned," with figures from Republican and Imperial Rome, and Donatello's original **"Judith and Holofernes" ★** bronze (1455), one of his last works. In the palace basement is the **Scavi del Teatro Romano ★** exhibit, remnants of the Roman Florentia theater, upon which the medieval palace was built, with walls and an intact paved street.

If you can bear small spaces and 218 steps, the views from the top of the **Torre di Arnolfo ★★,** the palace's crenelated tower, are sublime. The 95m (312-ft.) Torre is closed in bad weather; the minimum age to climb it is 6, and children ages 17 and under must be accompanied by an adult.

Piazza della Signoria. ticketsmuseums.comune.fi.it. ✆ **055/276-8325.** Palazzo 12.50€; Torre 12.50€; Palazzo plus Scavi 16€. Fri–Wed 9am–7pm (Torre closes 5pm); Thurs 9am–2pm. Bus: C1 or C2.

**Ponte Vecchio ★** ARCHITECTURE   The oldest and most famous bridge across the Arno, the Ponte Vecchio was built in 1345–50 by Taddeo Gaddi to replace an earlier version. Overhanging shops have lined a bridge here since at least the 12th century. In the 16th century, it was home to butchers, until Duke Ferdinand I moved into the Palazzo Pitti across the river. He couldn't stand the stench, so he evicted the meat cutters and moved in goldsmiths, silversmiths, and jewelers, who occupy it to this day.

The enclosed passageway that runs along the top of the Ponte Vecchio is part of the **Corridoio Vasariano (Vasari Corridor) ★,** a private elevated link between the Palazzo Vecchio and Palazzo Pitti. Duke Cosimo I found the idea of mixing with the hoi polloi on his way to work distressing—and assassination was a real danger—so he commissioned Vasari to design his V.I.P. route in 1565. His former secret commuter passageway is now hung with the world's best collection of artists' self-portraits. The corridor has been closed since 2016, but is scheduled to open for public access in 2022. Inquire at the tourist office or check **www.uffizi.it/corridoio-vasariano** for updates.

In 1944 the Ponte Vecchio's fame saved it from the Nazis, who had orders to blow up all the bridges before retreating out of Florence as Allied forces advanced. They couldn't bring themselves to reduce this span to rubble, so instead they blew up the ancient buildings on either end to block it off. Even less discriminating was the **Great Arno Flood** of 1966, which severely damaged the shops. A private night watchman saw waters rising alarmingly and called many of the goldsmiths at home. They rushed to remove valuable stock before it was washed away. *Tip:* The Ponte Vecchio is a busy bottleneck for people crossing the river. If you are not comfortable in crowds, we recommend you take another bridge, any of which will be much quieter.

Via Por Santa Maria/Via Guicciardini. Bus: C3 or C4.

**Santa Trínita ★★** CHURCH   Behind Bernardo Buontalenti's late-16th-century facade lies a dark church, rebuilt in the 14th century but founded by the Vallombrosan order before 1177. The third chapel on the right has remains of 14th-century frescoes of the "Madonna Enthroned" by Spinello Aretino, found beneath Lorenzo Monaco's 1424 "Scenes from the Life of the Virgin" frescoes in the next chapel along. The chapel's iron gate is contemporaneous (1420). In the right transept, Ghirlandaio frescoed the **Cappella Sassetti ★** in 1485 with a cycle on the "Life of St. Francis," setting all the scenes against Florentine backdrops peopled with portraits of contemporary notables. His "Francis Receiving the Order from Pope Honorius" (in the lunette) takes place under an arcade on the north side of Piazza della Signoria; you'll recognize the Loggia dei Lanzi in the middle, and on the left, the Palazzo Vecchio (the Uffizi hadn't yet been built), Take .50€ coins for the chapel lights. *Tip:* The south end of the piazza leads to the **Ponte Santa Trínita ★★,** Florence's most graceful bridge. In 1567, Ammannati built this span, set with four 16th-century statues of the seasons, for the wedding of Cosimo II. After the Nazis blew up the bridge in 1944, it was rebuilt, and all was set into place—save the head on the statue of "Spring," which remained lost until a team dredging the river in 1961 found it by accident. If you want to photograph the Ponte Vecchio, head here at dusk.

Piazza Santa Trínita. ⓒ **055/216-912.** Free. Mon–Sat 8am–noon and 4–6pm; Sun 8:15–10:45am and 4–6pm. Bus: C3, C4, 6, 11.

The Renaissance **Palazzo Strozzi** ★★, Piazza Strozzi (www.palazzostrozzi.org; ✆ **055/264-5155**), is Florence's major space for temporary and contemporary art shows, and has been experiencing a 21st-century rebirth of its own. Hit shows in recent years have included Bill Viola's "Electronic Renaissance" in 2017 and Jeff Koons in 2021. There's usually plenty going on around each show, including talks, late openings (usually Thurs), and free downloadable activity kits for kids of different ages. Check the website for the latest updates. Admission to headline exhibitions is usually around 15€.

# Around San Lorenzo & the Mercato Centrale

The church of San Lorenzo was once lost behind the leather and souvenir stalls of Florence's vast **San Lorenzo Street Market** (see p. 205), until the carts were moved out of the piazza and into adjacent streets almost a decade ago. A bustle of commerce characterizes this whole neighborhood, centered on both the tourist market and the nearby **Mercato Centrale,** whose upper floor is a showcase for Italian street food (see p. 204).

**Cappelle Medicee (Medici Chapels)** ★ MONUMENT/MUSEUM When Michelangelo built San Lorenzo's New Sacristy between 1520 and 1533 (finished by Vasari in 1556), it was to be a tasteful monument to Lorenzo the Magnificent and his generation of relatively enlightened Medici. When work got underway in 1604 on the adjacent **Cappella dei Principi** (Chapel of the Princes), it was to become one of Italy's most god-awful and arrogant memorials, dedicated to the grand dukes, whose ranks include some of Florence's most decrepit tyrants. The Cappella dei Principi is an exercise in bad taste, a mountain of cut marbles and semiprecious stones—jasper, alabaster, mother-of-pearl, agate, and the like—slathered onto the walls and ceiling with no regard for composition and still less for chromatic unity. The pouring of ducal funds into this monstrosity lasted until Gian Gastone de' Medici drank himself to death in 1737, without an heir. Teams kept doggedly at the thing, and they were still finishing the floor in 1962. It was once again restored in 2019; judge for yourself.

Michelangelo's **Sagrestia Nuova (New Sacristy)** ★★, built to jibe with Brunelleschi's Old Sacristy in San Lorenzo proper (see p. 191), is much calmer. (An architectural tidbit: The windows in the dome taper as they get near the top to fool you into thinking the dome is higher.) Michelangelo was supposed to produce three tombs here (perhaps four) but ironically got only the two less important ones done. So, Lorenzo de' Medici ("the Magnificent")— wise ruler of his city, poet of note, grand patron of the arts, moneybags behind much of the Renaissance, and subject of his own Netflix miniseries—ended up with a mere inscription of his name next to his brother Giuliano's on a plain marble slab against the entrance wall. They did get one Michelangelo sculpture to decorate their slab, an unfinished **"Madonna and Child"** ★. On the left wall of the sacristy, Michelangelo's **"Tomb of Lorenzo"** ★ commemorates the duke of Urbino (Lorenzo the Magnificent's grandson), whose seated statue symbolizes the contemplative life. Below him on the curves of the tomb stretch a pair of sculptures, "Dawn" (female) and "Dusk" (male). Observing them, one might wonder if Michelangelo perhaps hadn't seen many naked women.

Piazza Madonna degli Aldobrandini (behind San Lorenzo, where Via Faenza and Via del Giglio meet). ☎ **055/238-8602.** 8€. Sat–Mon 8:45am–1:30pm; Tues, Thurs & Fri 1:45–6:30pm. Closed 1st, 3rd, and 5th Sun of each month. Bus: C1, C2, 22.

**Palazzo Medici-Riccardi ★** PALACE   Built by Michelozzo in 1444 for Medici "godfather" Cosimo il Vecchio, this is the prototype Florentine *palazzo,* on which the more overbearing Strozzi and Pitti palaces were later modeled. It remained the Medici private home until Cosimo I (not the same guy) officially declared his power as duke by moving to the Palazzo Vecchio, the city's civic nerve center. A door off the grandiose courtyard designed by Michelozzo leads up a staircase to the **Cappella dei Magi,** the oldest chapel to survive inside a private Florentine palace; its walls are covered with dense and colorful Benozzo Gozzoli **frescoes ★★** (1459–63), classics of the International Gothic style. The walls depict an extended "Journey of the Magi" to see the Christ child, who's being adored by Mary in the altarpiece.

Via Cavour 3. www.palazzomediciriccardi.it. ☎ **055/276-8224.** 7€ (10€ during temporary exhibitions); courtyard and citrus garden free admission. Thurs–Tues 9am–7pm. Bus: C1, 14, 23.

**San Lorenzo ★** CHURCH   A rough brick anti-facade fronts what is most likely the oldest church in Florence, founded in A.D. 393. It was later the Medici family's parish church, and Cosimo il Vecchio, whose wise behind-the-scenes rule made him popular with Florentines, is buried in front of the high altar. The plaque marking the spot is inscribed PATER PATRIAE, "Father of the Homeland." Off the left transept, the **Sagrestia Vecchia (Old Sacristy) ★** is one of Brunelleschi's purest pieces of early Renaissance architecture. The focal sarcophagus contains Cosimo il Vecchio's parents, Giovanni di Bicci de' Medici and his wife, Piccarda Bueri. A side chapel is decorated with a star map showing the night sky above the city in the 1440s—a scene that also features, precisely, in Brunelleschi's Pazzi Chapel in Santa Croce; see p. 197. On the wall of the main church's left aisle is Bronzino's huge fresco of the **"Martyrdom of San Lorenzo" ★** (1568), showing the poor saint being roasted on a grill in Rome. Round the corner in the transept is another highlight: Filippo Lippi's **"Annunciation" ★** (1447), heavily influenced by Flemish art. The church's two pulpits are thought to be the last works completed by Donatello.

Piazza San Lorenzo. www.operamedicealaurenziana.org. ☎ **055/214-042.** 7€. Mon–Sat 10:30am–4pm. Bus: C1.

## Near Piazza Santa Maria Novella

The two squat obelisks in **Piazza Santa Maria Novella ★,** resting on tortoises by Giambologna, once served as turning posts for "chariot" races held here from the 16th to the mid–19th century. Down-at-heel just a couple of decades ago, this neighborhood now has some of Florence's priciest hotels.

**Museo Marino Marini & Cappella Rucellai** ★ MUSEUM   One of Florence's quirkiest museums showcases the work of sculptor Marino Marini (1901–80). A native of nearby Pistoia, Marini worked mostly in bronze, with "horse and rider" a recurring theme in his semi-abstract work. The open spaces, minimal crowds, monumental sculptures, and fun themes in Marini's work make this museum—revamped in 2018—a good bet if kids are weary of the Renaissance. They won't escape it entirely, however: Tagged onto the side of the museum is the **Cappella Rucellai,** a Renaissance chapel housing the **Tempietto ★★,** a polychrome marble tomb completed by L. B. Alberti for Giovanni de' Rucellai in 1467. Decorated with symbols of both the Rucellai and Medici families, and frescoed on the inside, the tomb was supposedly based on drawings of the Holy Sepulcher in Jerusalem.

Piazza San Pancrazio. www.museomarinomarini.it. (C) **055/219-432.** 6€. Sat–Mon 10am–7pm. Bus: C3, 6, 11.

**Museo Novecento** ★ MUSEUM   This 21st-century museum covers 20th-century Italian art in a multitude of media. Crowds are often sparse—let's face it, you're in Florence to experience the 1400s, not the 1900s. This is no reflection on the collection's quality, which spans 100 years of visual arts. Exhibits include works by major names such as De Chirico and Futurist Gino Severini, and close examinations of Florence's role in fashion and Italy's relationship with European avant-garde art. In a tiny top-floor room, a 20-minute movie-clip montage shows Florence through the lens of the century's filmmakers, from Arnaldo Ginna's 1916 "Vita Futurista" to more recent hits like "Room with a View" and "Tea with Mussolini."

Piazza Santa Maria Novella 10. www.museonovecento.it/en. (C) **055/286-132.** 9.50€. Apr–Sept Fri–Wed 11am–9pm; Oct–Mar Mon–Fri 11am–7pm (closes 2pm Thurs). Bus: 6 or 11.

**Ognissanti** ★ CHURCH   The Biblical Last Supper (*Cenacolo* in Italian) was a favorite commission for wealthy Renaissance monasteries and convents, usually for their refectory (dining hall). Florence has several, including in the old refectory at San Marco (p. 194). Ghirlandaio's 1480 version here is set in a vaulted loggia beside a citrus grove with abundant bird life, all painted precisely in fresco. (Check below for viewing hours, which are limited.)

The church itself has a baroque facade, a rare sight in Florence. It has long links to the Vespucci family, whose most famous son—Amerigo—made his name as a seafaring explorer. Painted shortly before he did his Last Supper, Ghirlandaio's "Madonna della Misericordia" on the aisle wall is basically a Vespucci family portrait.

Borgo Ognissanti 42. (C)**055/239-8700.** Free. Cenacolo: Mon & Sat 9am–1pm. Church: Mon, Tues & Thurs–Sat 9:30am–12:30pm and 4–7:15pm; Wed & Sun 4–7:15pm. Bus: C4.

**Santa Maria Novella** ★★ CHURCH   Of all Florence's major churches, the home of the Dominicans is the only one with an original, unadulterated **facade ★★.** The lower Romanesque half was started in the 1300s by architect

Fra Jacopo Talenti. Renaissance architect Leon Battista Alberti finished the facade, adding a classically inspired top that not only chimed seamlessly with the lower half but also created a Cartesian plane of perfect geometry. Inside, Masaccio's **"Trinità"** ★★★ (ca. 1425) was the first painting ever to use linear mathematical perspective. Florentine citizens and artists flooded in to see the fresco's unveiling, many remarking in awe that it seemed to punch a hole into space, creating a chapel out of a flat wall. Frescoed chapels by Filippino Lippi and others fill the **transept.** The **Sanctuary** ★ behind the main altar was frescoed after 1485 by Ghirlandaio with the help of his assistants and apprentices, probably including a young Michelangelo. The left wall is covered with a cycle on the "Life of the Virgin," and the right has a "Life of St. John the Baptist," works that are also snapshots of the era's fashions, stuffed with portraits of the Tornabuoni family who commissioned them.

The church and convent cloisters are now accessible on one admission ticket. The **Chiostro Verde (Green Cloister)** ★★ was partly frescoed between 1431 and 1446 by Paolo Uccello, a Florentine painter who became increasingly obsessed with the mathematics behind perspective. His Old Testament scenes include a "Universal Deluge," which ironically was badly damaged by the Great Arno Flood of 1966. Off the cloister, the **Spanish Chapel** ★ is a complex piece of Dominican propaganda, frescoed in the 1360s by Andrea di Bonaiuto. The **Chiostro dei Morti (Cloister of the Dead)** ★, one of the oldest parts of the convent, was also badly damaged in 1966. Its low-slung vaults were decorated by Andrea Orcagna and others. Visitors can also access the **Chiostro Grande** (Florence's largest cloister) and papal apartments frescoed by Florentine Mannerist Pontormo. Allow at least 90 minutes to explore the complex fully.

*Tip:* Take home some of the divinely scented soaps and skincare products of Florence's famed herbal pharmacy **Officina Profumo-Farmaceutica di Santa Maria Novella,** next door at Via della Scala 16. It traces its roots to 13th-century Dominican friars who founded the Santa Maria Novella convent (see "Shopping," p. 203).

Piazza Santa Maria Novella/Piazza della Stazione 4. www.smn.it. (*055/219-257.* 7.50€ (10€ during exhibition). Mon–Sat 10am–5pm; Sun 1–5pm. Bus: C2, 6, 11, 22.

# Near San Marco & Santissima Annunziata

**Cenacolo di Sant'Apollonia** ★ CONVENT/MUSEUM  Andrea del Castagno (1421–57) learned his trade painting portraits of condemned men in city prisons, and the influence of this apprenticeship is apparent on the faces of the disciples in his version of **"The Last Supper,"** the first of many painted in Florence during the Renaissance. This giant fresco, completed around 1447, covers an entire wall at one end of the former convent refectory. Judas is banished to the far side of a communal table. Castagno's "Crucifixion," "Deposition," and "Entombment" complete the sequence.

Via XXVII Aprile 1. (*055/238-8608.* Free. Daily 8:15am–1:50pm. Closed 1st, 3rd, and 5th Sat and Sun of each month. Bus: 1, 6, 11, 14, 17, 23.

**Galleria dell'Accademia** ★★ MUSEUM   The Accademia's star exhibit, **"David"** ★★★—"Il Gigante"—is much larger than you imagine, looming 4.8m (16 ft.) on top of a 1.8m (6-ft.) pedestal. He hasn't faded with time, either; the marble still gleams as if it were unveiling day in 1504. Viewing the statue is a pleasure in the bright and spacious room custom-designed for him after his move to the Accademia in 1873, following 300 years of pigeons perching on his head in Piazza della Signoria. (Replicas now take the abuse there, and at Piazzale Michelangelo; the spot high on the northern flank of the Duomo, for which he was originally commissioned, stands empty.) But the Accademia is not only about "David"; you will be delighted to discover he is surrounded by an entire museum of Renaissance works. Michelangelo's unfinished **"Prisoners"** ★★ statues are a contrast to "David," their rough forms struggling to emerge from the raw stone. Michelangelo famously said he tried to free the sculpture from within every block, and you can appreciate this technique here. Rooms showcase paintings by Perugino, Filippino Lippi, Giotto, Giovanni da Milano, Andrea Orcagna, and others.

Via Ricasoli 60. www.galleriaaccademiafirenze.it. ✆ **055/294-883** (ticket office). 12€; prebooking compulsory on weekends. Tues–Sun 9am–6:45pm. Bus: C1, 1, 6, 14, 19, 23, 31, 32.

**Museo Archeologico (Archaeological Museum)** ★ MUSEUM   If you can force yourselves away from the Renaissance, rewind a millennium or two at one of the most important archaeological collections in central Italy. It has a particular emphasis on the Etruscan period. You'll need a little patience, however: The collection inside 17th-century Palazzo della Crocetta is not easy to navigate, though you will easily find the **"Arezzo Chimera"** ★★, a bronze figure of a mythical lion–goat–serpent dating to the 4th century B.C., perhaps the most important bronze sculpture to survive from the Etruscan era. It's displayed alongside the "Arringatore," a life-size bronze of an orator dating to the 1st century, just as Etruscan culture was being subsumed by Ancient Rome. On the top floor is the **"Idolino"** ★, an exquisite and slightly mysterious, lithe bronze. The collection is strong on Etruscan-era *bucchero* pottery and funerary urns, and Egyptian relics including several sarcophagi displayed in a series of eerie galleries. In 2018, the museum inaugurated a section dedicated to the vast collection of gems, cameos, and intaglio gathered by generations of Medici and Lorraine dukes. Some pieces date back many centuries B.C. With other travelers so focused on medieval and Renaissance sights in the city, you may have this museum almost to yourself.

Piazza Santissima Annunziata 9b. ✆ **055/23-575.** 8€ (free with Uffizi ticket). Sun–Wed & Sat 8:30am–2pm; Thurs 1:30–7pm. Closed 2nd, 3rd, 4th, and 5th Sun of each month. Bus: 6, 19, 31, 32.

**San Marco** ★★★ CHURCH   Showcasing the work of Fra Angelico, Dominican monk and Florentine painter in the International Gothic style, this is the most important collection in the world of his altarpieces and painted panels, residing in a deconsecrated 13th-century convent this multitasking artist-monk once called home. Seeing it all in one place—around a courtyard and upstairs library designed by Michelozzo—helps you to appreciate how his decorative impulses and the sinuous lines of his figures place his work right on the cusp of the Renaissance. The most moving and unusual is his **"Annunciation"** ★★★, but a close second are the intimate frescoes of the life of Jesus—painted not on one giant wall, but scene by scene on the individual walls of small monks' cells that honeycomb the upper floor. The idea was for these scenes, painted by both Fra Angelico and his assistants, to aid in the monks' prayer and contemplation. The final cell on the left corridor belonged to firebrand

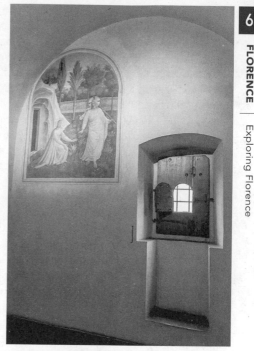

At San Marco, masterpieces by Fra Angelico are painted simply right onto the convent walls.

preacher Savonarola, who briefly incited the people of the most art-filled city in the world to burn their "decadent" paintings, illuminated manuscripts, and anything else he felt was a worldly betrayal of Jesus's ideals. You'll see his rosary, chair, and what's left of the clothes he wore in his cell, as well as an anonymous panel painted to show the day in 1498 when—having fallen out with everyone, including the pope—he was burned at the stake in Piazza della Signoria. There's much more Fra Angelico secreted around the cloisters, including a **"Crucifixion"** ★ in the Chapter House. The former Pilgrims' Hospice is now a gallery dedicated to Fra Angelico and his contemporaries; look especially for his **"Tabernacolo dei Linaioli"** ★★, painted for the linen workers' guild in the 1430s, and a seemingly weightless **"Deposition"** ★★.

Piazza San Marco 3. ⓒ **055/238-8608.** 8€. Daily 8:15am–1:50pm. Closed 1st, 3rd, and 5th Sun and Mon after 2nd and 4th Sun of month. Bus: C1, 1, 6, 7, 10, 11, 14, 17, 19, 20, 23, 25, 31, 32.

**Santissima Annunziata** ★★ CHURCH   This church's story begins humbly, in 1233, when seven Florentine nobles had a spiritual crisis, gave away their possessions, and retired to the forest to contemplate divinity. In 1250, they returned to what were then fields outside the city walls and founded a small oratory, proclaiming themselves Servants of Mary (the

"Servite Order"). Over the years, thanks to a miraculous painting (more on that later), the oratory grew into a grand basilica, enlarged by Michelozzo (1444–81) and later redecorated in unrestrained baroque style.

Visitors enter through the **Chiostro dei Voti (Votive Cloister),** which is today the church's main art draw, decorated with some of the city's finest **Mannerist frescoes** ★★ (1465–1515). A 5-year restoration reinstated their original vibrancy. Rosso Fiorentino provided an "Assumption" (1513) and Pontormo the "Visitation" (1515) just to the right of the door. Their master, Andrea del Sarto, contributed a "Birth of the Virgin" (1513), in the far-right corner, one of his finest works. To the right of the door into the church is a damaged but still fascinating "Procession of the Magi" (1514) by del Sarto, who included a self-portrait at the far right, looking out at us from under his blue hat.

The church's interior is a flamboyant affair, smothered in multicolored marble and topped with a gilded coffered ceiling. In a side chapel to the left of the entrance, look for the ornate tabernacle housing a small 14th-century painting of the "Annunciation." Why such a grandiose setting? Well, according to legend, the friar who was painting the picture became vexed that he couldn't paint the Madonna's face as beautifully as she should be, and went to take a nap. When he awoke, he found an angel had completed the face for him. The miraculous painting became an object of cult worship, and a once-humble church was changed forever.

On **Piazza Santissima Annunziata** ★★ outside, flanked by elegant Brunelleschi porticos, an equestrian statue of Grand Duke Ferdinand I was Giambologna's last work, cast in 1608 after his death by his student Pietro Tacca, who also did the two fountains of fantastical mermonkey-monsters. *Tip:* You can stay right on this spectacular piazza, at one of our favorite Florence hotels, the **Loggiato dei Serviti** ★★ (p. 162).

Piazza Santissima Annunziata. ✆ **055/266-181.** Free. Cloister: daily 7am–12:45pm and 4–5pm. Church: daily 4–5pm. Bus: 6, 19, 31, 32.

**Spedale degli Innocenti** ★★ MUSEUM/ARCHITECTURE Originally funded by the silkworkers' guild, the "Nocenti" opened in 1419, and ever since has been one of the world's most famous childcare institutions. (The Institute still works with UNICEF.) Their landmark building was designed by Brunelleschi himself, with elegant Renaissance loggias on the facade and surrounding its interior "Women's" and "Men's" **courtyards.** Inside, a three-floor museum has multimedia exhibits tracing the history of the place and the personal stories of many who benefited from its care. The Institute also has a fine **art collection,** including Renaissance works by Botticelli and Ghirlandaio displayed in a top-floor gallery, alongside original painted ceramic roundels by Della Robbia, which elegantly completed Brunelleschi's facade. As you leave, notice the little grated window on the north wall of the main loggia, where for centuries babies were delivered anonymously to the orphanage's care.

Piazza Santissima Annunziata. www.museodeglinnocenti.it. ℂ **055/203-7308.** 10€; 15€ family. Wed–Mon 11am–6pm. Bus: 6, 19, 31, 32.

6

FLORENCE | Exploring Florence

# Around Piazza Santa Croce

**Piazza Santa Croce** is pretty much like any grand Florentine square—an open space ringed with souvenir and leather shops and thronged with tourists. Once a year (during late June), it's covered with dirt for a violent, Renaissance-style football tournament known as **Calcio Storico Fiorentino.** In December, you'll also find Florence's main **Christmas market**—a fun, if boilerplate German-style affair.

**Santa Croce** ★★ CHURCH The center of Florence's Franciscan universe was begun in 1294 by Gothic master Arnolfo di Cambio to rival the church of Santa Maria Novella being raised by the Dominicans across the city. The church wasn't consecrated until 1442, and even then it remained faceless until the neo-Gothic **facade** was added in 1857. This art-stuffed complex demands a couple hours of your time to see properly.

The Gothic **interior** is vast, and populated with the tombs of famous Florentines. Starting from the front door, immediately on the right is the tomb of the most venerated Renaissance master, **Michelangelo Buonarroti,** who died in Rome in 1564 at the ripe age of 89. The pope wanted him buried in the Eternal City, but Florentines snuck his body home. Two berths along from Michelangelo's monument is a pompous 19th-century cenotaph to **Dante Alighieri,** one of history's great poets, whose "Divine Comedy" laid the basis for the modern Italian language. (Exiled from Florence, Dante is buried in Ravenna.) Elsewhere are monuments to philosopher **Niccolò Machiavelli,** composer **Gioacchino Rossini,** sculptor **Lorenzo Ghiberti,** and scientist **Galileo Galilei.**

The church's right transept is richly decorated with **frescoes.** The **Cappella Castellani** was frescoed with stories of saints' lives by Agnolo Gaddi. His father, Taddeo Gaddi—one of Giotto's closest followers—painted the **Cappella Baroncelli** ★ (1328–38) at the transept's end. The frescoes depict scenes from the "Life of the Virgin," and include an "Annunciation to the Shepherds," the first night scene in Italian fresco. Giotto himself frescoed the two chapels to the right of the high altar. Whitewashed over in the 17th century, they were uncovered in the 1800s and inexpertly restored. The **Cappella Peruzzi** ★ is a late work with many references to antiquity, reflecting Giotto's trip to Rome's ruins. The more famous **Cappella Bardi** ★★ appeared in the movie "A Room with a View"; key panels, featuring episodes in the life of St. Francis, include the "Trial by Fire Before the Sultan of Egypt" on the right wall; and one of Giotto's best-known works, the "Death of St. Francis," in which monks weep and wail with convincing pathos.

Outside in the cloister is the **Cappella Pazzi** ★, one of Filippo Brunelleschi's architectural masterpieces (faithfully finished after his death in 1446). Giuliano da Maiano probably designed the porch that now fronts the chapel, set with glazed terracottas by Luca della Robbia. The chapel is one of Brunelleschi's signature pieces, decorated with his trademark *pietra serena* gray stone. It's a defining example of early Renaissance architecture. Note the ceiling of the smaller dome depicts the same night sky as his Old Sacristy in San Lorenzo (p. 191). It is unclear why this was done. In the church **Sacristy** is a Cimabue **"Crucifix"** ★ that was almost destroyed by the Arno Flood of 1966. It became an international symbol of the ruination wreaked that November.

Piazza Santa Croce. www.santacroceopera.it. © **055/246-6105.** 8€. Mon & Wed–Sat 9:30am–5:30pm; Sun 1–5:30pm. Bus: C1, C2, C3.

## The Oltrarno, San Niccolò & San Frediano

**Giardino Bardini (Bardini Garden)** ★ PARK/GARDEN Hemmed in on the north by the city's medieval wall, the handsome Bardini Garden is less famous—and therefore less hectic—than its neighbor down the hill, the Boboli (see below). From a loftier perch over the Oltrarno, it beats the Boboli hands down for views and new angles on the city. The side view of Santa Croce—with the synagogue's copper dome in the background—shows how the church's 19th-century facade was bolted onto a building dating to the 1200s.

Costa San Giorgio 2. www.villabardini.it. © **055/2006-6233.** Combined ticket with Boboli Garden Mar–Oct 10€, Nov–Feb 6€. Same hours as Boboli; see below. Bus: C3 or C4.

**Giardino di Boboli (Boboli Garden)** ★★ PARK/GARDEN The statue-filled park behind the Pitti Palace is one of the earliest and finest Renaissance gardens, laid out mostly between 1549 and 1656 with box hedges in geometric patterns, groves of ilex (holm oak), dozens of statues, and rows of cypress. Just above the entrance through the courtyard of the Palazzo Pitti is an oblong **amphitheater** modeled on Roman circuses, with a **granite basin** from Rome's Baths of Caracalla and an **Egyptian obelisk** of Ramses II. In 1589 this was the setting for the wedding reception of Ferdinand de' Medici and Christine of Lorraine. For the occasion, the family commissioned entertainment from Jacopo Peri and Ottavio Rinuccini, who decided to set a classical story entirely to music and called it "Dafne"—the world's first opera. (Later, they wrote a follow-up hit, "Erudice," performed here in 1600; this is the first opera whose score survives.) At the south end of the park, the **Isolotto** ★ is a dreamy island in a pond full of huge goldfish, with Giambologna's "L'Oceano" sculptural composition at its center. At the north end, around the end of the Pitti Palace, are fake caverns filled with statuary, attempting to invoke a classical sacred grotto. The most famous, the **Grotta Grande,** was designed by Giorgio Vasari, Bartolomeo Ammannati, and Bernardo Buontalenti between 1557 and 1593. Dripping with phony stalactites, it's set with replicas of Michelangelo's unfinished "Prisoners" statues. You can usually get inside on the hour (but not every hour) for 15 minutes.

Entrance via Palazzo Pitti. www.uffizi.it/en/boboli-garden. © **055/238-8791.** Mar–Oct 10€, Nov–Feb 6€; includes Giardino Bardini. Nov–Feb daily 8:15am–4:30pm; Mar daily 8:15am–5:30pm; Apr–May and Sept–Oct daily to 6:30pm; June–Aug daily to 7pm. Closed 1st and last Mon of month. Bus: C3, C4, 11, 36, 37.

**Palazzo Pitti (Pitti Palace)** ★★ MUSEUM/PALACE   Although built by and named after a rival of the Medici—the merchant Luca Pitti—in the 1450s, this gigantic *palazzo* soon came into Medici hands. It was the Medici family's principal home from the 1540s, and continued to house Florence's rulers until 1919. The Pitti contains five museums, including one of the world's best collections of canvases by Raphael. Out back are elegant Renaissance gardens, the **Boboli** (see above).

In the art-crammed rooms of the Pitti's **Galleria Palatina** ★★, paintings are displayed like cars in a parking garage, stacked on walls above each other following the Enlightenment method of exhibition. Rooms are alternately dimly lit, or garishly bright; this is how many of the world's great art treasures were seen and enjoyed by their original commissioners. You will find important historical treasures amid the Palatina's vast and haphazard collection; some of the best efforts of Titian, Raphael, and Rubens line the walls. Botticelli and Filippo Lippi's **"Madonna and Child"** ★ (1452) provide the key works in the **Sala di Prometeo** (Prometheus Room). The latter looks suspiciously like another portrait of his nun/lover, Lucrezia Buti (see Uffizi, p. 182). Two giant canvases of the "Assumption of the Virgin," both by Mannerist painter Andrea del Sarto, dominate the **Sala dell'Iliade** (Iliad Room). Here you will also find another Biblical woman painted by Artemisia Gentileschi, "Judith." The **Sala di Saturno** (Saturn Room) ★ overflows with

The walls of the Pitti Palace's Galleria Palatina are crammed with art.

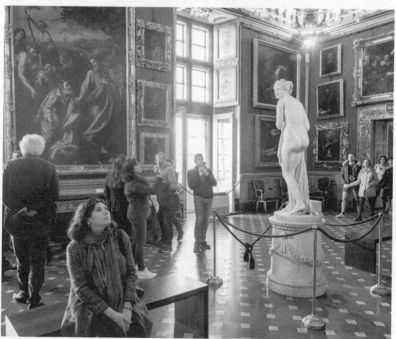

Raphaels; in the **Sala di Giove** (Jupiter Room) is his sublime, naturalistic portrait of **"La Velata"** ★★, as well as **"The Ages of Man"** ★. The current attribution of the latter painting is awarded to Venetian Giorgione, although this has been disputed.

At the **Appartamenti Reali** (Royal Apartments) you get a feeling for the conspicuous consumption of the Medici Grand Dukes and their Austrian and Belgian Lorraine successors—and see some notable paintings in their original, ostentatious setting. Italy's first king lived here for several years during the 19th-century unification process—when Florence was the second national capital, after Turin—until Rome was finally conquered and the court moved there. Much of the gilded stucco, fabrics, and general decoration is in thunderously poor taste.

The Pitti's "modern" gallery, the **Galleria d'Arte Moderna** ★, has a good collection of 19th-century Italian paintings with a focus on Romanticism, Neoclassical works, and the **Macchiaioli,** a school of Italian painters who worked in an "impressionistic style" chronologically before the French Impressionists. Highlights hunters with limited time should head straight for major works of the latter, in Sala 18 through 20, where landscapes by **Giovanni Fattori** ★ (1825–1908) and Telemaco Signorini (1835–1901) hang. The Pitti's two lesser museums—the **Galleria del Costume** (Costume Gallery) and **Museo degli Argenti** (Museum of Silverware)—combine to show that wealth and taste do not always go hand in hand. One thing you will notice in the Costume Gallery: how much smaller locals were a few centuries ago.

Piazza Pitti. www.uffizi.it. Mar–Oct 16€, Nov–Feb 10€. Tues–Sun 1:30–6:50pm (prebooking compulsory on weekends). Bus: C3, C4, 11, 36, 37.

**Piazzale Michelangelo** ★★ SQUARE   This pedestrianized, panoramic piazza is on the itinerary of every tour bus. The balustraded terrace was laid out in 1869 to give a sweeping **vista** ★★ of the Renaissance city, spread out in the valley below and backed by the green hills of Fiesole beyond. You will get the classic photo of Florence's skyline from here. Nearby, a bronze replica of "David" points directly at his original home, the Palazzo Vecchio.

Viale Michelangiolo. Bus: 12 or 13.

**San Miniato al Monte** ★★ CHURCH   High atop a hill, its gleaming white-and-green marble facade visible from the city below, San Miniato is one of few ancient churches of Florence to survive the centuries virtually intact. The current building took shape in 1013, under the auspices of the powerful Arte di Calimala guild, whose symbol, a bronze eagle clutching a bale of wool, perches on the **facade** ★★. Above the central window is a 13th-century mosaic of "Christ Between the Madonna and St. Minias" (a theme repeated in the apse). The interior has a few Renaissance additions, but they blend well with the overall medieval aspect—an airy, stony space with a raised choir at one end, painted wooden trusses on the ceiling, and tombs interspersed with inlaid marble symbols of the zodiac paving the floor. Below the choir is an 11th-century **crypt** with remains of frescoes by Taddeo Gaddi. Off to the right of the raised choir is the sacristy, which Spinello Aretino covered in 1387 with elaborate frescoes depicting the **"Life of St. Benedict"** ★. Off the left of the nave is the 15th-century **Cappella del Cardinale del Portogallo** ★★, a collaborative effort by Renaissance artists to honor the Portuguese humanist Cardinal Jacopo di Lusitania. It's worth timing your visit to come here when the Benedictine monks are celebrating mass in Gregorian chant (usually 5:30pm). Around the back of the church is San Miniato's monumental **cemetery** ★, its streets lined with tombs and mausoleums built in elaborate pastiches of every generation of Florentine architecture. It's a peaceful, often deserted spot, soundtracked only by birdsong and an occasional tolling of church bells.

Via Monte alle Croci/Viale Galileo Galilei (behind Piazzale Michelangelo). ℂ**055/234-2731.** Free. Mon–Sat 9:30am–12:30pm and 3–6pm; Sun 3–5:30pm. Bus: 12 or 13.

**Santa Felicita** ★ CHURCH    Greek sailors who lived in this neighborhood in the 2nd century brought Christianity to Florence, and this little church was probably the second to be established in the city, the first structure rising in the late 4th century. The current church was remodeled in the 1730s. The star works are in the first chapel on the right, the Brunelleschi-designed **Cappella Barbadori-Capponi,** with paintings by Mannerist master Pontormo (1525–27). Pontormo's **"Deposition"** ★★ and frescoed "Annunciation" are rife with his garish color palette of oranges, pinks, golds, lime greens, and sky blues, and exhibit his trademark surreal sense of figure.

Piazza Santa Felicita (on left off Via Guicciardini across the Ponte Vecchio). ℂ**055/213-018.** Free (1€ to illuminate chapel lights). Mon–Sat 9:30am–12:30pm and 3:30–5:30pm. Bus: C3 or C4.

**Santa Maria del Carmine** ★★★ CHURCH    Following a 1771 fire that destroyed everything but the transept chapels and sacristy, this Carmelite church was almost entirely reconstructed in high baroque style. To see the much older **Cappella Brancacci** ★★★, in the right transept, you have to enter through the cloisters and pay admission. The frescoes here were commissioned by an enemy of the Medici, Felice Brancacci, who in 1424 hired Masolino and his student Masaccio to decorate it with the "Life of St. Peter." Masolino probably worked out the cycle's scheme and painted a few scenes along with his pupil before taking off for 3 years to serve as court painter in Budapest. Masaccio kept painting, quietly creating the early Renaissance's greatest frescoes. Masaccio eventually left for Rome in 1428, where he died at age 27; the cycle was completed between 1480 and 1485 by Filippino Lippi. Masolino painted "St. Peter Preaching," the upper panel to the left of the altar, and the two top scenes on the right wall, which shows his fastidious, decorative style in a long panel of "St. Peter Healing the Cripple" and "Raising Tabitha," and his "Adam and Eve." Contrast this first man and woman, about to take the bait offered by the snake, with Masaccio's **"Expulsion from the Garden"** ★★★, opposite it. Masolino's figures are highly posed, expressionless models, while Masaccio's Adam and Eve burst with intense emotion. The top scene on the left wall, Masaccio's **"Tribute Money"** ★★, showcases his use of linear perspective. The scenes to the right of the altar are Masaccio's as well; the **"Baptism of the Neophytes"** ★★ is among his masterpieces.

Piazza del Carmine. ticketsmuseums.comune.fi.it. ☏ **055/276-8224.** Church free; Cappella Brancacci 8€ (10€ Sat–Mon). Mon and Wed–Sat 10am–5pm; Sun 1–5pm. Bus: C4.

**Santo Spirito** ★ CHURCH   One of Filippo Brunelleschi's masterpieces of architecture, this 15th-century church doesn't look much from the outside (no proper facade was ever built). But the **interior** ★ is a marvelous High Renaissance space—an expansive landscape of proportion and mathematics in classic Brunelleschi style, with coffered ceiling, lean columns with Corinthian capitals, and the stacked perspective of arched arcading. Late Renaissance and baroque paintings are scattered throughout, but the best stuff lies in the transepts, especially the **Cappella Nerli** ★, with a panel by Filippino Lippi (right transept). The church's extravagant baroque altar has a ciborium inlaid in *pietre dure* around 1607—and frankly, looks a bit silly against the restrained elegance of Brunelleschi's architecture. A separate entrance (with a 3€ admission fee) gets you into the **Sacristy**—to see a wooden "Crucifix" that has, controversially, been attributed to Michelangelo—as well as Santo Spirito's 17th-century cloister and refectory. *Tip:* Tree-shaded **Piazza Santo Spirito** ★ is one of the focal points of the Oltrarno, lined with cafes and outdoor tables. Sometimes a few farmers sell fresh produce on the piazza.

Piazza Santo Spirito. www.basilicasantospirito.it. ☏ **055/210-030.** Free (3€ sacristy & cloister). Mon–Tues and Thurs–Sat 10am–1pm and 3–5pm; Sun 11:30am–1:30pm and 3–6pm. Bus: C3, C4, 11, 36, 37.

## Organized Tours

Florence's best-kept secret is a regular small group trip to the north-facing roof **Terraces of the Cathedral** ★★, where until recently very few travelers got to stand. Views are spectacular; not just a close-up of the iconic dome from its base and down into the cathedral nave, but also the Baptistery's marble top, the green copper roof on the Mercato Centrale, and the hills of Fiesole beyond Florence. A 1-hour guided visit, conducted in English, costs 25€ per person. The tour departs from the Duomo ticket office (not Sun).

Insightful culture tours with **Context Travel** ★★ (www.contexttravel.com/cities/florence; ☏ **800/691-6036** in the U.S. or 06-96727371 in Italy) are led by academics and other experts in their field on a variety of themes, from the gastronomic to the archaeological and artistic. Tours are limited to six people and generally cost around 95€ per person. The quality of Context's walks is unmatched, and well worth their above-average cost. To book a private tour costs around $400.

**Food tours** are booming. A few hours in city markets, or in the company of street vendors or a pro chef, gives you an insight into traditions and trends in Florentine cooking. The glass-fronted Arclinea kitchens upstairs at the Mercato Centrale host the **Lorenzo de' Medici Cooking School** ★ (www.cucinaldm.com; ☏ **334/304-0551**), where 2-hour small-group courses (65€) teach the skills needed to create authentic staples such as stuffed fresh pasta.

**Eating Europe** (www.eatingeurope.com/florence) offers themed small-group tours (68€–95€) covering gelato-making, Oltrarno foodie haunts, and more. They can also customize a Florence food experience for you. **Curious Appetite Travel ★** (www.curiousappetitetravel.com) runs offbeat small-group market walks, a four-stop "dinner crawl," cocktail making, and artisan beer tastings. Prices range from $105 to $145 per person, which includes food and drink. **I Just Drive** (www.ijustdrive.us; ℭ **055/093-5928**) offers fully equipped cars (Wi-Fi, complimentary bottle of Prosecco) plus an English-speaking driver for various themed visits. For example, you can book a ride in a luxury Bentley or Mercedes up to San Miniato al Monte at dusk (1½ hr.; 129€). They also operate full-day and half-day food and wine tours into the Chianti hills.

## Especially for Kids

You have to put in a bit of work (and reserve ahead) to reach some of Florence's best views. The climbs, up claustrophobic medieval staircases, are a favorite with many kids. The cupola of the **Duomo** (p. 180), the **Palazzo Vecchio's** (p. 187) Torre di Arnolfo, and the **Campanile di Giotto** (p. 177) are perfect for any youngster with a head for heights.

The best family activities with an educational component are run by **Mus.e ★★** (www.musefirenze.it; ℭ **055/276-8224**), including child's-eye tours in English around the Palazzo Vecchio led by guides in period costumes. Lively, affordable activities focus on life at the ducal court, including "The Turtle and the Snail," pitched at children ages 4 to 7. Programs cost 5€ per person; book online or at the desk next to the Palazzo Vecchio ticket booth.

When youngsters need a crowd-free timeout space, head for the ground floor of the **Biblioteca delle Oblate,** Via dell'Oriuolo 24 (www.biblioteche. comune.fi.it; ℭ **055/261-6526**), a public library with a children's section for little ones (including in English), as well as space to spread out, color, or draw, and air-conditioning. It's free and open 9am to 6:45pm, except for Monday morning and all day Sunday (closed 1 week mid-Aug). *Tip:* The Oblate's cafe is an excellent place to kick back, with fair prices and a view of Brunelleschi's dome that few visitors see.

**Cycling** is a socially distanced pleasure in the riverside Parco delle Cascine: See p. 153 for bike rental advice. And remember: You are in the **gelato** capital of the world. At least one multi-scoop gelato per day is the minimum recommended dose; see p. 174.

# SHOPPING IN FLORENCE

After Milan, Florence is **Italy's top shopping city**—beating even Rome. Here's what to buy: leather, designer fashion, shoes, marbleized paper and other stationery, hand-embroidered linens, Tuscan wines, handmade jewelry, *pietre dure* (known also as "Florentine mosaic," inlaid semiprecious stones), and antiques. *Note:* It is illegal to knowingly buy fake goods anywhere in the city (and yes, a "Louis Vuitton" bag at 10€ counts as *knowingly*). You may be served a hefty on-the-spot fine if caught.

Traditionally, Florentine **shopping hours** are Monday through Saturday from 9:30am to noon or 1pm and 3 or 3:30 to 7:30pm. Increasingly, larger shops and those in tourist areas stay open on Sunday and through the midafternoon *riposo,* or "nap." Some small or family-run places close Monday mornings instead of Sundays.

## The Top Shopping Streets & Areas

**AROUND SANTA TRÍNITA**   The cream of the crop of Florentine shopping lines both sides of elegant **Via de' Tornabuoni,** with an extension along **Via della Vigna Nuova** and other surrounding streets. Here you'll find the big Italian fashion names like **Gucci ★** (at no. 73R; www.gucci.com; ✆ **055/264-011**), **Pucci ★** (at no. 22R; www.emiliopucci.com; ✆ **055/265-8082**), and **Ferragamo ★** (at no. 5R; www.ferragamo.com; ✆ **055/292-123**), ensconced in old palaces or minimalist boutiques. Couture meets streetwear at concept sneaker store **SOTF ★** (at no. 17R; www.sotf.com; ✆ **055/588-302**). Florence-headquartered **Benheart ★★** (Via della Vigna Nuova 97R; www.benheart.it; ✆ **055/239-9483**) sells up-to-the-minute Italian leather clothing, footwear, and accessories.

**AROUND VIA ROMA & VIA DEI CALZAIUOLI**   These are some of Florence's busiest streets, lined with storefronts offering mainstream shopping. Here you'll find major department stores **Coin,** Via dei Calzaiuoli 56R (www.coin.it; ✆ **055/280-531**), and **La Rinascente,** Piazza della Repubblica (www.rinascente.it; ✆ **055/219-113**), alongside quality clothing chains such as Geox and Zara. **La Feltrinelli RED,** Piazza delle Repubblica 26 (www.lafeltrinelli.it; ✆ **199/151-173**), is the center's best bookstore. A three-floor branch of upscale food-market mini-chain **Eataly** lies just north of the Baptistery at Via de' Martelli 22 (www.eataly.net; ✆ **055/015-3601**). Online couture sales sensation **Luisa Via Roma ★** (www.luisaviaroma.com) also has its flagship physical store here, at Via Roma 21R.

**AROUND SANTA CROCE**   The eastern part of the center has seen a flourishing of one-of-a-kind stores, with an emphasis on young, independent fashions. **Borgo degli Albizi** and its tributary streets are worth roaming— **Sabatini ★** (at no. 75R; ✆ **055/234-0240**) is an established go-to for affordable casual footwear.

## Florence's Best Markets

**Mercato Centrale ★★**   The center's main market stocks the usual fresh produce, but you can also browse (and taste) cheeses, salamis and cured hams, Tuscan wines, takeout food, and more. This is picnic-packing heaven. It runs Monday to Saturday until 2pm (until 5pm Sat for most of the year). Upstairs is street-food nirvana, all day, every day; see p. 171. Btw. Piazza del Mercato Centrale and Via dell'Ariento. No phone. Bus: C1.

**Mercato di San Lorenzo** ★   The city's tourist street market is a fun place to pick up T-shirts, marbleized paper, a leather-bound notebook, or some other city souvenir. Leather wallets, purses, bags, and jackets are popular with international visitors—be sure to assess the workmanship, which can be variable, and haggle shamelessly. This busy market runs daily; watch for pickpockets. Via dell'Ariento and Via Rosina. No phone. Bus: C1.

**Mercato di Sant'Ambrogio** ★   A proper slice of Florentine life, six mornings a week (closed Sun). The piazza outside has fruit, vegetables, costume jewelry, preserves, and end-of-line discount clothing. Go inside the market building for meat, olive oil, or a tasty budget lunch at **Da Rocco** (p. 172). Piazza Ghiberti. No phone. Bus: C2 or C3.

## Crafts & Artisanal Goods

Florence has a longstanding reputation for its craftsmanship. Although storefront display windows along touristed streets are often stuffed with cheap imports and mass-produced goods, if you know where to look, you will still find handmade, top-quality items.

**Il Torchio** ★★   This small Oltrarno workshop sells hand-bound notebooks and marbleized paper. Bespoke designs available. Via de' Bardi 17. www.legatoriailtorchio.com. *C* **055/234-2862.** Bus: C3 or C4.

**Madova** ★★   For a century, this has been the best city retailer for handmade leather gloves, lined with silk, cashmere, or lambs' wool. You'll pay

Shopping for leather goods in San Lorenzo market.

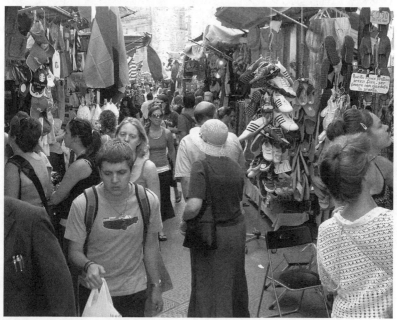

between 45€ and 80€ for a pair. Madova is the real deal, even this close to the Ponte Vecchio. Closed Sundays. Via Guicciardini 1R. www.madova.com. ☎ **055/239-6526.** Bus: C3 or D.

**Marioluca Giusti ★★**    The boutique of this renowned Florentine designer sells only his trademark synthetic acrylic crystal. The range includes colorful reinventions of cocktail and wine glasses, jugs, and tumblers—every piece tough, lightweight, and chic. Via della Spada 20R. www.mariolucagiusti.it. ☎ **055/214-583.** Bus: 6 or 11. Also at Via della Vigna Nuova 88R.

**Officina Profumo-Farmaceutica di Santa Maria Novella ★★★**    A shrine to scents and skincare, this is Florence's historic herbal pharmacy, with roots in the 13th century, when the adjacent convent of Santa Maria Novella was founded by Dominican friars. Nothing is cheap, but the perfumes, moisturizers, and candles are handmade from the finest natural ingredients and packaged exquisitely. Via della Scala 16. www.smnovella.com. ☎ **055/216-276.** Bus: C2.

**Parione ★**    This traditional Florentine stationer stocks notebooks, marbleized paper, fine pens, and souvenirs like handmade wooden music boxes and playing cards with 17th-century Florentine designs. Closed Sundays. Via dello Studio 11R. www.parione.it. ☎ **055/215-684.** Bus: C1 or C2.

**Scuola del Cuoio ★★**    Florence's leading leather school is also open house for visitors. You can watch trainee leatherworkers and gilders at work (Mon–Fri), then visit the small store to buy the best soft leather. Portable items like wallets, belts, and bags are a good buy. Closed Sundays in low season. Via San Giuseppe 5R (or enter through Santa Croce, via right transept). www.scuoladelcuoio.com. ☎ **055/244-534.** Bus: C3.

# ENTERTAINMENT & NIGHTLIFE

Florence has excellent, mostly free listings publications including *Informacittà* (www.informacitta.net), which is strong on theater, concerts, and other arts events, as well as one-off markets. Younger and hipper *Zero* (www.zero.eu/firenze) is hot on the latest eating, drinking, and edgy nightlife. *Firenze Spettacolo,* a 2€ Italian-language monthly sold at newsstands, is the most detailed and up-to-date listing of nightlife, arts, and entertainment. English-language magazine "The Florentine" includes weekly events and listings at **www.theflorentine.net/events**.

If you just want to wander and see what grabs you, you will find plenty of tourist-oriented action in bars close to the city's main squares, many with outdoor piazza seating. For something a little livelier—with a more local focus—visit **Borgo San Frediano, Piazza Santo Spirito,** or the northern end of **Via de' Macci,** near where it meets Via Pietrapiana. **Via de' Benci** is usually buzzing around *aperitivo* time and is popular with an expat crowd. **Via de' Renai** and the bars of San Niccolò around the **Porta San Miniato** are often lively too, with a mixed clientele of tourists and locals plus outdoor tables.

# Performing Arts & Live Music

Florence does not have the musical cachet of Milan, Venice, Naples, or Rome, but there are two symphony orchestras and a fine music school in Fiesole, as well as a modern opera house (see p. 210). The city's theaters are respectable, and most major touring companies stop in town. Buy tickets to cultural events online or in person from **Box Office,** Via delle Vecchie Carceri 1 (www.box officetoscana.it; ✆ **055/210-804**). Covid-related restrictions may include venue capacity limits, short-notice cancellations, or temporary closures.

Many classical music performances are sponsored by the **Amici della Musica** (www.amicimusicafirenze.it; ✆ **055/607-440**), so check the website to see what's on. Its venue is often **Teatro della Pergola,** where Verdi's opera "Macbeth" premiered in 1847; prices range 15€ to 30€. Florence's **Chamber Orchestra** runs an annual concert program, including in churches and other historic spaces in the city: See **www.orchestrafiorentina.it**. The restored Art Deco **Odeon Firenze ★** (Piazza Strozzi; www.odeonfirenze.com; ✆ **055/214-068**) theater shows the latest movies in their original language (9€).

**Libreria-Café La Cité ★** A relaxed cafe-bookshop by day, after dark this place becomes a bar and small-scale live music venue. The lineup is eclectic, often offbeat or world music, one night forrò or swing, the next Italian folk or chanteuse. Check its Facebook page to see what's on. Borgo San Frediano 20R. ✆ **055/210-387.** Bus: C3, C4, 6, 11, 36, 37.

**Opera di Firenze ★★** This vast new concert hall and arts complex seats up to 1,800 in daring postmodernist surrounds on the edge of the Cascine Park. Its program incorporates opera, ballet, and orchestral music: Restricted-view or "listening only" seats can be very cheap. Each May and June, the venue hosts the **Maggio Musicale Fiorentino,** one of Italy's most prestigious music festivals. Piazzale Vittorio Gui. www.operadifirenze.it. ✆ **055/277-9350.** Tickets 15€–200€. Tram: T1.

**Volume ★** By day, it's a laid-back cafe and art space selling coffee, books, and fresh juices. By night, it serves *aperitivo* from 6:30pm, then becomes a buzzing cocktail bar with live acoustic sets. Piazza Santo Spirito 5R. www.volume firenze.com. ✆ **055/238-1460.** Bus: C3, 11, 36, 37.

## Cafes

Florence no longer has a glitterati or intellectuals' cafe scene, and when it did—from the late-19th-century Risorgimento era through 1950s *Dolce Vita*—it was basically copying the idea from Paris. Although they're often overpriced tourist spots today—especially around **Piazza della Repubblica**—Florence's high-toned piazza cafes are fine if you want pastries while you sit and people-watch.

**Cantinetta dei Verrazzano ★★** One of the coziest little cafe-bars in the center is decked out with antique wooden wine cabinets, in genuine *eno-teca* style. Wines come from their own first-rate Verrazzano estate in Chianti.

Light breakfast and morning cappuccino is a delight. Closed evenings. Via dei Tavolini 18R. www.verrazzano.com.℘ **055/268-590.** Bus: C2.

**Ditta Artigianale ★★** This on-trend spot mixes modernist Scandinavian design with a bit of everything, at any time of day. Highlights are evening gin cocktails (10€) and fantastic coffee from its own small-batch roastery in Arezzo. (You can buy beans to take home.) There's also daily brunch, wines by the glass, and artisan beers. Via dello Sprone 5R. www.dittaartigianale.it. ℘ **055/045-7163.** Bus: C3 or C4. Also at Via dei Neri 32R; Via G. Carducci 4R.

**La Menagère ★** In the former premises of a vast 19th-century home-wares store, this trendy all-day cafe is a lively stop for breakfast, brunch, lunch, a caffeine pick-me-up, aperitif, or even to buy a bunch of fresh flowers. Via de' Ginori 8R. www.lamenagere.it.℘ **055/0750-600.** Bus: C1.

**Procacci ★** The second you walk through the door, you're hit with the perfume of Procacci's specialty: panini *tartufati,* brioche rolls spread with truffle butter. Via Tornabuoni 64R. www.procacci1885.it.℘ **055/211-656.** Bus: C3.

**Rivoire ★** If you want to pick one overpriced sidewalk cafe in Florence, make it this one. The steep prices (6€ for a cappuccino) help pay the rent beside one of the prettiest slices of real estate on the planet. Piazza della Signoria (at Via Vacchereccia). www.rivoire.it.℘ **055/214-412.** Bus: C2.

**Terrazza-Rooftop @Rinascente ★** The prices, like the perch, are a little elevated (3€–5€ for a coffee). But you get to enjoy your drink on a hidden terrace in the sky, with just the rooftops, towers, and Brunelleschi's dome for company. Top floor of La Rinascente, Piazza della Repubblica. www.larinascente.it. ℘ **055/219-113.** Bus: C2.

## Wine Bars, Cocktail Bars & Craft Beer Bars

Florence's iconic cocktail is the **Negroni.** It was invented in the city in 1919.

**Bitter Bar ★★** New-breed craft cocktails and twisted classics are served in a speakeasy-style bar with low lighting and moody midcentury decor. Mixology is first rate. Reserve a table on weekends. Via di Mezzo 28R. www.bitterbar firenze.it.℘ **340/549-9258.** Bus: C2 or C3.

**Fermento ★** Right opposite the Medici Chapels, this tiny bar with outdoor tables serves Italian and Belgian craft beers in every style from IPA to stout, plus carb-rich food to soak it up. Via Canto dei Nelli 38R. http://fermento firenze.com.℘ **055/267-5817.** Bus: C1.

**Il Santino ★★** This snug wine bar stocks niche labels from across Italy and serves exquisite "Florentine tapas" (7€–9€) to munch while you sip. Via Santo Spirito 60R.℘ **055/230-2820.** Bus: C4, 11, 36, 37.

**Mayday ★** A Florence original, this laidback bar offers signature cocktails commemorating famous Tuscans and events in 20th-century history. It's delightfully decked out like a mismatched junk store, with everything from old school desks to low-watt lamps dangling from the ceiling. Via Dante Alighieri 16R. www.maydayclub.it.℘ **055/238-1290.** Bus: C2.

**Mostodolce** ★    Burgers, pizza, snacks, Wi-Fi, and sports on the screen—so far, so good. And Mostodolce also has its own artisan beers on tap, brewed just outside Florence at Prato (some are very strong). Via Nazionale 114R. www.mostodolce.it.℃ **055/230-2928.** Bus: 1, 6, 11, 14, 17, 23.

**Rifrullo** ★    This friendly San Niccolò bar has one of Florence's most filling *aperitivo* spreads, perennially popular with locals and visitors. For 13€, choose a cocktail, beer, or glass of wine and enjoy crostini, seasonal salads, ribollita, and more, including vegan and gluten-free options. You won't need dinner reservations afterward. Via San Niccolò 55R. www.ilrifrullo.com.℃ **055/234-2621.** Bus: C4 or 23.

**Sant'Ambrogio** ★    This wine and cocktail bar is in a lively part of the center, northeast of Santa Croce. It is popular with locals without being too achingly hip. In summer, everyone spills out onto the little piazza and church steps outside. Piazza Sant'Ambrogio 7R. No phone. Bus: C2 or C3.

**Terrazza Rooftop Bar at the Continentale** ★★    There are few surprises on the list here—a classic Negroni, Moscow Mule, Bellini, and the like—and prices are a little steep at 19€ to 20€ a cocktail. But the setting, on a rooftop right by the Ponte Vecchio, makes them practically a steal. Arrive at sundown to see the city start to twinkle. Closed in bad weather. Continentale Hotel, Vicolo dell'Oro 6R. www.lungarnocollection.com/Continentale. ℃ **055/2726-5806.** Bus: C3.

## Spectator Sports

There's only one game in town when it comes to spectator sports: *calcio.* To Italians, soccer/football is akin to a second religion, and an afternoon at the stadium offers more insight into local culture than a lifetime in the Uffizi. Florence's team, **Fiorentina** ★ (nicknamed *i viola,* "the purples"), usually plays in Italy's top league, *Serie A.* You can generally catch them alternate Sundays from September through May at the **Stadio Comunale Artemio Franchi,** Via Manfredo Fanti 4 (www.violachannel.tv). Book tickets online at **acffiorentina.ticketone.it** or head to the official ticket office (with photo ID in hand) on arrival, at Via dei Sette Santi 28R, open from 10am matchdays. With kids, get seats in a Tribuna (stand) rather than a Curva, where the fanatics sit.

   To reach the stadium, take matchday bus no. 52 or no. 17 from Santa Maria Novella. You can get kitted out in home colors at **AleViola,** Via del Corso 58R (℃ **055/295-306**), or at stalls around the ground on matchday.

# DAY TRIPS FROM FLORENCE

By Donald Strachan

Even for other Italians, Florence's home region of Tuscany epitomizes everything good about their country: beguiling landscapes carpeted with cypresses and vineyards, delicious food and wine, and some of the greatest art and architecture of the Renaissance—including the Leaning Tower of Pisa, Ambrogio Lorenzetti's "Allegories" in Siena's Palazzo Pubblico, and the perfectly preserved Gothic hill town of San Gimignano. As Tuscany's transportation hub, Florence is perfectly situated within easy daytrip range of many of these sights: You don't even need to switch hotels to see these highlights of central Italy.

## FIESOLE ★

7km (4 miles) NE of Florence

An oasis of cultivated greenery separates hilltop Fiesole from Florence. Fiesole preserves the character of a Tuscan small town, which makes it a perfect escape from peak-season crowds. As you sit at a cafe on Piazza Mino, sipping an iced cappuccino, the lines at the Uffizi and throng around the Duomo seem very distant indeed.

Fiesole predates Florence by centuries. Etruscans from Arezzo probably founded a town here in the 6th century B.C., on the site of an earlier Bronze Age settlement. *Faesulae* grew into the most important Etruscan center in the region, and although it became a Roman town in 90 B.C., it retained a bit of otherness. A place in late Roman history was assured when, in A.D. 406, Ostrogoth King Radagaisus was defeated and executed near Fiesole, after an unsuccessful siege of Florence. Following later barbarian invasions, in the 9th century Fiesole became part of Florence's administrative district yet continued to struggle for self-government. Florence settled things in 1125 by attacking and razing the entire settlement. Archeologists have since unearthed several structures from the Roman and Etruscan eras.

# Essentials

**ARRIVING** Bus no. 7 from Florence departs from Largo Fratelli Alinari, at the station end of Via Nazionale. The journey to Fiesole takes 25 minutes, arriving in Fiesole's main square, Piazza Mino. The one-way fare is 1.50€.

**VISITOR INFORMATION** The Fiesole **tourist office** is at Via Portigiani 3 (www.fiesoleforyou.it; ℂ **055/596-1311**). Opening hours vary year to year; generally it's open daily from March to October (Apr–Sept 9am–7pm; Mar and Oct 10am–6pm). November through February is low season, when typical hours are weekends from 10am to 1pm. At the tourist office, you can buy a single admission ticket to all of Fiesole's linked sights for 12€ adults, 8€ ages 7–18; family ticket 24€. It's 2€ per person less without the Museum Bandini (which is missable). A **Firenzecard** (p. 148) is valid in Fiesole. For more information, visit **www.museidifiesole.it** or call ℂ **055/596-1293.**

# Exploring Fiesole

Uphill from Piazza Mino, the high point of the town is occupied by a tiny 14th-century church and monastery, **San Francesco ★** (Via San Francesco 13; www.fratifiesole.it; ℂ **055/59-175**; admission free; Tues–Sun 9:30am–noon and 2:30–5pm [6pm in summer]). At the end of a small nave hung with devotional works—Piero di Cosimo and Cenni di Francesco are both represented—is a fine "Crucifixion and Saints" altarpiece by Neri di Bicci. Off the cloisters, a quirky little ethnographic museum is stuffed with objects picked up by Franciscan missionaries, including an Egyptian mummy and Chinese jade and ceramics. Entrance to the church's painted, vaulted crypt is through the museum. To reach San Francesco, you will climb a sharp hill—pause close to the top, where a balcony provides perhaps the best **view ★★★** of Florence and the wine hills of the Chianti beyond.

Terraced into a hill with views over the olive groves and forests north of Florence, Fiesole's romantically overgrown **archaeological area** (enter at Via Portigiani 1) is scattered with sections of columns, broken friezes, and other ancient remnants. Beyond the **Roman Theater ★★** (which seated 1,500 in its heyday), three rebuilt arches mark the remains of 1st-century-A.D. **baths.** Near the arches, a cement balcony over the far edge of the archaeological park offers a view of the best remaining stretch of Fiesole's 4th-century-B.C. **Etruscan walls.** At the other end of the park from the baths, the floor and steps of a 1st-century-B.C. **Roman Temple** were built atop a 4th-century-B.C. Etruscan one dedicated to Minerva. To the left are oblong **Lombard tombs** from the 7th century A.D., when this part of Fiesole was a necropolis. The archaeological area is open year-round: April to September daily 9am to 7pm; March and October daily 10am to 6pm; and November to February Wednesday through Monday 10am to 3pm.

> ## Tuscany Protocols
>
> All sites and attractions require a Green Pass or your national equivalent (like a vaccination card) (see p. 147). Mask wearing has also often been required on Tuscany's buses. For details on Italy protocols, see chapter 10.

# SIENA ★★★

With a uniquely preserved medieval core, Siena is for many admirers the most beautiful town in Italy. Viewed from the summit of the Palazzo Pubblico's tower, a sea of roof tiles and red brick blends into a labyrinth of steep, twisting stone alleys. This cityscape hides dozens of Gothic palaces and pastry shops galore, longstanding neighborhood rivalries, and painted altarpieces of unsurpassed elegance.

Founded as a Roman colony by Emperor Augustus, Siena enjoyed its heyday in the 13th and 14th centuries. In 1270, Sienese merchants established the Council of Nine, an oligarchy that ruled over Siena's great republican era, when civic projects and artistic prowess reached their heights. Artists such as Duccio di Buoninsegna, Simone Martini, and the Lorenzetti brothers invented a distinctive Sienese art, a highly developed Gothic style that became an artistic foil to the emerging Florentine Renaissance. Then in 1348, a plague known as the "Black Death" hit the city, killing perhaps three-quarters of its 100,000 population, destroying the social fabric and devastating the economy. Siena never recovered, and much of it has barely changed since.

## Essentials

**ARRIVING**   The **bus** is more convenient than the train, because Siena's rail station is way outside of town. **Tiemme** (www.tiemmespa.it) runs express (80 min.) and slower buses (100 min.) from Florence's main bus station to Siena's Piazza Gramsci. It costs 8.40€ each way and there is no need to reserve ahead. Buses run at least hourly in the morning. Try not to make the trip on Sundays when the service is much reduced. The last bus back usually departs at 8:45pm (7:10pm is generally the last express service on weekends; but check ahead as schedules change).

If you have a **car,** there's a fast road direct from Florence (it has no route number; follow the green or blue signs toward Siena), about a 90-minute drive. The more scenic route, down the **Chiantigiana wine road,** the **SS222,** takes 2 hours or so. But for daytrips, the bus makes more sense than driving.

**VISITOR INFORMATION**   The **tourist office** is at Piazza del Campo 7 (www.terresiena.it/en/siena; ℰ **0577/280-551**). It is open daily from 9am to 6pm, although winter hours are often a little shorter.

**PARKING**   Siena's most convenient **parking lots** (www.sienaparcheggi. com; ℰ **0577/228-711**) charge around 2€ per hour. All lots are well marked, and locations are just outside the city gates. An especially handy lot is **Santa Caterina,** where escalators whisk you up to town.

## Exploring Siena

Be prepared for one *seriously* busy day (and even then, you can't see it all). Stepped alleys lead down into **Piazza del Campo ★★** ("Il Campo"), arguably the most beautiful piazza in Italy. Crafted like a sloping scallop shell, the

Campo was first laid out in the 1100s on the former site of the Roman forum. The herringbone brick pavement is divided by white marble lines into nine sections representing the city's medieval ruling body, the Council of Nine.

Overlooking the Campo, the crenellated town hall, **Palazzo Pubblico ★★** (built 1297–1310), is the city's finest Gothic palace (many would say Tuscany's finest), and the **Museo Civico** inside (© **0577/292-615**) is home to Siena's best artworks. Frescoed on the wall of the Sala del Mappamondo, Simone Martini's 1315 **"Maestà" ★★** honors the Virgin Mary, Siena's saintly protector. Next door, in the Sala della Pace, Ambrogio Lorenzetti covered

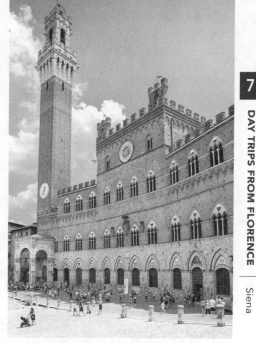

Bell tower of the Palazzo Pubblico in Siena.

the walls in his **"Allegories of Good and Bad Government" ★★★** (1338), full of detail of medieval Sienese life; it was painted to provide encouragement to the city's governing body, which met inside the room. The museum is open daily from 10am to 7pm (until 6m Nov–Feb). Admission costs 10€, 9€ for students and seniors, free for ages 10 and under.

Having seen Siena's civic heart, visit its religious monuments on **Piazza del Duomo** (www.operaduomo.siena.it; © **0577/286-300**) on a single ticket, the **Opa Si Pass** (15€ peak season, 13€ spring and holiday periods, 8€ winter), sold at the Museo dell'Opera (see below). Siena's **Duomo ★★** is stuffed with art treasures, including Bernini's **Cappella Chigi ★** (1659) and the **Libreria Piccolomini ★★**, frescoed in 1507 with scenes from the life of Sienese Pope Pius II, by Pinturicchio. If you are visiting in July or from mid-August to mid-October, you will find the **Cathedral Floor ★★★** uncovered; its 59 etched and inlaid marble panels were created between 1372 and 1547 by Siena's top artists, including Domenico di Bartolo, Matteo di Giovanni, Pinturicchio, and especially Domenico Beccafumi. The **Battistero ★★** (Baptistery) has a baptismal font (1417–30) with gilded brass panels cast by the foremost Sienese and Florentine sculptors of the early Renaissance, including Jacopo della Quercia, Lorenzo Ghiberti, and Donatello. Inside the **Museo dell'Opera del Duomo ★** is Siena's most precious work of art, Duccio di Buoninsegna's 1311 **"Maestà" ★★★**. It shows the Virgin and Child in majesty, adored by a

# REAL flavors OF THE CITY

**Taste Siena ★★** (www.sienafoodtour. com) runs a culinary adventure in the streets of the city. A 4-hour guided walk provides eight unique encounters with traditional Sienese cuisine—with stops for breakfast pastries, light lunch, *panforte* (a dense honey and nut cake), artisan cheese, wine, and more. Along the way, you'll hear lively insight into the history and culture of this little city. Tours run from 10am Tuesday to Saturday. It costs 85€ per person (55€ ages 11 and under), all tastings included.

litany of saints including St. Paul (holding the sword) and St. John the Baptist (pointing at Jesus and wearing animal skins). From the museum, climb to the top of the **Facciatone ★★** for the best view in Siena, over the rooftops and down into the Campo. Opening hours for most of the Duomo sights are 10:30am to 5:30pm, stretching to 7pm in summer. The cathedral is closed to visitors on Sunday mornings.

You also just about have time for **Santa Maria della Scala ★★** (www. santamariadellascala.com; ✆ **0577/286-300**), facing the cathedral facade. It's always much less busy than other sites in the city—and we have no idea why. An "old hospital" might not sound too enticing, but this huge building has treasures hidden away in its eerie corridors. The **Pellegrinaio ★★** was frescoed in the 1440s with sometimes grisly scenes of life in this medieval hospital; the Old Sacristy has an even more gruesome **"Massacre of the Innocents" ★★,** painted in 1482 by Matteo di Giovanni. Also here is the spooky oratory where St. Catherine of Siena used to pray during the night; the city's **National Archaeological Museum** occupies a labyrinthine lower floor; in **Bambimus,** art is displayed at child's-eye height. The most cost-efficient way to enter Santa Maria

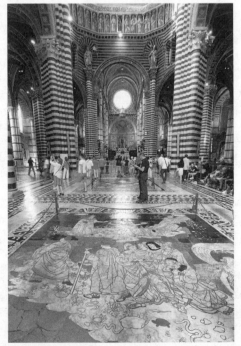

Mosaic floors inside Siena's Cathedral can only be viewed from mid-August to October.

Scala is to buy an **Acropoli Pass** (5€ extra) instead of the Opa Si Pass (see above). Admission to just this museum costs 9€, or 7€ for students 12 to 19 and seniors 65 and over. Discount combo tickets for Santa Maria Della Scala and the Museo Civico cost 14€. Santa Maria Della Scala is open 10am to 7pm; November through March it closes at 5pm Monday, Wednesday, and Thursday, and all day Tuesday.

## Where to Eat in Siena

Sienese cooking is rustic and simple, making liberal use of meat from the local *Cinta Senese* breed of pig. **L'Osteria ★★,** Via de' Rossi 81 (© 0577/287-592), does a mean line in local grilled meats, including veal and *Cinta;* main courses range from 8€ to 17€. Close to the cathedral the **Osteria del Gusto ★,** Via dei Fusari 13 (www.osteriadelgusto.it; © 0577/271-076), serves great-value pasta dishes in filling portions. Think *pici* (fat, hand-rolled spaghetti) served with a *ragù* of *Cinta* and porcini mushrooms for around the 10€ mark.

If you prefer a sandwich to a sit-down meal, walk around the back of the Palazzo Pubblico to **Gino Cacino di Angelo ★★,** Piazza del Mercato 31 (© 0577/223-076). Sublime offerings include aged pecorino cheese, Tuscan salami, anchovies, porchetta, and pretty much anything else that can go on bread or a tasting platter, all carefully sourced. It is open daily until 8pm, but often closes for a couple of weeks in August. The best gelato in the city is churned at **Kopakabana ★,** Via de' Rossi 52–54 (© 0577/284-124); it's open daily 11am to midnight mid-February through mid-November.

# PISA ★★

76km (47 miles) W of Florence

On a grassy lawn against the northwest corner of the city walls, medieval Pisans created one of the most dramatic (and now most photographed) squares in the world. Dubbed the **Campo dei Miracoli** (or "Field of Miracles"), Piazza del Duomo contains an array of elegant buildings that heralded the Pisan-Romanesque style—including the *Torre Pendente,* better known as the **Leaning Tower of Pisa.**

Founded as a seaside settlement around 1000 B.C., Pisa expanded into a naval trading port under the Romans in the 2nd century B.C. By the 11th century, it had grown into one of Europe's most powerful maritime republics. Extensive trading in the Middle East helped Pisa import Arab ideas—decorative and scientific—to Italy. In 1284, Pisa's battle fleet was destroyed by Genoa at Meloria, off Livorno, a staggering defeat that helped the Genoese take control of the Tyrrhenian Sea and forced Pisa's long gradual slide into twilight. Florence took Pisa in 1406 and, despite a few minor rebellions, remained in charge until Italian unification in the 1860s.

## Essentials

**ARRIVING**   From Florence's Santa Maria Novella station, around 50 daily **trains** make the trip (45–90 min.; 8.70€ one-way) to Pisa Centrale station.

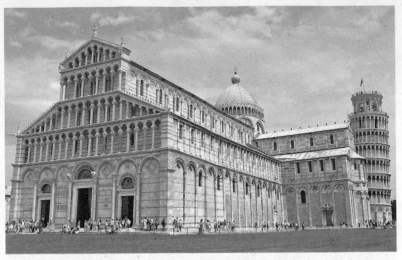

Visiting Pisa's Campo dei Miracoli, you can see the Leaning Tower as part of a whole elegant ensemble.

The last fast connection back to Florence departs around 9:30pm, but check **www.trenitalia.com** for timetable updates. There's also a fast, direct, and (for now) free **road**—the so-called *FI–PI–LI*—from Florence to Pisa along the Arno valley. Journey time is usually around 1¼ hours, subject to traffic.

**VISITOR INFORMATION**  The most convenient tourist office for the sights is at Piazza del Duomo 7 (www.turismo.pisa.it; ✆ **050/550-100**). It is open daily 10am to 6pm. It also offers walking tours and has a luggage storage service (3€–4€ per item per day).

**GETTING AROUND**  It's a long walk from the main station to the major sights. Every 10 minutes a **CPT** (www.pisa.cttnord.it) LAM Rossa bus runs from the train station to the "Torre" stop near the Leaning Tower (10 min.; 1.50€). Buy tickets from the station newsstand; it's 2.50€ per person if you purchase your ticket onboard.

**PARKING**  Much of central Pisa is a controlled traffic zone. However, city-managed lots are conveniently located within walking distance of the Campo, along Via Cammeo and Via Piave (2€/hr.). See **www.pisamo.it**.

## Exploring Pisa

At the **Campo dei Miracoli ★★★,** your likely main destination in Pisa, monuments are linked on various combo tickets. The cathedral plus any other site except the Tower costs 7€; to access everything except the Leaning Tower costs 10€. The **Leaning Tower** costs 20€ (includes cathedral admission; no reductions). To enter everything on the square costs 27€. Accompanied children under 10 do not pay, except at the Tower.

Tower admission is via timed half-hour slots. To buy tickets and book a slot, visit **www.opapisa.it**. *You should reserve up to 20 days ahead of arrival in* *peak season, or if you are on an inflexible schedule.* Anyone under 18 must be accompanied by an adult; children 8 and under are not allowed in the Tower. Main ticket offices are behind the Tower and Duomo, on the north edge of the piazza, and inside the Museo delle Sinopie: If you have no Tower reservation, head to one of the offices immediately to book for later in the day.

First, spend a moment looking at the layout of **Piazza del Duomo.** A hidden part of the square's appeal is its spatial geometry: If you take an aerial photo of the square and draw connect-the-dot lines between the centers, doors, and other focal points, you'll come up with an array of perfect triangles and tangential lines of mathematical grace.

Buscheto, the architect who laid the **Cathedral**'s first stone in 1063, kicked off a new era in art by building what was to become the model for the Pisan-Romanesque style. All its key elements are here on the **facade ★,** designed and built by Buscheto's successor, Rainaldo: alternating light and dark banding, rounded blind arches with Moorish-inspired lozenges at the top and colored marble inlay designs, and Lombard-style open galleries of mismatched columns, stacked to make the facade much higher than the roof. The **main door** was cast by students of Giambologna after a 1595 fire destroyed the original (the last surviving original door, which you can see in the **Museo dell'Opera,** was cast by Bonnano Pisano in 1180). On the back of the right transept, across from the bell tower, is a 2008 cast of the bronze **Door of San Ranieri ★★★.** Inside the Cathedral, on the north side of the nave, is Giovanni Pisano's masterpiece **pulpit ★★** (1302–1311)—it's the last and perhaps greatest of the Pisano pulpits. Head over to the **Battistero (Baptistery) ★** to see its prototype: a carved stone **pulpit ★★** by Nicola Pisano (1255–60), Giovanni's father. This father-and-son team created multiple masterful pulpits over the years, following this model. Heavily influenced by classical works, Nicola's high-relief panels (a synopsis of Christ's life) include pagan gods converted to Christianity as Madonnas and saints.

Now on to the main attraction. Why does the **Leaning Tower ★★★** lean? The main problem—and the bane of local engineers for eight centuries—is that you can't stack this much heavy marble on shifting subsoil and keep it all upright. Building began in 1173 under Guglielmo and Bonnano Pisano, who also cast the Duomo's doors (see above). They reached the third level in 1185 when they noticed a lean, at that point only about 3.8cm (1½ in.). Work stopped until 1275, under Giovanni di Simone. He tried to correct the tilt by curving the structure back toward the perpendicular, giving the tower its slight banana shape. In 1284, work stopped yet again. In 1360, Tommaso di Andrea da Pontedera capped it off at about 51m (167 ft.) with a vaguely Gothic belfry. In 2018, scientists discovered the lean was 4cm (1½ in.) less than originally thought.

The walls of the **Camposanto ★,** or cemetery, were once covered with important 14th- and 15th-century frescoes by Taddeo Gaddi, Spinello Aretino, and Benozzo Gozzoli, among others. On July 27, 1944, however, American warplanes launched an attack against the city (which was still in German hands) and the Camposanto was accidentally bombed. The most fascinating panel to survive the bombing is a 1341 **"Triumph of Death"** ★, attributed to Florentine Buonamico Buffalmacco.

## Where to Eat in Pisa

If you want a genuine taste of Pisa, get away from the crowds around the Tower. Head south on Via Santa Maria as far as Piazza Cavalotti, then along Via dei Mille into Piazza dei Cavalieri. Continue through this vast, polygonal square to the center of the "real" city—less than a 10-minute walk away. At **Osteria dei Cavalieri** ★★, Via San Frediano 16 (www.osteriacavalieri.pisa. it; ✆ **050/580-858**), you'll find grilled meats, daily fresh fish, and traditional Pisan dishes like rabbit stewed with oregano. Main courses range from 13€ to 18€. Osteria dei Cavalieri is closed Wednesdays and for 3 weeks in August. Just across the River Arno, you'll find a great-value lunch at **La Taverna di Pulcinella** ★, Via Garofani 10 (✆ **050/520-2704**). Wood-oven pizzas cost around 10€, including a range of vegan versions, or you can opt for a value 10€ two-course Pisan menu, which may be the likes of spelt with garbanzo beans and porcini mushrooms followed by a rustic pork steak with garlic and rosemary. It's closed Sundays.

For pizza or *cecina* (warm chickpea-flour flatbread) and a cold beer, stop at **Il Montino** ★★, Vicolo del Monte 1 (✆ **050/598-695**), a by-the-slice spot often busy with students.

# SAN GIMIGNANO ★★

52km (32 miles) SW of Florence

An otherworldly scene hits you when you pass through the Porta San Giovanni gate, inside the walls of **San Gimignano:** a thoroughly medieval center peppered with the tall towers which made *San Gimignano delle Belle Torri* ("of the beautiful towers") the poster child for Italian hill towns everywhere. At one time, around 70 of the things spiked the sky above this outsized village. Today, only a dozen or so remain. The towers started rising in the bad old days of the 1200s, partly to defend against outside invaders but mostly as command centers for San Gimignano's warring families. As successive waves of plague swept through (1348, 1464, and 1631 were bad), the economy—then based on textiles and hospitality for pilgrims walking the Via Francigena route to Rome—crumbled. San Gimignano slowly became a provincial backwater. As a result, when tourism picked up in the 19th century, visitors found a delightfully preserved medieval village of decaying stone towers.

## Essentials

**ARRIVING** Your best bet is the **bus.** From Florence's main bus station, **Tiemme** (www.tiemmespa.it) runs buses for most of the day, a 50-minute journey to Poggibonsi, where many services are timed to connect on to San Gimignano (a further 20–25 min.). Buy through-tickets for the whole journey

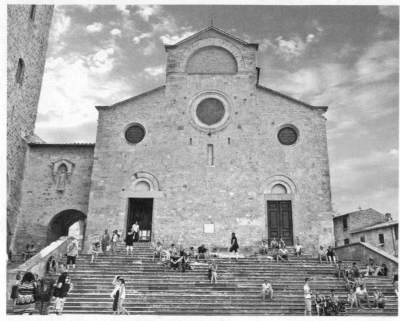

Piazza del Duomo, San Gimignano.

in Florence (around 8€). The last bus back usually departs around 8:30pm, but check when you leave Florence or in San Gimignano's tourist information office. *Tip:* Avoid making this daytrip on a Sunday when bus service is much reduced.

Arriving by **car,** take the Poggibonsi Nord exit off the Florence–Siena highway or the SS2. San Gimignano is 12km (7½ miles) from Poggibonsi, through very pretty countryside.

**VISITOR INFORMATION**    The friendly **tourist office** at Piazza Duomo 1 (www.sangimignano.com/en; ✆ **0577/940-008**) is open daily 10am to 1pm and also Saturday 3 to 7pm (Nov–Feb 2–6pm).

**PARKING**    The most convenient parking is at Parcheggio Montemaggio (signposted "P2"), outside the Porta San Giovanni (2€ an hour, 15€ per day). You can stroll into town from here. P1 (Giubileo), the farthest lot from town, is the cheapest (1.50€ an hour, 6€ per day). Drive up to the town gate, drop any passengers, then return to park—it is a stiff uphill walk of 7 to 10 minutes back from P1.

## Exploring San Gimignano

Anchoring the town at the top of Via San Giovanni are interlocking triangular *piazze:* **Piazza della Cisterna ★★,** centered on a 1237 well, and **Piazza del Duomo,** flanked by the city's main church and civic palace. It is easy to find them: From any direction, just keep walking uphill.

The town's key art site is the **Collegiata ★★,** Piazza del Duomo (www.duomosangimignano.it; ✆ **0577/286-300**). The right wall of this collegiate church was frescoed from 1333 to 1341—most likely by Lippo Memmi—with three levels of **New Testament scenes** (22 in all) on the life and Passion of Christ. In 1367, Bartolo di Fredi frescoed the left wall with 26 scenes from the **Old Testament;** Taddeo di Bartolo added a **"Last Judgment"** peppered with gruesome details (just above and left of the main door) in 1410.

In 1468, Giuliano da Maiano built the **Cappella di Santa Fina ★★** off the right aisle; his brother Benedetto carved relief panels for the altar. Florentine painter Domenico Ghirlandaio decorated the tiny chapel's walls with some of his finest, airiest works, including two scenes depicting the life of Santa Fina, a local girl who, although never officially canonized, is one of San Gimignano's patron saints. Admission to the Collegiata costs 5€, 3€ ages 6 to 17. From April through October it's open Monday to Friday 10am to 6:30pm, Saturday 10am to 6pm, and Sunday 12:30 to 6:30pm; November to March hours are Monday to Saturday 10am to 5pm, Sunday 12:30 to 5pm. It's closed the second half of November and the second half of January.

The town's small **Museo Civico ★** (Civic Art Museum), Piazza del Duomo 2 (www.sangimignanomusei.it; ✆ **0577/286-300**), inside the Palazzo Comunale, houses a **"Maestà" ★★** (1317) by Sienese painter Lippo Memmi and rather racy medieval "wedding night" frescoes by Lippo's father, Memmo di Filippuccio. Admission costs 9€. The same ticket gets you up the tallest tower still standing, the **Torre Grossa ★.** From 54m (175 ft.) up, you can gaze for miles across hills and grapevines. The museum and tower are open daily 10am to 6pm. *Tip:* A **San Gimignano Pass** combo ticket gets you into all the above sites. It costs 13€—a grand savings of 1€.

At **Sant Agostino,** Piazza Sant'Agostino (✆ **0577/907-012**), Florentine painter Benozzo Gozzoli spent 2 years frescoing the walls behind the main altar floor to ceiling with scenes rich in architectural detail from the **"Life of St. Augustine" ★★.** The church is generally open daily 10am to noon and 3 to 7pm (Nov–Mar it closes at 6pm; Jan–Mar it's also closed Mon mornings). Admission is free.

## Where to Eat in San Gimignano

The handiest restaurant for daytrippers, **Chiribiri ★,** Piazzetta della Madonna 1 (✆ **0577/941-948**), is open all day—you can dine early before heading for the bus or car parks. It is a small place, with a simple, well-executed menu of Italian and Tuscan classics such as lasagna, *osso buco,* and wild boar stew. Main courses are priced fairly at 8€ to 12€; no credit cards accepted. The town's essential foodie stop, however, isn't a restaurant, but the **Gelateria Dondoli ★★,** Piazza della Cisterna 4 (www.gelateriadondoli.com; ✆ **0577/942-244**), for creative combinations like raspberry and rosemary (it works) and their signature *crema di Santa Fina,* made with saffron and pine nuts.

# VENICE

By Stephen Keeling

No other place in the world quite looks like Venice. This vast, floating city of grand *palazzi*, elegant bridges, gondolas, and canals is a magnificent spectacle, truly magical when approached by sea for the first time, when its golden domes and soaring bell towers seem to rise straight from the sea. While it can sometimes appear that Venice is little more than an open-air museum where tourists outnumber locals—by a large margin—it is still surprisingly easy to lose the crowds. Indeed, the best way to enjoy Venice is simply to get lost in its labyrinth of narrow streets, stumbling upon a quiet *campo* (square), market stall, or cafe far off the beaten track, where even the humblest medieval church might contain masterful work by Tiepolo, Titian, or Tintoretto.

The origins of Venice—known as "La Serenissima" for centuries—are as muddy as parts of the lagoon it now occupies, but most histories begin with the arrival of refugees from Attila the Hun's invasion of Italy in the mid-5th century (though the official foundation date is A.D. 421). The mudflats were gradually built over and linked together, channels and streams eventually becoming canals. By the 11th century, Venice had emerged as a major independent trading city, and by the 13th century a seaborne empire (which included Crete, Corfu, and Cyprus) was held together by a huge navy and commercial fleet. Though embroiled with wars against rival Italian city Genoa and the Turks for much of the ensuing centuries, these were golden years for Venice, when booming trade with the Far East funded much of its grand architecture and art. Although it remained an outwardly rich city, by the 1700s the good times were over, and in 1797 Napoleon dissolved the Venetian Republic without a shot (handing it over to the Austrians shortly afterward). You'll gain a sense of some of this history touring **Piazza San Marco** and **St. Mark's Basilica,** or by visiting the **Accademia,** one of Italy's great art galleries, but only when you wander the back *calli* (streets) will you encounter the true, living, breathing side of Venice, still redolent of those glory days.

## TRAVEL DISRUPTIONS IN venice

In 2020, Venice was rocked by the Covid-19 pandemic, which shuttered businesses and devastated the tourist industry. The city fared better than other areas of Italy, however, and by 2021 Venice had largely reopened for business. As we go to press, some restrictions are still in place (and they may be when you come to visit): It is mandatory to **wear a mask on all public transport** (including boats), and **in museums, churches, bars, restaurants, and shops**—fines of 25€ to 500€ can be imposed for non-compliance. Always carry a mask with you. Everyone is encouraged to stand 1m (3.3 ft.) apart (again, even on boats and in the open). As with the rest of Italy, everyone over 12 years of age must show a digital Green Pass or your national equivalent, such as **proof of vaccination,** for consumption at tables indoors and to enter museums, cinemas, and concert venues.

In late 2021, most **museums were operating at limited capacity** during the week (first-come, first served), while weekend tickets had to be purchased in advance, online (with the exception of churches, which were still selling tickets on-site). At hotels, buffet-style meals had been discontinued; but other amenities (bars, restaurants, spa, pools, gyms, etc.) were available. Do check with your hotel to see what's being offered. **Capacity limits** were also in place for restaurants, bars, and live music venues.

Most Venice bus, water taxi, and boat services were operating as normal by the end of 2021, and all are sanitized daily.

For details on Italy protocols, see chapter 10.

## Strategies for Seeing Venice

Wandering aimlessly off the beaten path is a marvelous way to experience Venice, but you'll still want to hit all the must-see sights—preferably without over-spending or getting stuck in San Marco tourist gridlock. These strategies and time-tested tips will help you make the most of your time here.

o **Avoid the lines:** It pays to book ahead (online) for the Palazzo Ducale and the Accademia, which guarantees you an entry time (advance bookings are mandatory at weekends; see "Venice Pandemic Protocols" below). Venice offers several discount cards (see p. 272) that also let you skip ticketing lines (the **Museum Pass** is recommended).

o **Plan your sightseeing around lunch:** Some sights do close for lunch in Venice (12:30–3pm), but most (including the churches) stay open, meaning a lot fewer people at each location.

o **Walk:** Aside from on boats, the only way to explore Venice is on foot. Though the layout of the city is confusing, getting lost in its streets is part of the fun. Indeed, explore the far reaches of the city and you'll be guaranteed to lose the crowds, even in summer—most folks rarely stray beyond the main routes. See p. 229 for tips on getting around Venice.

o **Be prepared for Sunday closures:** While most sights in Venice are open every day (some museums close on Tues), much of the city's art is in churches, and many of those are closed to tourists on Sundays, either for the morning or all day. There's one way to get around this: Attend a Sunday

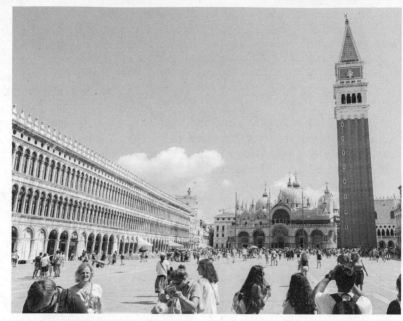

Piazza San Marco (St. Mark's Square).

service as a worshipper. You may not be able to study the art at length, but it's the best way to put this great religious art in context.

o **Avoid the crowds:** Late February and March, just after Carnevale, is a great time to visit; it can be cool and misty, but you'll have the streets and canals (largely) to yourself. Otherwise, get up at sunrise in summer at least once, just to wander the city before the crowds emerge—it's a magical experience.

o **Save money on meals:** Eating in Venice can be expensive, but there are plenty of budget options (see p. 247). You'll save loads by frequenting neighborhood bars known as *bàcari* (normally 5–7pm), where you can stand or sit with small plates of *cicchetti* (tapas-like finger foods), washed down with a small glass of wine. Anywhere near Piazza San Marco is likely to be expensive; it's best to avoid places with *menù turistico* options.

# ESSENTIALS

## Arriving

**BY PLANE**   From North America, the cheapest flights to Venice tend to route through Rome or Milan via **Alitalia,** though **Swissair** (via Zurich), **Lufthansa** (via Frankfurt), **KLM** (via Amsterdam), and **Air France** (via Paris) usually offer cheap fares in low season (code-sharing with U.S. carriers). If traveling in the peak spring and summer seasons, however, it's worth considering far more convenient seasonal nonstop flights, which are often priced competitively—assuming you buy far enough in advance. **Delta Airlines** (www.delta.com) flies from Atlanta (late June–Aug) and New York-JFK (Apr–Sept); **United Airlines** (www.united.com) from Newark (June–late Sept); and **American Airlines** (www.aa.com) from Chicago and Philadelphia (May–Oct). For those already in Europe, numerous budget airlines serve Venice, offering rock-bottom prices. No-frills **easyJet** (www.easyjet.com) flies from Amsterdam, Berlin, London-Gatwick, Manchester, and Paris; while **Ryanair** (www.ryanair.com) flies from Bristol, Barcelona, and London-Stansted, with many other flights routed through nearby **Treviso** (a 1-hr. bus ride to Venice).

Flights land at the **Aeroporto di Venezia Marco Polo (VCE),** 7km (4¼ miles) north of the city on the mainland (www.veniceairport.it; ℂ **041/2609260**). There are several alternatives for getting into town. The cheapest is by **bus,** though this is not recommended if you have heavy luggage; buses can't drive into Venice itself, so you'll have to walk to or from the final stop, Piazzale Roma, to the nearby *vaporetto* (water bus) stop for the final connection to your hotel. (See "The Vaporetto Lowdown," below.) It's rare to find porters who'll help with luggage, so pack light.

The **ATVO airport shuttle bus** (www.atvo.it; ℂ **0421/594672**) runs between Piazzale Roma and the airport about every 20 minutes, costing 8€ (15€ roundtrip); the trip takes about 20 minutes. Buy tickets at the automatic ticket machines in the arrivals baggage hall, or the Public Transport ticket office (daily 8am–midnight). The local **ACTV bus no. 5** (actv.avmspa.it; ℂ **041/2424**) also costs 8€, also takes 20 minutes, and runs between two and four times an hour depending on the time of day; the best option here is to buy the combined ACTV and "Nave" ticket for 14€ (valid for 90 min.), which includes your first *vaporetto* ride at a slight discount. Buy tickets at machines just outside the airport terminal.

It's also possible to take a **land taxi** (www.radiotaxivenezia.com; ℂ **041/5964**) from the airport to Piazzale Roma (where you get the *vaporetto*) for a fixed 40€ (it's 35€ to Mestre). While this is more convenient and a bit faster (15 min.) than the bus, it still doesn't take you to your hotel (unless you're staying right by Piazzale Roma)—you are better off spending the extra euros on water transport.

The most evocative and traditional way to arrive in Venice is by sea. For 15€, the **Cooperative San Marco/Alilaguna** (www.alilaguna.it; ℂ **041/2401701**) operates a large *motoscafo* (shuttle boat) service from the airport boathouse (a short, covered walk from the terminal) with two primary routes. The *Linea Blu* (blue line) runs almost every 30 minutes from 6:15am to 12:30am, stopping at Murano (8€) and the Lido before arriving, after about 1 hour and 30 minutes, in Piazza San Marco. The *Linea Arancio* (orange line) runs almost every 30 minutes from 7:45am to midnight, taking 1 hour and 15 minutes to arrive at San Marco, but gets there through the Grand Canal, which is much more spectacular and offers the possibility to get off at one of the stops along the way. This might be convenient to your hotel and could save you from having to take another

# THE vaporetto LOWDOWN

Whether you're arriving by train, bus, or car, your first challenge upon arriving in Venice will be to take a *vaporetto* (water bus) on to your final destination. The *vaporetto* is the seagoing streetcar of Venice, going to all parts of the city. Here's how to do it right.

Finding the right boat is a little easier if you're arriving by bus or car, because you'll be in Piazzale Roma, the route **no. 1** *vaporetto* terminus, and all these boats will be going the right direction. (See "By Vaporetto," p. 230, for information on tickets.) Exiting the train station, however, you'll find the Grand Canal immediately in front of you, with the docks for a number of *vaporetti* lines to your left and right. Head to the booths to your left, near the bridge, to buy tickets, then head for the docks farther to your right. The most useful routes are the two lines plying the Grand Canal: the **no. 2 express** (from bay "D"), which stops only at the San Marcuola, Rialto Bridge, San Tomà, San Samuele, and Accademia before hitting San Marco (30 min. total); and the slower **no. 1** (from bay "E"), which makes 13 stops before arriving at San Marco (a 36-min. trip). Both leave every 10 minutes or so, but before 9am and after 8pm, the no. 2 sometimes stops short at Rialto, meaning you'll have to disembark and hop on the next no. 1 or 2 that comes along to continue to San Marco.

***Word to the wise:*** The *vaporetti* go in two directions from the train station. Those heading left go down the Grand Canal toward San Marco—which is the (relatively) fast and scenic way. The no. 2 route heading right also eventually gets you to San Marco (at the San Zaccaria stop) but takes more than twice as long because it goes the long way around Dorsoduro (this line serves mainly commuters). As for the no. 1 line going to the right from the train station, it will go only one more stop before it hits its terminus at Piazzale Roma. **Make sure the vaporetto you get on is heading to the left.** Departing from **Piazzale Roma, make sure no. 2 is going to the right** (no.1 will only go right).

means of transportation. If you arrive at Piazza San Marco and your hotel isn't in the area, you'll have to make a connection at the *vaporetto* launches. (If you're booking a hotel in advance, ask for specific advice how to get there.)

A good alternative is the **Venice Shuttle** (www.venicelink.com; daily 4am–11pm; minimum two people for reservations), a shared water taxi (carrying six to eight people) that will whisk you directly from the airport to many hotels and most of the major locations in the city for 22€ to 32€ (add 6€ after 8pm). You must reserve online in advance.

A **private water taxi** (20–30 min. to/from the airport) is the most convenient option but costly—a trip to the city costs 115€ (discounted rates at www.venicelink.com) for up to four passengers with one bag each (10€ more for each extra person up to a maximum of 10, 5€ for each extra suitcase, and another 20€ for trips 10pm–7am). It's worth considering if you're pressed for time, have an early flight (taxis run 24 hr.), are carrying a lot of luggage (a Venice no-no), or can split the cost with a friend or two. It may be able to drop you off at the front (or side) door of your hotel or as close as it can maneuver given your hotel's location (check with the hotel before arriving). Your taxi captain should be able to tell you before boarding just how close he can get you. Try **Corsorzio Motoscafi Venezia** (www.motoscafivenezia.it; ℂ **041/5222303**) or **Venezia Taxi** (www.veneziataxi.it; ℂ **041/723112**).

**BY TRAIN** High-speed **Frecciarossa** or **Frecciargento** trains (www.tren italia.com) or rival high-speed trains operated by **Italo** (www.italotreno.it) from Rome (4 hr.), Milan (2½ hr.), Florence (2¼ hr.), and all over Europe arrive at the **Stazione Venezia Santa Lucia.** To get there, all must pass through (although not necessarily stop at) a station marked Venezia-Mestre. Don't be confused: Mestre is a charmless industrial city that's the last major stop on the mainland (some trains also stop at the next station, Venezia Porto Marghera, before continuing to Venice proper). Occasionally trains end in Mestre, in which case you'll have to catch one of the frequent 10-minute shuttles connecting with Venice; it's inconvenient, so when you book your ticket, confirm that the final destination is Venezia Santa Lucia.

**BY BUS** Although rail travel is more convenient and commonplace, Venice is serviced by long-distance buses from all over mainland Italy and some international cities. Most regional buses terminate at Piazzale Roma, where you'll need to pick up *vaporetto* no. 1 or no. 2 (see box p. 225) to connect you with stops in the heart of Venice and along the Grand Canal. **Eurolines** (www.euro lines.eu) buses drop off on the adjacent island of **Tronchetto,** which is a much longer walk from the action. Buses stop at the Tronchetto **People Mover** station where a light railway whisks you to Piazzale Roma in just 3 minutes

---

### Tourist Tax: New Start for Venice?

Pre-Covid-19, Venice was attracting an astounding 30 million visitors a year, or around 80,000 visitors per day—dwarfing the local population of just 55,000. The 2020 lockdown resulted in less pollution and crystal-clear canals for the first time in decades. Though most Venetians recognize the importance of tourism to the local economy, few want to return to the pre-lockdown bad old days of overtourism. Organizations such as the **Venetian Heritage Foundation** (www.venetianheritage.org) and **Save Venice** (www.savevenice.org) have called for restrictions on Airbnb apartments in Venice and support for cheaper long-term rentals to encourage locals to come back from the mainland. In a move widely applauded, cruise ships were banned from the inner lagoon in August 2021 (with ships diverted to the ports of Monfalcone or Marghera, or eventually to a new permanent passenger terminal at the Lido). And to encourage "slow tourism" and longer stays—as opposed to *"mordi e fuggi,"* or "hit-and-run" tourism—the city also plans to charge entry fees for day-trippers. From the summer of 2022, even the diverted cruise-ship passengers will pay a flat 5€ fee (eventually rising to 7€). For everyone else, the rate will vary according to season and demand, ranging from 3€ to 10€ per day. Day-trippers will also have to make an online booking just to enter Venice (entry will be monitored via electronic turnstiles). Still, the whole scheme may be delayed further or shelved in light of the pandemic, with tourist traffic to Venice still massively reduced in 2021.

(1.50€ one-way), though you will mostly likely need onward transportation from there. *Vaporetto* line 2 does stop at Tronchetto (facing the water, boats depart left to the train station and Grand Canal, right to San Marco).

**BY CAR**    The only wheels you'll see in Venice are those attached to luggage. **No cars are allowed,** or more to the point, no cars could drive through the narrow streets and over the footbridges—even the police, fire department, and ambulance services use boats. You can drive across the Ponte della Libertà from Mestre to Venice, but you can go no farther than Piazzale Roma at the Venice end, where many garages eagerly await your euros (and in high season are often full). The **Autorimessa Comunale garage** (avm.avmspa.it; © **041/2727301**) charges 26€ for a 24-hour period (23.40€ on-line), while **Garage San Marco** (www.garagesanmarco.it; © **041/5232213**) costs 32€ for 24 hours. From Piazzale Roma, you can catch *vaporetti* lines 1 and 2 (see box p. 225), which go down the Grand Canal to the train station and, eventually, Piazza San Marco. Cheaper (and in some cases free) parking is available on the adjacent island of **Tronchetto** (see "By Bus," above), first right as you cross the Ponte della Libertà.

## Visitor Information

**TOURIST OFFICES**    The most central **Venezia Unica** (www.venezia unica.it) information office lies in the arcade at the western end of **Piazza San Marco** (Calle Larga de l'Ascensione 71F), near Museo Correr (daily 9am–7pm; © **041/2424**). There are also offices at **Piazzale Roma** (kiosk near Ponte della Costituzione; daily 7am–8pm), the **train station** (opposite platforms 2 and 3; daily 7am–9pm), and in the arrivals hall at **Marco Polo Airport** (daily 8:30am–7pm). These offices do not offer free maps—they charge 3€.

The info-packed monthly *Un Ospite di Venezia* (www.unospitedivenezia.it) is a useful source of information (published in Italian and English); most hotels have free copies. Also useful is *VeNews* (www.venezianews.it), a monthly sold at newsstands all over the city (also in English and Italian).

## City Layout

Even armed with the best map or a hefty smartphone data plan, expect to get a little bit lost in Venice, at least some of the time (GPS directions are notoriously unreliable here). Just view it as an opportunity to stumble across Venice's most intriguing corners. Keep in mind as you wander seemingly hopelessly among the *calli* (streets) and *campi* (squares) that the city wasn't built to make sense to those on foot but rather to those plying its canals.

Venice lies 4km (2½ miles) from terra firma, connected to the mainland burg of Mestre by the Ponte della Libertà, which leads to Piazzale Roma. Snaking through the city is the **Grand Canal,** the wide main artery of aquatic Venice. Central Venice refers to the built-up block of islands in the lagoon's center, the six main *sestieri* (districts) that make up the bulk of the tourist city. Greater Venice includes all the inhabited islands of the lagoon—central Venice plus Murano, Burano, Torcello, and the Lido.

# Venice Neighborhoods in Brief

**San Marco** The most visited, and most central, *sestiere* is anchored by the magnificent Piazza San Marco and St. Mark's Basilica to the south and the Rialto Bridge to the north. This has been the commercial, religious, and political heart of the city for more than a millennium. Unfortunately, ever-rising rents have persuaded most locals to look for housing in other neighborhoods, but the area is laced with first-class hotels. See p. 238 for suggestions on where to stay in the heart of Venice without going broke.

**Castello** Just east of Piazza San Marco, Castello's tony waterside esplanade Riva degli Schiavoni follows the Bacino di San Marco (St. Mark's Basin), skirting Venice's most congested area to the north and east. Riva degli Schiavoni is often thronged, but if you head farther east in the direction of the Arsenale or inland away from the *bacino*, the crowds thin out. Here you'll find such major sights as Campo SS. Giovanni e Paolo and the Scuola di San Giorgio.

**Dorsoduro** Residential Dorsoduro, the largest of the *sestieri*, lies across the Accademia Bridge from San Marco. Home to the Accademia and Peggy Guggenheim museums, it was known as an artists' haven until rising rents forced many residents to relocate. Come here for good neighborhood restaurants, a charming gondola boatyard, lively Campo Santa Margherita, and the sunny canalside quay of le Zattere.

**San Polo** This mixed bag of residential corners and tourist sights stretches northwest of the Rialto Bridge to the church of Santa Maria dei Frari. At the foot of the bridge you'll find the bustling Rialto Market. Some of the city's best restaurants flourish here, alongside some of its worst tourist traps. Spacious Campo San Polo is the main piazza.

**Santa Croce** North and northwest of the San Polo district and across the Grand Canal from the train station, Santa Croce stretches all the way to Piazzale Roma. Less lively than San Polo but just as authentic, it feels light-years away from San Marco; its little-visited eastern section is a great place for curious visitors to explore. Quiet, lovely Campo San Giàcomo dell'Orio is its heart.

**Cannaregio** On the same side of the Grand Canal as San Marco and Castello, Cannaregio stretches north and east from the train station to include the old Jewish Ghetto. One-quarter of Venice's ever-shrinking population of 55,000 lives here. Many one-star hotels are clustered about the train station—not a dangerous neighborhood but not known for its charm, either. Strada Nova is Cannaregio's main thoroughfare, leading to the Rialto bridge.

**La Giudecca** Across the Giudecca Canal from Piazza San Marco and Dorsoduro, tranquil La Giudecca is a residential island where you'll find a youth hostel and a few hotels (including the deluxe Cipriani; see p. 247).

**Lido di Venezia** This slim, 11km-long (6¾-mile) island, the only spot in the Venetian lagoon where cars circulate, is the city's beach, fronting the open sea. It's also the home of the annual Venice Film Festival.

## A Note on Addresses

Within each *sestiere* is a most original system of numbering the *palazzi,* using one continuous string of 6,000 or so numbers. The format for addresses in this chapter is, where possible, the number with the actual street or *campo* on which you'll find that address. But official mailing addresses (and what you'll see written down in most places), are simply the *sestiere* name followed by the building number, which isn't especially helpful—for example, San Marco 1471 may not necessarily be found close to San Marco 1473. Many buildings aren't numbered at all.

# Getting Around Venice

Aside from traveling by boat, the only way to explore Venice is by walking—and by getting lost repeatedly. You'll navigate many twisting streets whose names change constantly and don't appear on any map, and streets that may very well end in a blind alley or spill abruptly into a canal. You'll also cross dozens of footbridges. Treat getting bewilderingly lost in Venice as part of the fun, and budget more time than you'd think necessary to get wherever you're going.

**STREET MAPS & SIGNAGE**    The map sold by the tourist office (3€) and free maps provided by most hotels don't always show—much less name or index—all the *calli* (streets) and pathways of Venice. For that, pick up a more detailed map (ask for a *pianta della città* at news kiosks—especially those at the train station and around San Marco or most bookstores). The best (and most expensive) is the highly detailed **Touring Club Italiano map,** available in a variety of forms (folding from 8.50€) and scales. If using your phone, note that GPS directions are often unreliable in Venice, though Google Maps has definitely improved in recent years (and has added its "streetview" option to the city).

Still, Venice's confusing layout confounds even the best maps and navigators. You're often better off just stopping and asking a local to point you in the right direction (always know the name of the *campo*/square or major sight closest to the address you're looking for and ask for that).

As you wander, look for the ubiquitous yellow signs (well, *usually* yellow) whose destinations and arrows direct you toward five major landmarks:

In summer, the beaches of the Lido offer a cool escape.

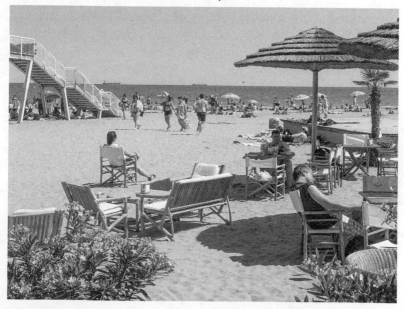

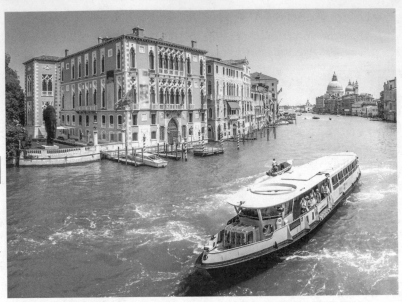

A vaporetto cruises up the Grand Canal.

**Ferrovia** (the train station), **Piazzale Roma** (the parking garage), **Rialto** (one of the four bridges over the Grand Canal), **San Marco** (the city's main square), and the **Accademia** (the southernmost Grand Canal bridge).

**BY VAPORETTO**  The various *sestieri* are linked by a comprehensive *vaporetto* (water bus/ferry) system of about a dozen lines operated by the **Azienda del Consorzio Trasporti Veneziano** (**ACTV;** actv.avmspa.it; ℂ **041/5287886**). Transit maps are available at the tourist office and most ACTV ticket offices. It's easier to get around the center on foot, as the *vaporetti* principally serve the Grand Canal, the outskirts, and the outer islands. The crisscross network of small canals is the province of delivery vessels, gondolas, and private boats.

A *vaporetto* ticket (good for 75 min. after validation) is a steep 7.50€, while the 24-hour **ACTV travel card** is 20€—it only takes three rides to begin saving money with the card. (For even more savings, there are also ACTV travel cards for 48 hr. [30€] and 72 hr. [40€]). Most lines run every 10 to 15 minutes from 7am to midnight, and then hourly until morning. Most *vaporetto* docks have timetables posted. You can buy tickets at Venezia Unica offices, authorized retailers displaying the ACTV/Venezia Unica sticker, and usually at the dock itself, though not all have machines or kiosks that sell tickets. If you haven't bought a pass or tickets beforehand, you can pay the conductors onboard (find them immediately upon boarding—they won't come looking for you) or risk a stiff fine of at least 60€ (plus ticket price and administrative fees), no excuses accepted. You **must validate** (stamp) all tickets in the yellow machines at the docks before getting aboard. *Tip:* If you're staying in Venice

# CRUISING THE canals

A leisurely cruise along the **Grand Canal** ★★★ (p. 263 from Piazza San Marco to the train station (Ferrovia)—or the reverse—is one of Venice's must-dos. It's the world's most unusual Main Street, a watery boulevard whose *palazzi* have been converted into condos. Lower water-lapped floors are now deserted, but the higher floors are still coveted by the city's titled families, who have inhabited these glorious residences for centuries; others have become the summertime dream homes of privileged expats, drawn here as irresistibly as the romantic Venetians-by-adoption who preceded them: Richard Wagner, Henry James, Robert Browning, and Lord Byron among them.

As much a symbol of Venice as the winged lion, the **gondola** ★★★ is one of Europe's great traditions, incredibly and inexplicably expensive but truly as romantic as it looks (detractors who write it off as too touristy have most likely never tried it). The official fixed rate is 80€ for a 30-minute gondola tour for up to six passengers. The rate bumps up to 100€ from 7pm to 8am (for 35 min.), and it's 40€ for every additional 20 minutes (50€ at night). That's not a typo: 150€ for a 1-hour evening cruise. **Note:** Although the price is fixed by the city, a good negotiator at the right time of day (when business is slow) can sometimes grab a small discount for a shorter ride. And at these ridiculously inflated prices, there is no need to tip the gondolier. You might also find **discounts online.**

Aim for late afternoon before sundown, when the light does its magic on the canal reflections (and bring a bottle of prosecco and glasses). If the gondola price is too high, find someone—other hotel guests, say—to share it. Though the price is "fixed," before setting off establish with the gondolier the cost, time, and route (back canals are preferable to the trafficked and often choppy Grand Canal). They're regulated by the **Ente Gondola** (www.gondolavenezia.it; ℂ **041/5285075**), so call if you have any questions or complaints.

And what of the serenading gondolier immortalized in film? Frankly, you're better off without. But if warbling is de rigueur for you, here's the scoop. An ensemble of accordion player and tenor is so expensive that it's shared among several gondolas traveling together. A number of travel agents around town book the evening serenades for around 50€ per person.

Venice has 12 gondola stations, including Piazzale Roma, the train station, the Rialto Bridge, and Piazza San Marco. There are also a number of smaller stations, with *gondolieri* in striped shirts standing alongside their sleek 11m (36-ft.) black wonders looking for passengers. All speak enough English to communicate the necessary details. Remember, if you just want a quick taste of being in a gondola, you can take a cheap *traghetto* across the Grand Canal.

for more than a week and intend to use the *vaporetto* service a lot, it makes sense to get a **Venezia Unica City Pass** (see "Venice Discounts," p. 272), which lets you buy *vaporetto* tickets for 1.50€.

**BY TRAGHETTO**    Just four bridges span the Grand Canal, and to fill in the gaps, *traghetti* skiffs (oversize gondolas rowed by two standing *gondolieri*) cross the Grand Canal at several intermediate points (during daylight hours only). You'll find a station at the end of any street named Calle del Traghetto on your map (though not all of them have active ferries today; ask a local before walking to the canal), indicated by a yellow sign with the black gondola symbol. These days only a handful operate regularly, primarily at San Tomà, Santa Maria del Giglio, and Santa Sofia (check with a local if in doubt). The fare is 5€, which you hand to the gondolier when boarding. Most Venetians cross standing up. For the experience, try the Santa Sofia crossing (Mon–Sat 7:30am–7pm, Sun 9am–7pm; Oct–Mar last crossing 6:30pm) that connects the Ca' d'Oro and the Pescheria fish market, opposite each other on the Grand Canal just north of the Rialto Bridge—the gondoliers expertly dodge water traffic at this point of the canal, where it's the busiest and most heart-stopping.

**BY WATER TAXI** *Taxi acquei* (water taxis) charge high prices and aren't for visitors watching their euros. Trips in town are likely to cost at least 50€ to 90€, depending on distance, time of day, and whether you've booked in advance or just hired on the spot. Each trip includes allowance for up to four to five pieces of luggage—beyond that there's a surcharge of 3€ to 5€ per piece (rates differ slightly according to company and how you reserve a trip). Plus there's a 20€ supplement for service from 10pm to 7am, and a 5€ charge for taxis on-call. Those rates cover up to four people; if any more squeeze in, it's another 5€ to 10€ per extra passenger (maximum 10 people). Taking a water taxi from the train station to Piazza San Marco or any of the hotels in the area will put you back about 90€ (the Lido is around 100€), while fixed fees to the airport range 110€ to 120€ (for up to four people). Taxis to Burano

A gondola near the Rialto Bridge.

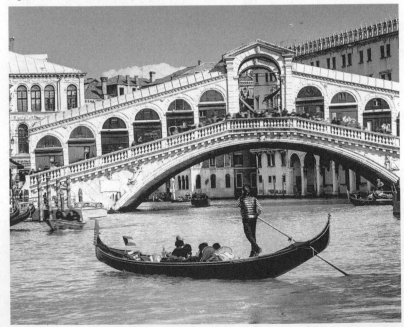

# COME HELL OR high water

During the tidal *acqua alta* (high water) floods, Venice's lagoon rises until it engulfs the city, leaving up to 1.5 to 1.8m (5–6 ft.) of water in the lowest-lying streets. Piazza San Marco, as the lowest point in the city, goes first. As many as 50 floods a year have been recorded since they first started keeping track in the late 1700s. One of the most devastating was in 1966, though the second-highest occurred in November 2019, and they seem to be getting worse—in 2021 flooding affected the city in August, much earlier than usual.

Significant *acqua alta* can begin as early as late September or October, but usually takes place November to March (there is no way to predict them in advance). Remember, though, the waters usually recede after just a few hours—there is no need to get wet and the city doesn't shut down. Walkways are set up along the main routes, but if you intend to wander around, do as the locals do and buy rubber wading boots, available from most stores from 20€ (for about 10€, souvenir shops and stands in Piazza San Marco also sell disposable knee-high plastic waterproof slippers, good for a couple of days). A complex system of hydraulic gates—the Modulo Sperimentale Elettromeccanico or **MOSE**—began operating in 2021. MOSE is controversial because of its environmental impact—keeping the gates closed for long periods could result in parts of the lagoon becoming stagnant, for example—but in the short run, key sights such as St. Mark's Square will be spared the worst of the flooding. Note however, MOSE is only activated to block tides of more than 130cm (4 ft., 3 in.), which means light flooding is still likely to occur.

or Torcello will be at least 140€. Note that only taxi boats with a yellow strip are the official operators sanctioned by the city. You can book trips with Consorzio Moscafi Venezia online at **www.motoscafivenezia.it** or call ☎ **041/5222303.** Six water-taxi stations serve key points in the city: the Ferrovia, Piazzale Roma, the Rialto Bridge, Piazza San Marco, the Lido, and Marco Polo Airport.

**BY GONDOLA**    If you've come all this way and don't indulge in a gondola ride, you might be kicking yourself long after you have returned home. Yes, it's touristy, and, yes, it's expensive (see "Cruising the Canals" on p. 231), but only those with a heart of stone will be unmoved by the quintessential Venetian experience. Don't initiate your trip, however, until you have agreed on a price and synchronized watches. Oh, and don't ask them to sing.

# [FastFACTS] VENICE

**Doctors & Hospitals**
The **Ospedale Civile Santi Giovanni e Paolo** (☎ **041/5294111**), on Campo Santi Giovanni e Paolo, has English-speaking staff and provides emergency service (go to the emergency room, *pronto soccorso*) 24 hours a day (*vaporetto* Ospedale).

**Emergencies**   The best number to call with a **general emergency** is ☎ **112;** this connects you to the military-trained (and English-speaking) **Carabinieri** who

233

will transfer your call as needed. For the local **police,** dial ⓒ **113;** for a medical emergency and to call an **ambulance,** the number is ⓒ **118;** for the **fire department,** call ⓒ **115.** All are free calls.

**Internet Access** Venice offers citywide Wi-Fi through the **Wi-Fi Venezia** (www.veneziaunica.it) network of 200 hotspots. Buy packages online (5€/24 hr., 15€/3 days, or 20€/7 days); access codes are then sent via e-mail.

**Mail** The most convenient post offices are:

**Venezia Centro** at Calle de la Acque, San Marco (ⓒ **041/2404149;** Mon–Fri 8:25pm–7:10pm and Sat 8:25am–12:35pm); **Venezia 4** at Calle de l'Ascension 1241 (ⓒ **041/2446711**), off the west side of Piazza San Marco (Tues–Fri 8:25am–1:35pm, Sat 8:25am–12:35pm); and **Venezia 3** at Campo San Polo 2012 (ⓒ **041/5200315;** same hours as Venezia 4).

**Pharmacies** Venice's pharmacies take turns staying open all night. To find out which one is on call in

your area, ask at your hotel or check the rotational duty signs posted outside all pharmacies.

**Safety** Be aware of pickpocketing on crowded *vaporetti,* particularly on tourist routes, where passengers are more intent on the passing scenery than on watching their bags. Venice's often deserted back streets are virtually crime-free, though occasional tales of theft have circulated. Generally speaking, Venice is one of Italy's safest cities.

# WHERE TO STAY IN VENICE

Few cities boast as long a high season as that of Venice, beginning with the Easter period. May, June, and September are the best months weather-wise and, therefore the most crowded. July and August are hot (few of the one- and two-star hotels offer air-conditioning, and when they do, it usually costs extra). Like everything else, hotels are more expensive here than in any other Italian city, with no apparent upgrade in amenities. The least special of those below are clean and functional; at best, they're charming and thoroughly enjoyable, with the serenade of a passing gondolier thrown in for good measure. Some may even provide you with your best stay in all of Europe. Try to reserve your lodging as far in advance as possible, even in the off-season. For Covid-19 restrictions, see p. 222.

## Hotels by Price
### EXPENSIVE
Al Ponte Antico ★★★, p. 246
Antiche Figure ★★★, p. 244
Baglioni Hotel Luna ★★★, p. 235
Belmond Hotel Cipriani ★★★, p. 247
Corte Di Gabriela ★★★, p. 238
Londra Palace ★★, p. 239
Metropole ★★★, p. 240
Moresco ★★★, p. 241

Arcadia ★★★, p. 246
Ca' Barba B&B ★★, p. 243
Casa Verardo ★★★, p. 240
Galleria ★★, p. 242
Giorgione ★★, p. 246
Locanda Fiorita ★★, p. 238
Pensione Accademia ★★, p. 243
Pensione Guerrato ★★★, p. 244
Violino d'Oro ★★, p. 239

### MODERATE
Ai Due Fanali ★★, p. 244
Al Piave ★★, p. 240
Al Ponte Mocenigo ★★★, p. 245
American Dinesen ★★, p. 242
Antica Locanda al Gambero ★, p. 238

### INEXPENSIVE
Ai Tagliapietra ★★★, p. 241
B&B San Marco ★★★, p. 241
Bernardi ★★, p. 247
Falier ★, p. 245

# Self-Catering Apartments

Anyone looking to get into the local swing of things in Venice should stay in a **short-term rental apartment.** For the same price or less than a hotel room, you could have your own one-bedroom apartment with a washing machine, air-conditioning, and a fridge to keep your wine in. Properties of all sizes and styles, in every price range, are available for stays of 3 nights to several weeks.

In terms of **location,** San Marco is the most convenient part of the city, though anywhere near the Grand Canal will allow you easy access to the best of Venice. Apartments in the farther reaches of Santa Croce, Cannaregio, Giudecca, and Castello may be slightly cheaper and allow a glimpse of residential life in the city, but getting to and from the main sights will take a lot of time.

For those renting apartments, rather than staying in hotels, secure **luggage storage facilities** are available through Radical Storage (which acts as an agent for businesses prepared to look after your bags throughout the city), from 5€ per day (radicalstorage.com).

## RECOMMENDED AGENCIES

**Airbnb** (www.airbnb.com), **VRBO.com**, and **Homeaway.com** are now major players in Venice, each with hundreds of properties listed. On Airbnb you can rent a room in someone's home from just 30€ per night. **Couchsurfing** (www.couchsurfing.com) is also popular and generally safe in Venice, though take the usual precautions (for those who don't know the company, it allows locals to offer free rooms to travelers). **Cities Reference** (www.cities reference.com; ℂ **06/48903612**) is the best traditional rental agency for Venice, with around 50 properties listed. The company's no-surprises property descriptions come with helpful information and lots of photos. **Cross Pollinate** (www.cross-pollinate.com; ℂ **06/99369799**) is a multi-destination agency with a decent roster of personally inspected apartments and B&Bs in Venice, created by the American owners of the Beehive hotel in Rome (p. 66). **Rental in Venice** (www.rentalinvenice.com; ℂ **041/718981**) has an alluring website—with video clips of the apartments—and the widest selection of midrange and luxury apartments in the prime San Marco zone (there are less expensive ones, too).

It's standard practice for local rental agencies to collect 30% of the total rental amount upfront to secure a booking. When you check in, the balance of your rental fee is normally payable in cash only, so make sure you have enough euros in hand. Upon booking, the agency should provide you with detailed check-in procedures. Most apartments provide a list of nearby shops and services; beyond that, you're on your own, which is what makes an apartment stay a great way to do as the Venetians do.

## San Marco
### EXPENSIVE

**Baglioni Hotel Luna ★★★** Perfectly situated on the lagoon just around the corner from the bustle of Piazza San Marco, this is the oldest hotel in Venice,

# Venice Hotels

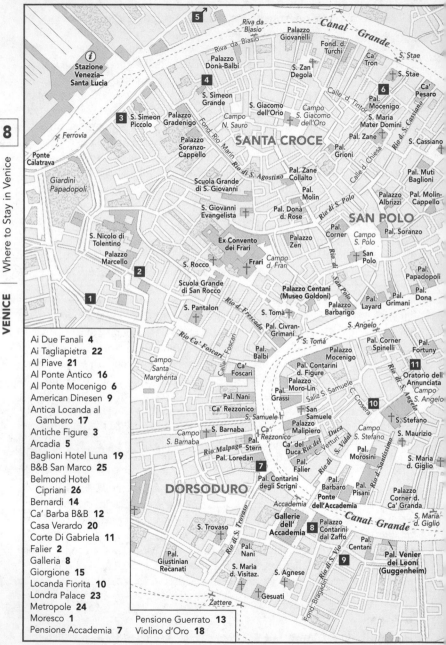

**5**

Riva da Biasio

Palazzo Giovanelli

Canal Grande

Fond. d. Turchi

Ca' Tron

S. Stae

S. Stae

Ca' Pesaro

Riva da Biasio

Palazzo Donà-Balbi

S. Zan Degola

**6**

(i) Stazione Venezia– Santa Lucia

**4**

S. Simeon Grande

S. Giacomo dell'Orio

Calle d. Tinto.

Pal. Mocenigo

S. Maria Mater Domini

S. Cassiano

**3**

S. Simeon Piccolo

Palazzo Gradenigo

Campo N. Sauro

Campo S. Giacomo dell'Oro

Pal. Zane

Rio di S. Cassiano

✕ Ferrovia

Fond. Rio Marin

**SANTA CROCE**

Pal. Grioni

Calle d. Chiesa

Ponte Calatrava

Palazzo Soranzo-Cappello

Pal. Zane Collalto

Pal. Muti Baglioni

Giardini Papadopoli

Scuola Grande di S. Giovanni

Rio di S. Agostino

Pal. Molin

Rio di S. Polo

Palazzo Albrizzi

Pal. Molin-Cappello

S. Nicolo di Tolentino

S. Giovanni Evangelista

Pal. Donà d. Rose

**SAN POLO**

Palazzo Marcello

Pal. Corner

Campo S. Polo

Pal. Soranzo

**2**

Ex Convento dei Frari

Palazzo Zen

San Polo

Pal. Papadopoli

S. Rocco

Frari

Campo d. Frari

Rio di San Polo

**1**

Scuola Grande di San Rocco

Rio d. Frescada

Palazzo Centani (Museo Goldoni)

Pal. Layard

Pal. Grimani

Pal. Dona

S. Pantalon

S. Tomà

Palazzo Barbarigo

S. Angelo

Pal. Civran-Grimani

S. Tomà

Rio Ca' Foscari

Calle Foscari

Pal. Balbi

Palazzo Mocenigo

Pal. Corner Spinelli

Pal. Fortuny

Campo Santa Margherita

Ca' Foscari

Pal. Contarini d. Figure

Saliz S. Samuele

C. Crosera

**11**

Oratorio dell' Annunciata

Campo S. Angelo

Pal. Nani

Palazzo Moro-Lin

Pal. Grassi

San Samuele

**10**

Rio di S. Angelo

Ca' Rezzonico

S. Samuele

Palazzo Malipiero

S. Stefano

S. Maurizio

Campo S. Barnaba

S. Barnaba

Ca' Rezzonico

Ca' del Duca

Rio del Duca

C. Venturi

Campo S. Stefano

S. Maria d. Giglio

Rio Malpaga

Pal. Stern

Pal. Loredan

Ca' del Duca

Rio di S. Vidal

Pal. Morosini

S. Maria d. Giglio

**DORSODURO**

**7**

Pal. Contarini degli Scrigni

Pal. Falier

Pal. Barbaro

Pal. Pisani

Rio di S. Santissimo

Palazzo Corner d. Ca' Granda

Accademia

Ponte dell'Accademia

S. Maria d. Giglio

Gallerie dell' Accademia

**8**

Palazzo Contarini dal Zaffo

Pal. Centani

Canal Grande

S. Trovaso

Rio di S. Trovaso

Pal. Nani

**9**

Pal. Venier dei Leoni (Guggenheim)

Pal. Giustinian Recanati

S. Maria d. Visitaz.

S. Agnese

Rio di S. Vio

Fond. Braggadin

Zattere

Gesuati

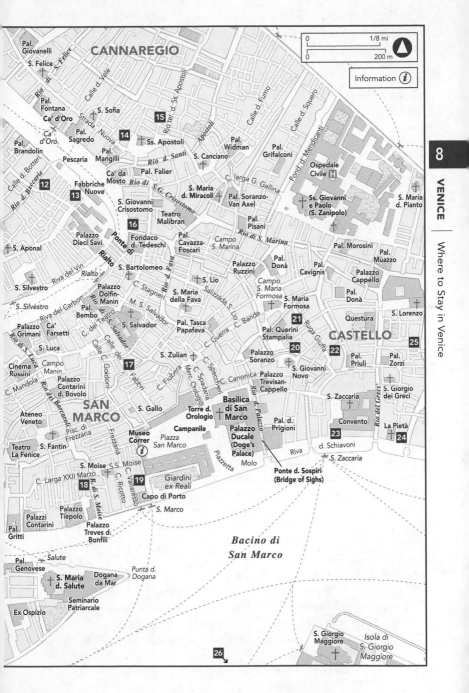

CANNAREGIO

Pal. Giovanelli

S. Felice

Rio di S. Felice

Pal. Fontana

Ca' d'Oro

Ca' d'Oro

Pal. Brandolin

Calle d. Botteri

Rio d. Becarie

12

13

Pescaria

Pal. Sagredo

S. Sofia

Strada Nuova

Calle d. Vele

Rio ter d. SS. Apostoli

15

14

Ss. Apostoli

Apostoli

Pal. Mangilli

Ca' da Mosto

Fabbriche Nuove

Rio di S. Canciano

Rio d. Santi

S. Giovanni Crisostomo

Pal. Falier

S. G. Crisostomo

Rio di

Palazzo Dieci Savi

16

Ponte di

Rialto

Teatro Malibran

Fondaco d. Tedeschi

Pal. Widman

S. Maria d. Miracoli

Pal. Cavazza-Foscari

Calle d. Furno

Calle d. Squero

Pal. Grifalconi

Fond d. Mendicanti

Ospedale Civile H

Pal. Soranzo-Van Axel

C. larga G. Gallina

Ss. Giovanni e Paolo (S. Zanipolo)

S. Maria d. Pianto

S. Aponal

Rialto

Riva del Vin

S. Bartolomeo

Rio d. Fava

Pal. Pisani

Campo S. Marina

Rio di S. Marina

Pal. Morosini

Pal. Muazzo

S. Silvestro

C. Stagneri

S. Lio

Palazzo Ruzzini

Pal. Donà

Pal. Cavignis

Palazzo Cappello

S. Silvestro

Palazzo Dolfin-Manin

Riva del Carbon

Pal. Bembo

C. del Teatro

M. S. Salvador

S. Maria della Fava

Salizzada S. Lio

Campo S. Maria Formosa

S. Maria Formosa

Pal. Donà

S. Lorenzo

Palazzo Grimani

Rio di S. Luca

Ca' Farsetti

S. Salvador

Pal. Tasca Papafava

C. Guerra

C. Bande

Pal. Querini Stampalia

Ruga Giuffa

Questura

Pal. Donà

S. Luca

Campo Manin

Calle C. Goldoni

17

S. Zulian

C. Fiubera

Merc. Orologio

C. Spadaria

C. Specchieri

C. Canonica

Palazzo Soranzo

Palazzo Trevisan-Cappello

20

CASTELLO

22

Pal. Priuli

Pal. Zorzi

25

Cinema Rossini

C. Mandola

Palazzo Contarini d. Bovolo

Rio di Barcaroli

Faben

S. Giovanni Novo

S. Giorgio dei Greci

Ateneo Veneto

Teatro La Fenice

S. Fantin

SAN MARCO

Pisc. di Frezzaria

Frezzaria

S. Gallo

Torre d. Orologio

Campanile

Museo Correr

Piazza San Marco

Basilica di San Marco

Palazzo Ducale (Doge's Palace)

Piazzetta

Pal. d. Prigioni

Rio d. Palazzo

S. Zaccaria

Convento

Rio dei Greci

S. Zaccaria

S. Giorgio dei Greci

La Pietà

23

24

S. Moise

S.S. Moise

18

C. Larga XXII Marzo

C. Valaresso

C. Ricotto

19

Giardini ex Reali

Capo di Porto

S. Marco

Molo

Riva

d. Schiavoni

S. Zaccaria

Ponte d. Sospiri (Bridge of Sighs)

Palazzi Contarini

Palazzo Tiepolo

Pal. Gritti

Palazzo Treves d. Bonfili

Pal. Genovese

Salute

S. Maria d. Salute

Dogana da Mar

Ex Ospizio

Seminario Patriarcale

Punta d. Dogana

Bacino di San Marco

26

S. Giorgio Maggiore

Isola di S. Giorgio Maggiore

Information (i)

0    1/8 mi
0    200 m

housed in a building from 1118 that was once a church before Napoleon destroyed its sacristy. Today, the boutique property, a member of Leading Hotels of the World, is a cocoon of privacy and comfort; the bright lobby with Murano chandeliers gives way to plush rooms decorated with antique furnishings, brocade, and original artwork from the 1700s. The breakfast room is especially noteworthy: With a room-length mural and intricately painted ceiling frescoes created in the 18th century by students of Tiepolo, it makes every cup of coffee feel like a regal break. Staff here is especially attentive and professional.

San Marco, 1243. www.baglionihotels.com. © **041/5289840.** 91 units. 260€–670€ double. *Vaporetto:* San Marco. **Amenities:** Restaurant; lounge; babysitting; concierge; Wi-Fi (free).

**Corte Di Gabriela** ★★★ This gorgeous boutique hotel just a short walk from Piazza San Marco combines contemporary design and classical Venetian style—ceiling murals, marble pillars, and exposed brick blend with designer furniture and appliances (including free use of iPads, strong Wi-Fi, and satellite TV). The fully renovated property dates from 1870, once serving as the home and offices of Venetian lawyers. Breakfast is one of the highlights and well worth lingering over: fresh pastries made by the owners the night before, crepes and omelets made on request, and decent espresso.

Calle degli Avvocati 3836. www.cortedigabriela.com. © **041/5235077.** 10 units. 180€–350€ double. Rates include breakfast. *Vaporetto:* Sant' Angelo. **Amenities:** Bar; babysitting; concierge; room service (limited hours); Wi-Fi (free).

## MODERATE

**Antica Locanda al Gambero** ★ The best attribute of this small, typically cute Venetian hotel is the location, just a 2-minute walk from Piazza San Marco. Rooms are dressed in a bright rococo style with modern extras like satellite TV and air-conditioning, and most have lovely views of the local canal (but not all—check when you book to avoid disappointment). It has no elevator (remember that a "fourth floor" room in Italy is actually on the fifth floor, quite a climb) and the breakfast buffet is small, but it does have free Internet terminals in the lobby and a small rooftop patio that few guests seem to use.

Calle dei Fabbri 4687. www.locandaalgambero.com. © **041/5224384.** 30 units. 60€–328€ double. Rates include breakfast. *Vaporetto:* Rialto (turn right along canal, cross bridge over Rio San Salvador, then left onto Calle Bembo/Calle dei Fabbri; hotel is five blocks ahead on left). **Amenities:** Restaurant; bar; concierge; Wi-Fi (free).

**Locanda Fiorita** ★★ Hard to imagine a more picturesque location for this little hotel, a charming, quiet *campiello* draped in vines and blossoms—no wonder it's a favorite of professional photographers. Standard rooms are small (bathrooms are tiny), but all are furnished in an elegant 18th-century style, with wooden floors, shuttered windows, and richly patterned fittings (air-conditioning and satellite TV are included). The helpful staff more than make up for any deficiencies, and breakfast is a real pleasure, especially when taken outside on the *campiello*.

Campiello Novo 3457a. www.locandafiorita.com. ☎ **041/5234754.** 10 units. 102€–170€ double. Rates include breakfast. *Vaporetto:* Sant'Angelo (walk to tall brick building and go around it, turn right into Ramo Narisi; at small bridge turn left and follow Calle del Pestrin to Campiello Novo on your right. **Amenities:** Babysitting; concierge; room service; Wi-Fi (free).

**Violino d'Oro** ★★   The relatively spacious rooms in this handsome 18th-century building have been adorned in a neoclassical Venetian style with exposed wooden beams, crystal chandeliers, and heaps of character. Most rooms also overlook the romantic San Moisè canal, and Piazza San Marco is just a 5-minute stroll. At this price (with incredible low-season deals), it's reassuring to know you get air-conditioning, satellite TV, and an elevator. Breakfast is a vast spread of homemade cakes and muffins paired with one of the best cappuccinos in the city.

Calle Larga XXII Marzo 2091. www.violinodoro.com. ☎ **041/2770841.** 26 units. 60€–260€ double. Rates include breakfast. *Vaporetto:* San Marco–Vallaresso (walk up Calle di Ca' Vallaresso, turn left on Salizada San Moisè and cross footbridge; hotel is across the *campiello* on the left). **Amenities:** Bar; concierge; room service; Wi-Fi (free).

## Castello
### EXPENSIVE
**Londra Palace** ★★   This white-marble beauty, part of the Relais & Chateaux stable, occupies a prime location overlooking the waterfront promenade—get a room with a balcony to make the most of the spectacular views. All rooms are spacious, with lofty ceilings, 19th-century Biedermeier-style

The Londra Palace, one of Venice's grande dame hotels.

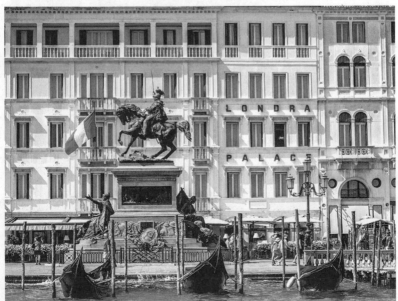

furniture, and satellite TV. This is another place with an intriguing history: The core of the hotel dates back to 1853 when it was the Hotel d'Angleterre, beefed up in the 1860s by a "neolombardesque-style" extension. Tchaikovsky was a guest here in December 1877; legend has it he composed the first three movements of his Symphony No. 4 in room no. 106.

Riva degli Schiavoni 4171. www.londrapalace.com. © **041/5200533.** 53 units. 257€– 725€ double. Rates include breakfast. *Vaporetto:* San Zaccaria. **Amenities:** Restaurant; bar; babysitting; concierge; room service; Wi-Fi (free).

**Metropole ★★★**    This five-star behemoth with a waterfront location is part luxury hotel, part eclectic art museum, with antiques, Asian artworks, and tapestries dotted throughout. But it's no dusty grand dame; on the contrary, the hotel is a chic boutique with rooms opulently furnished in white, red, and gold color schemes. It began life in the Middle Ages as the Ospedale della Pietà, serving as a charitable institution for orphans and abandoned girls, and later became the music school where Vivaldi taught violin in the early 1700s. After it was converted into a hotel in 1895, Sigmund Freud was an early guest, as was Thomas Mann, who allegedly wrote parts of *Death in Venice* here.

Riva degli Schiavoni 4149. www.hotelmetropole.com. © **041/5205044.** 67 units. 230€–675€ double. Rates include breakfast. *Vaporetto:* San Zaccaria (walk along Riva degli Schiavoni to right; hotel is next to La Pietà church). **Amenities:** Restaurant; bar; babysitting; concierge; room service; Wi-Fi (free).

## MODERATE

**Al Piave ★★**    Al Piave is a cozy, old-fashioned family-run hotel just 5 minutes from Piazza San Marco. Rooms are simply but attractively furnished with richly woven rugs, marble floors, and original wood beams exposed (some come with a terrace). Family suites are good value for groups. Bathrooms are relatively big, and the air-conditioning is a welcome bonus in the summer, but the four-floor hotel has no elevators, so be prepared if you get a higher floor. Outside of peak months (May, July, Sept), Piave offers exceptionally good value, given its proximity to the *piazza.*

Ruga Giuffa 4838. www.hotelalpiave.com. © **041/5285174.** 20 units. 120€–240€ double. Rates include breakfast. Closed Jan 7–Carnevale. *Vaporetto:* San Zaccaria (beyond Palazzo Danieli, find Calle delle Rasse and walk to end of street; turn left and then immediately right; cross tiny Ponte Storto, continue to Ruga Giuffa—hotel is on left). **Amenities:** Babysitting; concierge; Wi-Fi (free).

**Casa Verardo ★★★**    Tucked away across a small bridge in the warren of central Castello, this enchanting hotel occupies a 16th-century *palazzo,* though it's been a hotel since 1911. Rooms sport an old-fashioned Venetian style, with Florentine furniture, hand-painted beds, and colorful textiles (antiques and paintings are scattered throughout), but are updated with air-conditioning and satellite TV. Some rooms have a view over a canal, others over the shady courtyard and the city.

Calle Drio La Chiesa 4765 (at foot of Ponte Storto). www.casaverardo.it.© **041/5286138.** 25 units. 80€–233€ double. Rates include breakfast. *Vaporetto:* San Zaccaria (walk straight on Calle delle Rasse to Campo SS. Filippo e Giacomo; cross *campo* to Calle della Sacrestia, then Calle Drio La Chiesa to Ponte Storto, look for hotel on left). **Amenities:** Bar; babysitting; concierge; room service; Wi-Fi (free).

## INEXPENSIVE

**Ai Tagliapietra** ★★★   This cozy guesthouse is run by the amicable Lorenzo, who works hard to make guests' stay a memorable one. Rooms are basic but spotless, modern, and relatively spacious, with private bathrooms and air-conditioning. Rooms also come with a small refrigerator and kettle and use of a tiny kitchenette in the common area (microwave, coffee pots). Lorenzo usually meets guests at San Zaccaria, gives them a map, prints boarding passes, and generally organizes the trip, making this a highly recommended budget option for first-time visitors.

Salizada Zorzi 4943. www.aitagliapietra.info. ℂ **347/3233166.** 3 units. 75€–110€ double. *Vaporetto:* San Zaccaria (walk straight on Calle delle Rasse to Campo SS. Filippo e Giacomo; cross *campo* to Calle della Sacrestia; take first left; cross Salita Corte Rotta and continue to Salizada Zorzi). **Amenities:** Wi-Fi (free).

**B&B San Marco** ★★★   With just three rooms, this exquisite B&B in a peaceful residential neighborhood fills up fast, so book ahead. It's a comfortable, charming, yet convenient option, not too far from the main sights. Your hosts are the bubbly Marco and Alice Scurati, who live in the attic upstairs and are always happy to provide help and advice. Rooms, which are furnished with antiques, overlook the Scuola di San Giorgio degli Schiavoni and offer wonderful views of the canal. Two rooms share a bathroom; the third has private facilities. Breakfast is self-service in the shared kitchen, a spread of yogurts, pastries, espresso, cappuccino, juice, and tea.

Fondamenta San Giorgio dei Schiavoni 3385. www.realvenice.it. ℂ **041/5227589.** 3 units. 75€–135€ double. Rates include breakfast. Closed Aug and Jan 7–Carnevale. *Vaporetto:* San Zaccaria (walk on Calle delle Rasse to Campo SS. Filippo e Giacomo; cross *campo* to Calle della Sacrestia, cross canal and turn left at Campo S Provolo along Fondamenta Osmarin; turn left where canal ends, walk to bridge that connects to Calle Lion; at end of street turn left along canal onto Fondamenta San Giorgio dei Schiavoni). **Amenities:** Babysitting; Wi-Fi (free).

# Dorsoduro

## EXPENSIVE

**Moresco** ★★★   An incredibly attentive staff, a decadent breakfast that includes prosecco (to mix with orange juice, ahem), and lavish 19th-century Venetian decor make this a popular choice, away from the tourist hubbub. Rooms seamlessly blend Venetian style with modern design. Some have a terrace (with canal or garden views), while others have spa bathtubs; all come with flatscreen TVs with satellite channels. If the weather cooperates, take breakfast in the courtyard garden. The hotel is a 5- to 10-minute walk from Piazzale Roma and the train station, but you'll have a number of bridges and stairs to negotiate along the way.

Fondamenta del Rio Novo 3499, Dorsoduro. www.hotelmorescovenice.com. ℂ **041/2440202.** 23 units. 160€–465€ double. Rates include breakfast. *Vaporetto:* Ferrovia/Piazzale Roma (from train station walk SW along Fondamenta Santa Lucia, cross Ponte della Costituzione, turn left onto Fondamenta Santa Chiara; cross Ponte Santa Chiara and turn right onto Fondamenta Papadopoli; continue across Campiello Lavadori then along Fondamenta del Rio Novo). **Amenities:** Bar; concierge; free trips to Murano; room service; Wi-Fi (free).

## MODERATE/EXPENSIVE

**American Dinesen** ★★ Overlooking the San Vio Canal close to the Accademia, this 17th-century Venetian town house offers elegant rooms decorated in a classical Venetian style, with all the usual modern amenities including LCD TV. All the "superior canal"–view rooms have picture-perfect vistas of the San Vio, many with a balcony (check if this is important to you), and even partial views of the Grand Canal. Cheaper, modern "dependence rooms" are located in the annex next door and do not include breakfast.

San Vio 628 (on Fondamenta Bragadin). www.hotelamerican.it. © **041/5204733.** 30 units. 100€–480€ double. Rates include breakfast. *Vaporetto:* Accademia (veer left around Accademia, take 1st left turn, go straight to cross 1st small footbridge; turn right along Fondamenta Bragadin; hotel is on left). **Amenities:** Bar; babysitting; concierge; room service; free Murano trips; Wi-Fi (free).

**Galleria** ★★ Just around the corner from the Accademia, right on the Grand Canal, this hotel occupies a 19th-century *palazzo* in one of the most inviting locations in the city. It's been a hotel since the 1800s, hosting poet Robert Browning in 1878, and maintains an 18th-century Venetian theme in the rooms, with wood furniture and rococo decor. Hosts Luciano and Lucio serve a simple breakfast in your room. The smallest rooms here really are tiny, and there is no TV or air-conditioning (rooms are supplied with fans

A character-filled room at the Hotel Galleria.

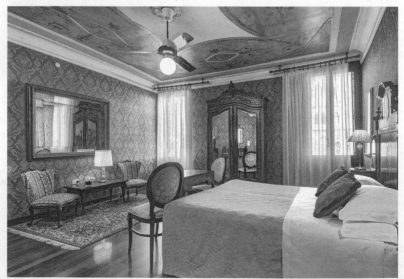

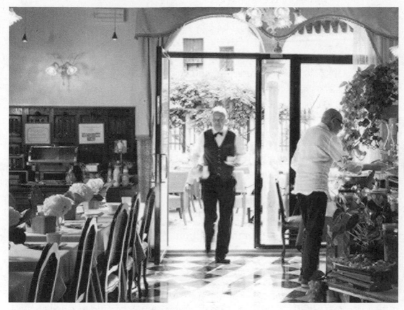
The dining room and patio at Pensione Accademia.

when it gets hot), but the fridge of free water and sodas is a lifesaver in summer.

Dorsoduro 878a (at foot of Accademia Bridge). www.hotelgalleria.it. © **041/5232489.** 10 units. 98€–290€ double. Rates include breakfast. *Vaporetto:* Accademia (with Accademia Bridge behind you, hotel is just to your left). **Amenities:** Babysitting; concierge; room service; Wi-Fi (free).

**Pensione Accademia** ★★  This spellbinding hotel with a tranquil blossom-filled garden has a fascinating history. The Gothic-style Villa Maravege was built in the 17th century as a family residence, but served as the Russian Embassy between World Wars I and II before becoming a hotel in 1950. If that's not enticing enough, the rooms are fitted with Venetian-style antique reproductions, wood furnishings, handsome tapestries, and air-conditioning, with views over either the Rio San Trovaso or the garden. Breakfast is served in your room, in the dining hall, or on the patio.

Fondamenta Bollani 1058. www.pensioneaccademia.it. © **041/5210188.** 27 units. 115€–365€ double. Rates include breakfast. *Vaporetto:* Accademia (turn right down Calle Gambara/Calle Corfu, which ends at a side canal; walk left to cross over bridge, turn right back toward Grand Canal and the hotel). **Amenities:** Bar; babysitting; concierge; room service; Wi-Fi (free).

## San Polo
### MODERATE/INEXPENSIVE

**Ca' Barba B&B** ★★  What you'll remember most about Ca' Barba may well be the host, Alessandro, who usually meets guests at the Rialto *vaporetto* stop; inspires daily wanderings with tips, maps, and books; and provides fresh breads and pastries from the local bakery for breakfast. Of the four rooms, no. 201 is the largest and brightest, with a Jacuzzi tub (no. 202 also has one). All rooms come with antique furniture, 19th-century paintings, wood-beamed ceilings, LCD TVs, air-conditioning, and strong Wi-Fi.

Calle Campanile Castello 1825. www.cabarba.com. ☏ **041/5242816.** 4 units. 90€–160€ double. Rates include breakfast. *Vaporetto:* Rialto (walk back along Grand Canal, turn left at Calle Campanile Castello). **Amenities:** Concierge; Wi-Fi (free).

**Pensione Guerrato ★★★**   Dating, incredibly, from 1227, this is definitely one of the city's most historic places to stay. The building's long history—it was once the "Inn of the Monkey," run by nuns, with the original structure mostly destroyed by fire in 1513—is worth delving into (the owners have all the details). Rooms are simply but classically furnished, with wood floors, exposed beams, air-conditioning, and private baths—many with original frescos that may date from the medieval inn. Note that some rooms have shared bathrooms and some are on the seventh floor—and there's no elevator.

Calle Drio La Scimia 240a (near the Rialto Market). www.hotelguerrato.com. ☏ **041/5227131.** 20 units. 70€–180€ double. Rates include breakfast. Closed Dec 22–26 and Jan 8–early Feb. *Vaporetto:* Rialto (from N side of Ponte Rialto, walk through the market to corner with UniCredit Banca; go one more short block and turn right; hotel is halfway along Calle Drio La Scimia). **Amenities:** Babysitting; concierge; Wi-Fi (free).

## Santa Croce
### EXPENSIVE
**Antiche Figure ★★★**   The most convenient luxury hotel in Venice lies directly across the Grand Canal from the train station, a captivating 15th-century *palazzo* adjacent to an ancient gondola workshop. History aside, this is a very plush choice, its rooms decorated in neoclassical Venetian style with gold leaf, antique furniture, red carpets, silk tapestries, and aging Murano glass and chandeliers, but also LCD satellite TVs and decent Wi-Fi. There is an elevator, just in case you were wondering.

Fondamenta San Simeone Piccolo 687. www.hotelantichefigure.it. ☏ **041/2759486.** 22 units. 98€–552€ double. Rates include breakfast. *Vaporetto:* Ferrovia (from train station, cross Scalzi Bridge on your left and turn right). **Amenities:** Restaurant; bar; babysitting; concierge; room service; Wi-Fi (free).

### MODERATE
**Ai Due Fanali ★★**   Originally a wooden oratory frequented by fishermen and farmers (later rebuilt), this beguiling hotel features small but artsy rooms, even for Venice: Headboards have been hand-painted by a local artist, exposed wood beams crisscross the ceiling, and vintage drapes and curtains add a cozy feel (work by Jacopo Palma the Younger, the 16th-century Mannerist painter, adorns the public areas). The bathrooms are embellished with terracotta tiles and Carrera marble. The location is excellent for proximity to the train station, while the roof terrace is the best place to soak up a panorama of the city (breakfast is served here). It's incredibly popular—book months ahead.

Campo San Simeon Profeta 946. www.aiduefanali.com. 📞 **041/718490.** 16 units. 60€–200€ double. Rates include breakfast. Closed most of Jan. *Vaporetto:* Ferrovia (cross Scalzi bridge over Grand Canal, continue straight, take second left, keep walking to Campo San Simeon Profeta). **Amenities:** Bar; concierge; room service; Wi-Fi (free).

**Al Ponte Mocenigo ★★★**   This gem of a hotel shows it is possible to live that Golden Age Venetian fantasy without breaking the bank (rates are a real bargain in the low season). The especially spacious rooms here are pure 18th-century Venice, with big beds, Murano glass chandeliers, and varnished furniture in pastel greens, creams, and golds. Traditional ceiling beams (in the second-floor rooms) and original Venetian wood and stone floors complete the effect. Breakfasts—served in an enchanting interior courtyard when weather allows—are substantial, with bacon, scrambled eggs, and sausage in addition to all the usual cheeses, fruits, and cold cuts. Another huge plus: It's steps away from the Stan Stae *vaporetto* stop, meaning easy transfers to/from the airport and elsewhere along the Grand Canal. Advanced reservations highly recommended. Note that there is usually a discount for paying in cash.

Fondamenta Mocenigo 2063. alpontemocenigo.com. 📞 **041/5244797.** 10 units. 75€–190€ double. Rates include breakfast. *Vaporetto:* San Stae. **Amenities:** Bar; baby-sitting; concierge (24 hr.); Wi-Fi (free).

### INEXPENSIVE

**Falier ★**   This tranquil budget hotel is set in a quiet neighborhood, next to the Frari Church and just a 10-minute walk from the train station. Rooms are fairly compact (and could be a little cramped for some), but par for this price

Breakfast is prepared at Hotel Al Ponte Antico.

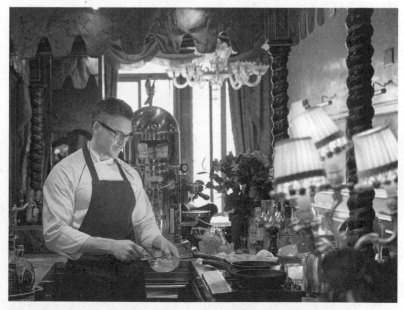

point in Venice; all are air-conditioned and come with free Wi-Fi and satellite TV (although there rarely seem to be any English-language channels). The elegant garden is a great place for breakfast (optional; you can also have it in the dining room), with warm croissants, cheese, and a selection of yogurts and cereals, teas and coffees, and fruit juices.

Salizada San Pantalon 130. www.hotelfalier.com. © **041/710882.** 19 units. 110€–175€ double. *Vaporetto:* Ferrovia (from train station, cross Scalzi Bridge, turn right along Grand Canal, walk to first footbridge; turn left before crossing bridge and continue along smaller canal to Fondamenta Minotti; turn left here—the street becomes Salizada San Pantalon). **Amenities:** Concierge; Wi-Fi (free).

## Cannaregio

### EXPENSIVE

**Al Ponte Antico ★★★** Yes it's expensive, but this is one of the most exclusive hotels in Venice, steps from the Rialto Bridge, with a private wharf on the Grand Canal—to indulge your James Bond fantasy, look no further. Part of the attraction is its relatively small size: With just seven rooms, it feels far more intimate than most hotels in this price range, and service is always superior. Rococo wallpaper, rare tapestries, elegant beds, and Louis XV–style furnishings make this place seem like Versailles on the water. The building was originally a 16th-century *palazzo;* one of the many highlights is the charming balcony where breakfast is served and where Bellinis are offered in the evenings.

Calle dell'Aseo 5768. www.alponteantico.com. © **041/2411944.** 7 units. 240€–530€ double. Rates include breakfast. *Vaporetto:* Rialto (walk up Calle Large Mazzini, take second left to cross Campo San Bartolomeo; walk north on Salizada S.G. Grisostomo to Calle dell'Aseo on left). **Amenities:** Bar; concierge; room service; Wi-Fi (free).

### MODERATE

**Arcadia ★★★** This sensational, modestly advertised boutique lodging set in a 17th-century *palazzo* has an appealing blend of old and new: The theme is Byzantium east-meets-west, combining elements of Venetian and Asian style, but the rooms are full of cool, modern touches: rainfall showers, air-conditioning, flatscreen TVs, bathrobes, and posh toiletries. The lobby is crowned with a Murano glass chandelier. It's just a 5-minute walk from the train station.

Rio Terà San Leonardo 1333, Cannaregio. www.hotelarcadia.net. © **041/717355.** 17 units. 100€–315€ double. Rates include breakfast. *Vaporetto:* Guglie (take left into Rio Terà San Leonardo; Arcadia is 30m [98 ft.] on left). **Amenities:** Bar; concierge; room service; Wi-Fi (free).

**Giorgione ★★** Set in a grand 18th-century building, the Giorgione is an elegant gem of a hotel—staying here really is like taking a trip back to old Venice. The combination of old and new works well, where antique furniture, Venetian decor, sumptuous fabrics, and Murano glass chandeliers meet satellite TV and air-conditioning. Rooms are a little worn, but that only adds to the historic ambience. In the summer, a generous breakfast is served in the pretty fountain courtyard.

Campo SS. Apostoli 4587. www.hotelgiorgione.com. ⓒ **041/5225810.** 76 units. 88€–240€ double. Rates include breakfast. *Vaporetto:* Ca' d'Oro (walk up Calle Ca' d'Oro and turn right onto Strada Nuova, which ends in Campo SS Apostoli). **Amenities:** Bar; babysitting; concierge; room service; Wi-Fi (free).

## INEXPENSIVE

**Bernardi** ★★    An excellent deal, this hotel offers small, basic, but spotless rooms in a 16th-century *palazzo* (the superior rooms are bigger), owned and managed by the congenial Leonardo and his wife, Teresa. Most rooms come with one or two classical Venetian touches: Murano chandeliers, hand-painted furniture, exposed wood beams, or tapestries. The shared showers are kept very clean (11 rooms have private bathrooms), and fans are provided in the hot summer months for the cheaper rooms with no air-conditioning. Breakfast is very basic, however, and note that the more spacious annex rooms (near the main building), have air-conditioning but don't appear to get good Wi-Fi coverage.

Calle de l'Oca 4366. www.hotelbernardi.com. ⓒ **041/5227257.** 18 units, 11 w/private bath. 45€–140€ double, includes breakfast. *Vaporetto:* Ca' d'Oro (walk to Strada Nova, turn right to Campo SS. Apostoli; in square, turn left and take first left onto Calle de l'Oca). **Amenities:** Concierge; room service; Wi-Fi (free).

## Giudecca

A quick ferry straight across from the cacophony of Piazza San Marco brings you to the quiet charms of Giudecca Island and its spectacular views across the lagoon to Venice. This is where you'll find **Belmond Hotel Cipriani** ★★★ (Giudecca 10; www.belmond.com; ⓒ 041/240801), the most famous hotel in Venice, if not all of northern Italy (founded in 1958 by Giuseppe Cipriani, of Harry's Bar fame), with its enormous saltwater pool, decadent spa, and rambling gardens. It's extremely expensive, but keep an eye out for shoulder-season deals (the hotel is closed Nov–late Mar). Or just ferry over to Giudecca for a meal or cocktail at the hotel's waterside **Cip's Club** ★★★ (daily 12:30–2:30pm and 7:30–10:30pm) where dinner comes with a sparkling view of Piazza San Marco.

# WHERE TO EAT IN VENICE

Eating cheaply in Venice is not easy, though it's by no means impossible. The city's reputation for mass-produced menus, bad service, and wildly overpriced food is, sadly, well-warranted, and if you've been traveling in other parts of the country, you may be a little disappointed here. Having said that, everything is relative—this is still Italy after all—and you'll find plenty of excellent dining options in Venice. As a basic rule, value for money tends to increase the farther you travel *away* from Piazza San Marco, and anything described as a *menù turistico,* while cheaper than a la carte, is rarely any good in Venice (exceptions listed below). Note also that compared with Rome and other points south, Venice is a city of early meals: You should be seated by 7:30 to 8:30pm. Most kitchens close at 10 or 10:30pm, even though the restaurant may stay open later.

# Venice Restaurants

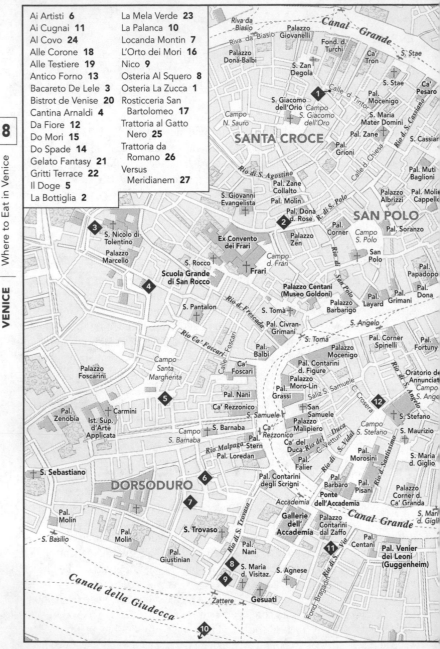

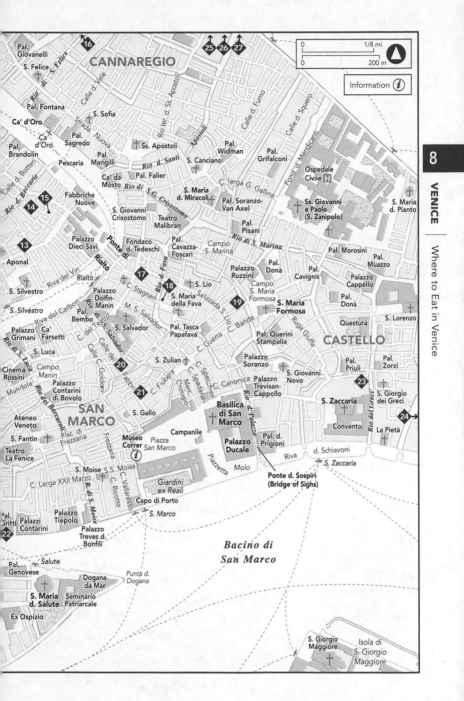

CANNAREGIO

Pal. Giovanelli
S. Felice
Pal. Fontana
Ca' d'Oro
Ca' d'Oro
Pal. Brandolin
Pal. Sagredo
S. Sofia
Strada Nuova
Pal. Mangilli
Pescaria
Ca' da Mosto
Pal. Falier
Rio di S.G. Crisostomo
Fabbriche Nuove
S. Giovanni Crisostomo
S. Maria d. Miracoli
Teatro Malibran
Palazzo Dieci Savi
Fondaco d. Tedeschi
Pal. Cavazza-Foscari
Ss. Apostoli
Pal. Widman
S. Canciano
Pal. Grifalconi
C. larga G. Gallina
Pal. Soranzo-Van Axel
Pal. Pisani
Campo S. Marina
Rio di S. Marina
Ospedale Civile
Ss. Giovanni e Paolo (S. Zanipolo)
S. Maria d. Pianto
Pal. Morosini
Pal. Muazzo
Palazzo Cappello

Aponal
Rialto
Riva del Vin
Rialto
Palazzo Dolfin-Manin
Pal. Bembo
Palazzo Grimani
Ca' Farsetti
S. Luca
Cinema Rossini
Campo Manin
Palazzo Contarini d. Bovolo
Ateneo Veneto
S. Fantin
Teatro La Fenice
Ponte di Rialto
C. Stagneri
Rio d. Fava
M. S. Salvador
S. Salvador
Pal. Tasca Papafava
S. Zulian
S. Maria della Fava
S. Lio
Salizzada S. Lio
C. Bande
C. Guerra
Campo S. Maria Formosa
Palazzo Ruzzini
Pal. Donà
Pal. Cavignis
S. Maria Formosa
Pal. Donà
Questura
Pal. Querini Stampalia
Riga Giuffa
S. Lorenzo
CASTELLO
Palazzo Soranzo
S. Giovanni Novo
Palazzo Trevisan-Cappello
Pal. Priuli
Pal. Zorzi
S. Zaccaria
S. Giorgio dei Greci
Rio del Greci
La Pietà

SAN MARCO
C. del Teatro
Calle d. Salvador
C. del Fabbri
Calle C. Goldoni
S. Gallo
Campanile
Piazza San Marco
Basilica di San Marco
Palazzo Ducale
Pal. d. Prigioni
Ponte d. Sospiri (Bridge of Sighs)
Museo Correr
S. Moise
S.S. Moise
C. Vallaresso
C. Ricotto
R. di S. Moise
C. Larga XXII Marzo
Frezzaria
Pisc. di Frezzaria
Mandola
Rio del Barcaroli
Giardini ex Reali
Capo di Porto
S. Marco
Riva
S. Zaccaria
Convento
Molo
Piazzetta
d. Schiavoni

Pal. Gritti
Palazzi Contarini
Palazzo Tiepolo
Palazzo Treves d. Bonfili
Pal. Genovese
Salute
S. Maria d. Salute
Dogana da Mar
Seminario Patriarcale
Ex Ospizio
Punta d. Dogana

Bacino di San Marco

Punta d. Dogana

S. Giorgio Maggiore
Isola di S. Giorgio Maggiore

Information ⓘ

0        1/8 mi
0        200 m

While most restaurants in Italy include a cover charge *(coperto)* that usually runs 1.50€ to 5€, in Venice they tend to instead tack on 10% to 12% to the bill for "taxes and service." Some places in Venice will very annoyingly charge you the cover and still add on 12%. A menu should state clearly what extras the restaurant charges (sometimes you'll find it in fine print at the bottom) and if it doesn't, take your business elsewhere. For Covid-19 protocols, see p. 222.

**VENETIAN CUISINE**   Venice has a distinguished culinary history, much of it based on its geographical position on the sea. For first courses, both pasta and risotto are commonly prepared with fish or seafood: Risotto *al nero di seppia* or *alle seppioline* (tinted black by the ink of cuttlefish, also called *risotto nero* or black risotto) or *spaghetti alle vongole* (with clams; clams without their shells are not a good sign) are two specialties. Both appear with *frutti di mare* ("fruit of the sea"), which is mixed shellfish. *Bigoli,* a thick spaghetti that's perfect for catching lots of sauce, is a Venetian staple, as is creamy polenta, often served with *gamberetti* (small shrimp) or tiny shrimp called *schie,* or as an accompaniment to *fegato alla veneziana* (calf's liver cooked with onions and white wine). Some of the fish and seafood dishes Venice does particularly well include *branzino* (a kind of seabass), *rombo* (turbot or brill), *moeche* (soft-shelled crab) or *granseola* (crab), and *sarde in saor* (sardines in onions, vinegar, pine nuts, and raisins).

Try the dry white Tocai and pinot from the Friuli region to the northeast of Venice and the light, sparkling prosecco that Venetians consume almost like a soft drink. Popular local red wines include Bardolino, Valpolicella, and Soave, all of which come from the surrounding Veneto region. *Grappa,* the local firewater, is an acquired taste and is often offered in many variations.

## Restaurants by Cuisine

# San Marco

## EXPENSIVE

**Bistrot de Venise** ★★★ VENETIAN It may look a bit like a wood-paneled French bistro, but the menu here is old-school Venetian, specializing in rare wines and historical recipes from the 14th to 18th centuries. It's gimmicky but it works; think fried soft crabs with artichoke salad; scallops with fennel and squid ink mayonnaise; and suckling pig with *civiro* (spices), quince, and bitter orange compote. The "historical" tasting menu is a splurge, but we recommend it as the best introduction.

4685 Calle dei Fabbri. www.bistrotdevenise.com. ⓒ **041/5236651.** Entrees 26€–42€; 4-course tasting menu 74€; historical 6-course menu 110€. Daily noon–3pm and 7–11:30pm (bar 11am–11pm). *Vaporetto:* Rialto (turn right along canal, cross footbridge over Rio San Salvador, turn left onto Calle Bembo, which becomes Calle dei Fabbri; Bistrot is about 5 blocks ahead).

**Da Fiore** ★★ VENETIAN At this classy but laid-back Venetian trattoria (not to be confused with the posher *osteria* with the same name), the menu features typical Venetian dishes like squid ink pasta, but the specials here are the most fun, with *moeche* (local soft-shell crab) a particular treat (the two main seasons are Mar–Apr and Oct–Nov). Desserts see all sorts of sugary *golosessi* on offer, from *buranelli* to *zaletti* (cornmeal cookies, typically eaten dipped in sweet wine or chocolate) and an exceptional *sgroppino al limone* (lemon sherbet). Make sure you visit the bar and *cicchetteria* next door, the **Bacaro di Fiore** (Wed–Mon 9am–10pm), which has been around since 1871, serving cheap wine (spritz 3€) and finger food like fried sardines and squid, fried vegetables, and crostini with creamed cod.

Calle delle Botteghe 3461, off Campo Santo Stefano. www.dafiore.it. ⓒ **041/5235310.** Entrees 18€–30€. Wed–Mon noon–3pm and 7–10pm. Closed 2 weeks Jan and 2 weeks Aug. *Vaporetto:* Accademia (cross bridge to San Marco side and walk straight to Campo Santo Stefano; at *campo*'s north end, take a left onto Calle delle Botteghe); also close to Sant'Angelo *vaporetto* stop.

## MODERATE

**Rosticceria San Bartolomeo** ★ DELI/VENETIAN Also known as Rosticceria Gislon, this no-frills spot is incredibly popular with locals, with a handful of small tables and bar stools and bigger tables in the upstairs dining room (which tends to be quieter). Don't be fooled by appearances—the food here is excellent, with a range of grilled fish and cheap seafood pastas and a tasty *"mozzarella in carrozza"* (fried cheese sandwich; 3.50€). Note that the food displayed on the countertop is reheated to order, but still tastes good. Otherwise just sit at the counter and soak up the animated scene, as cooks chop, customers chat, and people come and go.

Calle della Bissa 5424. ℭ **041/5223569.** Entrees 9€–25€ (pasta downstairs 7€–9€, cicchetti 1.50€–3€). Daily 9am–9:30pm. *Vaporetto:* Rialto (with bridge at your back on San Marco side, walk straight to Campo San Bartolomeo; take underpass to your left marked SOTTOPORTEGO DELLA BISSA; *rosticceria* is on first corner on your right; look for GISLON above the entrance).

## Castello
### EXPENSIVE

**Al Covo** ★★ SEAFOOD/VENETIAN   For years, this high-quality Venetian restaurant from Diane and Cesare Benelli has been deservingly popular with American food writers and TV chefs, so expect to be eating with plenty of fellow tourists. It features two cozy dining rooms adorned with art (plus some outdoor seating in summer), but it's the food that takes center stage here: fresh fish from the lagoon or the Adriatic, fruits and vegetables from local farms, and meat sourced from esteemed Franco Cazzamali Butchers. The pasta, desserts, and sauces are all homemade. Begin with Venetian *saor* (sweet-and-sour fish and shellfish), or fried zucchini flowers, followed by salt cod in cocotte, taggiasca olives, salina capers, and rosemary, or Piemontese beef tagliata with potato fries, chicory sprouts, and homemade ketchup. Diane's desserts might include rustic pear and prune cake with grappa-cinnamon sauce or green apple sorbet with Calvados.

Campiello della Pescheria 3968. www.ristorantealcovo.com. ℭ **041/5223812.** Reservations required. Entrees 23€–28€. Fri-Tues 12:45–3:30pm (kitchen closes 2pm) and 7:30pm–midnight (kitchen closes 10pm); closed usually in Jan and 10 days in Aug. *Vaporetto:* Piazza San Marco (walk along Riva degli Schiavoni toward Arsenale, take third narrow street left [Calle della Pescaria] after Hotel Metropole).

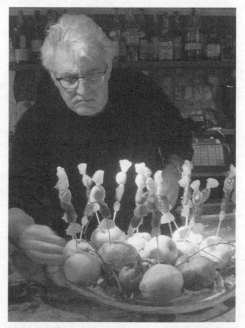

Al Covo chef Cesare Benelli preparing Carmelli Veneziani, a dessert of caramelized fruits and nuts.

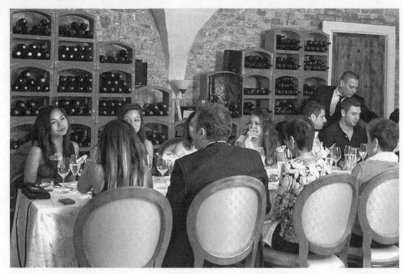
Dining room of Alle Corone.

**Alle Corone** ★★★ SEAFOOD/VENETIAN   This is one of Venice's finest restaurants, an elegant 19th-century dining room inside the Hotel Ai Reali and overlooking the canal. Start with a selection of classic Venetian seafood *cicchetti* (35€) before moving on to risotto with Sicilian red prawns and dried fruit (23€) or main courses such as fillets of seabass with artichokes, small squid, and olives, or beef sirloin with mashed potatoes, burrata cheese, baby carrots, and hazelnuts. To finish, the homemade tiramisu is spectacular. Reservations recommended.

Campo della Fava 5527 (Hotel Ai Reali). www.ristoranteallecorone.com. ℭ **041/2410253.** Entrees 19€–31€; 6-course tasting menu 95€. Daily noon–2:30pm and 7–10:30pm. *Vaporetto:* Rialto (walk east along Calle Larga Mazzini, turn left at Merceria then right on Calle Stella until you reach hotel).

**Alle Testiere** ★★★ ITALIAN/VENETIAN   This tiny restaurant (with only nine tables) is the connoisseur's choice (and an alleged favorite of Meryl Streep, Emily Blunt, and Stanley Tucci) for fresh fish and seafood, with a menu that changes daily. Dinner is served at two seatings, where you choose from appetizers such as scallops with orange and leeks, or grilled razor clams that seem to have been plucked straight from the sea. Fresh seabass fillet with capers and Ligurian black olives is always an exceptional main choice, and seasonal pastas—like pumpkin-and-ricotta ravioli with prawns, or spaghetti with clams—are all superb. Finish off with homemade peach pie or chestnut pudding. In peak season, make reservations at least 1 month ahead, and note that the second seating offers a less-rushed experience.

Calle del Mondo Novo 5801. www.osterialletestiere.it. ℭ **041/5227220.** Entrees 24–54€; many types of fish sold by weight. Tues–Sat 12:30–1pm; dinner seatings 7pm and 9:30pm. *Vaporetto:* Rialto or San Marco (look for Salizada San Lio west of Campo Santa Maria Formosa; from there ask for Calle del Mondo Novo).

# bàcari & CICCHETTI

One of the essential culinary experiences of Venice is trawling the countless neighborhood bars known as **bàcari,** where you can stand or sit with *tramezzini* (small, tri-angular white-bread half-sandwiches filled with everything from thinly sliced meats and tuna salad to cheeses and vegetables), and **cicchetti** (tapas-like finger foods, such as calamari rings, speared fried olives, potato croquettes, or grilled polenta squares), traditionally washed down with a small glass of wine, Veneto Prosecco, or spritz (a fluorescent cocktail of Prosecco and orange-flavored Aperol). All of the above will cost approximately 1.50€ to 6€ if you stand at the bar, as much as double when seated. Bar food is displayed on the countertop or in glass counters and usually sells out by late afternoon, so though it can make a great lunch, don't rely on it for a light dinner. A concentration of popular, well-stocked bars can be found along the **Mercerie** shopping strip that connects Piazza San Marco with the Rialto Bridge; on the always lively **Campo San Luca** (look for Bar Torino, Bar Black Jack, or the character-filled Leon Bianco wine bar); and on **Campo Santa Margherita.**

## Dorsoduro
### EXPENSIVE

**Ai Artisti** ★★★ VENETIAN   This unpretentious family-owned osteria enoteca is one of the best dining experiences in Venice, with a menu that changes daily according to what's available at the market (no fish is served on Monday, when the fish market is closed). Grab a table by the canal and feast on octopus salad, swordfish steak, or an amazing buttery beef cheek with corn polenta. Or opt for one of the wonderful pastas, such as fettuccine with spider crab. Reservations recommended—this tiny place has seating for just 20.

Fondamenta della Toletta 1169A. www.enotecaartisti.com. ✆ **041/5238944.** Entrees 26€–28€. Tues–Sat 12:45–2:30pm; dinner seatings 7–9pm and 9:30–11pm. *Vaporetto:* Accademia (walk around Accademia, turn right onto Calle Gambara; at Rio di San Trovaso, turn left onto Fondamenta Priuli; take first bridge onto road that leads into Fondamenta della Toletta).

**Locanda Montin** ★★ VENETIAN   Montin was the famous ex-hangout of Peggy Guggenheim in the 1950s and later frequented by Jimmy Carter, Robert De Niro, and Brad Pitt, among many other celebrities, but is the food still any good? Well, yes. Grab a table in the wonderfully serene back garden (covered by an arching trellis), itself a good reason to visit, and sample Venetian classics such as sardines in *saor* (a local marinade of vinegar, wine, onion, and raisins) or an exquisite *seppie in nero* (cuttlefish cooked in its ink). For a main course, it's hard to beat the crispy seabass *(branzino)* or legendary monkfish, while the lemon sorbet with vodka is a perfect, tangy conclusion to any meal.

Fondamenta di Borgo 1147. www.locandamontin.com. ✆ **041/5227151.** Entrees 18€–30€. Daily 12:15–2:30pm and 7:15–10pm (usually closed Nov–Feb). *Vaporetto:* Ca'Rezzonico (walk straight along Calle Lunga San Barnaba, then turn left along Fondamenta di Borgo).

## MODERATE

**Ai Cugnai ★★** VENETIAN   The name of this small trattoria means "at the in-laws," and in that spirit the kitchen knocks out solid, home-cooked Venetian food, beautifully prepared and very popular with locals and hungry gondoliers. The classics are done especially well: The *spaghetti vongole* here is crammed with sea-fresh mussels and clams, the *caprese* and baby octopus salad are perfectly balanced appetizers, and the house red is top value. Our favorite, though, is the sublime spaghetti with scallops, a slippery, salty delight. Just two small tables outside, so get here early if you want to eat alfresco.

Calle Nuova Sant'Agnese (Piscina Forner) 857. ✆ **041/5289238.** Entrees 13€–19€. Wed–Mon noon–3pm and 6–10pm. *Vaporetto:* Accademia (head east of bridge toward Guggenheim Collection; restaurant is on right, on street connecting two museums).

**Osteria Al Squero ★★★** WINE BAR/VENETIAN   Perhaps the most beguiling view in Venice is from this enticing *osteria,* right opposite the Squero di San Trovaso (p. 276). Sip coffee or wine and nibble *cicchetti* while observing the activity at the medieval gondola boatyard and workshop, on the other side of the Rio di San Trovaso (drinks served in glasses inside, but in plastic cups if you want to stand outside). It's essentially a place for a light lunch or *aperitivi* rather than a full meal. Snack on such delights as Carnia smoked sausage, baccalà crostini (cod), anchovies, blue cheese, tuna, and sardines in *saor* for a total of around 13€ to 16€ per person. Spritz from 3€.

Fondamenta Nani 943–944.✆ **335/6007513.** *Cicchetti* 1.50€–2.80€ per piece. Thurs–Tues 11am–8:30pm. *Vaporetto:* Zattere (walk west along waterside to Rio di San Trovaso, then turn right up Fondamenta Nani).

## San Polo
### MODERATE

**Do Spade ★** VENETIAN   It's tough to find something so authentic this close to the Rialto Bridge these days, but Do Spade ("Two Swords") has been around since 1448; Casanova ate here. Most locals come for the *cicchetti* small plates such as fried calamari, its famed *polpetta di spianata calabra* (meatballs of Calabrian sausage, smoked cheese. and potatoes), and salted cod (1.50€–3.50€), as well as decent Italian wines (3€ a glass). The more formal restaurant section is also worth a try, with seafood highlights including a delicately

## tours **FOR FOODIES**

While it's relatively easy to explore Venice's culinary scene solo, it can be fun and more enlightening to enlist the services of a local guide. Indie outfit **The Roman Guy** (theromanguy.com; ✆ **06/94804747**) offers more focused evening food tours in Cannaregio (100€ for 2½ hr.), while **Food Tours** **of Venice** (foodtoursofvenice.com; ✆ **393/1670961**) offers Rialto and Jewish Ghetto culinary tours (from 50€). **Cesarine** (cesarine.com), Italy's oldest network of home cooks, runs excellent cooking classes in Venice, as well as lunches in local homes, market tours, and wine tastings.

prepared monkfish, scallops served with fresh zucchini, and a rich seafood lasagna. The seasonal pumpkin ravioli is one of the best dishes in the city.

Calle de le Do Spade 860. www.cantinadospade.com. ⓒ**041/5210574.** Entrees 14€– 18€. Daily 10am–3pm and 6–10pm. *Vaporetto:* Rialto Mercato (with your back to Grand Canal, walk up Ruga Vecchia San Giovanni, turn right on Ruga dei Spezieri; at end turn left on Calle de le Beccarie O Panataria; take second right onto covered Sottoportego do Spade).

## INEXPENSIVE

**Antico Forno** ★★★ ITALIAN/PIZZA   Venice is not known for pizza, partly because fire codes restrict the use of traditional wood-burning ovens, but the big, fluffy-crusted pies here are the best in the city. Little more than a hole-in-the-wall (take-out only), *Antico Forno* has been selling pizza by the slice since 2001, thick and thin-crust. Its "La Pizzaccia-style" pizza is a soft focaccia topped with fresh chopped tomatoes, *mozzarella fior di latte* (from Treviso farms), and everything from Trevisan sausage to gorgonzola and mushrooms.

Ruga Rialto 973. www.anticofornovenezia.it. ⓒ**041/5204110.** Pizza slices 3.50€–4.50€. Daily 11:30am–9:30pm. *Vaporetto:* Rialto Mercato (walk into Campo de la Pescaria, follow Ruga Vecchia San Giovanni for around 300m [32 yds.], just beyond Calle del Paradiso).

**Do Mori** ★★★ WINE BAR/VENETIAN   Serving good wine and *cicchetti* since 1462 (check out the antique copper pots hanging from the ceiling), Do Mori is above all a fun place to have a genuine Venetian experience, a small, dimly lit *bàcari* that can barely accommodate 10 people standing up. Sample the baby octopus and ham on mango, lard-smothered *crostini,* and pickled onions speared with salty anchovies, or opt for the *tramezzini* (tiny sandwiches). Local TV (and BBC) star Francesco Da Mosto is a regular, but note that this institution is very much on the well-trodden tourist trail—plenty of *cicchetti* tours stop by in the early evening. Sip local wine for 3€ to 5€ a glass. Cash only.

Calle Do Mori 429 (also Calle Galeazza 401). ⓒ**041/5225401.** *Tramezzini* and *cicchetti* 1.80€–3.50€ per piece. Mon–Fri 8am–7:30pm, Sat 8am–5pm (June–Aug closed daily 2–4:30pm). *Vaporetto:* Rialto Mercato (with your back to Grand Canal, walk straight up Ruga Vecchia San Giovanni and turn right on Calle Galeazza).

**La Bottiglia** ★★ WINE BAR/VENETIAN   This more contemporary *bàcari* (it opened in 2015) features wonderful cheese and meat boards, a well-curated wine list (exceptional Amarone red wine is served here) and excellent panini sandwiches stuffed with prosciutto and cheeses. As you might expect, it's a tiny place, with a few tables outside near the Rio San Stin and just five bar stools inside (most visitors stand).

Campo San Stin (Calle de la Chiesa) 2537. ⓒ**041/4762426.** Sandwiches from 7€. Daily 10am–11pm. *Vaporetto:* Ferrovia or San Tomà.

## Santa Croce
### VERY EXPENSIVE

**Gritti Terrace** ★★ ITALIAN   One of the city's most famous restaurants remains one of its most magical experiences, despite the high prices.

First-time Venice visitors in particular should not miss the chance to dine on this venerable deck overlooking the Grand Canal on a sunny day, or especially, on a clear evening, when the city lights begin to reflect off the water. The view across to Punta della Dogana and Santa Maria della Salute is spectacular (the signature "Basil-i-ca" cocktail was inspired by the latter church). The menu features light salads, pasta, risotto, and platters of seasonal seafood. A sumptuous afternoon tea is also served, along with the usual selection of champagne, Bellini, and Negroni cocktails. Reservations required.

Campo Santa Maria del Giglio 2467 (Gritti Palace Hotel). www.marriott.com. ℂ **041/794611.** Entrees 38€–48€. Apr–Oct daily noon–10:30pm; closed Nov–Mar. *Vaporetto:* Santa Maria del Giglio.

## MODERATE

### Osteria La Zucca ★★ ITALIAN/VEGETARIAN
Though not specifically a vegetarian restaurant, the romantic, canal-side dining room of La Zucca (aka "the pumpkin") does offer a huge range of high-quality vegetable dishes, from the signature pumpkin-and-ricotta flan and potato cakes to zucchini-and-almond lasagne. The seasonal menu (Italian only, but the staff speak English) also includes plenty of meat dishes, such as succulent rabbit with white wine, and lamb with spices. End with one of the homemade cakes—pear cake with ginger or the "spices tart" with red wine and raspberry.

Calle dello Spezier 1762. lazucca.it. ℂ **041/5241570.** Reservations recommended. Entrees 10€–23€; 3-course tasting menu from 35€. Mon–Sat 12:30–2:30pm and 7–10:30pm. *Vaporetto:* San Stae (walk straight down Salizada San Stae, turn right on Calle del Tentor; turn left at Calle Del Meglio and follow it as it turns right).

## INEXPENSIVE

### Bacareto Da Lele ★★★ WINE BAR/VENETIAN
This tiny hole-in-the-wall *bàcaro* is worth seeking out for its cheap, fresh snacks, sandwiches, and *cicchetti*. Tiny glasses, or *ombras,* of wine and Prosecco are just 0.70€ to 1.50€. There are no seats, so do as the locals do and grab a space on the nearby church steps, or outside by the canal, while you sip and nibble. Opt for a tiny porchetta and mustard or the bacon and artichoke panini (around 2.50€), antipasti plates (cheese and salami), or a simple, freshly baked crostini for 1€ to 2€. Expect long lines here in peak season; the secret is definitely out. Cash only.

Campo dei Tolentini 183. No phone. *Cicchetti* 1€–2.50€ per piece. Mon–Fri 6am–8pm; Sat 6am–2pm. *Vaporetto:* Piazzale Roma (walk left along Grand Canal past Ponte della Costituzione, into Giardino Papadopoli; turn right on Fondamenta Papadopoli, then left. Cross park at first bridge; at next canal [Rio del Tolentini] cross bridge to campo; Da Lele is on SW corner).

### Cantina Arnaldi ★★★ WINE BAR/VENETIAN
This welcoming *bàcaro* offers some of the freshest snacks in the city, washed down with quality wines, spritz, and Prosecco (3€–5.50€). The thing to order is the delicious board of cheese and cold cuts, all sourced from the region and enhanced with fresh fruits, fig jam, local bread, and a small pot of roasted potatoes. The

extensive wine list includes natural/organic options as well as some of the best cellars from Italy. It's a small place, so reservations are recommended if you want a table (there are also a handful of barstools).

Salizada San Pantalon 35. ℅ **041/718989.** Meat/cheese platter for one 15€; for 2 from 26€. Sun–Tues & Thurs 11am–midnight; Fri–Sat 11am–2am. *Vaporetto:* San Tomà (walk up Calle Traghetto Vecchio Galeazza, turn left at Calle del Campanile and right on Fondamenta del Forner; turn left and cross canal on Calle Gozzi, follow to Calle Crosera; turn right and walk straight, crossing Rio de San Pantalon and on to Salizada San Pantalon).

## Cannaregio
### EXPENSIVE

**L'Orto dei Mori** ★★ VENETIAN  Everything on the relatively small menu is exceptional—the codfish and clams stewed with artichokes especially so—and the setting next to a small canal is enhanced by candlelight at night. This place can get very busy—the waiters are normally friendly, but expect brusque treatment if you turn up late or early for a reservation. Don't be confused: The restaurant prefers to serve dinner, broadly, within two seatings, one early (7–9pm) and one late, and waiters will be reluctant to serve diners who arrive early for the second sitting—even if there's a table available, you'll be given water and told to wait.

Campo dei Mori 3386. www.osteriaortodeimori.com. ℅ **041/5243677.** Entrees 21€– 32€. Wed–Mon 12:30–2:30pm and 7pm–midnight, usually in 2 seatings (no weekday lunch July–Aug). *Vaporetto:* Madonna dell'Orto (walk through campo to canal, turn right; take first bridge on left, walk down street and turn left at canal onto Fondamenta dei Mori; go straight to reach Campo dei Mori).

## La Giudecca
### MODERATE

**La Palanca** ★★ SEAFOOD/VENETIAN  For simple, no-frills Venetian cuisine with a stellar view across to the spires of Dorsoduro, this Giudecca spot, well off the tourist trail, is hard to beat. Grab a table on the waterside for coffee and cake (most locals take breakfast standing at the bar), or have a sandwich, a more substantial lunch, or sunset spritz (meals usually served noon to 2:30pm; it's just *cicchetti* and drinks thereafter). Standouts include the tuna tartare, swordfish carpaccio, and anchovies with pink peppercorns. Some of the friendliest staff in the city seem to work here.

Fondamenta Sant'Eufemia 448. ℅ **041/5287719.** Entrees 8€–17€. Mon–Sat 7am–9pm. Reserve for lunch. *Vaporetto:* Palanca (restaurant is 80m [260 ft.] along canal to left).

## Murano & Burano

The glass-making island of **Murano** isn't especially known for its food, though there are plenty of decent trattorias scattered along the main streets. For a real treat, make for **Versus Meridianem** ★★ (Fondamenta Manin 1; www.versusmeridianem.com; ℅ **041/5275408;** Tues–Sun noon–2:30pm and 7–10pm), a spacious, contemporary restaurant in a restored glass furnace,

# EATING alfresco IN VENICE

You don't have to eat in a fancy restaurant to enjoy good food in Venice. Prepare a picnic, and while you eat alfresco, you can observe the life in the city's *campi* or the aquatic parade on its main thoroughfare, the Grand Canal.

**Mercato Rialto**  Venice's principal open-air market has two parts, beginning with the produce section, with many stalls unfolding north on the San Polo side of the Rialto Bridge. Vendors are here Monday to Saturday 7am to 1pm, with some staying on in the afternoon. Behind these stalls are a few permanent food stores that sell cheese, cold cuts, and bread. At the market's farthest point, you'll find the covered **fish market,** still redolent of the days when it was one of the Mediterranean's great fish bazaars. The fish merchants take Monday off and work mornings only.

**Campo Santa Margherita**  On this spacious *campo* in Dorsoduro, Tuesday through Saturday from 8:30am to 1pm, open-air stalls set up, selling fresh fruit and vegetables. A conventional supermarket, **Conad City** (Mon–Sat 7:30am–8:30pm, Sun 9am–2pm & 4–7:30pm), is just off the *campo* in the direction of the quasi-adjacent *campo* San Barnaba, at no. 3017.

**San Barnaba**  Venice's heavily photographed **floating market** (mostly fruit and vegetables), now operates from just one boat moored off San Barnaba at the Ponte dei Pugni in Dorsoduro.

This market is open daily 8am to 1pm and 3:30 to 7:30pm, except Wednesday afternoon and Sunday.

**The Best Picnic Spots**  Given its aquatic roots, you won't find much in the way of green space in Venice (if you are really desperate for green, walk 30 minutes past San Marco along the water to the **Giardini Pubblici,** Venice's only green park). An easier alternative is to find one of the larger *campi* that have park benches, such as Campo San Giacomo dell'Orio (in the quiet *sestiere* of Santa Croce). The two most central are **Campo Santa Margherita** in Dorsoduro and **Campo San Polo** in San Polo.

The **Punta della Dogana** (Customs House; see p. 275) is a prime viewing site at the mouth of the Grand Canal. Perch on the embankment here and watch the water activity against a backdrop deserving of the Accademia Museum. In this same area, **Campo San Vio** (near the Guggenheim), is another superb spot directly on the Grand Canal; it boasts two benches and the option of sitting on an untrafficked small bridge.

A bit farther afield, you can take the *vaporetto* to Burano and then a 5-minute ride on no. 9 to the near-deserted island of **Torcello.** Bring a basketful of bread, cheese, and wine to reenact the romantic scene between Katharine Hepburn and Rossano Brazzi from the 1955 film *Summertime.*

with gorgeous views of the lagoon. It's best known for traditional Venetian dishes and pizzas.

The island of **Burano** makes a wonderful culinary excursion for its seafood restaurants, notably **Trattoria al Gatto Nero ★★,** the "Black Cat" (Fondamenta della Giudecca 88; www.gattonero.com; ℗ **041/730120;** Tues–Sat 12:30–3pm and 7–9:30pm, Sun 12:30–3pm; usually closed Nov), which has been around since the 1940s. Signature dishes include Burano-style risotto (made with *ghiozzi,* a small, long-bodied fish from the lagoon), local turbot and seabass, and the tagliolini with spider crab. Another favorite is **Trattoria da Romano** ★★ (Via Baldassarre Galuppi 221; daromano.it; ⓒ **041/730030;** Mon and Wed–Sat noon–3pm and 6:30–11:30pm, Sun noon–3pm), its dining room adorned with more than 400 artworks donated by visiting artists since the 1940s. Rolling Stone Keith Richards, designer Philippe Starck, and actor Sylvester Stallone have been regulars here for years.

## Gelato

Is the gelato any good in Venice? Italians might demur, but by international standards, the answer is most definitely yes. As always, remember that gelato parlors aimed exclusively at tourists are notorious for poor quality and extortionate prices, especially in Venice. Try to avoid places near Piazza San Marco altogether. Below are some of our favorite spots in the city. Each generally opens midmorning and closes late. Winter hours are more erratic.

**Gelato Fantasy** ★ GELATO   Since 1998, this tiny gelato shop has been doling out tasty scoops dangerously close to Piazza San Marco, but the quality remains high and portions generous. Fresh, strong flavors, with standouts including the pistachio, tiramisu, and strawberry cheesecake. Calle dei Fabbri 929, San Marco. www.gelatofantasy.com. ⓒ**041/5225993.** Cones and cups from 3.50€. Daily 10am–11.30pm. Vaporetto: Rialto or San Marco.

**Il Doge** ★★ GELATO   A definite contender for best gelato in Venice, with a great location at the southern end of the Campo Santa Margherita since 1986. These guys use only natural, homemade flavors and ingredients, from an exceptional spicy chocolate to their specialty, "Crema de Doge," a rich concoction of eggs, cream, and real oranges. Try a refreshing *granita* in summer. Campo Santa Margherita, Dorsoduro. ⓒ **041/5234607.** Cones and cups 1.80€– 5.80€. Open daily 11am–10pm. Vaporetto: Ca'Rezzonico.

**La Mela Verde** ★★ GELATO   The popular rival to Il Doge for best scoop in the city, with sharp flavors and all the classics done sensationally well: pistachio, chocolate, *nocciola* (hazelnut), and a mind-blowing lemon-and-basil. The overall champions: *mela verde* (green apple), like creamy, frozen fruit served in a cup, and the addictive tiramisu. Fondamenta de L'Osmarin, Castello. www.facebook.com/lamelaverdevenezia. ⓒ **349/1957924.** Cones or cups from 2€. Daily 11am–11pm. Usually closed mid-Nov to mid-Feb. Vaporetto: Zaccaria.

**Nico** ★ GELATO   Founded in 1935, this is one of the city's more historic gelato counters, with a handful of chairs on the waterfront (these are only for "table service," at extra charge). Quality is good (the mint, amaretto, and the signature *gianduiotto,* a chocolate and nut blend, are crazy good), but lines are always long in the afternoons and evenings, and service can be a little surly. Fondamenta Zattere al Ponte Longo 922, Dorsoduro. www.gelaterianico.com. ⓒ **041/5225293.** Cone 2€–3.50€. Mon–Wed & Fri–Sat 6:45am–8:30pm; Sun 7:30am– 8:30pm. Vaporetto: Zattere.

# EXPLORING VENICE

Venice is notorious for changing and extending the opening hours of its museums and, to a lesser degree, its churches (often due to special events). Before you begin your exploration of Venice's sights, ask at the tourist office for the season's list of museum and church hours.

## San Marco

### Basilica di San Marco (St. Mark's Cathedral) ★★★ CATHEDRAL

One of the grandest, and certainly the most exotic of all cathedrals in Europe, **Basilica di San Marco** is a treasure heap of Venetian art and all sorts of booty garnered from the eastern Mediterranean. Legend has it that **St. Mark,** on his way to Rome in the 1st century A.D., was told by an angel his body would rest near the lagoon that would one today become Venice. Hundreds of years later, the city fathers were looking to replace their original patron St. Theodore with a saint of high stature, someone more in keeping with their lofty aspirations. In 828 the prophecy was fulfilled when Venetian merchants stole the body of St. Mark from Alexandria in Egypt (the story goes that the body was packed in pickled pork to avoid the attention of the Muslim guards). Today the high altar's green marble canopy on alabaster columns is believed to cover the remains of St. Mark (despite a devastating fire in 976), and continues to be the focus of the basilica, at least for the faithful.

Modeled on Constantinople's Church of the Twelve Apostles, the original shrine of St. Mark was consecrated in 832, but in 976 the church burned down. The present incarnation was completed in 1094, then extended and embellished over the years it served as the doge's personal church. Today San Marco looks more Byzantine cathedral than Roman Catholic church, with a cavernous interior gilded with Byzantine mosaics added over 7 centuries, covering every inch of both ceiling and pavement.

For a closer look at many of the most remarkable ceiling mosaics and a better view of the Oriental-carpet-like patterns of the pavement mosaics, pay the admission to go upstairs to the **Museo di San Marco** (the entrance is in the atrium at the principal entrance); this was originally the women's gallery, or *matroneum,* and includes access to

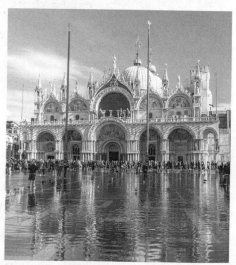

The facade and dome of the Basilica di San Marco, reflected in *acqua alta* floodwaters.

○ **Access:** Full access to St. Mark's resumed in 2021 after being limited during the Covid-19 pandemic, but it's prudent to check the latest opening times and regulations on the **Basilica website** (www.basilicasanmarco.it) or **VenetoInsider** (www.veneto inside.com). The latter website normally offers "Skip the Line" entry April through October, for an additional 3€ fee—well worth it—but this was suspended indefinitely in 2020.

○ **Attire:** The guards at St. Mark's entrance are serious about forbidding entry to anyone in inappropriate attire: shorts, sleeveless shirts, cropped tops, and skirts above the knee. Note also that you also cannot enter the basilica with luggage.

○ **Photos:** Photos and filming inside the basilica are forbidden.

the outdoor **Loggia dei Cavalli.** Here you can admire a panoramic view of the piazza below and replicas of the celebrated *Triumphal Quadriga,* four gilded bronze horses dating from the 2nd or 3rd century A.D.; the Roman originals were moved inside in the 1980s for preservation. (The word *quadriga* actually refers to a car or chariot pulled by four horses, though in this case there are only the horses.) The horses were transported to Venice from Constantinople in 1204, along with lots of other loot from the Fourth Crusade.

The basilica's greatest treasure is the magnificent altarpiece known as the **Pala d'Oro** (Golden Altarpiece), a Gothic masterpiece encrusted with over 2,000 precious gems and 83 enameled panels. It was created in 10th-century Constantinople and embellished by Venetian and Byzantine artisans between the 12th and 14th centuries. Second to the Pala d'Oro in importance is the 10th-century **"Madonna di Nicopeia,"** a bejeweled icon also purloined from Constantinople and exhibited in its own chapel. Also worth a visit is the **Tesoro** (Treasury), a collection of crusaders' plunder from Constantinople and other icons and relics amassed over the years. Much of the loot has been incorporated into the interior and exterior of the basilica in the form of marble, columns, capitals, and statuary.

Although guided tours were suspended indefinitely at the start of the pandemic in 2020, if they've been reinstated by the time you visit, it's worth taking one. The 1-hour tours normally run April to October Monday to Saturday (at least one daily, from noon on; guides speak English). Book them (32€) online at www.venetoinside.com. The church also organizes free tours, in English Monday to Friday at 11am, April to October only.

Piazza San Marco. www.basilicasanmarco.it. © **041/2708311.** Basilica 3€; Museo di San Marco (includes Loggia dei Cavalli) 7€, Pala d'Oro 5€, Tesoro 5€. Basilica Mon–Sat 9:30am–5:15pm, Sun 2–5pm (Nov–mid-Apr closes 4:30pm Sun). Tesoro and Pala d'Oro Mon–Sat 9:45am–5pm, Sun 2–5pm (Nov–mid-Apr Mon–Sat 9:45am–4:45pm, Sun 2–4:30pm). Museo di San Marco daily 9.30am–5:15pm (Nov–mid-Apr 9:45am–4:45pm). *Vaporetto:* San Marco.

**Campanile di San Marco (Bell Tower)** ★★★ LANDMARK  An elevator whisks you to the top of this 97m (318-ft.) brown brick bell tower, where you get an awe-inspiring view of St. Mark's cupolas. With a gilded angel atop its spire, the bell tower is the highest structure in the city, offering a pigeon's-eye panorama that includes the lagoon, neighboring islands, and the red rooftops and church domes and bell towers of Venice. Originally built in the 9th century, the bell tower was reconstructed in the 12th, 14th, and 16th centuries, when the pretty marble loggia at its base was added by Jacopo Sansovino. It collapsed in 1902, miraculously hurting no one except a cat. Nine years later it was rebuilt exactly as before, using most of the same materials, even one of the five historical bells still in play today. Check www.venetoinside.com to see if "Skip the Line" tickets, which were suspended indefinitely in 2020 due to Covid-19, have been reinstated.

Piazza San Marco. www.basilicasanmarco.it. ℂ **041/2708311.** 10€. Daily: mid-Apr–Sept 9:45am–9:15pm; Oct–Mar 9:45am–5pm; Apr 1–mid-Apr 9:45am–5:30pm (closes Jan for maintenance). *Vaporetto:* San Marco.

**Canal Grande (Grand Canal)** ★★★ LANDMARK  A leisurely cruise along the "Canalazzo" from Piazza San Marco to the Ferrovia (train station), or the reverse, is one of Venice's (and life's) must-do experiences (see box, p. 231). Hop on the **no. 1** *vaporetto* in the late afternoon (try to get a coveted outdoor seat in the prow), when the weather-worn colors of the former homes of Venice's merchant elite are warmed by the soft light and reflected in the canal's rippling waters, and the busy traffic of delivery boats, *vaporetti,* and gondolas that fills the city's main thoroughfare has eased somewhat.

Best stations to start/end a tour of the Grand Canal are Ferrovia (train station) or Piazzale Roma on the NW side of the canal and Piazza San Marco in the SE. Tickets 7.50€.

**Casanova Museum & Experience** ★★ MUSEUM  One of the city's newer attractions pays homage to one of its most famous sons, **Giacomo Casanova** (1725–1798). The absorbing, interactive exhibition features information boards and multimedia installations, set in the otherwise bare rooms of the Palazzo Malipiero (you're given a headset that wirelessly translates the audio in each room as you enter). The first section covers aspects of Casanova's exceptional life as adventurer, writer, diplomat, and spy, though his more infamous role as seducer and libertine gets most attention. In one segment you even don headgear for a virtual-reality jaunt through 18th-century Venice. Other rooms add context to the fashions and popular parlor games of the time (Casanova claimed to have mastered at least 22). *Note:* The museum was closed indefinitely in 2020 due to the pandemic—check to see if it has reopened before visiting.

Palazzo Malipiero, Salizada Malipiero 3198. ℂ **041/237-9736.** 13€; 9€ over 65 and students under 26. Temporarily closed due to Covid-19 pandemic. *Vaporetto:* San Samuele.

**Palazzo Ducale** ★★★ PALACE  The pink-and-white marble Gothic-Renaissance **Palazzo Ducale** (Doge's Palace), residence of the doges who ruled Venice for more than 1,000 years, stands between the Basilica di San

# Venice Attractions

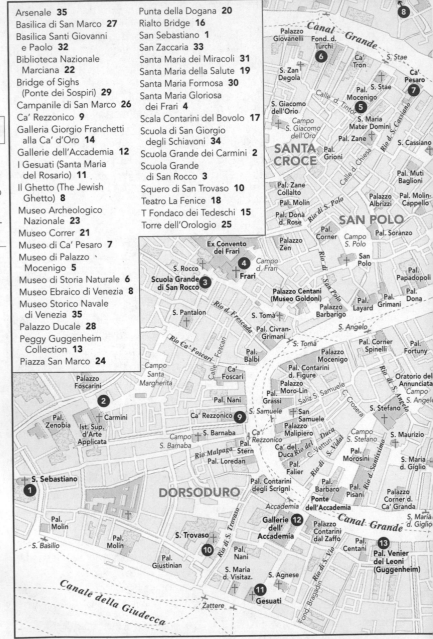

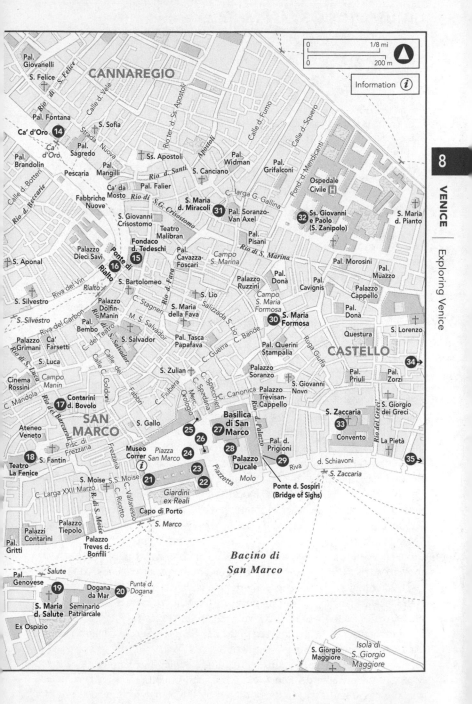

## museums **OF SAN MARCO**

Your ticket to the Palazzo Ducale also includes entry to several other museums around Piazza San Marco, though these are recommended for ancient-history and art aficionados only—with limited time you won't miss a lot by skipping them. Much of the **Museo Correr** (www.correr.visitmuve.it; ✆ **041-2405211;** daily 11am–5pm) is dull, comprising lesser-known artworks, archaeological remains, and odd bits and pieces from the city's later history, but it does have one spark of gold: the **"Courtesans"** ★★, a captivating painting by **Vittore Carpaccio.** The **Museo Archeologico Nazionale** (✆ **041-2967663;** same hours) contains a collection of Roman and Greek bits and pieces, while the ticket also includes a look at the two original reading rooms of the **Biblioteca Nazionale Marciana** (same hours), accessed via the Museo Correr—the current library is next door in the old mint of the Republic of Venice.

Marco and the sea. A symbol of prosperity and power, the original was destroyed by a succession of fires, with the current building started in 1340, extended in the 1420s, and redesigned again after a fire in 1483. If you want to understand something of this magnificent place, the fascinating history of the thousand-year-old maritime republic, and the intrigue of the government that ruled it, take the **Secret Itineraries tour** ★★★ (see box, p. 270). Failing that, at least download the free iPhone/Android app (see the website) or shell out for the audioguide tour (available at entrance, 5€) to help make sense of it all. Unless you can tag along with an English-speaking tour group, you may otherwise miss out on the importance of much of what you're seeing.

The 15th-century **Porta della Carta** (Paper Gate) opens onto a splendid inner courtyard with a double row of Renaissance arches (today visitors enter through a doorway on the lagoon side of the palace). The self-guided route through the palace begins on the main courtyard, where the **Museo dell'Opera** contains assorted bits of masonry preserved from the Palazzo's exterior. Beyond here, the first major room you'll come to is the spacious **Sala delle Quattro Porte** (Hall of the Four Doors), with a worn ceiling by Tintoretto. The **Sala dell'Anticollegio,** where foreign ambassadors waited to be received by the doge and his council, is covered in four works by Tintoretto, including "Mercury & the Three Graces" and **"Bacchus and Ariadne"** ★★, the latter deemed one of his best by some critics. The Tintorettos are outshone, however, by Veronese's **"Rape of Europa"** ★★, one of the palazzo's finest paintings.

The highlight of the adjacent **Sala del Collegio** (the Council Chamber itself) is the spectacular cycle of **ceiling paintings** ★★, a Veronese masterpiece completed between 1575 and 1578. Next door lies the most impressive of the interior rooms, the richly adorned **Sala del Senato** (Senate Chamber), with Tintoretto's ceiling painting "The Triumph of Venice." After passing again through the Sala delle Quattro Porte, you'll enter the Veronese-decorated **Stanza del Consiglio dei Dieci** (Room of the Council of Ten), where justice was dispensed and decapitations ordered by the Republic's dreaded security police. Formed in the 14th century to deal with emergency situations, the Ten became more powerful than the Senate and feared by all. In the **Sala della Bussola** (the Compass Chamber), notice the **Bocca dei Leoni** (Lion's Mouth), a slit in the wall into which secret denunciations and accusations of enemies of the state were placed for quick action by the much-feared Council.

The main sight on the next level down—indeed, the main sight in the entire palace—is the **Sala del Maggior Consiglio** (Great Council Hall). This enormous space is animated by Tintoretto's huge **"Paradiso"** ★ at the far end of the hall above the doge's seat. Measuring 7×23m (23×75 ft.), it is said to be the world's largest oil painting; together with Veronese's gorgeous **"Il Trionfo di Venezia"** ★★ ("The Triumph of Venice") in the oval panel on the ceiling, it affirms the power emanating from the council sessions held here. Tintoretto also did the portraits of the 76 doges encircling the top of this chamber; note that the picture of the Doge Marin Falier, who was convicted of treason and beheaded in 1355, has been blacked out—Venice has never forgiven him. Tours culminate at the enclosed **Ponte dei Sospiri** (Bridge of Sighs), built in 1600, which connects the Doge's Palace with the grim **Palazzo delle Prigioni** (Prison). The bridge took its current name in the 19th century—Lord Byron popularized it in his epic poem "Childe Harold's Pilgrimage" (1812–1818), romantically imagining the prisoners' final breath of resignation upon viewing the outside world one last time. Some attribute the name to Casanova,

who, following his arrest in 1755 (he was accused of being a Freemason and spreading antireligious propaganda), crossed this very bridge. One of the rare few to escape, he did so 15 months after his imprisonment began; it was 20 years before he dared return to Venice. Some of the cells still have the original graffiti of past prisoners, many of them locked up interminably for petty crimes.

San Marco, Piazza San Marco. www.palazzoducale.visitmuve.it. ✆ **041/2715911.** Admission only with San Marco Museum Pass (26€). For Secret Itineraries tour in English, see box p. 270. Restricted Covid-19 hours daily 10am–6pm; otherwise Sun–Thurs 8:30am–9pm, Fri–Sat 8:30am–11pm (Nov–Mar daily 8:30am–7pm). *Vaporetto:* San Marco.

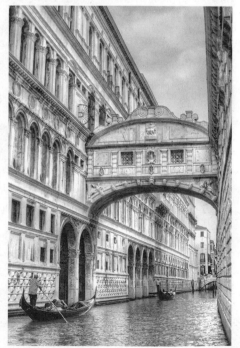

**The Bridge of Sighs.**

| **St. Mark's & the Doge's Palace in 1 Day?** |

Yes, it is possible (and not too exhausting) to see the Basilica di San Marco and the Palazzo Ducale in 1 day. Start at the church, arriving 30 minutes before opening (ideally get an online reservation in advance; see p. 262). Take a break before heading across to the Doge's Palace, where you can spend the rest of the day. You can buy palace tickets in advance online (**muve.vivaticket. it**). Your palace ticket also includes entry to the Museo Correr, Museo Archeologico Nazionale, and Biblioteca Nazionale Marciana, but it's safe to save these for another day—tickets are valid for up to 3 months.

**Piazza San Marco** ★★★ SQUARE   Dubbed "the finest drawing-room in Europe" by Napoleon, San Marco Square is undeniably one of Italy's most beautiful spaces, despite being terribly congested in high season (and often flooded during *acqua alta*). Today, the square is a focal point for Carnevale, as well as the spectacular Basilica and the most **historic cafes** in Venice—it's worth spending time in at least one of them for the ambience alone. The oldest (1720) is **Caffè Florian** (see p. 289), with compact **Caffè Lavena** ★ (founded on the opposite side of the *piazza* in 1750) said to be Wagner's favorite (look for the plaque inside) and the hangout of fellow composer Franz Liszt in the 19th century. The final member of the San Marco "big three," **Gran Caffè Quadri** ★ opened in 1638 as "Il Rimedio" ("The Remedy"), but it was more of a retail coffee operation at first, with the cafe upstairs added in 1830. It's been revitalized by chef Max Alajmo of Le Calandre restaurant in Padua, who added a fancy restaurant (**Ristorante Quadri;** https://alajmo.it). Expect the same high prices and surcharges at all three.

**Rialto Bridge** ★★ LANDMARK   This graceful arch over the Grand Canal, linking the San Marco and San Polo districts, is lined with overpriced boutiques and teeming with tourists and overflow from the daily market on the San Polo side. Until the 19th century, it was the only bridge across the Grand Canal, originally built as a pontoon bridge at the canal's narrowest point. Wooden versions of the bridge followed; the 1444 incarnation was the first to include shops, interrupted by a drawbridge in the center. In 1592, this graceful stone span was finished to the designs of Antonio da Ponte (whose last name fittingly enough means "bridge"), who beat out Sansovino, Palladio, and Michelangelo with plans that called for a single, vast, 28m-wide (92-ft.) arch in the center to allow trading ships to pass.

Ponte del Rialto. *Vaporetto:* Rialto.

**Scala Contarini del Bovolo** ★★ VIEW   Part of a palazzo built in the late 15th century, this multi-arch spiral staircase (a mini-Tower of Pisa) was artfully restored in 2016, featuring a belvedere with fabulous views of Venice. Halfway up, the **Sala del Tintoretto** (Tintoretto Room) contains the rare portrait of Lazzaro Zen, an African who converted to Christianity in Venice in 1770, as well as a preparatory painting by Tintoretto of his monumental

"Paradise" (the final version is in the Palazzo Ducale). You can buy **timed entry tickets** in advance at www.ticketlandia.com (advisable in peak season).

Corte Contarini del Bovolo 4299, San Marco. www.gioiellinascostidivenezia.it. ℃ **041/3096605.** 7€. Daily 10am–6pm. Vaporetto: Rialto.

**Teatro La Fenice** ★★★ THEATER   One of Italy's most famous opera houses (it ranks third after La Scala in Milan and San Carlo in Naples), La Fenice was originally completed in 1792 but has been completely rebuilt twice after devastating fires; in 1837 and most recently in 2004. Self-guided tours (audio guides included) take in the opulent main theater, ornate side rooms, the gilded "royal box," and a small exhibit dedicated to feted soprano Maria Callas. For tickets to performances, see p. 288.

Campo San Fantin 1965, San Marco. www.teatrolafenice.it. Buy tour tickets on-site or in advance at festfenice.com. ℃ **041/2424.** 11€. Daily 9:30am–6pm. Vaporetto: Giglio.

**T Fondaco dei Tedeschi** ★★ STORE/VIEW   The Harrods of Italy? In 2016, architect Rem Koolhaas and friends converted one of the city's great 16th-century *palazzi* (originally headquarters of the city's German or *Tedeschi* merchants) into a posh department store, centered on an elegant courtyard (featuring cafe/restaurant **AMO,** run by the Alajmo brothers). The **Rooftop Terrace** has rotating art exhibitions and quite possibly the greatest view of Venice. It's worth making reservations for the terrace in peak season (up to 21 days in advance), either on the store website or via a QR Code scanner on the 4th floor. The building is actually owned by Benetton and leased by the LVMH–owned luxury travel company DFS.

Calle de Fontego dei Tedeschi, Ponte di Rialto, San Marco. www.dfs.com/en/venice. ℃ **041/3142000.** Daily 10am–7pm. Roof deck (free) open daily 10:30am–6:30pm; visits limited to 15 min. Vaporetto: Rialto.

**Torre dell'Orologio (Clock Tower)** ★★ MONUMENT   As you enter the magnificent **Piazza San Marco,** this Renaissance clock tower is one of the first things you see, standing on the north side, the centerpiece of the stately white **Procuratie Vecchie** (the ancient administration buildings for the Republic). With its distinctive blue face ringed by astrological symbols, the tower was built between 1496 and 1506, and the clock still keeps perfect time (although most of its original workings have been replaced). On top, two bronze figures, known as "Moors" because of the dark color of the bronze, pivot to strike the hour. Visits inside are by guided tour only (included in the price of admission), but unless you are interested in the clock's history, these are easily skipped, especially if you've already been up the Campanile di San Marco.

Piazza San Marco. www.torreorologio.visitmuve.it. ℃ **848/082000** or 041/42730892. 12€, 7€ ages 6–14 and students 15–25; ticket also includes Museo Correr, Museo Archeologico Nazionale, and Biblioteca Nazionale Marciana. Restricted Covid-19 tours (1 hr.) Thurs 3pm in English; otherwise Mon–Wed 11am and noon, Thurs–Sun 2pm and 3pm (must be reserved in advance online); tours start at Museo Correr ticket office. Tours also in Italian and French. *Vaporetto:* San Marco.

# secrets **OF THE PALAZZO DUCALE**

The **Itinerari Segreti ★★★ (Secret Itineraries)** guided tours of the Palazzo Ducale are a must-see for any visit to Venice of more than 1 day. The tours offer an unparalleled look into the world of Venetian politics over the centuries and are the only way to access otherwise restricted quarters and hidden passageways of this enormous palace, such as the doges' private chambers and the torture chambers where prisoners were interrogated. The tour must be reserved in advance online (**muve.vivaticket.it**), by phone (**℃ 041/4273-0892**), or in person at the ticket desk. Tours often sell out at least a few days ahead, especially from spring through fall. Tours in English are daily at 10:15am (check the website to see if more times have been added post-pandemic) and cost 28€ for adults, 15€ for ages 6 to 14 and students 15 to 25. There are also tours in Italian at 11:30am and French at 12:45pm. The tour lasts about 75 minutes.

## Castello

While the highlight of this neighborhood is the huge **Santi Giovanni e Paolo** (see below), within a few minutes' walk from here are two more magnificent Renaissance churches: **Santa Maria Formosa** (3€; Mon–Sat 10:30am– 4:30pm), on Campo Santa Maria Formosa, and **San Zaccaria** (free; Mon–Sat 10am–noon and 4–6pm, Sun 4–6pm), at Campo San Zaccaria, which contains Giovanni Bellini's exceptional **San Zaccaria Altarpiece ★★.** Pay 3€ to enter the side chapels for Tintoretto's "Birth of St. John the Baptist" and the creepy flooded crypt, which houses the bodies of eight doges.

Several attractions lie on the far eastern side of Castello. The sprawling **Museo Storico Navale di Venezia** (Riva San Biasio 2148; www.marina.difesa. it) is worthwhile for folks with a deep interest in maritime history, but can be skipped by most others. Nearby is the **Ponte del Paradiso** and the famous twin-towered entrance to the **Arsenale** (only open during the Biennale).

**Basilica Santi Giovanni e Paolo ★** CHURCH    Built by the Dominican order from the 13th to the 15th century, this massive Gothic church, together with the Frari Church in San Polo, is second in size only to the Basilica di San Marco. An unofficial Pantheon where 25 doges are buried (a number of tombs are part of the unfinished facade), the church, commonly known as Zanipolo in Venetian dialect, is also home to many artistic treasures. The brilliantly colored **"Polyptych of St. Vincent Ferrer"** (ca. 1465), attributed to a young Giovanni Bellini, is in the right aisle. You'll also see the mummified foot of St. Catherine of Siena—considered a holy relic—encased in glass near here. Visit the **Cappella del Rosario ★,** through a glass door off the left transept, to see three restored ceiling canvases and one oil painting by Paolo Veronese, particularly "The Assumption of the Madonna."

Anchoring the large and impressive *campo* outside the church, a popular crossroads for this area of Castello, is the **statue of Bartolomeo Colleoni ★★,** the Renaissance *condottiere* (mercenary) who defended Venice's interests at the height of its power until his death in 1475. The 15th-century sculpture by the Florentine **Andrea Verrocchio** is considered one of the world's great equestrian monuments and Verrocchio's best.

Campo Santi Giovanni e Paolo 6363. santigiovanniepaolo.it. ℂ **041/5235913.** 3.50€. Daily 7:30am–7pm (open to tourists Mon–Sat 9am–6pm, Sun noon–6pm). *Vaporetto:* Rialto.

**Scuola di San Giorgio degli Schiavoni** ★★ MUSEUM   One of the most mesmerizing spaces in Europe, the tiny main hall of this *scuola* once served as a meeting house for Venice's Dalmatian community (Dalmatia is a region of Croatia, and *schiavoni* means "Slavs"). Venetian *scuole,* or schools, were Middle Age guilds that brought together merchants and craftspeople from certain trades or similar religious devotions. Guilds functioned as social clubs, credit unions, even sources of spiritual guidance, and many commissioned elaborate headquarters, hiring the best artists of the day to decorate them. The *scuole* that remain in Venice today house some of the city's finest art treasures. Built beside its sister church, San Giovanni di Malta, in the early 16th century, San Giorgio degli Schiavoni offers a big reason to visit: to admire the awe-inspiring cycle of paintings on its walls, created by Renaissance master Vittore Carpaccio between 1502 and 1509. The paintings depict the lives of the Dalmatian patron saints George (of dragon-slaying fame), Tryphon, and Jerome. In the upper hall (Sala dell'Albergo), you'll also find Carpaccio's masterful "Vision of St. Augustine."

Calle dei Furlani 3259A. www.scuoladalmatavenezia.com/en. ℂ **041/5228828.** 6€. Restricted Covid-19 hours Wed–Mon 10am–5:30pm; otherwise Mon 1:30–5:30pm, Tues–Sat 9:30am–5:30pm, and Sun 9:30am–1:30pm (reserve entry 1 day in advance at segreteria@scuoladalmatavenezia.com). *Vaporetto:* Rialto.

# Dorsoduro

**Ca' Rezzonico** ★★★ MUSEUM   Overlooking the Grand Canal, the palatial **Ca' Rezzonico** has a storied history that begins in the 1750s with the noble Rezzonico family. Later tenants included the poet Robert Browning (who died here in 1889) and Cole Porter, who rented the premises from 1926 to 1927.

---

## The Biennale

Venice hosts the latest in contemporary art and sculpture from dozens of countries during the prestigious **Biennale d'Arte** ★★★ (www.labiennale.org; ℂ **041/5218711**), one of the world's top international art shows. It fills the pavilions of the **Giardini** (public gardens) at the east end of **Castello** and at the **Arsenale,** as well as in other spaces around the city from April to November every other year. (The 2021 Biennale was postponed to 2022 because of the Covid-19 epidemic.) It's usually open Tuesday to Sunday 10am to 6pm; tickets cost around 25€, 20€ seniors 65 and over, 16€ students and ages 26 and under. The **Biennale Architettura** (international architecture exhibition) takes place in alternate years (2023, 2025, and so on).

# VENICE discounts

Venice offers a somewhat bewildering range of passes and discount cards. For short stays, we recommend buying a 1-day to 7-day **ACTV travel card** (p. 230) and combining that with one of the first two passes listed below. The more complex Venezia Unica card scheme is recommended if you intend to stay up to 7 days and do a lot of sightseeing. The **Venezia Unica website** (www.veneziaunica.it) is a one-stop shop for all the passes listed below.

The **Museum Pass (MUVE)** grants admission to all city-run museums over a 6-month period, and also lets you skip ticketing lines, a useful perk in high season. The pass covers the museums of St. Mark's Square—**Palazzo Ducale, Museo Correr, Museo Archeologico Nazionale,** the **Biblioteca Nazionale Marciana** (it's 25€ to visit just these museums with a San Marco Museum Pass)—as well as the **Museo di Palazzo Mocenigo** (Costume Museum), **Ca' Rezzonico, Ca' Pesaro,** the **Museo del Vetro** (Glass Museum) on Murano, and the **Museo del Merletto** (Lace Museum) on Burano. The Museum Pass is available online (for an extra 1€), or at any participating museum. It costs 35€ for adults and 18€ for students under 26, kids ages 6 to 14, and seniors over 65. It's a good deal, as the Doge's Palace alone will set you back 26€; visit two more of the larger museums (e.g., Ca' Rezzonico, 10€, and Ca' Pesaro, 14€) and you've made a decent saving.

The **Chorus Pass** (www.chorusvenezia. org) grants admission to almost every major church in Venice, 17 in all, for 12€ (8€ for students under 30), for up to 1 year. For 24€, the **Chorus Pass Family** gives you the same perks for a family of two adults and their children up to 18 years old. Most churches charge 3€ admission, which means you'll need to visit more than four to make this pass worthwhile.

The **Venezia Unica card** (www.vene-ziaunica.it) combines the above passes, transport, discounts, and even Internet access on one card via a "made-to-order" online system, where you choose the services you want. Of these, the 7-day passes (if available) are the best value. You can also buy various transportation packages from Venezia Unica (1-, 2-, 3- and 7-day ACTV passes 20€–60€), which cover all *vaporetto* and bus travel, or just Wi-Fi access (from 5€ for 24 hr.).

For visitors between the ages of 6 and 29, the **Rolling Venice card** (also available at www.veneziaunica.it) costs just 6€. Valid through the end of the year in which you buy it, it entitles the bearer to significant (20%–30%) discounts at participating restaurants (cardholder's meal only) and discounted ACTV travel cards (22€ for 3 days), along with discounts in museums, stores, hotels, and bars across the city (it comes with a thick booklet listing all the places you're entitled to get discounts).

Today its lavish rooms pay tribute to 18th-century Venetian art and decor, with works by Tintoretto, four major ceiling frescoes by Tiepolo (plus his wonderfully preserved **Frescoes from the Villa at Zianigo ★★**), a couple of masterpieces from Francesco Guardi, and rare paintings by Francesco Maffei.

Calle San Bernardo 3136. carezzonico.visitmuve.it. ✆ **041/2410100.** 10€. Restricted Covid-19 hours Thurs–Sun 11am–5pm; otherwise daily April–Oct 10:30am–6pm, Nov–March 10:30am–5pm. *Vaporetto:* Ca' Rezzonico.

**Gallerie dell'Accademia (Academy Gallery)** ★★★ MUSEUM
Along with San Marco and the Palazzo Ducale, the **Accademia** is one of the highlights of Venice, a magnificent collection of European art and especially Venetian painting from the 14th to the 18th centuries. There's a lot to take in here, so buy a catalog in the store, as these contain detailed descriptions of the core paintings and plenty of context—the audio guides are a little muddled and not worth 6€. Note also that one of the museum's prize holdings, Da Vinci's iconic **Vitruvian Man** ★★★ ("L'Uomo Vitruviano"), is an extremely fragile ink drawing and rarely displayed in public; check the website before you visit, as exhibitions featuring the painting are rare but well publicized.

Visitors are currently limited to 300 at one time and lines can be long in high season—so advance reservations are essential (these are timed entry, letting you skip the line). In general, the least crowded times tend to be at opening in the morning, and around 2 hours before closing.

Rooms are laid out in rough chronological order, though renovations and closures mean some rooms may be off-limits when you visit (call ahead to check on specific paintings; the website is updated monthly). Work began on the second-floor galleries in 2018—rooms 6 to 12, plus 15, each are likely to be closed at some point over the next few years. The following artworks should be on display somewhere in the museum, though locations will change (again, check the website for the latest).

Visits normally begin upstairs on the second floor, where room 1 (the grand meeting room of the Scuola Grande di Santa Maria) displays a beautifully presented collection of lavish medieval and early Renaissance art, primarily religious images and altarpieces on wood panels from 1300 to 1450. The giant canvases in room 2 include Carpaccio's "Presentation of Jesus in the Temple," and works by Giovanni Bellini (one of Bellini's images of St. Peter lies in room 3). Rooms 6 to 8 feature Venetian heavyweights Tintoretto, Titian, Veronese, and Lorenzo Lotto, while Room 10 is dominated by Paolo Veronese's mammoth **"Feast in the House of Levi"** ★★. Vast Tintoretto canvases make up the rest of the room, including his four paintings of the legends of St. Mark. Opposite is Titian's last painting, a "Pietà" intended for his own tomb. Room 11 contains work by Tiepolo, the master of 18th-century Venetian painting, but also several paintings by Tintoretto, including a "Crucifixion."

The next rooms contain a relatively mediocre batch of 17th- and 18th-century paintings, though Canaletto's **"Capriccio: A Colonnade"** ★ (Room 17), which he presented to the Academy when he was made a member in 1763, certainly merits a closer look for its elegant contrast between diagonal, vertical, and horizontal lines.

Room 19 traditionally contains a monumental cycle of nine paintings by Carpaccio illustrating the **Story of St. Ursula** ★★; most of these continue to undergo restoration, with "Arrival in Cologne" the only one likely to be displayed for some time. Room 20 is filled by Gentile Bellini's cycle of **"The Miracles of the Relic of the Cross"** ★, painted around 1500. While renovations are ongoing, room 23 will contain some of the museum's most famous paintings—check with the information desk (or online) if there's a particular work you want to see. Finally, room 24 is adorned with Titian's "Presentation of the Virgin," created between 1534 and 1538 specifically to hang in this space.

Downstairs, the renovated ground-floor galleries cover the late 18th to 19th centuries, a far more mediocre collection of baroque and romantic works, though delicate paintings by Tiepolo share space with his large tondo "Feast of the Cross" in gallery 2, along with Veronese's "Venice Receives Homage from Hercules and Ceres." Sculpture galleries (featuring the work of Canova) should also be open on this level.

Campo della Carità 1050, at foot of Accademia bridge. www.gallerieaccademia.it. *C* **041/5200345.** 12€ adults (admission price subject to change during temporary exhibitions). 1.50€ reservation charge by phone or online. Daily 8:15am–7:15pm (Mon closes 2pm). *Vaporetto:* Accademia.

### I Gesuati (Santa Maria del Rosario) ★ CHURCH

Built from 1724 to 1743 by Giorgio Massari to mirror the Redentore across the Canale della Giudecca, this cavernous church counters the latter's Palladian sobriety with rococo flair. The interior is graced by airy 1738–39 ceiling frescoes (some of the first in Venice) by **Giambattista Tiepolo.** Tiepolo also created the "Virgin with Saints Rosa of Lima, Catherine of Siena, and Agnes of Montepulciano" on the first altar on the right. The third altar on the left is adorned with a Tintoretto "Crucifixion" (1565).

Fondamenta delle Zattere ai Gesuati. *C* **041/2750462.** 3€ adults, free for children 5 and under. Mon–Sat 10am–4:30pm. *Vaporetto:* Zattere.

### Peggy Guggenheim Collection ★★ MUSEUM

Though this is one of the best museums in Italy exhibiting American and European art of the 20th century, you might find the experience a little jarring, given its location in a city so heavily associated with the High Renaissance and the baroque. Nevertheless, art aficionados will find some fascinating work here, and the galleries occupy Peggy Guggenheim's wonderful former home, the 18th-century Palazzo Venier dei Leoni, right on the Grand Canal (you can access the waterfront from the main building). Guggenheim bought the mansion in 1949 and lived here, on and off, until her death in 1979 (the history of this once-derelict palace is wonderfully brought to life in Judith Mackrell's *The Unfinished Palazzo*). Today the entire villa has been converted into galleries. Highlights include Picasso's extremely abstract "Poet" and his more gentle "On the Beach," several works by Kandinsky ("Landscape with Red Spots No. 2" and "White Cross"), Miró's expressionistic "Seated Woman II," Klee's mystical "Magic Garden," and some unsettling works by Max Ernst ("The Kiss," "Attirement of the Bride"), who was briefly married to Guggenheim in the 1940s. Look for Magritte's "Empire of Light," Dalí's typically surreal "Birth of Liquid Desires," and a couple of gems from Pollock (who was especially championed by Guggenheim): his early "Moon Woman," which recalls

Picasso, and "Alchemy," a more typical "poured" painting. The Italian Futurists are also well represented here, with a rare portrait from Modigliani ("Portrait of the Painter Frank Haviland"). Adjacent buildings added later to the complex (serving as temporary exhibition space, a cafe, and a shop) are connected to the main building by the pleasantly shady **Nasher Sculpture Garden;** Guggenheim is buried in the corner, marked by a simple headstone. *Tip:* It's not a good idea to visit the Guggenheim and St. Mark's on the same day—it's a fairly long walk between the two. We also don't advise

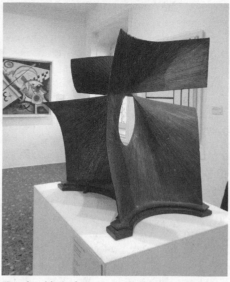

"Developable Surface," a 1941 sculpture by Antoine Pevsner made of bronze rods, is on display at the Peggy Guggenheim Collection.

seeing it on the same day as the Accademia, even though they are only 10 minutes apart; the artistic overload is likely to prove too much for even the most avid art aficionado.

Fondamenta Venier dai Leon 704. www.guggenheim-venice.it. ℂ**041/2405411.** Tickets (must be purchased online in advance) 15€ adults, 13€ 65 and over, 9€ students 26 and under and children ages 10–18 (plus 1.50€ online booking fee); printed guide 5€; audio guide 7€). Wed–Mon 10am–6pm. *Vaporetto:* Accademia (walk around left side of Accademia, take first left, and walk straight ahead following the signs).

**Punta della Dogana ★★★** MUSEUM   The eastern tip *(punta)* of Dorsoduro is crowned by the distinctive triangle of the 17th-century **Dogana di Mare** (Customs House), which once monitored all boats entering the Grand Canal. Transformed by architect Tadao Ando into a beautiful exhibition space, it's now a showcase for the contemporary art collection of billionaire François Pinault (officially dubbed the **Centro d'Arte Contemporanea Punta della Dogana**). It's pricey, but expect to see quality work from Cindy Sherman, Cy Twombly, Jeff Koons, and Marlene Dumas, among many others.

Fondamenta della Dogana alla Salute 2. www.palazzograssi.it. ℂ**041/2719031.** 15€–20€ (includes admission to Palazzo Grassi). Wed–Mon 10am–7pm (usually closed Jan–late March; check ahead). *Vaporetto:* Salute.

**San Sebastiano ★★** CHURCH   Lose the crowds as you make a pilgrimage to the parish church of **Paolo Veronese,** home to some of his finest work. Veronese painted the coffered nave ceiling with the florid "Scenes from the Life of St. Esther." In the 1560s he also decorated the organ shutters and panels in the chancel with scenes from the life of St. Sebastian. Although Veronese is the main event here, don't miss Titian's sensitive "St. Nicholas" (just inside the church on the right). Veronese's sepulchral monument (with bust by Mattia Carneri) is to the left of the altar. The real highlight is the sacristy (go through the door under the organ), a tiny jewel box of a room adorned with more wonderful Veronese paintings of the "Coronation of the Virgin" and the "Four Evangelists."

Campo San Sebastiano. ℂ **041/2750462.** 3€. Mon–Sat 10:30am–4:30pm. *Vaporetto:* San Basilio.

**Santa Maria della Salute** ★ CHURCH   The church of the Virgin Mary of Good Health, known as "La Salute," is a crown jewel of 17th-century baroque architecture, proudly reigning over a landmark point, almost directly across from the Piazza San Marco, where the Grand Canal empties into the lagoon.

The first stone was laid in 1631 after the Senate decided to honor the Virgin Mary for delivering Venice from a plague that had killed around 95,000 people. They accepted the revolutionary plans of a young, relatively unknown architect, Baldassare Longhena. He dedicated the next 50 years of his life to overseeing its progress (he would die 1 year after its inauguration but 5 years before its completion). Today the dome of the church is an iconic presence on the Venice skyline, recognized for its exuberant exterior of volutes, scrolls, and more than 125 statues. The most revered image inside is the **Madonna della Salute,** a rare black-faced sculpture of Mary brought back in 1670 from Candia in Crete as war booty. The otherwise sober interior is enlivened by the **sacristy,** with a number of important ceiling paintings and portraits by **Titian.** On the right wall of the sacristy (4€ admission) is Tintoretto's **"Marriage at Cana"** ★, often considered one of his best paintings.

Campo della Salute. www.basilicasalutevenezia.it. ℂ **041/5225558.** Church free; sacristy 4€. Daily 9:30am–noon and 3–5:30pm; sacristy Mon–Sat 10am–noon & 3–5pm, Sun 3–5pm. *Vaporetto:* Salute.

**Scuola Grande dei Carmini** ★★ CHURCH   The former Venetian base of the Carmelite religious order, finished in the 18th century, is now a shrine of sorts to **Giambattista Tiepolo,** who painted the ceiling of the upstairs hall between 1739 and 1744. It's truly a magnificent sight. Tiepolo's elaborate rococo interpretation of "Simon Stock Receiving the Scapular" is now fully restored along with various panels throughout the building.

Campo San Margherita 2617. www.scuolagrandecarmini.it. ℂ **041/5289420.** 7€. Daily 11am–5pm. *Vaporetto:* San Basilio.

**Squero di San Trovaso** ★★ HISTORIC SITE   One of the most intriguing sights in Venice is this small *squero* (boatyard), which first opened in the 17th century on the narrow Rio San Trovaso (not far from the Accademia Bridge). It is surrounded by Tyrolean-looking wooden structures (a true rarity in this city of stone built on water) that are home to the multigenerational

# THE ART OF gondola

Putting together one of these sleek black boats is a fascinatingly exact science that is still done in the revered traditional manner at boatyards such as the **Squero di San Trovaso** (see p. 276). Gondolas have been painted black since the 16th century, when local legislators passed a law designed to restrict the gaudy outlandishness so prevalent at the time.

Propelled by the strength of a single *gondoliere*, these boats, unique to Venice, have no modern equipment. They move with no great speed but with unrivaled grace. The right side of the gondola is lower because the *gondoliere* always stands in the back of the boat on the left.

The San Trovaso *squero*, or boatyard, is the city's oldest and one of only three remaining (the other two are immeasurably more difficult to find). Its predominant focus is on maintenance and repair, although they will occasionally build a new gondola (which takes some 40–45 working days), carefully crafting it from the seven types of wood—mahogany, cherry, fir, walnut, oak, elm, and lime—necessary to give the shallow and asymmetrical boat its various characteristics. After all the pieces are put together, the painting, the *ferro* (the iron symbol of the city affixed to the bow), and the woodcarving that secures the oar are commissioned out to various local artisans.

Although some 10,000 of these elegant boats floated on the canals of Venice in the 16th century, today there are only around 425, almost all catering to the tourist trade. The job of *gondoliere* remains a coveted profession, passed down from father to son over the centuries, but nowadays it's open to anyone who can pass 400 hours of rigorous training—including Giorgia Boscolo, who passed the exam in 2010 and became the first-ever *gondoliera*; her father was also in the profession.

owners and original workshops for traditional Venetian boats (see "The Art of the Gondola," above). Aware that they have become a tourist site themselves, the gondoliers don't mind if you watch them at work from across the narrow Rio di San Trovaso, but don't try to invite yourself in. *Tip:* It's the perfect midway photo op after a visit to the Accademia and a trip to **Gelateria Nico** (Zattere 922; see p. 260), where the chocolate *gianduiotto* is a decadent delight.

Dorsoduro 1097 (on the Rio San Trovaso, SW of the Accademia). *Vaporetto:* Zattere.

## San Polo & Santa Croce

The eastern portion of Santa Croce contains several minor attractions. The grand **Museo di Palazzo Mocenigo** (Salizada San Stae 1992; mocenigo.visitmuve.it) is worthwhile for visitors with a keen interest in historic costumes and perfumes, but can be skipped by most others, while the nearby **Museo di Ca' Pesaro** (Fondamenta de Ca' Pesaro 2076; capesaro.visitmuve.it) is home to modernist work from the likes of Rodin and Klimt, plus a large Asian art collection. The **Museo di Storia Naturale** (Salizada del Fontego dei Turchi 1730; msn.visitmuve.it) is a well-presented natural history museum aimed squarely at children.

**Santa Maria Gloriosa dei Frari (Church of the Frari)** ★★

CHURCH  Known simply as "i Frari," this immense 14th-century Gothic basilica was built by the Franciscans and is the largest church in Venice after San Marco. It houses a number of important artworks, including two Titian masterpieces: the **"Assumption of the Virgin"** ★★ over the main altar, painted when the artist was only in his late 20s, and "Virgin of the Pesaro Family" in the left nave. For the latter work, Titian's wife posed for the figure of Mary (and died soon afterward in childbirth). Don't miss Giovanni Bellini's **"Madonna & Child"** ★★ over the altar in the sacristy, of which novelist Henry James wrote, "it is as solemn as it is gorgeous." The grand **mausoleum of Titian** is on the right as you enter the church, opposite the incongruous 18th-century monument to sculptor **Antonio Canova,** shaped like a pyramid—designed by Canova himself, this was originally supposed to be Titian's tomb.

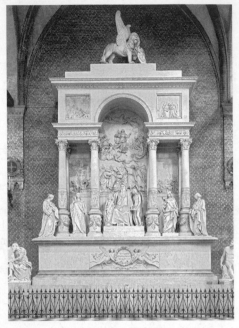

The mausoleum of the painter Titian, in Santa Maria Gloriosa dei Frari.

Campo dei Frari. www.basilicadeifrari.it. ℂ **041/2728611.** 3€; audio guide 2€. Mon–Sat 9:30am–12:30pm and 3–6pm; Sun 1–6pm. *Vaporetto:* San Tomà (walk straight on Calle del Traghetto, turn right and immediately left across Campo San Tomà; walk straight on Ramo Mandoler, then Calle Larga Prima, turn right at beginning of Salizada San Rocco).

**Scuola Grande di San Rocco** ★★★ MUSEUM  Like many medieval saints, French-born San Rocco (St. Roch) died young, but thanks to his work healing the sick in the 14th century, his cult became associated with the power to cure the plague and other serious illnesses. When his body was brought to Venice in 1485, this *scuola* began to reap the benefits, and by 1560 the current complex was completed. Work soon began on more than 50 paintings by **Tintoretto,** and today the *scuola* is primarily a shrine to the masterful Venetian artist. You enter at the **Ground Floor Hall** (Sala Terrena), where the paintings were created between 1583 and 1587, led by one of the most frenzied "Annunciations" ever made. The "Flight into Egypt" here is undeniably one of Tintoretto's greatest works. Upstairs is the **Great Upper Hall** (Sala Superiore), where Old Testament scenes such as "Moses Striking Water From the Rock" cover the ceiling. The paintings around the walls, based on the New Testament, are generally regarded as a master class of perspective, shadow, and color. In the **Sala dell'Albergo,** an entire wall is adorned by Tintoretto's mind-blowing "Crucifixion" (as well as his "Glorification of St. Roch," on the ceiling, the painting that actually won him the contract to paint the *scuola*). Way up in the loft, the **Tesoro** (Treasury) is a tiny space dedicated primarily to gold reliquaries containing venerated relics such as the fingers of St. Peter and St. Andrew, and one of the thorns that crowned Christ during the crucifixion.

Campo San Rocco 3052, adjacent to Campo dei Frari. www.scuolagrandesanrocco.it. ℂ **041/5234864.** 10€ adults, 8€ ages 18–26 and over 65, free 18 and under; audio guide 3€. Daily 9:30am–5:30pm. *Vaporetto:* San Tomà (walk straight ahead on Calle del Traghetto, turn right and immediately left across Campo San Tomà; walk straight on Ramo Mandoler, Calle Larga Prima, and Salizada San Rocco, which leads into the *campo*—look for the crimson sign behind Frari Church).

## Cannaregio

**Galleria Giorgio Franchetti alla Ca' d'Oro ★★** MUSEUM    A magnificent *palazzo* overlooking the Grand Canal, the "golden house," was built between 1428 and 1430 for the noble Contarini family. Baron Giorgio Franchetti bought the place in 1894, and it now serves as an atmospheric art gallery for his exceptional collection (mostly early Renaissance Italian and Flemish). The highlight is **"St. Sebastian" ★★** by Paduan artist Andrea Mantegna, displayed in its own marble chapel. The so-called "St. Sebastian of Venice" was the third and final painting of the saint by Mantegna, created around 1490 and quite a contrast to the other two (in Vienna and Paris, respectively); it's a bold, deeply pessimistic work, with none of Mantegna's usual background details to detract from the saint's suffering. Don't miss three panels from Carpaccio's "Stories of the Virgin" series on the second floor.

Strada Nuova 3932. polomusealeveneto.beniculturali.it. ℂ **041/520-0345.** 6€; audio guide 4€. Restricted Covid-19 hours Wed–Sat 9am–1:30pm; otherwise Mon 9am–2pm, Tues–Sun 9am–7pm. *Vaporetto:* Ca' d'Oro.

**Museo Ebraico di Venezia ★** MUSEUM/SYNAGOGUE    In the heart of the Ghetto Nuovo, the Jewish Museum contains a small but precious collection of artifacts related to the long history of the Jews in Venice, beginning with an exhibition on Jewish festivities in the first room; chandeliers, goblets, and spice-holders used to celebrate Shabbat, Shofàrs (ram's horns), and a Séfer Torà (Scroll of Divine Law). The second room contains a rich collection of historic textiles, including Torah covers, and a rare marriage contract from 1792. A newer area explores the immigration patterns of Jews to Venice, and their experiences once here. For many, the real highlight is the chance to tour the area's historic synagogues (ladies must have shoulders covered and men must have heads covered; no photos): **German** (Scuola Grande Tedesca), founded in 1528; **Italian** (Scuola Italiana), founded in 1575; **Sephardic** (Scuola Levantina), founded in 1541 but

Jews began settling in Venice in great numbers in the 15th century, and the Republic soon came to value their services as moneylenders, physicians, and traders. In 1516, however, fearing their growing influence, the Venetians forced the Jewish population to live on an island with an abandoned foundry (*ghetto* is old Venetian dialect for "foundry"), and drawbridges were raised to enforce a nighttime curfew. By the end of the 17th century, as many as 5,000 Jews lived in the Ghetto's cramped confines. Napoleon tore down the Ghetto gates in 1797, but it wasn't until the unification of Italy in 1866 that Jews achieved equal status. Il Ghetto remains the spiritual center for Venice's ever-diminishing community of Jewish families, with two synagogues and a Chabad House; although accounts vary widely, it's said that anywhere from 500 to 2,000 Jews live in all of Venice and Mestre, though very few now live in the Ghetto.

Aside from its historic interest, this is also one of the less touristy neighborhoods in Venice and makes for a pleasant and scenic place to stroll. Venice's first kosher restaurant, **Gam Gam,** opened here in 1996, at 1122 Ghetto Vecchio right on the canal (www.gamgamkosher.com; *©* **366/2504505**), close to the Guglie *vaporetto* stop. Run by Orthodox Jews, it is open Sunday to Thursday noon to 10pm, Friday noon to 2 hours before Shabbat begins at sunset, and Saturday from 1 hour after sunset until 11pm (excluding summer).

rebuilt in the second half of 17th century; **Spanish** (Scuola Spagnola), rebuilt in the first half of 17th century; and the baroque-style **Ashkenazi** (Scuola Canton), largely rebuilt in the 18th century. Museum tickets include a tour of the Scuola Levantina (and the Luzzatto midrash), but it is also possible to book private guided tours to two other synagogues (from 90€).

Campo del Ghetto Nuovo. www.museoebraico.it. *©* **041/715359.** Museum 10€ adults, 8€ kids and students ages 6–26 (includes guided tour to the Levantina Synagogue and the Luzzatto midrash). Museum Mon–Wed, Fri & Sun 10am–5:30pm, Thurs 11am–6.30pm; synagogue guided tours in English hourly 10:30am–5:30pm (Oct–May last tour 4:30pm). Closed Jewish holidays. *Vaporetto:* Guglie.

**Santa Maria dei Miracoli** ★ CHURCH   Hidden in a quiet corner of the residential section of Cannaregio northeast of the Rialto Bridge, the small and exceedingly attractive 15th-century Miracoli has one side of its precious polychrome-marbled facade running alongside a canal, creating colorful and shimmering reflections. It was built from 1481 to 1489 by Pietro Lombardo, a local artisan whose background in monuments and tombs is obvious. He would go on to become one of the founding fathers of the Venetian Renaissance.

The less romantic are inclined to compare it to a large tomb with a dome, but untold couples have made this jewel-like church their choice for weddings. The small square in front is the perfect place for gondolas to drop off and pick up the newlyweds, and inside is decorated with early Renaissance reliefs in a pastel palette of pink, gray, and white marble, an elegant nuptial setting. The church was constructed for a venerated image of the Virgin Mary, credited with working miracles—including bringing back to life someone who'd spent half an hour at the bottom of the Giudecca Canal. The icon is now displayed over the main altar.

Campiello di Miracoli, Rio di Miracoli. No phone. 3€. Mon–Sat 10:30am–4:30pm. *Vaporetto:* Rialto (located midway btw. Rialto Bridge and Campo SS. Giovanni e Paolo).

## Giudecca & San Giorgio

**Il Redentore** ★★ CHURCH   Many consider this the finest church ever designed by Andrea Palladio, the great Renaissance architect from nearby Padua most known for his country villas built for Venice's wealthy merchant families. It was commissioned by Venice to give thanks for being delivered from the great plague (1575–77), which claimed over a quarter of the population (some 46,000 people). The doge established a tradition of visiting this church by crossing a long pontoon bridge made up of boats from the Dorsoduro's Zattere, every third Sunday of July, a tradition that survived the demise of the doges and remains one of Venice's most popular festivals ("Festa del Redentore," see p. 40). The interior is done in austere but elegant classical Palladian style. The artworks tend to be workshop pieces (from the studios or schools, but not the actual brushes, of Tintoretto and Veronese), but there is a fine "Baptism of Christ" by Veronese himself in the sacristy (accessed through a door in the last chapel on the right), which also contains Alvise Vivarini's "Madonna with Child & Angels" alongside works by Jacopo da Bassano and Palma il Giovane.

Campo del Redentore 195.✆ **041/5231415.** 3€. Mon–Sat 10:30am–4:30pm. *Vaporetto:* Redentore.

**San Giorgio Maggiore** ★★ CHURCH   Sitting on the little island of San Giorgio Maggiore across from Piazza San Marco, this church is another Andrea Palladio masterpiece (see "Il Redentore," above), designed in 1565 and completed in 1610. To impose a classical front on the traditional church structure, Palladio designed two interlocking facades, with repeating triangles, rectangles, and columns harmoniously proportioned. Palladio also reinterpreted the interior with whitewashed stucco surfaces, an unadorned but harmonious space. The main altar is flanked by two epic paintings by Tintoretto, "The Fall of Manna," to the left, and the more noteworthy **"Last Supper"** ★★ to the right, famous for its chiaroscuro. Accessed by free guided tour only (usually Apr–Oct only; times vary), the adjacent Cappella dei Morti (Chapel of the Dead) contains Tintoretto's "Deposition," and the upper chapel contains Carpaccio's "St. George Killing the Dragon." To the left of the choir is an elevator that you can take to the top of the 1791 campanile—for a charge of 6€—to experience an unforgettable view of the island, the lagoon, and the Palazzo Ducale and Piazza San Marco across the way.

San Giorgio Maggiore island. ✆ **041/5227827.** Free. Daily 9am–7pm Apr–Oct, 8:30am–6pm Nov–Mar. *Vaporetto:* Take Giudecca-bound *vaporetto* no. 2 from Riva degli Schiavoni (San Marco/San Zaccaria) and get off at first stop.

# Exploring Venice's Islands

Venice shares its lagoon with four other principal islands: **Murano, Burano, Torcello,** and the **Lido.** Guided tours of the first three are available (25€–40€ for 3 to 4 hours), but while these can be informative, unless you are very short of time you'll enjoy exploring the islands in far more leisurely fashion on your own, easily done using the *vaporetti.*

Line nos. 4.1 and 4.2 make the journey to **Murano** from Fondamente Nove (on the north side of Castello). For **Murano, Burano,** and **Torcello,** line no. 12 departs Fondamente Nove every 30 minutes (for Torcello, change to the line 9 shuttle boat that runs from Burano, timed to match the arrivals from Venice). The islands are small and easy to navigate, but check the schedule for the next island-to-island departure (usually hourly) and plan your return so that you don't spend most of your day waiting for connections.

*Vaporetto* line nos. 1, 2, 5.1, 5.2, and LN cross the lagoon to the **Lido** from the San Zaccaria–Danieli stop near San Marco. Note that the Lido becomes chilly, windswept, and more or less deserted from October to April.

## MURANO ★★

The island of **Murano** has long been famous throughout the world for the products of its glass factories. The illuminating **Museo del Vetro (Museum of Glass)** ★★, Fondamenta Giustinian 8 (www.museovetro.visitmuve.it; *©* **041/739586**), provides context, charting the history of the island's glass-

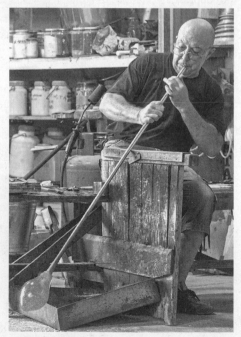

making; it's definitely worthwhile if you intend to purchase a lot of glassware, providing plenty of background so you know what you're buying in the stores outside. Normally it's open daily 10:30am to 6pm (Nov–Mar to 4:30pm); admission is 11€ adults, 8.50€ ages 6 to 14 and students 25 and under.

Dozens of *fornaci* (kilns) offer free (or cheap) shows of mouth-blown glassmaking, almost invariably hitched to a hard-sell tour of their factory outlet. Once you're on the island, you can't miss these places; they're pretty much of equal quality. A dependable choice is **Original Murano Glass** (Feb–Oct normally open daily 9:30am–4pm;

Traditional glassblowing in Murano.

reserve 5€ tours and demonstrations at www.visitmuranoglassfactory.com), at the Ellegi Glass *fornaci*, Fondamenta San Giovanni dei Battuti 4, a few minutes' walk from the Murano Faro *vaporetti* stop. Almost all shops will ship their goods, although that often doubles the price. On the other hand, these pieces are instant heirlooms.

Murano is also graced by two worthy churches (both free admission): the largely 15th-century **San Pietro Martire** ★ (Mon–Sat 9am–5:30pm, Sun noon–5:30pm), with its paintings by Veronese and Giovanni Bellini, and the ancient **Santa Maria e Donato** ★ (Mon–Sat 9am–6pm, Sun 12:30–6pm), with its intricate Byzantine exterior apse, 6th-century pulpit, stunning mosaic of Mary over the altar, and a fantastic 12th-century mosaic inlaid floor.

## BURANO ★★★

Lace is the claim to fame of tiny, historic **Burano,** a craft kept alive for centuries by the wives of fishermen waiting for their husbands to return from the sea. Sadly, most of the lace sold on the island these days is made by machine elsewhere. It's still worth a trip if you have time to stroll the back streets of the island, whose canals are lined with the brightly colored, simple homes of the Buranesi fishermen—it's quite unlike anything in Venice or Murano. The local government continues its attempt to keep its centuries-old lace legacy alive with subsidized classes.

Visit the **Museo del Merletto (Museum of Lace Making)** ★, Piazza Galuppi 187 (www.museomerletto.visitmuve.it; ✆ **041/730034**), to understand why something so exquisite should not be allowed to fade into extinction. It's normally open Tuesday to Sunday 10:30am to 5pm (Nov–Mar to 4pm); admission is 6€ adults, 4.50€ ages 6 to 14 and students 25 and under.

Butter biscuits known simply as *buranelli* are also a famous product of the island—expect to be offered them in almost every store.

## TORCELLO ★★

**Torcello** is perhaps the most charming of the islands, though today it consists of little more than one long canal leading from the *vaporetto* landing to a clump of buildings at its center. Hard to imagine this was once a thriving city in its own right, with at least 20,000 inhabitants in the 16th century.

Torcello boasts the oldest Venetian monument, the **Basilica di Santa Maria dell'Assunta** ★★★, whose foundation dates from the 7th century (✆ **041/2702464**). It's justly famous for its spectacular 11th- to 12th-century Byzantine mosaics—a "Madonna and Child" in the apse and a monumental "Last Judgment" on the west wall—rivaling those of Ravenna's and St. Mark's basilicas. The cathedral is open daily 10:30am to 6pm (Nov–Feb to 5pm), and admission is 5€ (audio guide an extra 2€; the bell tower another 5€). Also of interest is the adjacent 11th-century church of **Santa Fosca** (free admission), a simple Byzantine brick chapel with a plain interior, and the **Museo di Torcello** (✆ **041/730761**), with two small galleries showcasing archaeological artifacts from the Iron Age to the medieval era, many found on the island. The church closes 30 minutes before the basilica, and the museum is open Tuesday to Sunday 10:30am to 5:30pm (Nov–Feb 10am–5pm). Museum admission is 3€. You must buy tickets for all attractions at the Basilica entrance (museum, cathedral, and bell tower is 12€).

Peaceful Torcello is now uninhabited except for a handful of families (plus a population of feral cats) and is a favorite picnic spot. You'll have to bring food in from Venice—there are no stores on the island and only a handful of bars/trattorias plus one fabulous destination restaurant, **Locanda Cipriani** ★★★ (Wed–Mon noon–3pm and 7–9pm; closed Jan to mid-Feb; www.locandacipriani.com), of Hemingway fame; Queen Elizabeth II, Winston Churchill, and Princess Diana all dined here too). Opened in 1935 by Giuseppe Cipriani (it's still owned by the family), this spot is definitely worth a splurge. Once the tour groups have left, the island offers a very special moment of solitude and escape.

## THE LIDO ★

Although a convenient 15-minute *vaporetto* ride away from San Marco (see transport details above), Venice's **Lido beaches** are not much to write home about and certainly no longer a chic destination (the Grand Hotel des Bains depicted in Thomas Mann's *Death in Venice* closed in 2010). For bathing and sun-worshipping there are much better beaches nearby—in Jesolo, to the north, for example. But the parade of wealthy Italian and foreign tourists (plus a good number of Venetian families) who still frequent this coastal area makes an interesting sight indeed.

The Lido has two main beach areas. **Bucintoro** is at the opposite end of Gran Viale Santa Maria Elisabetta (referred to as the Gran Viale) from the *vaporetto* station Santa Elisabetta. It's a 10-minute stroll; walk straight ahead along Gran Viale to reach the beach. **San Nicolò,** about 1.5km (1 mile) away, can be reached by bus B from Santa Elisabetta. Renting loungers and parasols can cost from 10€ to 20€ per person (per day) depending on the time of year (it's just 1€ to use the showers and bathrooms). Keep in mind that if you stay at any of the hotels on the Lido, most have some kind of agreement with the different *bagni* (beach establishments). Note that the restored **Ancient Jewish Cemetery** (Antico Cimitero Ebraico), on the Lido (established in 1386), is open to the public but best appreciated on a tour from the Museo Ebraico (90€; p. 279).

## Organized Tours

Because of the sheer number of sights to see in Venice, some first-time visitors like to start out with an organized tour. Although few things can really be covered in any depth on these overviews, they're sometimes useful for getting your bearings. **Avventure Bellissime** (www.tours-italy.com; ✆ **041/970499**) coordinates a plethora of trips (in English), by boat and gondola, though the walking tours are the best value, covering all the main sights around Piazza San Marco in 2 hours for 39€ (includes "skip the line" tickets to St Mark's Basilica).

For those with more energy, learn to "row like a Venetian" (yes, literally standing up) at **Row Venice** (www.rowvenice.com; ✆ **347/7250637**), where 1½-hour lessons take place in traditional, hand-built "shrimp-tail," or *batele coda di gambero* boats for 85€ for up to 2 people. Or you could abandon tradition altogether and opt for a **Venice Kayak** tour (www.venicekayak.com; ✆ **346/4771327**), a truly enchanting way to see the city from the water. Despite restrictions imposed on kayaking by Venice authorities in 2018 and in 2019, the company is challenging the ruling in court and still offering tours (100€–160€)—check the website for the latest situation. **SUP in Venice** (www.supinvenice.com; ✆ **389/9851866**) offers guided SUP (standup paddleboard) trips (Apr–Oct), with 1-hour, 40-minute sessions starting at 70€.

## Especially for Kids

It goes without saying that a **gondola ride** (p. 277) will be the thrill of a lifetime for any child (or adult). If that's too expensive, consider the far cheaper alternative: a **ride on the no. 1** *vaporetto* (p. 225).

Judging from the squeals of delight, **feeding the pigeons in Piazza San Marco** could be the high point of your child's visit to Venice, and it's the ultimate photo op. Purchase a bag of corn and you'll be draped in pigeons in a nanosecond. Be sure your child won't be startled by all the fluttering and flapping.

A jaunt to the neighboring **island of Murano** (p. 282) can be as educational as it is recreational—follow the signs to any *fornace* (kiln), where a glassblowing performance of the island's thousand-year-old art is free entertainment. But be ready for the guaranteed sales pitch that follows.

Take the elevator to the **top of the Campanile di San Marco** (p. 263) for a scintillating view of Venice's rooftops and cupolas, or get up close and personal with the four bronze horses on the facade of the Basilica San Marco. The view from its **outdoor loggia** is something you and your children won't forget. Scaling the **Torre dell'Orologio** (p. 269) or the bell tower at **San Giorgio Maggiore** (p. 281) is also lots of fun.

The **winged lion,** said to have been a kind of mascot to St. Mark, patron saint of Venice, was the very symbol of the Serene Republic and to this day appears on everything from cafe napkins to T-shirts. Keep a running tab of who can spot the most flying lions—you'll find them on facades, atop columns, over doorways, as pavement mosaics, on government stamps, and on the local flag.

# SHOPPING

In a city that for centuries has thrived almost exclusively on tourism, remember this: **Where you buy cheap, you get cheap.** Venetians, centuries-old merchants, aren't known for bargaining. You'll stand a better chance of getting a good deal if you pay in cash or buy more than one item. In our limited space below, we've listed some of the more reputable places to stock up on classic Venetian items.

## Shopping Streets & Markets

A mix of low-end trinket stores and mid-market-to-upscale boutiques lines the narrow zigzagging **Mercerie** running north between Piazza San Marco and the Rialto Bridge. More expensive boutiques make for great window-shopping on **Calle Larga XXII Marzo,** the wide street that begins west of Piazza San Marco and wends its way to the expansive Campo Santo Stefano near the Accademia Bridge. Narrow **Calle Frezzaria,** which runs north-south just west of Piazza San Marco, offers bars, souvenir shops, and tony clothing stores like Louis Vuitton and Versace. The non-produce part of the **Rialto Market** is as good as it gets for basic souvenirs, such as cheap T-shirts, glow-in-the-dark plastic gondolas, and tawdry glass trinkets. The 3-day professional antiques market **Mercatino dell'Antiquariato** (www. mercatinocamposanmaurizio.it) takes place four to five times a year (usually Mar–Apr, May, Sept, Oct, and Dec; check website for dates), in Campo San Maurizio, San Marco.

## Arts & Crafts

Venice is uniquely famous for local crafts that have been produced here for centuries and are hard to get elsewhere: the **glassware** from Murano, the **delicate lace** from Burano, and the *cartapesta* **(papier-mâché) Carnevale masks** you'll find in endless *botteghe* (shops), where you can watch artisans paint amid their wares.

Now here's the bad news: There is such an overwhelming sea of cheap glass that buying **Venetian glass** can become something of a turnoff (shipping and insurance costs make most things unaffordable; the alternative is to hand-carry anything fragile). Plus, there are so few women left on Burano willing to spend countless tedious hours keeping alive the art of **lace-making** that the few pieces you'll see not produced by machine in China are sold at stratospheric prices; ditto the truly high-quality glass (although trinkets can be cheap and fun). The best place to buy glass is Murano itself—the **"Vetro Artistico Murano"** trademark guarantees its origin, but expect to pay as much as 60€ for just a wine glass.

**Atelier Segalin di Daniela Ghezzo** ★★ Founded in 1932 by master cobbler Antonio Segalin and his son Rolando, this old leather shoe store is now run by Daniela Ghezzo (Rolando's star apprentice), maker of exuberant

# carnevale A VENEZIA

Carnevale traditionally was the celebration preceding Lent, the period of penitence and abstinence prior to Easter; its name is derived from the Latin *carnem levare*, meaning "to take meat away." In Venice, the heyday of Carnevale was the 18th century; it was outlawed in 1797 and only revived in 1979 to boost winter tourism. Today Carnevale in Venice builds for a whole month until the big blowout, Shrove Tuesday, when fireworks illuminate the Grand Canal, and Piazza San Marco is turned into a giant open-air ballroom for the masses. The festival is a harlequin patchwork of cultural events, many of them free of charge, which appeals to all ages, tastes, nationalities, and budgets. Musical events from reggae and zydeco to jazz and baroque are staged in dozens of *piazze*. Book your hotel months ahead, especially for the two weekends prior to Shrove Tuesday. Check **www.carnevalevenezia.com** for details on upcoming events.

handmade shoes and boots, from basic flats to crazy footwear designed for Carnevale (custom footwear from 650€–1,800€). Calle dei Fuseri 4365, San Marco. www.danielaghezzo.it. (✆) **041/5222115.** Mon–Fri 10am–1pm and 3–7pm; Sat 10am–1pm. Vaporetto: San Marco.

**Ca' del Sol Maschere ★★**   Run by a group of artists since 1986, this shop is a treasure trove of Venetian masks (prices 35€–360€), along with elaborate 18th-century costumes; you can even take mask-making courses here. Fondamenta de l'Osmarin 4964, Castello. www.cadelsolmascherevenezia.com. (✆) **041/5285549.** Daily 10am–8pm. Vaporetto: San Zaccaria.

**Il Canovaccio ★**   Remember the creepy orgy scenes in Stanley Kubrick's film *Eyes Wide Shut*? The ornate masks used in the movie were made by the owners of this vaunted store. All manner of traditional, feathered, and animal masks are knocked out in their on-site workshop. Calle delle Bande 5369 (near Campo Santa Maria Formosa), Castello. kartaruga.com/il-canovaccio. (✆) **041/5210393.** Daily 10am–7pm. Vaporetto: San Zaccaria.

**Il Grifone ★★★**   Toni Peressin's handmade leather briefcases, satchels, bound notebooks, belts, and soft-leather purses have garnered quite a following, and justly so—his craftsmanship is truly magnificent (he makes everything in the workshop out back). Small items start at around 25€. Fondamenta del Gaffaro 3516, Dorsoduro. www.ilgrifonevenezia.it. (✆) **041/5229452.** Tues and Fri 10am–6pm; Wed, Thurs, Sat 10am–1pm and 4–7pm. Vaporetto: Piazzale Roma.

**La Bottega dei Mascareri ★★**   High-quality, creative masks—some based on Tiepolo paintings—have been crafted by the brothers Sergio and Massimo Boldrin since 1984. Basic masks start at around 15€ to 20€, but you'll pay over 75€ for a more innovative piece. The smaller, original branch lies at the foot of the Rialto Bridge (San Polo 80; (✆) **041/5223857**). Calle dei Saoneri 2720, San Polo. www.mascarer.com. (✆) **041/5242887.** Both locations daily 9am–6pm. Vaporetto: Rialto.

**Marco Polo International** ★ This vast showroom, just west of the Piazza San Marco, displays quality glass direct from Murano (although it's more expensive than going to the island yourself), including plenty of easy-to-carry items such as paperweights and small dishes. Frezzaria 1644, San Marco. www.marcopolointernational.it. ✆ **041/5229295.** Daily 10am–7pm. Vaporetto: San Marco.

**Venini** ★ Convenient, classy, but incredibly expensive, Venini has been selling quality glass art since 1921, supplying the likes of Versace and many other designer brands. Venini's **workshop** on Murano is at Fondamenta Vetrai 50 (✆ **041/2737211**). Piazzetta Leoncini 314, San Marco. www.venini.com. ✆ **041/5224045.** Both locations Mon–Sat 9:30am–5:30pm. Vaporetto: San Marco.

# ENTERTAINMENT & NIGHTLIFE

If you're looking for serious nocturnal action, you're in the wrong town—Verona and Padua are far livelier. Your best bet is to sit in the moonlit Piazza San Marco and listen to the cafes' outdoor orchestras, with the illuminated basilica before you—the perfect opera set—though this pleasure comes with a hefty price tag. Other popular spots to hang out include **Campo San Bartolomeo,** at the foot of the Rialto Bridge (admittedly a zoo in high season), and nearby **Campo San Luca.** In late-night hours, for low prices and low pretension, the absolute best place to go is **Campo Santa Margherita,** a huge open *campo* about halfway between the train station and the Accademia Bridge.

Visit one of the tourist information centers for current English-language schedules of the month's special events. The monthly *Ospite di Venezia* is distributed free or online at **www.unospitedivenezia.it** and is extremely helpful, but it's usually available only in the more expensive hotels. For Covid-19 restrictions, see p. 222.

## Performing Arts & Live Music

Venice has a long and rich tradition of classical music; this was, after all, the home of Vivaldi. People dressed in period costumes stand around in heavily trafficked spots near San Marco and Rialto passing out brochures advertising classical music concerts, so you'll have no trouble finding up-to-date information.

**Santa Maria della Pietà** ★★ The so-called "Vivaldi Church," built between 1745 and 1760, holds concerts throughout the year, mostly performed by lauded ensemble **I Virtuosi Italiani;** check the website for specific dates. Full-price tickets are usually 28€ to 35€. Riva degli Schiavoni 3701, Castello. www.chiesavivaldi.it. ✆ **041/5221120.** Vaporetto: San Zaccaria.

**Teatro La Fenice** ★★★ The opera season runs from late November through June, but there are also ballet performances and classical concerts. Tickets are expensive for the major productions (110€–200€ for the gallery and 190€ to 240€ for a decent seat). Those on a budget can opt for obstructed-view seats (from 35€). Campo San Fantin 1965, San Marco. www.teatrolafenice.it. ✆ **041/2424.** Vaporetto: Giglio.

# Cafes

For tourists and locals alike, Venetian nightlife mainly centers on the many cafes in one of the world's most remarkable *piazze:* Piazza San Marco. It is also a most expensive and touristed place to linger over a **spritz** (the Venetian classic cocktail of Prosecco and orange-flavored Aperol), but it's a splurge that should not be dismissed too readily.

**Caffè dei Frari** ★★★ Established in 1870, this inviting bar and cafe overlooking the Frari church has walls adorned with original murals, an antique wooden bar, and a wrought-iron balcony upstairs. The seafood is especially good here, and at least three excellent German beers are usually on tap. The whole place morphs into **Il Mercante Cocktail Bar** in the evenings (Tues–Thurs 6pm–1am; Fri and Sat 6pm–2am; Sun 6pm–midnight). Fondamenta dei Frari 2564, San Polo. www.ilmercantevenezia.com. © **041/5241877.** Tues–Sat 9am–5pm. Vaporetto: San Tomà.

**Caffè Florian** ★★ Occupying prime *piazza* real estate since 1720, this is one of the world's oldest coffee shops, with a florid interior of 18th-century mirrors, frescoes, and statuary. Sitting at a table, expect to pay 10.50€ for a cappuccino, 20€ for a Bellini (Prosecco and fresh peach nectar in season), and 14€ for a spritz—add another 6€ if the orchestra plays (Mar–Nov). Standing or sitting at the bar is much cheaper (5€ for a cappuccino, 10€ for a Bellini, etc.). Piazza San Marco 57. www.caffeflorian.com. © **041/5205641.** Mon–Thurs 10am–9pm; Fri & Sat 9am–11pm; Sun 9am–9pm. Vaporetto: San Marco.

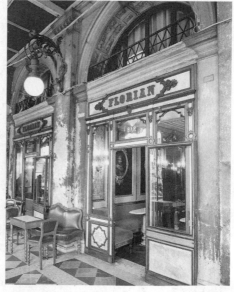

Caffè Florian, one of the world's oldest coffee shops, on Piazza San Marco.

**Il Caffè (aka Caffè Rosso)** ★★★ Established in the late 19th century, Il Caffè has a history almost as colorful as its clientele, a mixture of students, aging regulars, and lost tourists. This is an old-fashioned, no-nonsense Venetian cafe/bar, with reasonably priced drinks and sandwiches, and plenty of seating on the *campo* (plus small seating area inside). Cash only. Santa Margherita 2963, Dorsoduro. www.cafferosso.it. © **041/5287998.** Mon–Sat 7am–1am. Vaporetto: Ca'Rezzonico.

**Marchini Time ★★** The outlet for the famed Marchini *pasticcerie* (it opened in 1938), this plush modern cafe offers a range of addictive pastries, *biscotti,* chocolates, coffees, cakes, and savory *pizzette.* Campo San Luca 4589, San Marco.☏ **041/2413087.** Daily 7:30am–8.30pm. Vaporetto: Rialto.

**Pasticceria Nobile ★★** Founded in the 1930s, this is the most happening cafe in this section of town, celebrated for its tempting range of sweets, snacks, pastries, and chocolate. Locals congregate here for breakfast and for *aperitivo* after work. Calle del Pistor 1818, Cannaregio. ☏ **041/720731.** Daily 6:30am–8.30pm (closed July). Vaporetto: San Marcuola.

**Pasticceria Tonolo ★** This tiny bakery has had a cult following since 1886, thanks to its deep-fried sweet treats (*frittelle,* Italian-style doughnuts, 1.10€–1.30€), plus a vast range of sumptuous cakes and cookies. Coffee is served in charming, antique blue German porcelain cups (standing room only). Calle San Pantalon 3764, Dorsoduro.☏ **041/5237209.** Tues–Sat 7:30am–8pm; Sun 7:30pm–1pm (often closed through Aug). Vaporetto: San Tomà.

## Birreria, Wine & Cocktail Bars

Venice has never been a late-night clubbing hotspot. Evenings are better spent lingering over a late dinner or nursing a glass of Prosecco in one of the outdoor bars and cafes in Piazza San Marco or Campo Santa Margherita. It's also worth considering dressing up for a visit to one of the **historic bars** in Venice's grand-dame hotels, at least for a cocktail. It will be an expensive but memorable experience, often with mesmerizing views and impeccable service to match. You should also visit the neighborhood bars known as *bàcari* at least once (see p. 254).

**Al Prosecco ★★** Get acquainted with all things bubbly at this local enoteca, a specialist, as you'd expect, in Veneto Prosecco. It features plenty of tasty *cicchetti* to wash down the various brands, and plenty of outdoor tables from which to observe the laid-back Campo San Giacomo da l'Orio. Most drinks run 3€ to 5€. Campo San Giacomo da l'Orio 1503, Santa Croce. www.alprosecco.com. ☏ **041/5240222.** Mon–Sat 9am–10:30pm (closes 8pm in winter; closed Aug and Jan). Vaporetto: San Stae.

**Bar Dandolo ★★** Doge Dandolo built his glorious Venetian Gothic palace three doors down from the Palazzo Ducale in the 14th century, and current occupier Hotel Danieli has been one of the most sumptuous hotels in Venice since 1822. Nestled amid marble columns on the ground floor of the *palazzo,* this classic Venice bar serves everything from velvet-capped cappuccinos and a traditional afternoon tea (daily 3–6pm; 42€ per person) to a decadent Vesper Martini cocktail. You can also opt for an alfresco drink on the rooftop **Bar Terrazza Danieli** (Apr–Oct daily 3–11pm) in the same hotel. Riva degli Schiavoni 4196, Castello. www.terrazzadanieli.com. ☏ **041/5226480.** Daily 6:30am–1am (pianist plays daily 7pm–12:30am). Vaporetto: San Zaccaria.

**Bar Longhi ★★★** The Gritti Palace Hotel really was the 16th-century palace of Doge Andrea Gritti, whose portrait graces one of its antiques-filled lounges (it remains the city's most expensive hotel since opening in 1895). Bar Longhi is the quintessential Venetian watering hole, with lavish decor (hand-sculptured mirrors, Murano glass appliqués, and a marble bar counter), plus paintings belonging to the school of the celebrated 18th-century Venetian artist Pietro Longhi. Afternoon tea, cocktails, and champagne served. Campo Santa Maria del Giglio 2467 (Gritti Palace Hotel), San Marco. www.marriott.com. ℰ 041/794611. Daily 11am–1am. Vaporetto: Santa Maria del Giglio.

**Harry's Bar ★**    Possibly the most famous bar in Venice (and now a global chain), Harry's was established in 1931 by Giuseppe Cipriani and frequented by the likes of Ernest Hemingway, Charlie Chaplin, and Truman Capote. The Bellini was invented here in 1948 (along with *carpaccio* 2 years later), and you can sip the signature concoction of freshly-squeezed peach juice and Prosecco for a mere 22€. Go for the history, but don't expect a five-star experience—most first-timers are surprised just how ordinary it looks inside (though the bow-tied waitstaff still look the part). It's more restaurant than bar these days, serving very expensive food (main courses 40€–45€), but just stick to the drinks. Calle Vallaresso 1323, San Marco. www.cipriani.com. ℰ **041/5285777.** Daily 10:30am–11pm. Vaporetto: Vallaresso.

**Il Santo Bevitore ★★**    Beer aficionados will be pleased to learn that Italy has a growing craft beer scene, with this local spot showcasing the best brews from all over the country (many on tap). Sample Milan's Birrificio Lambrate and Birrificio Extraomnes, Parma's Birra Toccalmatto, Udine's Borderline Brewery, and Veneto's very own Mesh Brewery. The small bar overlooks the Rio de Servi just off the main drag (Strada Nova), with a few benches outside for warmer days. Fondamenta Diedo 2393, Cannaregio. www.ilsantobevitorepub.com. ℰ **335/8415771.** Daily 4pm–2am. Vaporetto: San Marcuola.

**Margaret DuChamp ★★**    This popular student and *fashionista* hangout has plenty of chairs on the *campo* for people-watching, cocktails, and a spritz or two (spritz is just 3€). It also serves decent panini (from 5€) and *tramezzini* (2€ at the table/1.50€ at the bar) and has free Wi-Fi. Cash only. Campo Santa Margherita 3019, Dorsoduro. ℰ **041/5286255.** Wed–Mon 9am–2am. Vaporetto: Ca' Rezzonico.

# DAY TRIPS FROM VENICE

By Stephen Keeling

I f you only have 3 days or so, you will probably want to spend them in the center of Venice. If, however, you are here for a week—or on your second visit to the city—head over to the mainland to see some fascinating old towns in the historic Veneto region.

**9**

## PADUA ★★★

40km (25 mi) W of Venice

Tucked away within the ancient heart of **Padua** lies one of the greatest artistic treasures in all Italy, the precious Giotto frescoes of the **Cappella degli Scrovegni.** Although the city itself is not especially attractive (it was largely rebuilt after bombing during World War II), don't be put off by the urban sprawl that now surrounds it; central Padua is refreshingly bereft of tourist crowds, a workaday Veneto town with a large student population and a small but intriguing ensemble of historic sights.

Like much of the region, Padua prospered in the Middle Ages, and Italy's second-oldest university was founded here in 1222. Its fortunes grew further when St. Antony of Padua died in the city in 1231, making it a place of pilgrimage ever since. In the 14th century, the da Carrara family presided over the city's golden age, but in 1405 Padua was conquered by Venice, losing its independence. With the fall of the Venetian Republic in 1797, the city was ruled by Napoleon and then became part of the Austrian Empire in 1814. Finally annexed to Italy in 1866, the city boomed again after World War II, becoming the industrial dynamo of northeast Italy.

### Essentials

**ARRIVING** The most efficient way to reach Padua (and the other destinations in this chapter) is to take the train from Venice's Santa Lucia station. Trains depart every 10 to 20 minutes and take 26 to 50 minutes depending on the class (tickets 5€–19€ one-way). The main Padua station ("Padova" in Italian) is a short walk north up Corso del Popolo from the Cappella degli Scrovegni and the old city.

**VISITOR INFORMATION**   The **tourist office** at Vicolo Pedrocchi 9 is usually open Monday to Saturday 9am to 6pm and Sunday 10am to 4pm (www.turismopadova.it; ✆ **049/5207415**).

## Exploring Padua

The one unmissable sight in Padua is the **Cappella degli Scrovegni ★★★** (www.cappelladegliscrovegni.it; ✆ **049/2010020;** daily 9am–7pm; check website for evening openings 7–10pm) at Piazza Eremitani, an outwardly unassuming chapel commissioned in 1303 by Enrico Scrovegni, a wealthy banker. Inside, however, the chapel is gloriously decorated with an astonishing cycle of frescoes by Florentine genius **Giotto.** The frescoes depict the life of the Virgin Mary and the life of Jesus, culminating with the Ascension and Last Judgment. Seeing Giotto's powerful work in the flesh is spine-tingling; this is where he made the decisive break with Byzantine art, taking the first steps toward the realism and humanism that would characterize the Renaissance in Italy.

Entrance to the chapel is limited, involving groups of 25 visitors spending 15 minutes in a climate-controlled airlock, used to stabilize the temperature, before going inside for another 15 to 20 minutes. To visit the chapel, you must **make a reservation at least 24 hours in advance.** You must then arrive 45 minutes before the time on your ticket. Tickets cost 14€ (5€ for kids ages 6–17 and students under 27).

If you have time, try to take in Padua's other historic highlights. The vast **Palazzo della Ragione** on Piazza delle Erbe (7€; Tues–Sun 9am–7pm, closes 6pm Nov–Jan) is an architectural marvel, a cavernous town hall completed in 1219 and decorated with frescoes by Nicola Miretto in the 15th century. The **Basilica di Sant'Antonio** (Piazza del Santo; www.santantonio.org; ✆ **049/8225652;** admission free; daily 6:20am–7:45pm, closes 6:45pm Nov–Mar), is the stately resting place of **St. Anthony of Padua,** the Portuguese Franciscan best known as the patron saint of finding things or lost people. While the exterior of the church is a bizarre 14th-century mix of Byzantine, Romanesque, and Gothic styles, the interior is richly adorned with statuary and murals. In the piazza outside, don't miss **Donatello**'s stupendous 1453 equestrian

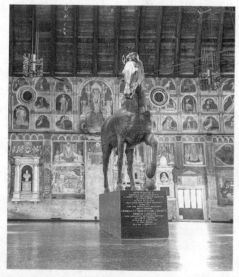

Donatello's imposing 1453 equestrian statue, in the piazza outside the Palazzo della Ragione, Padua.

9

DAY TRIPS FROM VENICE

Padua

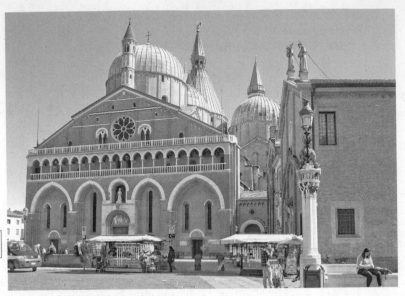

The Basilica of St. Anthony of Padua.

statue of the Venetian *condottiere* **Gattamelata** (Erasmo da Narni), the first large bronze sculpture of the Renaissance.

## Where to Eat in Padua

Padua offers plenty of places to eat and drink (Aperol was created here in 1919), and you'll especially appreciate the overall drop in prices compared with Venice. It's hard to match the location of **Bar Nazionale ★★,** Piazza delle Erbe 40 (Tues, Thurs, and Fri 7am–11:30am; Mon and Sat 7am–10:30pm; Sun 9am–9:30pm; Wed 7am–midnight), on the steps leading up to Palazzo della Ragione, though it's best for drinks and snacks (excellent *tramezzini* from 2€, panini from 4€, spritz 3€, and glasses of wine just 2.50€) rather than a full meal. For that, make for **Osteria dei Fabbri ★,** Via dei Fabbri 13, just off Piazza delle Erbe (www.facebook.com/osteriadeifabbripadova; *©* **049/650336;** Mon–Fri noon–2:30pm and 7–10:30pm, Sat noon–3pm & 7–11pm, Sun noon–3pm), which cooks up cheap, tasty pasta dishes for under 15€.

# VERONA ★★

115km (71 mi) W of Venice

The affluent city of **Verona,** with its Roman ruins and gorgeous medieval buildings in red and peach hues, is one of Italy's major tourist draws, though its appeal owes more to **William Shakespeare** than real history. He immortalized the city in his (totally fictional) *Romeo and Juliet, The Two Gentlemen of Verona,* and *The Taming of the Shrew.* Despite its popularity with tourists, Verona is not Venice; it's a booming commercial center with vibrant science and technology sectors.

Verona emerged as a city-state in the 12th century, ruled primarily by the bloodthirsty (and, in Renaissance tradition, art-loving) Scaligeri family until 1387. After a brief period of Milanese rule, Verona fell under the control of Venice in 1405. Like the rest of the region, the city was occupied by Napoleon in 1797, then Austria, and became part of Italy in 1866.

## Essentials

**ARRIVING**   The best way to reach Verona from Venice is by **train.** Direct services depart every 30 minutes and take anywhere from 1 hour and 10 minutes to 2 hours and 20 minutes, depending on the type of train you catch (one-way tickets 10€–28€). From Verona station (Verona Porta Nuova), it's a 15-minute walk to the historic center.

**VISITOR INFORMATION**   The **Visit Verona** tourist office is off Piazza Bra at Via Degli Alpini 9 (www.visitverona.it; ✆ **045/8068680;** Mon–Sat 9am–6pm, Sun 10am–5pm) and can supply maps and guided tour information.

## Exploring Verona

"Two households, both alike in dignity, in fair Verona…" So go the immortal opening lines of *Romeo and Juliet,* ensuring that the city has been a target for love-sick romantics ever since. Though Verona is crammed with genuine historic goodies, one of the most popular sites is the ersatz **Casa di Giulietta,** Via Cappello 23 (6€; Tues–Sun 8:30am–6pm), a 14th-century house (with balcony, naturally), claiming to be the Capulets' home. In the courtyard, the chest of a bronze statue of Juliet has been polished to a gleaming sheen thanks to a legend claiming that stroking her right breast brings good fortune. **Juliet's Wall,** at the entrance, is quite a spectacle, covered with the scribbles of star-crossed lovers (though the corridor is periodically scrubbed clean of graffiti and gum); love letters placed here are taken down and, along with 5,000 letters annually, are answered by the Club di Giulietta (a group of locally based volunteers). There's not much to see inside the house, though plenty of visitors line up for a chance of a selfie on the balcony.

Once you've made the obligatory Juliet pilgrimage, focus on actual historic sights. The 1st-century **Arena di Verona** ★ (10€; Mon 1:30–7:30pm and Tues–Sun 8:30am–7:30pm), in the spacious Piazza Bra, is the third-largest classical arena in Italy after Rome's Colosseum and the arena at Capua—it could seat some 25,000 spectators and still hosts performances today (see www.arena.it).

To the northwest on Piazza San Zeno, the **Basilica di San Zeno Maggiore** ★★ (www.basilicasanzeno.it; 3€, includes audioguide; Mar–Oct Mon–Fri 9:30am–1pm and 2:30–6pm, Sat 9:30am–6pm, Sun 1–6pm; Nov–Feb Tues–Fri 10am–1pm and 1:30–5pm, Sat 9am–6pm, Sun 12:30–5:30pm) is the greatest Romanesque church in northern Italy. The present structure was completed around 1135 over a 4th-century shrine to Verona's patron saint, St. Zeno (who died in 380). The church's massive rose window represents the Wheel of Fortune, lintels above the portal represent the months of the year. The highlight of the interior is Mantegna's "Madonna and Saints" above the altar.

## Where to Eat in Verona

The most authentic budget Verona restaurant is **Osteria Sottoriva,** Via Sottoriva 9 (✆ **045/8014323;** Thurs–Tues 11am–3pm and 6:30–10:30pm), one of the most popular places in town, try the *trippa alla Parmigiana* (braised tripe) or the hopelessly rich gorgonzola melted over polenta (main courses 10€–16€). **Caffè Monte Baldo,** Via Rosa 12 (www.osteriamontebaldo.com; ✆ **045/8030579;** Mon–Thurs 10am–11pm, Fri 10am–midnight, Sat 11am–midnight, Sun 11am–11pm), an old-fashioned cafe (open since 1909) transformed into a trendy *osteria,* serves classic pastas and scrumptious *crostini.*

# TREVISO ★★

30km (19 mi) N of Venice

Long overshadowed by Venice, **Treviso** is a small, prosperous city of narrow medieval streets, Gothic churches, and an enchanting network of canals, replete with weeping willows and waterwheels (it's known as "*piccola Venezia,*" or "little Venice"). Giotto's follower **Tomaso da Modena** (1326–79) frescoed many of its churches, and its maze of back streets makes for pleasant, often tourist-free exploring.

## Essentials

**ARRIVING**   Trains run two to four times an hour from Venice's Santa Lucia station; it's a 30- to 40-minute trip, definitely your fastest option. Tickets start at 3.60€ one-way. Arriving at Treviso Centrale station, you'll have an easy 10- to 15-minute walk to Piazza dei Signori, north across the River Sile (follow signs to "Centro"). Note also that most Ryanair **budget flights to Venice** actually arrive at Treviso airport (p. 224).

**VISITOR INFORMATION**   The **Visit Treviso** tourist office at Via Fiumicelli 30 (www.visittreviso.it; ✆ **0422/547-632**) is open Monday from 10am to 1pm, Tuesday to Saturday 10am to 5pm, and Sunday 10am to 4pm.

## Exploring Treviso

The historic heart of Treviso, **Piazza dei Signori ★** is anchored by the **Palazzo del Podestà,** rebuilt in the 1870s with a tall clock tower, and the **Palazzo dei Trecento,** the 13th-century town council hall (chic **Bar Beltrame** nestles beneath the arches). Just beyond the square, on adjacent Piazza San Vito, sit two handsome medieval churches: **Santa Lucia ★** (www.santaluciatreviso.it; ✆ **0422/5457200**), with a superb Tomaso da Modena fresco of the "Madonna del Pavegio" in the first shrine on the right; and **San Vito ★,** with its fine 13th-century Byzantine-style frescoes. Both are open Monday to Friday 8am to noon, and Saturday and Sunday 9am to noon and 3:30 to 6pm; admission is free.

Historic **Via Calmaggiore,** lined with posh boutiques, runs northwest from Piazza dei Signori toward Treviso's **Duomo ★** (admission free; Mon–Sat 7:30am–noon and 3:30–7pm, Sun 8am–1pm and 3:30–8pm). Its relatively dull neoclassical facade dates only from 1836, but its flanking Romanesque lions and seven Venetian-Byzantine–style green copper domes testify to the cathedral's 12th-century origins. The crypt is the most compelling part of the interior, with tombs of the city's bishops amid a forest of columns and fragments of 14th-century frescoes and mosaics. The cathedral also has a fine 1520 Titian altarpiece, the "Malchiostro Annunciation." Stroll southwest from the Duomo to the massive Italian Gothic **San Nicolò church ★** (admission free; daily 8am–noon & 3:30–6pm), with its intriguing Gothic frescoes. Tomaso da Modena and his school deco-

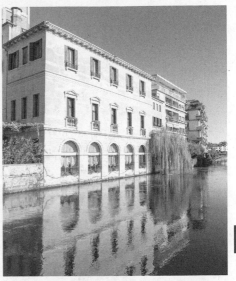

Treviso is called "Little Venice" for its many canals.

rated the huge, round columns with a series of saints, notably St. Jerome and St. Agnes. Antonio da Treviso painted the gargantuan St. Christopher—his .9m-long (3-ft.) feet strolling over biting fish—in 1410.

East of Piazza dei Signori, in Piazzetta Mario Botter, the **Museo di Santa Caterina** (www.museicivicitreviso.it; ✆ **0422/658442**; 6€; Tues–Sun 10am–6pm) is housed in a deconsecrated church. Its highlight is another fresco cycle by Tomaso da Modena, the "Story of the Life of Saint Ursula" (detached from a now-destroyed church and preserved here). There's also a cache of local archaeological finds, plus minor works by Titian, Lorenzo Lotto, and Francesco Guardi. South of there, the 15th-century church of **Santa Maria Maggiore** (admission free; daily 8am–noon and 3:30–6pm) houses a venerated frescoed image of Mary (the "Madonna Granda"), an ancient Byzantine-style image later touched up by Tomaso and members of his school.

## Where to Eat in Treviso

For atmosphere it's hard to beat the **Hostaria Dai Naneti ★★,** Vicolo Broli 2 (✆ **3403/783158;** Mon–Sat 9am–2:30pm and 5:30–9pm, Sun 11am–2pm and 5–9pm; closed Sun May–Sept), a cozy tavern, deli, and cheese shop where you can grab a delicious baguette and glass of wine, or just snack at the bar for around 6€ (standing-room only).

For a full meal in the center, reserve a table at **Trattoria All'Antico Portico ★★,** overlooking the church at Piazza Santa Maria Maggiore 18 (www.anticoportico.it; ✆ **0422/545259;** Mon 9am–4pm, Wed–Sun 9am–11pm), which serves local specialties such as radicchio risotto and *baccalà alla veneziana* (salt cod); main courses are 16€ to 19€.

# PLANNING
# YOUR TRIP

By Donald Strachan

This chapter provides a variety of planning tools, including information on how to get to Italy, how to get around in safety and comfort, and the inside track on local resources you can consult for up-to-date advice. If you do your homework, pick the right place for the right season, and pack for the climate, preparing for a trip to Italy should be as pleasant and uncomplicated as ever. For "When to Go" advice, see p. 38.

# GETTING THERE

## By Plane

**10**

If you're flying across an ocean, you'll most likely land at Rome's **Leonardo da Vinci–Fiumicino Airport** (FCO; www.adr.it/fiumicino), 40km (25 miles) from the center. This is almost always the cheapest intercontinental destination. Rome's much smaller **Ciampino Airport** (CIA; www.adr.it/ciampino) serves low-cost airlines connecting to European cities and some destinations within Italy. For information on getting to central Rome from its airports, see p. 42. Travelers can also board a direct high-speed train from Fiumicino to Florence or Venice **without** passing through central Rome.

Carriers within Europe fly direct to many smaller Italian cities, including Venice's **Marco Polo Airport** (VCE; www.veniceairport.it), **Florence Airport** (FLR; www.aeroporto.firenze.it/en), Bologna's **Marconi Airport** (BLQ; www.bologna-airport.it), and Pisa's **Galileo Galilei Airport** (PSA; www.pisa-airport.com). For information on getting into central Venice from the airport, see p. 224. For reaching central Florence from the airport—and from Pisa or Bologna airport—see p. 147. *Note:* Since the pandemic, airports have adopted strict cleaning protocols and mandated **mask wearing and social distancing.** Check airport websites for updated regulations (in English).

# VISITING ITALY IN THE covid-19 ERA

From the very first wave of the SARS-CoV-2 virus—which hit Italy, especially Lombardy, early and hard—the national government introduced strict measures to tackle infection rates, including compulsory mask-wearing, limited visitor numbers, stringent cleaning protocols, and contact tracing. You will find updated rules and guidance on a dedicated coronavirus page at **www.italia.it**. The website for the Ministry of Health (**www.salute.gov.it/portale/home.html**) is also worth bookmarking. For guidance on whether you can travel to Italy—and what proof of vaccination or testing you may need—consult the automated Italian government questionnaire (in English) at infocovid.viaggiaresicuri.it/returningtoitaly.html.

As you travel around, you may hear about the so-called **Green Pass.** Part of an EU-wide scheme, this digital pass certifies that the holder has been vaccinated against Covid-19, has tested negative within the last 48 hours, or is otherwise immune—say, after recent infection. Currently, you must show a Green Pass to **enter a museum or public building; use long-distance trains;** **attend the theater or enter a sports stadium; eat indoors at a restaurant; or access many other services or venues.** While the Green Pass itself is only available to EU citizens and those from participating non-EU countries, **carrying national proof of vaccination status will suffice.** You may need to share a few personal details for contact-tracing purposes, including the contact info for those you've traveled with and your lodging. Further information on the Green Pass scheme (in Italian only) is provided at www.dgc.gov.it.

At any time while traveling in Italy, if you should develop Covid-19 symptoms, *do not* visit a doctor, pharmacy, or emergency room: Instead, call Italy's national helpline, staffed 24/7, on ✆ **1500.** Many pharmacies do offer **antigen and PCR testing** for travelers (typically 20€ and 60€ respectively), as well as certificates in English. Check with your airline and national embassy in Italy if you need to arrange an antigen or PCR test before returning to your home country. The U.S. Embassy in Rome has a dedicated webpage at it.usembassy.gov/covid-19-information.

# By Train

Italy's major cities are well-connected to Europe's rail hubs. You can arrive in Milan on direct trains from France—including Paris and Lyon—by **TGV** (en.oui.sncf/en/tgv), or on a Swiss intercity service from Zurich, and connect in Milan to Venice or Rome (see "Getting Around," p. 300). **Nightjet** rail routes (www.nightjet.com/en) go from Munich, Germany and Vienna, Austria to Venice, Florence, and Rome. Direct trains from elsewhere in central Europe also arrive at Verona and Venice.

You can book European rail travel in advance online with agents such as **Rail Europe** (www.raileurope.com) or **International Rail** (www.international rail.com; ✆ **+44-871/231-0790**).

*Note:* It is likely that **mask wearing in stations and on trains** will remain mandatory for the foreseeable future. Rail Europe keeps its website updated with the latest public health–related regulations for rail travel.

# GETTING AROUND

## By Train

Italy, especially the northern half, has one of the best train systems in Europe, with most destinations connected. Consequently, the train is an excellent option to visit major sites without the hassle of driving. The vast majority of lines are run by state-owned **Ferrovie dello Stato,** or **Trenitalia** (www.trenitalia.com; ✆ **89/2021**). Private operator **Italo** (www.italotreno.it; ✆ **06/07-08,** or 89/2020) operates on the main Milan–Florence–Rome–Naples high-speed line; branches north from Bologna to Padua/Venice and Verona/Trento; and travels from Turin eastward to Venice via Milan and Verona.

Travel durations and the price of tickets vary considerably depending on the type of train you choose. The country's principal north–south high-speed line links Milan to Bologna, Florence, Rome, and Naples. Milan to Rome, for example, takes around 3 hours on the fast train, and costs 88€ to 95€—although you can find tickets as low as 40€ if you buy ahead and travel in off-peak hours. *Tip:* To grab the cheapest fares on high-speed trains, **book around 100 to 120 days before your travel dates.** The **Italo newsletter** (and homepage) regularly advertises limited-time promo code discounts offering up to 50% off advanced fares—making them crazy cheap. You can also book on Trenitalia and Italo via **Trainline** (www.thetrainline.com/trains/italy).

**TYPES OF TRAIN**   The speed, cleanliness, and overall quality of Italian trains vary. **High-speed trains** usually have four classes: Standard, Premium, Business, and Executive on Trenitalia; Smart, Comfort, Prima, and Club Executive on Italo. The cheapest of these, on both operators, is perfectly comfortable, even on long legs of a journey. *Tip:* Business class on Trenitalia's Frecciarossa is worth paying extra for, if it's reduced for advance ticket purchase.

The **Frecciarossa,** as well as Italo's rival high-speed train, is the fastest of the fast, Italy's bullet train. These trains operate on lines connecting both Milan and Venice with Florence–Rome–Naples, and normally run up to 300 kmph (186 mph). Frecciarossa services also connect Milan with Venice (with halts in Verona and Vicenza). The **Frecciargento** uses slightly lesser hardware and is a bit slower; it links Naples, Rome, and Florence with Pisa and Verona at speeds of up to 250 kmph (155 mph). Speed and cleanliness come at a price, however, with tickets for any of these high-speed trains usually around three times the cheapest, standard "regional" train. On high-speed services you **must make a seat reservation** when you buy a ticket. If you are traveling with a rail pass (see p. 302), you also pay a 10€ reservation fee to ride (which you can do from automated Trenitalia ticket machines in stations, as well by queuing at a teller window). Rail passes are not accepted on Italo.

**Intercity (IC)** trains are a step down, in both speed and comfort; specific seat reservations are also compulsory. The slower *Regionale* (**R**) and *Regionale Veloce* (**RV**) make many stops and are occasionally on the grimy side, but are also cheap: A Venice–Verona second-class ticket will put you back only 9.25€ compared with 28€ on a high-speed service. There's no need to book R or RV trains ahead of time, and no price advantage in doing so. Just turn up, buy a ticket, and go.

Old *Regionale* trains are slowly being replaced, and comfort is improving. However, **overcrowding** is still a problem on some standard services (that is, not the pre-bookable trains) on Friday evenings, weekends, and holidays, especially in and out of big cities, or just after a strike.

**TRAIN TRAVEL TIPS** If you don't have a reservation for a particular seat on a specific train, then you must **validate any paper ticket by stamping it in the little yellow box** on the platform before boarding the train. If you board a train without a ticket, or without having validated your ticket, you'll have to pay a hefty fine on top of the ticket or supplement, which the conductor will sell you. If you board a train without a ticket or realize once aboard that you have the wrong type of ticket, your best bet is to let the conductor know; she is likely to be more forgiving because you sought her out and made it clear you weren't trying to ride for free.

Rail **apps** for state and Italo services offer paperless ticketing and convenient in-app payment for tickets via credit card or PayPal. These represent the simplest, contactless way to buy and carry rail tickets—for both high-speed and regular services. They are available, in English, from the usual app stores. You can just show a copy (paper or electronic) of your booking confirmation email, which has a unique PNR code.

In big cities and tourist destinations, ticketing lines can be dreadfully long. Don't be intimidated by **automatic ticket machines.** These are easy to navigate, offer instructions in English, accept cash and credit cards, and save the stress of waiting in a slow line. *One caveat:* You cannot buy international tickets at automatic machines.

## Travel Times Between the Major Cities

| CITIES | DISTANCE | (FASTEST) TRAIN TRAVEL TIME | DRIVING TIME |
| --- | --- | --- | --- |
| Florence to Venice | 261km/162 miles | 2 hr. | 3 hr. |
| Rome to Florence | 277km/172 miles | 1½ hr. | 3 hr. |
| Rome to Venice | 528km/327 miles | 3hr., 20 min. | 5¼ hr. |

# COVID-19 & train TRAVEL

Mask-wearing mandates have been introduced when necessary, and when in force, apply on board all trains and in stations. In-train filters ensure circulating air is as germ-free as possible; trains are cleaned between journeys; and any prebooked seat allocations maximize distance between traveling groups, when required. For **long-distance train travel** between regions, a Covid-19 Green Pass or its international equivalent is compulsory (see p. 299).

**Schedules** for all trains leaving a given station are printed on yellow posters tacked up on the station wall (a corresponding white poster lists arrivals). These are good for general information. Keep your eye on electronic boards and screens updated with delays and track *(binario)* changes. You can get official schedules (also in English) at www.trenitalia.com and www.italo treno.it.

**SPECIAL PASSES & DISCOUNTS**   To buy the **Eurail Italy Pass,** available only outside Europe and priced in U.S. dollars, contact **Rail Europe** (www.raileurope.com) or **Eurail** (www.eurail.com). The pass gives you a month to use the train a set number of days; the base number of days is 3, and you can add up to 5 more. For adults, the first-class pass costs $201, second class is $151. Additional days each cost $35 to $40 more for first class, around $30 for second class. For youth tickets (27 and under), a 3-day second-class pass is $125 and additional days about $25 each. **Buying your pass early** in the year is often rewarded with an extra day's travel at no additional cost (such as, pay for 3 days, get 4) or significant discounts: We have seen up to 35% off some Eurail passes. The **Eurail Global Pass** covers rail travel in Italy, all its neighbors, and most of the rest of Europe (33 countries). The electronic **Trenitalia Pass** costs slightly more than a Eurail Pass, but seat reservations are free, and you can buy it in Italy or online at www. trenitalia.com.

*Note:* Booking individual rail journeys online ahead of arrival will often beat a pass on price, especially if you factor in the costs (and hassle) of making compulsory seat reservations on every high-speed train. However, the cheapest online fares are nonrefundable: You gain flexibility with a pass.

**Children 14 and under ride half-price** on Italian trains, and kids 3 and under don't pay—although they do not have the right to their own seat. On state railways, there are sometimes **free tickets for children 14 and under** traveling with a paying adult; ask about "Bimbi gratis" when buying your ticket (this option will appear automatically when available on automatic ticket machines). The **Italo Famiglia** fare, available at least 2 days before travel at the station or online, includes free travel for kids 13 and under accompanying an adult (in Smart [standard] class only, Mon–Sat).

**10**

Getting Around

**PLANNING YOUR TRIP**

# By Bus

Although trains are quicker and easier, you can get just about anywhere in Italy on a network of local, provincial, and regional bus lines. In bigger cities, the **bus station** for intercity trips is usually near the main train station. A small town's **bus stop** is generally in the main square, on the edge of town, or on a bend in the road just outside the main town gate. If there's no office, tickets are usually sold at the nearest newsstand or *tabacchi* (a sign with a white T) or occasionally a bar. Buses in cities often have the technology to accept **fare payment via contactless credit card**—a major convenience boost.

Two useful long-distance bus routes are the efficient **Florence–Siena** service and slightly more awkward **Florence–San Gimignano** run (see p. 218). If you are traveling on a tight budget, check intercity fares of **FlixBus** (www. flixbus.it), which often significantly undercut train prices. A long-distance bus is *un pullman*.

For details on urban bus transportation, see individual chapters—for Rome, p. 49; for Florence, p. 152; and for Venice's water buses, p. 230. *Note:* **Face masks** (either surgical or material coverings) have often been obligatory on buses. Check the current rules when you arrive—or just do as locals do.

# By Car

Much of Italy is accessible by public transportation, but to explore vineyards, countryside, and smaller towns, a car is essential. You may also feel more comfortable in a private car than a shared train carriage—although Italy's train operators have implemented strict hygiene and cleaning protocols. You'll get the **best rental rate** if you book your car far ahead of arrival. Try the website **AutoSlash.com**, which applies any coupons on the market to your rental; and then monitors your booking. If the price drops, they'll make you a new reservation. We've found AutoSlash to be the best search engine for rentals by far, though it's a bit clunky to use: You must wait for a return e-mail before you can see the options, but thankfully it usually comes within minutes of your request. Car-rental search companies generally report the **lowest rates available between 6 and 8 weeks ahead** of arrival. Rent the smallest car possible and request a diesel rather than petrol engine to minimize fuel costs. You must be 25 or older to rent from many agencies (although some accept ages 21 and up, at a premium price).

The legalities and contractual obligations of renting a car in Italy (where accident rates are high) are more complicated than those in almost any other country in Europe. You also must have nerves of steel, a sense of humor, a valid domestic driver's license, and, strictly speaking (for non-Europeans), an **International Driving Permit** (see below). Insurance on all vehicles is compulsory. *Tip:* If you're planning to rent a car in Italy during high season, you should **book well in advance.** It's not unheard of to arrive at Rome airport in June or July to find that every agent is out of cars, perhaps for the whole week.

It can sometimes be tricky to get to the *autostrada* (fast highway) from a city center or airport, so consider renting or bringing a GPS-enabled device or installing an offline navigation app on your smartphone. In bigger cities you will first have to get to the *tangenziale,* or beltway. The beltway in Rome is known as the *Grande Raccordo Anulare,* or "Big Ring Road."

The going can be slow on Friday afternoons out of Italian cities and Sunday nights on the way back into town, and an urban rush hour any day of the week can be epic. Gas costs around 1.60€ *per liter* at time of writing. (Diesel is usually around .10€ cheaper.) Add in the price of the rental, and it's often cheaper to take the train, even for two people.

**PERMITS & AUTO CLUBS**   Before leaving home, you can buy an **International Driving Permit** from the **American Automobile Association** (**AAA;** www.aaa.com; ✆ **800/622-7070** or 650/294-7400). In Canada, the permit is available from the **Canadian Automobile Association** (**CAA;** www.caa.ca; ✆ **800/222-4357**). Technically, you need this permit and your driver's license to drive in Italy, although at a rental desk, your license itself often suffices. But why take the risk? Traffic police can fine you for driving without an IDP. Visitors from within the EU need only take their domestic driver's license.

Italy's equivalent of AAA is the **Automobile Club d'Italia** (**ACI;** www.aci.it). They're the people who respond when you place an emergency assistance call to ✆ **803-116** for road breakdowns (✆ **800/116-800** from an overseas cellphone). You'll be charged for this service if you're not a member.

**ROAD TYPES**   **Autostrade** are toll highways denoted by green signs and a number prefaced with an *A,* like the A1 from Milan to Florence, Rome, and Naples. A few fast highways aren't numbered and are simply called a *raccordo,* a connecting road between two cities (such as Florence–Siena and Florence–Pisa). Autostrada tolls can get expensive, costing just over 1€ for every 15km (9 miles): it costs around 22€ to drive from Rome to Florence. See **www.autostrade.it** for live traffic updates and a road-toll calculator.

*Strade statali* (singular, *strada statale*) are state roads, usually without a center divider and two lanes wide (although sometimes they can be a divided four-way highway), indicated by blue signs. The route numbers are prefaced with an *SS,* as in the SS11 from Milan to Venice. On signs, however, these official route numbers are frequently omitted. Usually, you'll just see blue signs listing destinations by name with arrows pointing in the appropriate directions. It pays to study the map before coming to an intersection, or better yet, download an **offline navigation app** for your smartphone. Because they bisect many towns, the *strade statali* can be frustratingly slow: When feasible, pay the euros and take the autostrada.

**DRIVING RULES**   Italian drivers aren't maniacs; they only appear to be. Spend any time on a highway and you will have the experience of somebody driving up insanely close from behind while flashing their headlights. Take a deep breath and don't panic: This is the aggressive signal for you to move to the right so he (it's always he) can pass, and until you do he will stay mind-bogglingly close. On a two-lane road, the idiot swerving into your lane to pass

## Road Signs

Here's a brief rundown of road signs you'll frequently encounter:

- **Speed limit sign:** Black number inside a red circle on a white background
- **End of a speed zone:** Black and white, with a black slash through the number
- **Yield to oncoming traffic:** Red circle with a white background, a black arrow pointing down, and a red arrow pointing up
- **Yield ahead:** Point-down, red-and-white triangle
- **Pedestrian zone:** Simple white circle with a red border, or the words *zona pedonale* or *zona a traffico limitato* (if your hotel is in a pedestrian zone, ask if you can prearrange to drop baggage off by car)
- **One-way streets:** White arrow on a blue background
- **Do not enter:** Mostly red circle with a horizontal white slash
- **No parking:** Circular sign in blue with a red circle-slash
- Any image in black on a white background surrounded by a red circle means that whatever is portrayed is **not allowed** (for instance, if the image is two cars next to each other, it means no passing; and so on).

someone in oncoming traffic expects you to veer obligingly toward the shoulder so three lanes of traffic can fit. He would do the same for you. Probably. Many Italians seem to think turn signals are optional, so be aware the car in front could be ready to turn at any moment.

A few important rules:

When traveling outside of towns, it is compulsory to **keep your headlights illuminated**—set to dip—even during the day.

The **speed limit** on roads in built-up areas around towns and cities is 50 kmph (31 mph). On two-lane roads it's 90 kmph (56 mph) and on the highway it's 130 kmph (81 mph). Italians have an astounding disregard for these limits. However, police can ticket you and collect a fine on the spot.

The **blood-alcohol limit** in Italy is 0.05%, often achieved with less than two drinks; driving above the limit can result in a fine, driving ban, or imprisonment. The blood-alcohol limit is set at zero for anyone who has held a driver's license for less than 3 years.

**Seat belts** are obligatory in both front and back seats; ditto child seats or special restraints for minors under 1.5m (5 ft.) in height—although this latter regulation is often ignored.

Drivers may not use a **cellphone** while driving. This is yet another regulation locals treat as optional.

**PARKING**    Even savvy locals struggle to find convenient parking in Italy's cities. Hotels rarely have parking facilities, but many do negotiate deals with private city lots. Your hotel should be a first point of contact if you plan to park and leave the car for the duration of your stay. Should you prefer driving to the high-speed train, this is the only sensible option in big cities. On streets, **white lines** indicate free public spaces; **blue lines** are pay spaces; and **yellow**

**lines** indicate spots where only residents are allowed to park. Meters don't line the sidewalk; rather, there's usually a machine on the block where you punch in how long you want to park. The machine prints a ticket to place on your dashboard. If you park in an area marked *parcheggio disco orario,* root around in your rental car's glove compartment for a cardboard parking disc. With this device, you dial up the hour of your arrival and display it on your dashboard. You're allowed *un'ora* (1 hr.) *due ore* (2 hr.), or whatever the sign advises. If you do not have a disk, **write your arrival time clearly on a sheet of paper and leave it on the dash.**

Parking lots have ticket dispensers, but exit booths are not usually manned. When you return to the lot to depart, first visit the office or automated payment machine to exchange your ticket for a paid receipt. You then use this to pass through the exit gate.

**FUEL** Gasoline (gas or petrol), *benzina* in Italian, can be bought at pull-in gas stations along major roads and on the outskirts of towns, as well as in 24-hour stations along the autostrada. Almost all are closed for the *riposo* (midday siesta) and on Sundays (except along the autostrada), but most have an automatic machine that accepts cash. Unleaded gas is *senza piombo.* Diesel is *gasolio* (or just *diesel*).

# [FastFACTS] ITALY

**Area Codes** The **country code** for Italy is **39.** City codes (Florence is 055, Venice is 041, Rome is 06) are incorporated into the numbers themselves. Therefore, you must dial the entire number, *including the initial zero,* when calling from *anywhere* outside or inside Italy, and within the same town. To call Florence from the United States, dial **011-39-055,** then the rest of the phone number. Numbers in Italy can range anywhere from 6 to 12 digits in length.

**ATMs** Referred to in Italy as *un bancomat,* ATMs are easy to find in Italian cities; smaller towns usually have one, but it's good practice to fuel up on cash in urban centers before visiting rural areas.

Before traveling, confirm your card is valid for international withdrawals and that you have a four-digit PIN. (Some ATMs in Italy will not accept any other number of digits.) Also, be sure you know your daily withdrawal limit.

If at the ATM you get an on-screen message saying your card isn't valid for international transactions, don't panic: Most likely the bank can't make an electronic connection to check it (occasionally this can be a city-wide epidemic). Try another ATM or another town.

**Business Hours**

Access to almost any indoor public space requires a **Covid-19 Green Pass** or your country's equivalent; see p. 299. **Banks** tend to be open Monday through

Friday 8:30am to 1:30pm and 2:45 to 4:15pm. General opening hours for **stores, offices,** and **churches** are from 9:30am to noon or 1pm and again from 3 or 3:30pm (or later) to 7:30pm. The early afternoon shutdown is the *riposo,* the Italian siesta (in large cities, downtown stores don't usually close for *riposo*). Most small stores close all day Sunday and some also on Monday (morning only or all day). Some public services and business offices are open to the public only in the morning.

Traditionally, **state museums** are closed Mondays. Most large museums stay open all day otherwise, although some close for *riposo* or are only open in the morning (9am–2pm is popular). State museums usually offer free admission on the **first Sunday of the month**.

### Cellphones See "Mobile Phones," p. 308.

### Credit Cards The evolution of global computerized banking has heralded the triumph of plastic throughout Italy. It remains a good idea to carry some cash—small businesses may accept only cash or might even claim their credit card machine is broken to avoid card fees. **Visa** and **Mastercard** are almost universally accepted, and some businesses, typically at the luxe end, take **American Express. Diners Club** tends not to be accepted in Italy. Be sure to let your bank know you'll be traveling abroad to avoid having your card blocked after a few days of big purchases far from home.

**Note:** Many banks assess a 1% to 3% "transaction fee" on **all** charges you incur abroad, whether you're using the local currency or your native currency. If a card machine asks you to choose between your home currency or euros, pick euros. The "wholesale" exchange rate will be much more favorable. The same rule applies at ATMs.

### Customs Foreign visitors arriving by air can bring most items for personal use, including new merchandise bought duty-free for up to 430€. Returning to the United States, U.S. citizens

can bring with them up to $800 of goods, including 1 liter of alcohol, but no meats, fresh fruits, or vegetables. Vinegars, oils, preserves, chocolates, and certain cheeses are permissible (vacuum-packed cheeses, yes; raw milk cheese, no).

### Disabled Travelers

Most top museums and churches have installed ramps at entrances, and many hotels have converted first-floor rooms into accessible units. Otherwise, expect to find some parts of Italy tricky to tackle with a mobility impairment. Builders in the Middle Ages didn't have wheelchairs in mind when they built narrow doorways and spiral staircases, and heritage preservation laws keep Italians from doing much about this in some places.

Public transportation is improving, however. There is generally better access for passengers in wheelchairs, particularly on modern local buses and new transit infrastructure like Florence's tram. Dedicated seats or areas cater for those with disabilities, and Italians are quick to give up their place for somebody who looks like they need it. **Trenitalia** has a number for disabled travelers to call for assistance on the rail network: ✆ **323232**. The private rail network **Italo** has wheelchair spaces on every train: Call ✆ **060708** for any station assistance you need.

### Drinking Laws People of any age can legally consume alcohol in Italy, but a person must be 16 years old to be served alcohol in a restaurant or bar. Bars generally close around 2am, although alcohol is often served in clubs after that. Supermarkets carry beer, wine, and liquor.

### Electricity Italy operates on a 220-volt AC (50 cycles) system, as opposed to the U.S. 110-volt AC (60 cycles) system. You'll need a simple adapter plug to make American flat pegs fit Italian round holes. Most gadgets you will carry are dual voltage, so you are unlikely to need an additional converter. Buy all electrical accessories **before** you travel.

### Embassies & Consulates Most countries have embassies in Rome. The **U.S. Embassy** is at Via Vittorio Veneto 121 (it.usembassy.gov; ✆ **06/46-741**). There is also a **U.S. Consulate General** in Florence at Lungarno Vespucci 38 (✆ **055/266-951**). The **Canadian Embassy** is at Via Zara 30 (www.italy.gc.ca; ✆ **06/854-441**). The **Australian Embassy** is at Via Antonio Bosio 5 (www.italy.embassy.gov.au; ✆ **06/852-721**). The **New Zealand Embassy** is at Via Clitunno 44 (www.mfat.govt.nz/en/embassies; ✆ **06/853-7501**). The **U.K. Embassy** is at Via XX Settembre 80a (www.gov.uk/world/italy; ✆ **06/4220-0001**). Each national embassy website publishes the latest

Embassies & Consulates

coronavirus-related information for its citizens traveling to and from Italy.

**Emergencies**  The best number to call with a **general emergency** is ✆ **112,** which connects you to the *Carabinieri,* who will transfer your call as needed. For the **police,** dial ✆ **113;** for a **medical emergency** and to call an **ambulance,** the number is ✆ **118;** for the **fire department,** call ✆ **115.** If your car breaks down, dial ✆ **116** for **roadside aid** courtesy of the Automotive Club of Italy. All are free calls, but roadside assistance is a paid service for nonmembers.

**Family Travel**  Italy is a family-oriented society. A crying baby at a dinner table is greeted with a knowing smile rather than a stern look. Children almost always receive discounts, and maybe a special treat from the waiter, but the availability of such accoutrements as child seats for dinner tables is more the exception than the norm. There are plenty of parks, offbeat museums, markets, ice-cream parlors, and vibrant street life to amuse even the youngest children.

**Health & Hospitals**
Even if you don't have insurance, **you will be treated in an emergency.** Italy offers universal health care to its citizens and those of other European Union countries.

Others should be prepared to pay medical bills upfront. Before leaving home, find out what medical services your **health insurance** covers.

**Insurance**  Italy may be one of the safer places for travelers, but accidents and setbacks can happen, from lost luggage to car accidents. We recommend looking at the following online insurance marketplaces: **SquareMouth.com, InsureMyTrip.com**, and **TravelInsurance.com**. All three allow users to quickly and easily compare policies from different, vetted travel insurance companies. We find the user interface at SquareMouth to be the more intuitive, but all three are excellent resources.

**Internet Access**  For traveling with your own computer or smartphone, you'll find Wi-Fi in almost every accommodation, but if this is essential for your stay, verify before booking. In a pinch, hostels, local libraries, and some cafes and bars have web access. Several spots around Venice, Florence, Rome, and other big cities have free Wi-Fi access provided by the local government, but antiterrorism laws make it obligatory to register before you can log on. Take your passport or other photo ID when you go looking for an Internet point. **High-speed trains** often have free Wi-Fi (but throttle Skype/Zoom, streaming, file sharing, and similar data-hungry services). **Fiumicino Airport** has free Wi-Fi.

**LGBT Travelers**  Italy as a whole, and northern Italy in particular, is gay-friendly.

Homosexuality is legal and the age of consent is 16. Same-sex civil unions became legal in 2016. Italians are generally more affectionate and physical than North Americans in all their friendships, and even straight men occasionally walk down the street with their arms around each other. However, kissing anywhere other than on the cheeks at greetings and goodbyes may draw attention. Italy's national associations and support networks for gays and lesbians are **Arcigay** (www.arcigay.it) and **Arcilesbica** (www.arcilesbica.it); most cities have a local office. See **www.arcigay.it/sedi** for a map of local affiliates.

**Mail & Postage**  Sending a postcard or letter up to 20g, or a little less than an ounce, costs 1.15€ to European countries, 2.40€ to North America, and a whopping 3.10€ to Australia and New Zealand.

**Mobile Phones**  GSM (Global System for Mobile Communications) is a cellphone technology used by most of the world's countries. (In the U.S., Verizon uses a different technology—CDMA—and phones on those networks also need GSM or 4G/5G compatibility to work in Italy. Most current models do.) Before traveling, contact your home service provider to activate "international roaming."

But—and it's a *big* but—using roaming can be very expensive, especially if you access the Internet on your phone. It is usually much cheaper, once you arrive, to buy an Italian SIM card (a removable plastic card encoded with your phone number). This is an especially good idea if you will be in Italy for more than a week. You can **buy a SIM card** at one of the many cellphone shops you pass in every city. The main service providers are **TIM** (www.tim.it), **Vodafone** (www.vodafone.it), and **WINDTRE** (www.windtre.it). With an Italian SIM card in your phone, local and national calls may be as low as .10€ per minute and incoming calls are free. Deals on each network change regularly; check the individual websites, or visit a provider's store or an electronics chain such as **Euronics** (www.euronics.it). **Note:** U.S. contract cellphones are often "locked" and will only work with a SIM card from your own service provider, so check first that you have an unlocked phone.

**Buying a phone** is another option, and you shouldn't have any trouble finding one for about 20€. Use it, then recycle it when you get home. It will save you a fortune versus alternatives such as roaming or using hotel telephones.

**Money & Costs** Frommer's lists exact prices in local currency. The currency conversions quoted below were correct at press time. However, rates fluctuate, so before departing, consult a currency exchange website, such as **www.oanda.com/currency/converter**, to check up-to-the-minute rates.

Like many European countries, Italy uses the **euro** as its currency. Euro coins are issued in denominations of .01€, .02€, .05€, .10€, .20€, and .50€, as well as 1€ and 2€; bills come in denominations of 5€, 10€, 20€, 50€, 100€, 200€, and 500€. You'll get the best rate if you **exchange money** at a bank or take cash out from one of its **ATMs** (see p. 306).

Traveler's checks have gone the way of the Stegosaurus.

**Newspapers & Magazines** The *New York Times International Edition* and *USA Today* are available at most newsstands in big cities. At larger kiosks you can also find the *Wall Street Journal Europe*, European editions of *The Economist*, and most major European newspapers and magazines.

**Pharmacies** Pharmacies are ubiquitous (look for the green cross) and serve almost like mini-clinics, where pharmacists diagnose and treat minor ailments, like flu symptoms and general aches and pains, including with over-the-counter drugs. Carry the generic name of any prescription medicines you take, in case a local pharmacist is unfamiliar with your overseas brand. Pharmacies in cities take turns covering the night shift; normally a list is posted at the entrance of each pharmacy informing customers which ones are open each night of the week. Face masks and hand sanitizer are widely available. Many pharmacies offer certified **antigen and PCR testing** for travelers.

**Police** For emergencies, call *©* **112** or *©* **113.** Italy has several different police forces, but you'll likely need to deal with only two. The **Carabinieri** (*©* **112;** www.carabinieri.it) normally only concern themselves with serious crimes but point you in the right direction. The **Polizia** (*©* **113;** www.poliziadistato.it), whose city headquarters is called a *questura,* is the place to go for help with lost and stolen property or petty crimes.

**Safety** Italy is a remarkably safe country. The worst threats you'll likely face are pickpockets who sometimes frequent touristy areas and public buses; keep your hands on your camera at all

## THE VALUE OF THE EURO VS. OTHER POPULAR CURRENCIES

| €  | Aus$    | Can$    | NZ$      | UK£    | US$    |
|----|---------|---------|----------|--------|--------|
| 1  | A$1.57  | C$1.44  | NZ$1.63  | £0.85  | $1.14  |

times and valuables in an under-the-clothes money belt or inside zip-pocket. Don't leave anything valuable in a rental car overnight, and leave nothing visible in it at any time. If you are robbed, you can fill out paperwork at the nearest police station (questura), but this is mostly for insurance purposes or to get a passport issued—don't expect them to hunt down the perpetrator. In general, avoid public parks at night. Areas around rail stations are often unsavory, but rarely any worse.

**Senior Travel**   Seniors and older people are treated with respect and deference, but few specific programs or concessions are made for them. The one exception is admission prices for museums and sights, where those ages 60 or 65 and older often get in at a reduced rate or even free. As a senior in Italy, you're *un anziano* (if you're a woman: *un'anziana*). It's a term of respect and you should let people know if you think a discount may be due.

**Smoking**   Smoking has been eradicated from inside restaurants, bars, and most hotels, so smokers tend to take outside tables. If you pick an outdoor table, you are essentially choosing a seat in the smoking section; requesting that your neighbor refrain from smoking may not be politely received.

## Student Travelers
An **International Student Identity Card (ISIC)** qualifies students for savings on rail passes, plane tickets, entrance fees, and more. The card is valid for 1 year. You can apply at **www. myisic.org**. If you're no longer a student but are still 30 or under, you can get an **International Youth Travel Card (IYTC)** or an **International Teacher Identity Card (ITIC)** from the same issuer, which entitles you to some discounts.

**Taxes**   No sales tax is added to the price tag of purchases in Italy, but a 22% value-added tax (in Italy: IVA) is automatically included in just about everything, except food and a few specific goods and services, where rates of 4% and 10% apply. Entertainment, transport, hotels, and dining are among a group of goods taxed at a lower rate of 10%. For major purchases, non–EU residents can get IVA refunded. Several city governments have also introduced an **accommodation tax.** For example, in Florence, you are charged between 3€ and 5€ per person per night depending on the hotel or rental apartment's government-star rating. Children 11 and under are exempt. Venice, Rome, and many other popular destinations levy their own taxes. This tax is not usually included in any published room rate, even those prepaid online.

**Tipping**   In **hotels,** service is usually included in your bill. In family-run operations, additional tips are unnecessary and sometimes considered rude. In fancier places with a hired staff, however, you may want to leave a 1€ daily tip for the maid and pay any porter 1€ per bag. In **restaurants,** a 2€ to 3€ per person "cover charge" is automatically added to the bill, and in some tourist areas, especially Venice, another 10% to 15% is tacked on (except in the most unscrupulous of places, this will be noted on the menu; if unsure you should ask, "È *incluso il servizio?*"). It is not necessary to leave any extra money on the table, though it is not uncommon to leave up to 10€ for good service. Locals often leave nothing. It is not necessary to tip **taxi** drivers, although it is common to round up the bill to the nearest euro or two.

**Toilets**   Aside from toilets in train stations, which sometimes cost .50€ to 1€ to use, and gas/petrol stations, where they are free (with perhaps a basket seeking gratuities for cleaners), public toilets are few and far between. It is advisable to always make use of toilets in a hotel, restaurant, museum, or bar before setting off around town. Public toilets—and often those in bars, too—can be dirty, with no seat or toilet paper. It's best to carry a pack of tissues and hand sanitizer with you, especially if you're traveling with children or teens.

# USEFUL ITALIAN PHRASES

| English | Italian | Pronunciation |
|---|---|---|
| Thank you | Grazie | *graht*-tzee-yey |
| You're welcome | Prego | *prey*-go |
| Please | Per favore | *pehr* fah-*vohr*-eh |
| Yes | Si | see |
| No | No | noh |
| Good morning or Good day | Buongiorno | bwohn-*djor*-noh |
| Good evening | Buona sera | *bwohn*-ah *say*-rah |
| Good night | Buona notte | *bwohn*-ah *noht*-tay |
| It's a pleaswure to meet you. | Piacere di conoscerla. | pyah-*cheh*-reh dee *koh*-nohshehr-lah |
| My name is ___. | Mi chiamo ___. | mee *kyah*-moh |
| And yours? | E lei? | eh lay |
| Do you speak English? | Parla inglese? | *pahr*-lah een-*gleh*-seh |
| How are you? | Come sta? | *koh*-may stah |
| Very well | Molto bene | *mohl*-toh *behn*-ney |
| Goodbye | Arrivederci | ahr-ree-vah-*dehr*-chee |
| Excuse me (to get attention) | Scusi | *skoo*-zee |
| Excuse me (to get past someone) | Permesso | pehr-*mehs*-soh |

## GETTING AROUND

| English | Italian | Pronunciation |
|---|---|---|
| Where is . . . ? | Dovè . . . ? | *doh*-vey |
| the station | la stazione | lah stat-tzee-*oh*-neh |
| a hotel | un albergo | oon ahl-*behr*-goh |
| a restaurant | un ristorante | oon reest-ohr-*ahnt*-eh |
| the bathroom | il bagno | eel *bahn*-nyoh |
| I am looking for . . . | Cerco . . . | *chehr*-koh |
| the check-in counter | il check-in | eel check-in |
| the ticket counter | la biglietteria | lah beel-lyeht-teh-*ree*-ah |
| arrivals | l'area arrivi | *lah*-reh-ah ahr-*ree*-vee |
| departures | l'area partenze | *lah*-reh-ah pahr-*tehn*-tseh |
| gate number | l'uscita numero | loo-*shee*-tah *noo*-meh-roh |
| the restroom | la toilette | lah twa-*leht* |
| the police station | la stazione di polizia | lah stah-*tsyoh*-neh dee poh-lee-*tsee*-ah |
| the smoking area | l'area fumatori | *lah*-reh-ah foo-mah-*toh*-ree |
| the information booth | l'ufficio informazioni | loof-*fee*-choh een-*fohr*-mah-tsyoh-nee |
| a public telephone | un telefono pubblico | oon teh-*leh*-foh-noh *poob*-blee-koh |
| an ATM/cashpoint | un bancomat | oon *bahn*-koh-maht |
| baggage claim | il ritiro bagagli | eel ree-*tee*-roh bah-*gahl*-lyee |

| English | Italian | Pronunciation |
|---|---|---|
| I am looking for . . . | Cerco . . . | *chehr*-koh |
| a cafe | un caffè | oon kahf-*feh* |
| a restaurant | un ristorante | oon ree-stoh-*rahn*-teh |
| a bar | un bar | oon bar |
| a bookstore | una libreria | *oo*-nah lee-breh-*ree*-ah |
| To the left | A sinistra | ah see-*nees*-tra |
| To the right | A destra | ah *dehy*-stra |
| Straight ahead | Avanti (*or* sempre diritto) | ahv-*vahn*-tee (*sehm*-pray dee-*reet*-toh) |

## DINING

| English | Italian | Pronunciation |
|---|---|---|
| Breakfast | Prima colazione | *pree*-mah coh-laht-tzee-*ohn*-ay |
| Lunch | Pranzo | *prahn*-zoh |
| Dinner | Cena | *chay*-nah |
| How much is it? | Quanto costa? | *kwan*-toh *coh*-sta |
| The check, please | Il conto, per favore | eel kon-toh *pehr* fah-*vohr*-eh |

## A MATTER OF TIME

| English | Italian | Pronunciation |
|---|---|---|
| When? | Quando? | *kwan*-doh |
| Yesterday | Ieri | ee-*yehr*-ree |
| Today | Oggi | *oh*-jee |
| Tomorrow | Domani | doh-*mah*-nee |
| What time is it? | Che ore sono? | kay *or*-ay *soh*-noh |
| It's one o'clock. | È l'una. | eh *loo*-nah |
| It's two o'clock. | Sono le due. | *soh*-noh leh *doo*-eh |
| It's two-thirty. | Sono le due e mezzo. | *soh*-noh leh *doo*-eh eh *mehd*-dzoh |
| It's noon. | È mezzogiorno. | eh mehd-dzoh-*johr*-noh |
| It's midnight. | È mezzanotte. | eh mehd-dzah-*noht*-teh |
| in the morning | al mattino | ahl maht-*tee*-noh |
| in the afternoon | al pomeriggio | ahl poh-meh-*reed*-joh |
| at night | alla notte | dee *noht*-the |

## DAYS OF THE WEEK

| English | Italian | Pronunciation |
|---|---|---|
| Monday | Lunedì | loo-nay-*dee* |
| Tuesday | Martedì | mart-ay-*dee* |
| Wednesday | Mercoledì | mehr-cohl-ay-*dee* |
| Thursday | Giovedì | joh-vay-*dee* |
| Friday | Venerdì | ven-nehr-*dee* |
| Saturday | Sabato | *sah*-bah-toh |
| Sunday | Domenica | doh-*mehn*-nee-kah |

# Index

# Map List

# Photo Credits

*Frommer's EasyGuide to Rome, Florence & Venice*, 8th Edition

Published by

## FROMMER MEDIA LLC

Copyright © 2022 by Frommer Media LLC. All rights reserved. No part of this publication may be reproduced, stored in a retrieval system, or transmitted in any form or by any means, electronic, mechanical,
photocopying, recording, scanning or otherwise, except as permitted under Sections 107 or 108 of the
1976 United States Copyright Act, without the prior written permission of the Publisher. Requests to the
Publisher for permission should be addressed to support@frommermedia.com.

Frommer's is a registered trademark of Arthur Frommer. Frommer Media LLC is not associated with any
product or vendor mentioned in this book.

ISBN 978-1-62887-525-6 (paper), 978-1-62887-526-3 (ebk)

Editorial Director: Pauline Frommer
Editor: Alexis Lipsitz Flippin
Production Editor: Erin Geile
Cartographer: Liz Puhl
Photo Editor: Meghan Lamb
Indexer: Cheryl Lenser
Cover Design: Dave Riedy

Front cover photo: Roman Forum at sunrise. © mammoth | istockphoto.com
Back cover photo: Island Murano in Venice, Italy. © Yasonya | shutterstock.com

For information on our other products or services, see www.frommers.com.

FrommerMedia LLC also publishes its books in a variety of electronic formats. Some content that appears
in print may not be available in electronic formats.

Manufactured in the United States of America

5 4 3 2 1

## ABOUT THE AUTHORS

A longtime contributor to Frommer's guides, **Elizabeth Heath** is a writer and editor based in Umbria, central Italy, from where she writes about travel and culture in Italy, Europe, and farther afield. Her work has appeared in the *Washington Post*, *Travel + Leisure*, Trip-Savvy, Frommers.com, and many other outlets. When not traveling and writing about it, she enjoys rural life with her extended Italian family and houseful of pets.

**Stephen Keeling** has been traveling to Italy since 1985 (when a serving of gelato was 1,000 lire), and covering his favorite nation for Frommer's since 2007. He has written for *The Independent*, *Daily Telegraph*, various travel magazines, and numerous travel guides. Stephen lives in New York City.

**Donald Strachan** is a writer and journalist who has written about Italy for publications worldwide, including *National Geographic Traveler*, *The Guardian*, *Sunday Telegraph*, and *The Independent*. He resides in London, England.

## ABOUT THE FROMMER TRAVEL GUIDES

For most of the past 50 years, Frommer's has been the leading series of travel guides in North America, accounting for as many as 24% of all guidebooks sold. I think I know why.

Though we hope our books are entertaining, we nevertheless deal with travel in a serious fashion. Our guidebooks have never looked on such journeys as a mere recreation, but as a far more important human function, a time of learning and introspection, an essential part of a civilized life. We stress the culture, lifestyle, history, and beliefs of the destinations we cover, and urge our readers to seek out people and new ideas as the chief rewards of travel.

We have never shied from controversy. We have, from the beginning, encouraged our authors to be intensely judgmental, critical—both pro and con—in their comments, and wholly independent. Our only clients are our readers, and we have triggered the ire of countless prominent sorts, from a tourist newspaper we called "practically worthless" (it unsuccessfully sued us) to the many rip-offs we've condemned.

And because we believe that travel should be available to everyone regardless of their incomes, we have always been cost-conscious at every level of expenditure. Though we have broadened our recommendations beyond the budget category, we insist that every lodging we include be sensibly priced. We use every form of media to assist our readers, and are particularly proud of our feisty daily website, the award-winning Frommers.com.

I have high hopes for the future of Frommer's. May these guidebooks, in all the years ahead, continue to reflect the joy of travel and the freedom that travel represents. May they always pursue a cost-conscious path, so that people of all incomes can enjoy the rewards of travel. And may they create, for both the traveler and the persons among whom we travel, a community of friends, where all human beings live in harmony and peace.

Arthur Frommer